Ohio's Western Reserve
A Regional Reader

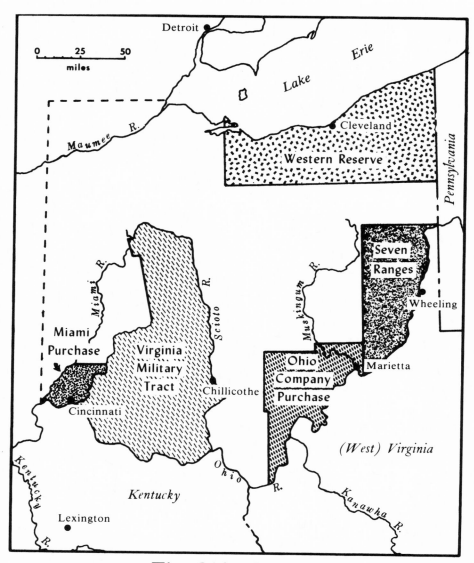

Detroit

Lake Erie

Western Reserve

Cleveland

Pennsylvania

Maumee R.

Miami R.

Scioto R.

Muskingum R.

Seven Ranges

Wheeling

Miami Purchase

Virginia Military Tract

Ohio Company Purchase

Marietta

Chillicothe

Cincinnati

(West) Virginia

Kentucky

Ohio R.

Kanawha R.

Kentucky R.

Lexington

0   25   50
miles

The Ohio Country

Ohio's Western Reserve
A Regional Reader

edited by

HARRY F. LUPOLD and
GLADYS HADDAD

THE KENT STATE UNIVERSITY PRESS
Kent, Ohio, and London, England

©1988 by The Kent State University Press, Kent, Ohio 44242
All rights reserved
Library of Congress Catalog Card Number 88-691
ISBN: 0-87338-372-9
Manufactured in the United States of America

Second printing, 1991

Library of Congress Cataloging-in-Publication Data

Ohio's Western Reserve.

       Includes bibliographies and index.
       1. Western Reserve (Ohio)—History. I. Lupold, Harry Forrest. II. Haddad,
Gladys.
F497.W5035 1988   977.1′36   88-691
ISBN 0-87338-372-9 (alk. paper) ∞

British Library Cataloguing-in-Publication data are available

Contents

Preface

The editors designed this reader to appeal to a wide audience: students and professors of regional and local history courses, students and teachers of American history or American literature courses, members of historical societies, local history "buffs," and the general reader who just wants to have a better understanding of his or her community or sectional development. *Ohio's Western Reserve: A Regional Reader* traces the social, economic, and political evolution of a special geographic area in Ohio's maturity as a state.

Once upon a time there was a Western Reserve, a New Connecticut, or a Western New England—to that we agree. But we also agree that the forces of industrialism, urbanism, and immigration or migration by the late nineteenth and early twentieth centuries had destroyed the uniqueness of this once transplanted New England. It is true that the landmarks, architecture, and placenames are still visible in the Reserve, but progress has caught up to the area, and the Western Reserve is now a part of the Midwest and, more importantly, has been assimilated into the American mainstream. Certainly this was the case by 1920.

A special thank you is in order to Bari Stith and Mark Pendleton, research assistants, and Lisa DiNallo, for her expert typing skills. The editors, however, owe another debt of gratitude to a man whose encouragement, enthusiasm, energy, and patience made this book a reality: John T. Hubbell, Director of the Kent State University Press. Dr. Hubbell gave invaluable advice (and consent) throughout the entire project, and we thank him for the faith he had in our dream, which we presented to him in the fall of 1986.

Harry F. Lupold
Lakeland Community College

Gladys Haddad
Lake Erie College

September 1, 1987

Acknowledgments

Phillip R. Shriver, "The Beaver Wars and the Destruction of the Erie Nation," *Timeline* (December 1984–January 1985). Reprinted with permission of *Timeline*.

Jaré R. Cardinal and Eric J. Cardinal, "Archaeology and History: Some Suggestions from the Historian's Viewpoint," *Ohio Archaeologist* 34, no. 2 (1984). Courtesy of the Archaeological Society of Ohio.

John Milton Holley's Journal (Transcripts), July 12–13, 1796 and Holley's Field Notes, September 21–28, 1796, MSS1. Courtesy of the Western Reserve Historical Society.

George W. Knepper, "Early Migration to the Western Reserve," *Western Reserve Magazine* (November-December 1977). Courtesy of the Western Reserve Historical Society.

Thomas A. Smith, "The Firelands and the Settlement of Vermilion," *The Western Reserve Story*. Garrettsville, Ohio, 1981. Courtesy of Thomas A. Smith, Head of Research, The Rutherford B. Hayes Presidential Center.

Jeffrey P. Brown, "Samuel Huntington: A Connecticut Aristocrat on the Ohio Frontier," *Ohio History* 89, no. 4 (Autumn 1980): 422–38. With the permission of the Ohio Historical Society, Columbus, Ohio.

Grace Goulder Izant, "The Howling Wilderness," *Hudson's Heritage*. Kent, Ohio: Kent State University Press, 1985. Reprinted with permission of the Kent State University Press.

William D. Ellis, "Cleveland as Canal Town," *Early Settlers in Cleveland*. Cleveland State University Press, 1976. Courtesy of Cleveland State University's Ethnic Heritage Studies Program and William D. Ellis.

Harry F. Lupold, "Fairport: The Transformation of a Lake Erie Port, 1812–1870," *Inland Seas* (Summer 1981). Reprinted from *Inland Seas*,® the Journal of The Great Lakes Historical Society.

Robert A. Wheeler, "Shakers and Mormons in the Early Western Reserve: A Contrast in Life Styles," *Western Reserve Magazine* (July-August 1978). Courtesy of the Western Reserve Historical Society.

Gladys Haddad, "The First Women's Colleges," *The Gamut: A Journal of Ideas and Information* (Winter 1984). Permission to reprint from *The Gamut*, Cleveland State University and Gladys Haddad.

C. H. Cramer, "Student Life at Western Reserve College," *Case Western Reserve University: A History 1826–1976.* Copyright 1976 by Case Western Reserve University. By permission of Little, Brown and Company.

Harry F. Lupold, "1820–1860 Anti-Slavery Activities in a Western Reserve County," *Negro History Bulletin* (October-November 1975). Reprinted with permission of the *Negro History Bulletin* and the Association for the Study of Negro Life and History.

Kenneth E. Davison, *Cleveland During the Civil War.* Columbus: Ohio State University Press for the Ohio Historical Society, 1962. Courtesy of the Ohio Historical Society.

Edward T. Downer, "Johnson's Island," *Civil War Prisons.* Kent, Ohio: Kent State University Press, 1962. Reprinted with permission of the Kent State University Press.

Harlan Hatcher, "Building the Railroads." Reprinted with permission of Macmillan Publishing Company from *The Western Reserve* by Harlan Hatcher. Copyright 1949 by Macmillan Publishing Company, renewed 1977 by Harlan Hatcher.

Frederick D. Williams, "Garfield's Front Porch Campaign: The Mentor Scene," *Lake County Historical Quarterly* 22, no. 3 (September 1980). Courtesy of the Lake County Historical Society.

Allan Peskin, "The Funeral of the Century," *Lake County Historical Quarterly* 23, no. 3 (September 1981). Courtesy of the Lake County Historical Society.

Gladys Haddad, "Personalities of an Era . . . Intersections: Rockefeller, Mather, Tarbell," *Allegheny College Magazine* (Autumn 1984). Reprinted with permission of *Allegheny College Magazine* and Gladys Haddad.

Peter Jedick, "When Euclid Avenue Was Somebody," *Cleveland Magazine* (December 1974). Reprinted with permission of *Cleveland Magazine* and Peter Jedick.

Eugene C. Murdock, "A Couple of Giants: Mark Hanna and Tom Johnson," *Western Reserve Magazine* (May-June 1980). Reprinted with permission of *Western Reserve Magazine.*

Thomas L. Newcomb, "Northeastern Ohio's Mennonite and Amish Folk," *Western Reserve Magazine* (July-August 1981). Reprinted with the permission of *Western Reserve Magazine* and Thomas L. Newcomb.

John J. Grabowski, "Social Reform and Philanthropic Order in Cleveland, 1896–1920," in Van Tassel and Grabowski, eds., *Cleveland: A Tradition of Reform.* Kent, Ohio: Kent State University Press, 1986. Reprinted with permission of Kent State University Press.

Kenneth L. Kusmer, "Racism at High Tide: Cleveland, 1915–1920," *A Ghetto Takes Shape.* Urbana: University of Illinois Press, 1976. Copyright 1976 by the Board of Trustees of the University of Illinois. Reprinted by permission of Kenneth L. Kusmer and the University of Illinois Press.

Eric J. Cardinal, "New England and the Western Reserve in the Nineteenth Century: Some Suggestions," *Western Reserve Studies* 1 (1986). Reprinted with permission of *Western Reserve Studies*.

OHIO IN 1856

MICHIGAN

Lake Erie

PENNSYLVANIA

Williams

Fulton

Lucas

Ottawa

CLEVELAND

Lake

Ashtabula

Defiance

Wood

Sandusky

Cuyahoga

Geauga

Henry

Erie

Lorain

Medina

Summit

Portage

Trumbull

Paulding

Putnam

Hancock

Seneca

Huron

Mahoning

Van Wert

Wyandot

Crawford

Richland

Ashland

Wayne

Stark

Columbiana

Mercer

Allen

Hardin

Marion

Holmes

Carroll

Jefferson

Auglaize

Shelby

Logan

Morrow

Knox

Coshocton

Tuscarawas

Harrison

Darke

Champaign

Union

Delaware

Licking

Guernsey

Belmont

Miami

Clark

Franklin

COLUMBUS

Muskingum

Noble

Monroe

Preble

Mont-
gomery

Madison

Greene

Pickaway

Fairfield

Perry

Morgan

Washington

Ohio

River

Butler

Warren

Clinton

Ross

Hocking

Vinton

Athens

Meigs

Hamilton

CINCINNATI

Clermont

Highland

Pike

Jackson

Gallia

Brown

Adams

Scioto

Lawrence

INDIANA

KENTUCKY

Ohio

River

VIRGINIA

CANALS ———

NATIONAL ROAD ·······

BOUNDARY OF THE
WESTERN RESERVE

PART I

Conquest and Settlement:
Native Americans to New Englanders

Over fifteen thousand years ago the land that is northeastern Ohio lay undisturbed by human inhabitants. The forests were wide and deep; animal life, including game birds such as the now extinct passenger pigeon, mountain lions, white-tailed deer, black bears, and timber wolves, abounded. Fish were plentiful in all the rivers along the south shore of Lake Erie. It was, in the words of the French explorers, a *paradis terrestre.*

Then about twelve thousand years ago, during the last ice age, all was changed, and the first "settlers" arrived. These nomadic hunters had emigrated from Western Asia to North America through Alaska and gradually made their journey to what is today Ohio. Termed Paleo-Indian, this prehistoric culture may be traced through archaeological evidence. Later, in a warmer climate, a new group of hunters, food gatherers, and fishermen, the Archaic Indians, succeeded to occupy the area with a strong stone-age culture.

Slowly, a distinct Woodland and Mississippian Tradition emerged from 1000 B.C. to A.D. 1200 or later. Various Indian nations and cultures left remnants of their life-styles, such as Indian mounds and earthworks (Adenas and Hopewells), as well as bows and arrows used for hunting and sticks and hoes used for farming. Village sites were occupied for longer periods of time, and a more sedentary way of life evolved.

By the time of the American Revolution the future state of Ohio was inhabited by a mixed Indian population whose ancestors had roamed the area for over ten thousand years. The major nations that lived within the state's present boundaries included the Shawnee, Delaware, Miami, Ottawa, and Wyandot. Since these tribes failed to recognize territorial boundaries, there was seldom warfare or serious rivalry. Actually, it was the white traders and settlers, and then during the Revolution the British and American soldiers, who encouraged the Indians to war on each other and on the whites.

Centuries before these historic Indians, however, another group of people, usually identified as Iroquois, walked the forest trails and fished the rivers of northeastern Ohio. Since they have left us no written or oral records, and since no white person ever visited their villages, their name and lineage as a nation are lost to history. It has become their destiny to be known as Ohio's forgotten people. Several generations of Jesuit missionaries wrote reports to their superiors in France and, when published, these documents became the *Jesuit Relations*. One of these *Relations*, in 1647–48, noted that "this lake, called Erie, was formally inhabited on its southern shore by certain tribes whom we call the Nation of the Cat."

Who were these once populous and warlike people—the Erie? Where were their villages located? How extensive was Erieland? And what happened to them? In an attempt to separate myth from fact and wrestle with the contemporary debate waged between historians and archaeologists, Phillip R. Shriver's article, "The Beaver Wars and the Destruction of the Erie Nation," clearly and logically presents answers to the mystery surrounding the Erie. More importantly, Shriver shows that the Iroquois Wars were intertwined with England's and France's worldwide colonial and commercial battles. William D. Ellis, in *Land of the Inland Seas*, pointed at the problem when he wrote, "Fur was the continent's cash crop and beaver its gold standard."

It has been traditional to assign most of northern Ohio and especially the southern shore of Lake Erie as the homeland of the Erie Indians. For instance, Harry F. Lupold, in *The Forgotten People*, placed their village sites and forts from west of the Cuyahoga River along the shoreline through northwestern Pennsylvania and western New York, possibly as far east as the Genesee River. Lupold also accepted the notion that the Erie were culturally and linguistically related to the Iroquois. But contemporary archaeological and ethnohistorical evidence suggests that these conclusions may not be valid. Certainly the recent work of David Bush at the Grantham Burial Site in Fairport Harbor, Ohio, warrants careful study of that region archaeologists call the Whittlesey Focus. Using as their model the issue of the location of the Erie Indians, Jaré R. Cardinal and Eric J. Cardinal show how researchers can approach a problem in different ways. "Archaeology and History: Some Suggestions from the Historian's Viewpoint" also allows the Cardinals to review the "battle of the maps," thus refining their argument on alternative interpretations of the same sources.

The nineteenth-century historian and lecturer, John Fiske, labeled the half decade from the end of the Revolutionary War in 1783 to the launching of the new Constitution in 1789 "the critical period." Recent scholars, such as Merrill Jensen, have taken issue with Fiske's thesis and have argued that there was reasonable prosperity and stability in the nation. However, as Gordon S. Wood presumed in 1969, the overall feeling of *contemporaries* was probably that they were passing through a critical era. After all, we had no strong national authority, no army or navy, the British and Spanish still occupied American soil, our foreign commerce was a mess, and paper money added to the debt-credit-inflation problems leading to demonstrations such as Shays' Rebellion in 1786–87.

It was under these conditions that the Confederation Congress, as part of a dying government, passed two land ordinances so vital to the future of the United States. Passed on May 20, 1785, the Land Ordinance required a survey of the congressional lands in preparation for sale. Of especial importance were the provisions that "there shall be reserved the lot No. 16, of every township, for the maintenance of public schools within the said township." The second of these land laws, the Northwest Ordinance of 1787, enacted into law on July 13, 1787, has been called one of the four great fundamental documents in United States history. The six articles of the Northwest Ordinance guaranteed historic rights that anticipated the Bill of Rights to the Constitution, encouraged education and the growth of schools, forbade slavery north of the Ohio River in the Northwest, and provided for an orderly plan whereby colonies could become states on an equal footing with older states.

There were many pressures on the Congress for the passage of the land laws. Members of Congress were alarmed at the amount of squatter sovereignty, land speculation, and illegal states being formed in the West. Certainly in the minds of the centralists and those desiring a stronger Union, these activities were a threat. On squatter sovereignty in the Northwest, George Washington wrote Richard Henry Lee: "The spirit of immigration is great; the people have got impatient; and though you cannot stop the road, it is yet to your power to mark the way; a little while and you will not be able to do either." Push for the Ordinance of 1787 particularly came from a group of land speculators, the Ohio Company of Associates and the Society of the Cincinnati, who wished to plant colonies in the Ohio country. Their leaders were Manasseh Cutler, Samuel Parsons, and Rufus Putnam.

With five of the thirteen states unrepresented, including, incidentally, Connecticut, a state so deeply committed to keeping its western lands, there were some irregularities in the passage of the land laws. First, Congress had no authority under the Articles to dispose of public lands. They therefore assumed such authority in 1785 by common consent. Second, the Articles required approval of at least nine states before any legislation could be passed. But with no quorum, the Ordinance of 1787 was approved by eight states and was, therefore, invalid. Finally, the Ordinance of 1787 was lobbied through Congress by speculators who desired a guarantee of a government framework that would make their small lots more attractive to potential buyers. Fortunately for posterity these irregularities were overlooked. The Confederation Congress held its last meeting on November 1, 1788. So for five months the country had no national government, until Washington was inaugurated president on April 30, 1789. "During this interim there was a state of quiet anarchy—literally no government," said professor Thomas A. Bailey.

The Northwest Ordinance of 1787 anticipated the Bill of Rights to the Constitution in two areas of concern to the emigrating settlers: education and religion. Article I, as part of the compact between the original states and the people of the Northwest, stated: "No person, demeaning himself in a peaceable and orderly manner, shall ever be molested on account of his mode of worship or religious sentiments, in the said territory." Article III stated : "Religion, morality, and knowledge, being necessary to good government and the happiness of mankind, schools and the means of education shall forever be encouraged." On September 16, 1876, future president James A. Garfield, in his address to the Geauga County Historical Society, reiterated the fact that the safety and prosperity of the nation depended on the "trinity of powers." "These pioneers," concluded Garfield, "knew well that the three great forces which constitute the strength and glory of a free government are, the family, the school and the church."

The question may now be asked as to where Connecticut and Ohio's Western Reserve fit into this process of land division and frontier state-building. In 1662, King Charles II of England granted the Connecticut colony a charter to all lands between the forty-first and forty-second parallels of north latitude. Connecticut's rights extended from Providence plantations in the East to the Pacific Ocean in the West, with the exception of the Pennsylvania and New York colonies. Trouble lay ahead because New York, Massachusetts, and Virginia all had overlapping claims to the same territory. Through compromise, Connecticut deeded to the government in 1786 all but that portion defined as the Western Reserve. In the words of one writer, "They had long been victims of a martyr complex tracing back to the time when big New York 'deprived' them of Long Island."

Many citizens of Connecticut were indeed martyrs, since the first "New Connecticut" occurred when colonists from that state settled the beautiful Wyoming Valley on the Susquehanna River in William Penn's domain. Here, in 1778, three thousand settlers lived in their own towns, had their own laws, and collected taxes and levies to support a Connecticut regiment in the Revolutionary Army. But tragedy struck on July 3, 1778, when an army of twelve hundred British and Indians swooped down on the Wyoming colony and shot, tomahawked, and murdered nearly three hundred men, while the women and children attempted to flee to safety. The final blow came in 1782 when the Trenton Federal Court ruled that the Wyoming Valley lands belonged to Pennsylvania and not to Connecticut.

Located in northeastern Ohio and bordered by Lake Erie on the north, Pennsylvania on the east, the parallel of forty-first degree north latitude on the south, and Sandusky and Seneca counties on the west, the Western Reserve measured 120 miles from east to west and an average of 50 miles from north to south. This was the area Connecticut sold to the Connecticut Land Company on August 3, 1795, for $1,200,000. The remaining 500,000 acres at the western end of the Reserve, today Erie and Huron counties, had earlier (May 11, 1792) been quitclaimed to citizens of Connecticut's coastal towns for damages suffered by British raids. Legal entanglements and delays of the law were slow for the eighteen hundred sufferers. An appraisal of the losses was required, and almost thirty years passed before the investigations were complete. By then, many of the claimants were dead; others were too old to consider migration once the survey was complete in 1807.

Now that the Connecticut Land Company had received its nearly three million acres of land from Connecticut, what power—juridical and territorial—did the company possess? What was its relationship to Hartford? Apparently, said Ohio historian B. A. Hinsdale, some members of the "syndicate" presumed that the land company had received enough political authority to found a new state. "They imagined themselves, like William Penn, to be proprietors, coupled with the rights of self-government." The company soon dismissed this nonsense when Connecticut took little interest in the whole business. Also, the governor of the Northwest Territory, Arthur St. Clair, arbitrarily included the Western Reserve in different counties he created for the Ohio territory. Finally, on July 10, 1800, St. Clair issued a proclamation making the entire Reserve a county, with the name Trumbull, and Warren as the county seat.

Now occurred the first great event in the development of the Western Reserve. The first surveying party into New Connecticut, under the direction of Moses Cleaveland, got under way in May 1796. Moses Cleaveland was a good choice to lead this expedition into the Reserve wilderness. He was a graduate of Yale College and had practiced law in Canterbury, Connecticut, for almost thirty years. He had served in the state legislature several terms and, in 1796, before leaving for the Reserve, he was elected general of the state militia. Cleaveland had married Esther Champion, sister of General Henry Champion, one of the agents of the Connecticut Land Company. Elroy M. Avery described Cleaveland as "a man of few words and prompt action, a man of true courage and as shrewd in his tactics as he was courageous." The general was of medium height, erect, portly, and wore such a sedate look strangers often took him to be a clergyman.

The journals, such as J. M. Holley's, of the fifty men in Cleaveland's surveying party are generally matter-of-fact and impersonal, and we are seldom permitted a glimpse into their hearts. Cleaveland (Range 12, Township 7) was fifty-five miles west of the Pennsylvania line and thirty miles north of the forty-first parallel. The going was tough, and it was even tougher hacking out the five-mile—square townships. The party encountered all the hardships known to man on the frontier: clouds of mosquitoes, rainstorms, swamps, hot sun, dysentery, and intermittent fevers, as well as having to eat boiled rattlesnake or go supperless when food supplies ran low, and getting cramps from eating berries. Still the axmen, rodmen, chainmen, and compassmen pushed on through the uninhabited Reserve. Harlan Hatcher summarized their courage: "The stalwart young men got thin and haggard from excessive labors, disease, and poor and inadequate diet, but for the most part their morale remained high." They would go into camp wet and cold, get a fire started and "push about the bottle. . . [and] were merry as grigs."

The mouth of the Cuyahoga River, which in the Iroquoian language meant "crooked river," was reached on July 22, 1796. A name was needed for this new frontier settlement. The members of the surveying party decided to name their settlement after their leader, Moses Cleaveland. Apparently taken by surprise, Cleaveland gracefully accepted the compliment, responding later: "While I was in New Connecticut I laid out a town on the bank of Lake Erie, which was called by my name, and I believe the child is now born that may live to see that place as large as Old Windham." Upon completing this survey in October 1796, Moses Cleaveland left the Reserve, never to return.

George W. Knepper's essay, "Early Migration to the Western Reserve," and Thomas A. Smith's, "The Firelands and the Settlement of Vermilion," are complementary analyses that relate the "Yankee Exodus" and outmigration westward from New England, New York, and Pennsylvania into the Old Northwest and New Connecticut. Walter Havighurst asserted that the Old Northwest began its political existence as a unified region, quickly won, with few obstacles in its landscape to dispute possession: "Most settlers had no part in the winning of the West—they came to a waiting welcome country." Why did they come? What caused this exodus? According to Knepper, the New England emigration to the Western Reserve was attributed to the desire for economic gain, hard times in New England, new opportunity, and cheap land in the West. David Abbot, pioneer settler of Chagrin, "anxious to make money in western lands," built a cabin at the mouth of the Chagrin River in 1797, and, in 1801, brought his wife and children to live there. In 1808, however, he bought 1,800 acres near Milan, Ohio and moved his family there.

Cheap land, of course, remained the primary lure. In part, it provided the "safety valve" relieving some of the pressure in old New England, especially after the War of 1812. One group in Geneva, Ashtabula County, purchased 900 acres at $1.50 per acre. Costs to individual buyers were often reduced by people grouping together for joint purchase of larger blocks of land. Boosterism and propaganda persuaded some emigrants. Letters home stressed the mild climate, rich soil, huge trees and huge crop yields, in addition to the cheap land. William Tear, from the Isle of Man, who had settled in Leroy Township, Geauga County, wrote a lengthy letter to his Manx relatives and friends. He pointed out that provisions were cheap; an axe was all that was needed to provide adequate fuel. He was also impressed by the social equality and freedom of religion and liberty. Tear exclaimed that he got a job one day after he arrived.

Jacob Morse, a tanner, came to Concord Township, Geauga County, in 1815, leaving his family behind in Franklin, Massachusetts. Morse wrote a long letter from Painesville to his wife, Betsy, giving her explicit instructions on how to bring the family west. In this letter, he advised her to bring all kinds of provisions, particularly butter, cheese, fish, and pork. "Bake up a good passel of bread before you start. It must be flour bread, for brown bread will not keep," said Morse. He asked his wife especially to bring items he assumed to be too expensive in Geauga County.

Did the stereotypical pattern of the "western movement" in America make the Western Reserve a miniature New England? B. A. Hinsdale, writing in 1888, enthusiastically concluded: "No other five thousand square miles of territory in the United States, lying in a body outside of New England, ever had, to begin with, so pure a New England population." Indeed, it is true that towns such as Hudson, Tallmadge, or Gates Mills retain their dignified, quiet, historical-minded New England heritage and flavor. Harlan Hatcher, for instance, described Gates Mills in the lush Chagrin River Valley as embodying twentieth-century man's dream of early nineteenth-century Connecticut peace and graciousness. But New Connecticut did not become an exact reproduction of the old. The Irish, Germans, Blacks, Hungarians, Czechs, and Italians now take their places beside the New Englanders, and cities such as Lorain, Youngstown, Akron, and Cleveland attest to this dramatic ethnic mixture.

The Connecticut Land Company was truly a speculator's enterprise. Few of the investors ever became settlers; most stayed in Connecticut and sought buyers through agents. One promoter and schemer was Gideon Granger, postmaster general in President Thomas Jefferson's administration. Granger held huge tracts of land in Ashtabula County and boasted that here would grow the "new" Washington of the West. Others were dreamers, such as Abraham Skinner, agent of Henry Champion, who envisioned a planned community along the banks of the Grand River, north of present-day Painesville. Some pioneers such as the Reverend David Bacon of Tallmadge, came to fight the devil. Others were more practical opportunists, such as Lorenzo Carter, Cleveland's first permanent settler and successful entrepreneur and politician.

As Jeffrey P. Brown makes clear in his article on Samuel Huntington, there were also ambitious, well-educated eastern politicians transplanted to the Reserve frontier. Fond of social and lively company, energetic, courteous, and gentlemanly, Huntington was one of the most versatile men to serve the new state of Ohio. Huntington arrived in the village of Cleveland in 1801, at a time when the various political factions throughout the territory were plotting Ohio's statehood. Working with George Tod of Warren, Huntington threw his prestige with northern Republicans and joined the Virginia Jeffersonian Republicans from Chillicothe and Marietta to work against Governor Arthur St. Clair's Federalists. The result was an Ohio loyal to President Jefferson. But more importantly, it was a boost to Huntington's personal career, as chief justice of the state supreme court and, from 1808 to 1810, as Ohio's third governor. It was indeed an era of personality and pragmatism in politics, and Huntington made the most of all opportunities.

PHILLIP R. SHRIVER

The Beaver Wars and the Destruction of the Erie Nation

Sometime, probably in the third or fourth decade of the seventeenth century, a European first stood on the shores of Lake Erie. Whether the intrepid agent of French imperialism ever traveled among the native peoples on the south shore is a question that may never be answered. Certainly at that time there were Indians still living and hunting on the lake plains along such rivers as the Maumee, Sandusky, Huron, Vermilion, Black, Rocky, Cuyahoga, Grand, and Ashtabula in Ohio; the Elk and Walnut in Pennsylvania; and the Cattaraugus, Eighteen-mile, and Buffalo in New York. Yet when Jolliet and Pere, Casson, and Galinee explored Lake Erie in 1669, the Indians of the south shore were gone, their villages destroyed, their fires cold.

Who were the Indians who had lived here, and what had happened to them? From the *Jesuit Relations* of 1640 and a series of mid-seventeenth-century maps, we know their names and their approximate locations. Through extensive and continuing archaeological and anthropological investigation, we know more. South-shore Lake Erie may have had at least three groups of Indians living along it in 1640: from west to east, the Assistaeronon, or Mascouten; the Ontarraronon, or Kickapoo; and the Eriehronon, or Erie, called by the French "Nation du Chat" or "Cat Nation."

The Assistaeronon (a Huron term meaning "People of Fire" or "Fire Nation") have the historic tribal name of Mascouten. They were a semi-sedentary Algonquian tribe who apparently preferred areas where they might have access to both prairie and forest; they planted corn and other crops and hunted deer, bear, and, where available, buffalo. David M. Stothers and James R. Graves of the University of Toledo believe the Mascouten occupied the area between the Maumee and Sandusky valleys in northwestern Ohio, as well as the southern Lower Peninsula of Michigan in the late sixteenth and early seventeenth centuries. The marshlands about the western basin of Lake Erie were rich in beaver, an attraction to Indians engaged, as were nearly all the eastern tribes either directly or indirectly, in fur trade with Europeans. From 1640 to 1643, the Attiwandaron (or Neutral Nation as they were called by the French) from the area north and east of Lake Erie warred against the Mascouten and their allies, the Kickapoo, Sauk, and Fox, forcing them to retreat from the western Lake Erie basin to the area about Lake Michigan.

The Ontarraronon (a Huron word meaning "Lake People") are known historically as the Kickapoo, a tribe of Algonquian tradition whose movements are said to have been so frequent and extensive that no particular area can be regarded as their homeland. In 1640, when they were first mentioned in the *Jesuit Relations*, they were living in Michigan or Ohio near the west end of Lake Erie. Stothers and Graves believe they may have occupied the Lake Erie shore between the Vermilion and Cuyahoga rivers in the late sixteenth and early seventeenth centuries.

In language and culture, the Kickapoo were closely related to the Sauk, Fox, and Mascouten, ties which they also shared with the Shawnee. Alternating between semipermanent villages and temporary winter camps, the Kickapoo lived in pole-framed houses sided and roofed with slabs of elm bark, and they subsisted on their own crops combined with hunting and food gathering. The attacks of the Neutral Nation against their Mascouten neighbors in the early 1640s appear also to have dislodged the Kickapoo, for the French found them in southern Wisconsin in 1665.

By the 1650s only the Erie remained near the southern shore of Lake Erie. Though it has long been speculated that they might have occupied the entire shore of the lake that still bears their name, they appear to have been concentrated between present Erie and Buffalo, with seasonal movement possibly extending as far east as the Genesee River and as far south and west as the headwaters of the Allegheny-Ohio. Their movement inland "to escape their enemies, who are farther to the West" may have reflected Neutral pressure from the northwest.

A nation of several tribes, the Erie in the 1650s were reported to have a total population of about twelve thousand (including some four thousand warriors) grouped in twenty-eight villages and twelve fortified (or palisaded) towns, though those figures were probably exaggerated. Historic contact materials have been found at Erie village sites in the vicinity of present Erie, Pennsylvania; at Ripley, New York; at two locations in the valley of the Cattaraugus Creek, New York; and at two communities in the Niagara Frontier. Other sites along Lake Erie, literally as far west as the Cuyahoga valley and designated by archaeologists as the Whittlesey Focus, were long-surmised to be associated with the Erie. The present consensus among archaeologists and anthropologists is that the Whittlesey Focus represents an Algonquian, perhaps Kickapoo, culture rather than that of the Iroquoian Erie.

French records respecting the Kickapoo and Mascouten are fragmentary; they are more extensive concerning the Erie. They begin with a report published in 1632 by the Recollect [a French Franciscan missionary] historian, Gabriel Sagard-Theodat. Sagard had spent a year (1623–24) among the Huron of the Georgian Bay area and had there learned about a people living to the south called by the Huron "Eriehronon", "Rhiierrhonon," or simply "Erie." To Sagard and the French, they were "*la Nation du Chat*," or the Cat Nation, named not for the bobcat, the lynx, or the panther, as many came to believe, but rather for the "wild cat" (*chat sauvage*), or raccoon, which still abounds in the forests along the Lake Erie shore. That the raccoon was an important source of food for the Erie is evident in an analysis of animal bones recovered from their village refuse pits. And, as Sagard reported, the raccoon was also the source of the fur from which the Eries made their robes and blankets, each fringed with the animals' distinctive ringed tails.

While it was the gray-frocked Recollect, Brother Sagard, who was the first to publish information about the Erie, our principal understanding of them comes from the records maintained by missionaries of another order, the Society of Jesus. These black-robed zealots were militant, tough, and fearless, and the order was a force to be reckoned with, despite being few in number, at home in France as well as on the frontiers of the French Empire. Embodied in letters, journals, reports, and recommendations to their superiors, the records of the Jesuit missionaries were published nearly annually in Paris as the *Jesuit Relations*—ultimately totaling seventy-three volumes. Extended direct quotations in the subsequent narrative are drawn from the *Relations* unless otherwise noted. Unlike their Recollect predecessors in the missions of New France, whose official policy was based on the Europeanization of the Indian (even to the expectation of his speaking French), the Jesuits sought to graft Christianity onto the native culture with as little disruption as possible, leaving intact so much of Indian spiritual perception and social organization as was not incompatible with Christian doctrine or the interests of the Jesuit order.

Despite incredible hardships and obstacles, the Jesuits and their philosophy proved enormously successful. Baptisms and conversions to Christianity soared beyond anything the Recollects had experienced. Nowhere did the Jesuits have greater impact than in the area north of Lake Erie among the Huron where, led by Jean de Brebeuf, they began to serve in 1625. Yet there is no record of their ever having direct contact with the Erie villages one hundred fifty miles away, on the south side of that same lake.

That the Jesuits knew of the Erie through the Huron and other Indians is evident in their occasional references to them throughout the *Jesuit Relations*, beginning in 1635 with a comment by Brebeuf and concluding in 1685 with praise for one who had become a singular Christian convert. In that half century of Jesuit commentary *about* the Erie, there were a number of instances of direct Jesuit contact *with* individual Erie, including prolonged contact with a few. Thus it is in the pages of the *Jesuit Relations* that the dawn mists which envelop the history of Lake Erie's aboriginal people begin to clear.

Whatever the extent of direct intercourse between the French and the Erie Nation, the European presence on the American Continent had profound consequences for all the woodland tribes. Traditional intertribal relationships and balances of power were turned topsy-turvy by the mechanisms of the fur trade. Attempts to control the hunting grounds, the transportation routes, and the favorable trading sites became a driving force in Indian diplomacy, aggravating old hatreds and creating new ones.

At stake in the newly fostered rivalry was material wealth of bonanza proportions in the eyes of the Indians: glass-beaded chokers (called "porcelain collars" by the French), iron axes and celts, blankets, rings, bracelets, clay pipes, brass kettles, liquor, and knives were all prized, but most coveted of all was the European's gun. At first, when royal monopolies were vested in private fur companies with taxable shares guaranteed the crown, the several European powers were wary of selling guns to the Indians. Then, as independent operators discovered the comparative ease of circumventing state monopolies in the vastness of the American wilderness, the restrictions on gun sales broke down, particularly in the areas of Dutch and British influence. Only in New France, where gun sales were limited to "Christian" Indians, did restriction persist, a policy which ultimately proved calamitous. The number of guns in the hands of the Iroquois, the Indians closest to the Dutch fur-trading centers of New York and the British settlements in Connecticut and Massachusetts, rose dramatically in the 1630s and 1640s. Tribes trading with the French were much less well armed. These tribes included the Montagnard and other Algonquians north of Quebec as well as the Huron in the Lake Simcoe-Georgian Bay area, the Neutrals north of Lake Erie and on both sides of the Niagara River, and the Tionontate (or Tobacco Huron) to the east of Lake Huron.

About 1575, when the great leader Hiawatha forged the Iroquois Confederation, the Huron, also an Iroquoian people but not part of the league, were a much more numerous and powerful people than the Five Nations. But in 1636, eleven years after the Jesuit missionaries first came into their villages, an epidemic—possibly bubonic plague—decimated the Huron population. By 1639, the thirty-two villages of "Huronia" had been reduced from a total population of approximately forty thousand to half that number.

It was at this time that forest economics compelled the Iroquois to look to the north and west for more furs. Quite simply, the beaver of the New York area were all but gone. Prices paid in guns and other trade goods for beaver pelts at Albany rose dramatically compared to those paid at Quebec, Tadoussac, Three Rivers, and other French posts. The thirty-five-to-forty-foot Chippewa and Ottawa canoes from the upper lakes, laden with beaver furs and passing through Huronia (and Huron middlemen) to the Ottawa and St. Lawrence rivers, proved too tempting to resist. Tempting too were the cargoes of furs of the Montagnard and other Algonquians coming down from the north. A decade of Iroquois piracy ensued, culminating in the outbreak of the "Wars of the Iroquois," an all-out attempt of the Iroquois to establish themselves as middlemen in the fur trade, in 1649. Their depredations against their fellow redmen have been aptly designated "The Beaver Wars."

In one brief week in March 1649, the Iroquois crushed their traditional enemies, the Huron, the key link to the distant Indian nations in the French sphere, and who were already decimated by pestilence and only lightly armed by their French allies. Nine months later, the Tobacco Nation was shattered. The Neutral Nation was next. Situated between the Iroquois and the Huron, the Attiwandaron had attempted for generations to remain aloof from the quarrels of their two powerful neighbors. Though nineteen thousand in number, they proved easy victims of the imperialist Iroquois, whose pretext for attacking them was that they had refused to surrender a Huron girl. In the first months of 1651, a well-armed Iroquois army of six hundred Mohawks and Senecas attacked the Neutral towns along the Niagara and north of Lake Erie, effectively destroying the Attiwandaron as a separate people.

With three of their neighboring competitors now eliminated, the Iroquois paused to lick their wounds, assimilate replacement captives (the combined indigenous populations of the Five Nations had dropped to scarcely twelve thousand), and engage in some diplomatic maneuvering. A deputation of their "most dignified and smooth-talking" chiefs arrived at Montreal and proceeded with Machiavellian guile to brighten the chain of friendship with the French. Blandly professing ignorance of any cause for grievance between two great peoples, they urged that amity henceforward exist between them. Louis XIV's operatives in the New World were, before all else, realists. Their all-but-ruined fur trade must be re-established immediately on some basis if New France were to survive. For the present the Iroquois looked like the only game in town, and they swallowed whatever indignation they felt at the recent devastation of their principal Indian allies and the destruction of their missions, and they embraced the perpetrators. Moreover, the Five Nations offered a fertile field to the Black Robes, whom they invited to come to their towns and establish missions. Thus it was that peace came between the French and the Iroquois, and on July 2, 1654, Father Simon Le Moyne was dispatched to the Onondaga, the "keepers of the fire" in the symbolic longhouse of the Five Nations.

The way was now clear for the Iroquois to attack their fourth neighbor, the Erie, to the west. Possibly the largest of the nations the Iroquois had determined to conquer, the Erie were well led and organized and had defeated the Iroquois in previous battles. Even the Dutch believed the Erie warriors were superior to the Iroquois, referring to them as *satanas* or devils. Yet direct Erie contact with Europeans was minimal to nonexistent. Guns among them were few in contrast to those possessed by the well-armed Iroquois. The bow and arrow was still the Erie warrior's primary weapon. The preponderance of power once held by the Erie had tilted at last towards the Iroquois, thanks to the white man's gun. And the Iroquois realized it.

The Iroquois war against the Erie began in the summer of 1654 and lasted intermittently until 1656—this in striking contrast to the single week of war required to break the Huron in 1649. Historical accounts of the Iroquois-Erie struggle depend almost entirely on the *Jesuit Relations* of those years and are based on the reports of Iroquois informants. Having neutralized the French through diplomacy, the Iroquois informed them at Montreal in May 1654 that "our young men will wage no more warfare with the French; but, as they are too warlike to abandon that pursuit, you are to understand that we are going to wage a war against the Ehriehronnons and this very summer we shall lead an army thither. The earth is trembling yonder, and here all is quiet."

Though acknowledging the aggressiveness of their own young warriors in precipitating the conflict, the Iroquois spokesmen informed the French that there were ample provocations for the attack on the Erie. They told of the burning of a Seneca village by an Erie war party and of the surprise attack by another Erie force against a group of Iroquois returning from the vicinity of Lake Huron. These depredations, they claimed, were incited by vengeful Huron now living among the Erie. A cycle of events, inflamed by the inextricable admixture of tribal policy and private retribution which characterized all Indian warfare, had begun—and would end only with the extirpation of the Erie Nation.

In an effort to ward off all-out war, the Erie now sent to the Seneca a peace mission of thirty ambassadors who arrived, inopportunely, at about the same time as a report that a Seneca had been killed by an Erie in an "unexpected accident." In retaliation, the Seneca put to death twenty-five of the Erie envoys, though five managed to escape. Returning to the Erie villages, the escapees reported the fate of their comrades, whereupon the Erie resolved to gain revenge. Two Onondaga warriors were captured, and one, a chief by the name of Annenraes, was sent as a prisoner to an Erie village from which one of the slain peace ambassadors had come. There he was turned over to the sister of the murdered ambassador, the expectation being that he would probably be adopted by the woman as replacement for her dead brother, this in keeping with a traditional practice among many American Indian tribes.

The woman was absent from the Erie village at that time, but the villagers were so confident of the likelihood of her adoption of the captive that they dressed him in fine clothing and gave a feast in his honor. To their dismay, when the woman returned, she rejected the prisoner and demanded that he be killed to avenge her brother's death. Village leaders pleaded with her in vain to change her mind, arguing that her personal vengeance would probably involve them all in a new war. Their fears were soon realized. Just before his death, Annenraes cried out "that an entire people would be burned in his person." When news of his death reached the Onondaga in early August 1654, an army of eighteen hundred warriors was assembled to accomplish the destruction of the Erie.

At that point, Simon Le Moyne arrived at Onnontague, the principal village of the Onondaga, to establish the first Jesuit mission among the Iroquois. On the tenth of August, he addressed a key council of the principal chiefs of all the Iroquois nations—except the often intransigent Mohawk—gathered to discuss the impending war against the Erie. In the words of Le Moyne, "I was occupied fully two hours in delivering this harangue, which I pronounced in the tone of a Captain—walking back and forth, as is their custom, like an actor on a stage." No less cynically than might have any of his soldier countrymen, Le Moyne seized the opportunity to further solidify relations with the Iroquois. To each of the four Iroquois nations (Onondaga, Seneca, Cayuga, and Oneida) on hand he gave a symbolic hatchet "to be used in the new war in which they were engaged with the Cat Nation." To the Seneca he offered renewed courage after the loss of "some of their number in this war." To all four nations he gave a "present" or blessing to "enable them to maintain a strong defense against the enemy" and another present of paint for their faces, "for it is the custom of the warriors here never to go into battle without having their faces painted—some with black, some with red, and some with various other colors." Finally, he symbolically "wiped away the tears of all the young warriors caused by the death of their great Captain Annenraes." As Le Moyne made each of his points, the assembled Iroquois "uttered a loud shout of applause from the depths of their chests in evidence of their delight."

After Le Moyne had finished, the chiefs and warriors gathered together by nations and called to them as representative of the fifth Iroquois nation a lone Mohawk "who by good luck happened to be present." After two hours of consultation, they asked Le Moyne to thank Onnontio (literally, "great mountain"), the governor of New France, Monsieur de Lauson, for "encouraging them to make a spirited fight against their new enemies of the Cat Nation, and for exhorting them never to wage war again with the French." And they asked Le Moyne to build a French mission on the shore of Onondaga Lake "in the heart of the country, since you are to possess our hearts." To help cement the new cordiality between the Five Nations and France, the Iroquois returned to Le Moyne the New Testament taken from the martyred Father Brebeuf, "whom they cruelly put to death five years ago, and another little book of devotion that had been used by the late Father Charles Garnier, whom these very people killed four years ago."

As the Iroquois army of eighteen hundred warriors, largely Onondaga, prepared to leave for the war against the Erie, their principal chief, a young man by the name of Achionagueras who had replaced the dead Annenraes, begged Le Moyne to baptize him. Asked the young Onondaga leader, "If from this day forth I possess the Faith, cannot I be a Christian?...Will our enemies' arrows become blunted for my sake? Dost thou wish me, at each step that I take in battle, to fear hell more than death? Unless thou baptize me, I shall be without courage, and shall not dare to face the conflict. Baptize me,...and I give thee my word that I will live and die a Christian."

Early in the morning of August 15, 1654, as Le Moyne prepared to return to Quebec and the Iroquois made ready to strike the Erie villages to the west, the Jesuit missionary baptized the Onondaga chief, giving him the Christian name of Jean Baptiste, or John the Baptist. It is not the least of the numerous ironies of seventeenth-century forest diplomacy that as John the Baptist, wearing a French uniform and carrying a French gun, Achionagueras led the Onondaga and other Iroquois in the war to destroy the Erie, who had dared to give refuge to the Huron, many of them Christian converts from earlier Jesuit missions.

The Iroquois attack came with stunning swiftness, catching the Erie villages by surprise. One by one they fell or were "abandoned to the mercy of the Conqueror, who after burning everything started in pursuit of the fugitives." The stream of refugees ultimately numbered more than six thousand, of whom at least two thousand were warriors. For five days, the Erie fled through the forest, closely pursued by their Iroquois enemies. Unable to escape, the Erie stopped and hastily built a fort of wood with palisaded walls and earthen entrenchments.

As the Iroquois approached the Erie fort, Achionagueras and another chief displayed themselves in French uniform, hoping to frighten the Erie, most of whom had never seen European attire. It was Achionagueras who called out to the Erie defenders to surrender or face certain destruction. Then invoking his new faith, he warned, "The Master of life fights for us; you will be ruined if you resist him." "Who is this Master of our lives?" came back the Erie reply. "We acknowledge none but our arms and hatchets." It was then that the "assault was made and the palisade attacked on all sides."

The siege of the Erie fort was a long and costly one. Though the Erie warriors outnumbered the Iroquois, they were burdened by the presence of their women and children. And they had few if any guns (and no powder) in contrast to the well-armed Iroquois. On the other hand, they were archers *extraordinaire*, the Jesuits grudgingly acknowledging that "they fight like Frenchmen, bravely sustaining the first discharge of the Iroquois, who are armed with our muskets, and then falling upon them with a hailstorm of poisoned arrows, which they discharge eight or ten times before a musket can be reloaded."

The end came with the near exhaustion of Erie arrows and an Iroquois stratagem. Simply, the Onondaga hit upon the plan of using their long war canoes as shields to ward off the volleys of poisonous arrows as they approached the Erie works. Driving back the entrenched defenders with musketry, they inverted their canoes to use them as scaling ladders to get up and over the palisaded walls. As their enemies scaled the walls, more than three hundred of the Erie defenders broke and ran, leaving their comrades and women and children behind. Once in the fort, the Iroquois commenced a systematic butchery of its occupants, the "carnage among the women and children" being so great "that blood was knee-deep in certain places." Shamed by their own cowardice, the three hundred Erie warriors who had bolted returned to the scene of the slaughter. For a brief moment, they caught the Iroquois off guard and exacted their own partial retribution. But the Iroquois recovered in time to crush the returning Erie and complete the annihilation, though their own losses overall were so heavy that they were compelled to remain two months in Erie country to bury their dead and care for their wounded.

On September 11, 1654, while the Iroquois were winning their signal though costly victory, Le Moyne arrived back in Quebec to report the success of his efforts to assure French peace with the Iroquois and their ultimate conversion to Christianity. Indeed, in the two years that followed, the Iroquois did keep the peace with France. And when Achionagueras returned to Onnontague from his conquest of the Erie, he fulfilled a battlefield pledge that if the Master of life would help him achieve victory, he would assist the Jesuit fathers in converting his people to Christianity. With his assistance, so successful was the Iroquois mission that by 1656 the Jesuits could report that "more Iroquois have become Christians in two months than there were Hurons converted in several years."

As for the Erie, the Iroquois war against them continued through 1655 and on into 1656. With the principal fortified towns already destroyed, Iroquois strategy now called for the elimination of the last remote villages and, indeed, the last remaining Erie wherever they could be found. Regrettably, much of the *Jesuit Relations* for 1665 is missing. From that portion which has survived, it is known that on September 12, 1655, an Onondaga delegation of eighteen arrived in Quebec to petition the governor of New France "for French soldiers to defend their villages against the inroads of the Cat Nation" as well as for more weapons. Two months later, Jesuit missionaries assigned to the Iroquois mission at Onnontague, Fathers Joseph Chaumonot and Claude Dablon, baptized a captured Erie boy of nine or ten years of age just before he was burned to death, "no quarter being now given between the two tribes." In late January 1656, they witnessed the "boiling of the war-kettle" as the Iroquois prepared for a new offensive against the Erie, while on the fifth of February, they "wiped away the blood" for a large war party of Seneca and Oneida returning "from their latest engagement with the Cat Nation."

On February 11, two more Erie captives, young men between twenty and thirty years of age, were brought in by Onondaga warriors. Each was given to a family to replace someone lost in combat. As reported by Father Dablon, "The younger and handsomer one, a Nephew of the other, was given to the greatest warrior of the Country, named Aharihon, a Captain famous for his warlike exploits, but as arrogant and bloodthirsty as he is brave." Though Aharihon already had sacrificed forty Erie captives to avenge the loss of one of his brothers in the war, he concluded that this young man too "must die in atonement for his brother's death." Accordingly, the young captive was roasted alive over a slow fire, his torture finally ending in death in the early morning hours of February 15, 1656.

Not all Erie captives were so unfortunate. An Erie woman captured and enslaved by the Oneida became a Christian convert and was baptized by the Bishop of Canada with the name Catherine Gandeaktena. In 1667 she persuaded her Iroquois husband and several of his relatives to go with her to found an Iroquois mission near Montreal, the celebrated Mission of la Prairie de la Magdeleine. By the time of her death in 1673, she had earned the acclaim of hundreds of Frenchmen and Iroquois alike for her virtue and saintliness and for her success in attracting some two hundred Iroquois converts to the mission.

Some Erie managed to elude the Iroquois for a time. As late as 1680, a remnant band of six hundred Erie men, women, and children surrendered voluntarily to the Iroquois south and east of the Ohio River and were then apparently absorbed into the Five Nations, their identities as Erie finally at an end.

Henry R. Schoolcraft, famed Indian authority of the nineteenth century, reported the Iroquois version of the Erie's ultimate fate: "Seneca tradition affirms that after the defeat of the most westerly bodies of the Eries, on the shores of

Lake Erie, the survivors fled to the Allegheny River, called Ohio by them, down which they fled. . . . Their council-fire was put out. Their name was obliterated from the number of tribes. The places where they once dwelt knew them no more."

JARÉ R. CARDINAL and
ERIC J. CARDINAL

Archaeology and History: Some Suggestions from the Historian's Viewpoint

In recent issues of *Ohio Archaeologist*, the archaeological uses of ethnohistorical sources have been critically discussed. The complementary nature of these two disciplines is evident: questions concerning the later prehistoric, proto-historic, and early historic periods are more effectively addressed through interdisciplinary rather than undisciplinary means and methods. It is equally clear that the practitioners of each discipline must exercise care when venturing into the realm of the other.

Researchers can approach a problem in different ways. Historians begin in the past and work toward the present, attempting not only to discover facts but sequence and causation as well. They sift historical materials to piece together a narrative of events. Too frequently, they are unaware of or ignore nondocumentary sources, and their construction of sequential narration can lack analytical synthesis. Anthropologists and archaeologists, on the other hand, explain the past by drawing analogies with the present. As a result, they may misinterpret historical source materials simply by failing to use proper historical methods.

Glenn A. Black has discussed some of these difficulties from an archaeologist's point of view:

> In order to approach prehistory from history the archaeologist is dependent entirely upon the records left by those who *first contacted and observed the Indian in his natural environment*, . . . some individual would have had to specifically describe . . . objects in detail . . . and describe the spot in *such a way that the site could be located today* and excavated for verification of the recorded statements.

It is therefore tempting to look for documents or other historical materials that provide a "missing link" which connects aboriginal populations to an accurate and reliable historic record. Yet no historical material can ever offer such a definitive key to understanding either anthropological or archaeological data. Isolated historical source materials all too often provide evidence that is incomplete, subtle, or tentative.

All of this is apropos to the long-standing but recently renewed discussion of the location of the Erie Indians. The authors would like to suggest from the historians' viewpoint some of the opportunities for, and the difficulties in, utilizing historical materials in studying this question.

Traditionally, most scholars—historians, anthropologists, and archaeologists alike—identified the late prehistoric and early historic inhabitants of what is now northeast Ohio as a powerful and populous tribe of Iroquoian-speaking people, the Erie. Before Europeans came to the American continents and until about 1656, the Erie (who were known to the early French invaders as "Nation du Chat" or "Cat Nation") occupied the southern shore of Lake Erie from the Cuyahoga River east to Cattaragus Creek, and possibly as far south as the Ohio River. In the mid-1650s, the Erie met near annihilation and dispersal at the hands of the Five Nations.

But archaeological fieldwork and analysis over the past fifty years have increasingly called the notion into question. As early as the 1930s, Emerson Greenman found indications at the Reeve Site in Eastlake, Ohio, of "the possibility of more than one culture" there, some of which were "more characteristic of Algonkian" than Iroquoian occupancy. More recent investigations have demonstrated that "it has become increasingly obvious that the name Erie was never applied to a single cultural unit recognizable in the archaeological record," and, further, that there is "considerable evidence to indicate that the group or groups the French Jesuits called Erie never inhabited Ohio, and we may never be able to apply the name to an archaeological component."

In 1976, after a lengthy analysis of the archaeological fieldwork in northeast Ohio, David Brose contended that "it is probable that re-evaluation of the ethnohistoric sources will conclude that if ethnic identity can be assigned to the late [prehistoric] components, it will be distinct from the Erie." Current archaeological fieldwork associates Native American occupancy in northeast Ohio more closely with Algonquian speakers, possibly the Ontarraronen (Kickapoo), than with Iroquoian speakers such as the Erie. In addition, archaeological and ethnohistorical analysis by Marian White shows that the Erie did occupy village sites between Ripley and Buffalo, New York until the mid-seventeenth century.

In short, the archaeological evidence accumulated and analyzed to date contradicts traditional histories by indicating that the Erie never occupied northeast Ohio. To bolster this view, scholars have turned anew to historical and ethnohistorical material for analysis. Documents, illustrations, and maps may shed light on the cultures and locations of aboriginal American populations. Early European-made maps in particular represent, as Brose has pointed out, "one of the most underutilized source[s] of potential data concerning the Protohistoric archaeological sites of Ohio."

Historian Francis Jennings has noted that many of the Woodland Amerindian peoples are "known today only by rumor or artifact." The Erie certainly are such a people. The essential difficulty in analyzing the Erie by means of historical materials is that "we know very little about them because no Caucasian reached their country until after their dispersion." The documentary evidence used by historians is, in this case, all second hand: derivative accounts written by Europeans that relied upon the often false and even mendacious testimony of Native

Americans. The early colonial maps were based upon such accounts and their depiction of topography, geography, and political geography was therefore often incorrect. These maps are useful and important tools, but usually deceptive ones as well.

The 1650 and 1656 maps of French Royal cartographer Nicolas Sanson d'Abbeville are cases in point. These works are often accepted as outlining the Great Lakes region more accurately than other contemporary charts. There are several reasons for this: Sanson placed Lake Erie on its correct north-east-southwest axis; he accurately represented both the St. Clair and the Niagara Rivers; and he also apparently placed ethnic groups which conform with subsequent discoveries of archaeological data. More importantly, Sanson located the Nation du Chat to the east of a crescent-shaped body of water that was later identified by White as Lake Chautauqua. This designation has been generally accepted by others, and it decidedly places the Erie Indians in the Niagara area of New York State.

It is quite tempting to believe that Sanson intended the lake to be Chautauqua and to locate the Nation du Chat there, especially because there has been no positive archaeological indications of Erie occupation further west. But did he? Sanson would have been at odds with contemporary French opinion had he deliberately pinpointed the Nation du Chat in such a limited area.

An analysis of the maps themselves in relation to other contemporaneous documents more clearly defines White's interpretation of these sources. Sanson never visited America and his maps were the product of aggregate French knowledge and his own acuity. It is doubtful that he was the beneficiary of information unavailable to others, as White, citing Nellis Crouse's 1924 work, hints. The cartographer himself noted on the 1656 map that his information concerning "the Great River of Canada or the St. Laurence, and all its environs are [taken] from the relations of the French." Most of seventeenth-century French knowledge about the Great Lakes region came from the *Jesuit Relations*, those detailed yet flawed documents of New France. The Jesuit Fathers never came into contact with the Erie. Yet they reported that the Nation du Chat was able to muster two thousand to four thousand warriors, a number that would conservatively suggest a total population of ten thousand to fifteen thousand.

These figures should not be accepted uncritically. It was common practice among a number of tribes from earliest contact times to inflate the numbers and the ferocity of populations further inland to discourage European penetration of the continent. It is quite likely that these figures on Erie population were intentionally exaggerated by Huron informants who wished to keep their privileged position in the Indian-European trade network, and later by the Iroquois who sought French aid and arms to fight the Erie during the "Beaver Wars." (The Iroquois received more aid from the Dutch and the English than they ever did from the French, but they sought French support as part of their strategy to "play off" European nations against each other.) In 1655, in response to repeated requests, Father Simon Le Moyne gave to the Seneca, Oneida, Onondaga, and Cayuga "a hatchet to be used in the New War in which they were engaged with the Cat

Nation." That same year, the Onondaga asked the French (without success) to provide a detachment of troops to fight the Erie. Certainly both the Huron and the Iroquois had greater motive to misinform the French than to reveal Erie strength accurately, given their own economic, diplomatic, and military considerations. The French, by no means inept at diplomacy, undoubtedly accepted this information with reservation. Nevertheless, it is reasonable to assume that they received an inaccurate and inflated picture not only of Erie population but of Erie strength and deployment as well. Based upon the *Relations*, it seems evident that the French would have believed the Erie's territory to be quite extensive.

More important in establishing Sanson's accuracy is the interpretation of the geographic landmarks themselves. Marian White has been instrumental in establishing this credibility, using a crescent-shaped lake and a river with its headwaters (both unidentified on the 1650 and 1656 maps) as ethnohistoric evidence of Erie occupation in western New York State. White identifies these two landmarks as Chautauqua Lake and the Allegheny River respectively. However, this crescent-shaped lake is shown far to the west and much further inland than Chautauqua's actual location. Sanson also charts a major stream that flows northwest from this nameless lake and enters Lake Erie at approximately the midpoint of its southern shoreline. In reality, no such stream exists if this body of water indeed represents Lake Chautauqua.

White reconciles these "inaccuracies" by noting that in both the 1650 and 1656 maps Lake Erie is "represented with too narrow an extent from east to west," and therefore other landmarks are slightly distorted. Yet, the lake's shape "is distinctive." No other lake with such characteristic shape appears on modern maps except Chautauqua. Furthermore, although White acknowledges that the stream "is incorrect if the lake is Chautauqua," she points out that a small creek (Little Inlet) does flow northwest from the lake toward the headwaters of Chautauqua Creek which does empty into Lake Erie. The "direction and shape of this Chautauqua Creek-Little Inlet connection corresponds quite well" with the stream/lake representation on Sanson's two maps. This stream, White argues, may have characterized "one" of the water-and-lake routes "probably" used between Lake Erie and the Susquehanna River, a route of which the French were "likely" to have been aware.

White's argument here is plausible, but not entirely persuasive as there are equally plausible alternative explanations of these geographic features. One may be that "the Indians spoke of a large river that flowed to the south of Lake Erie; with only that amount of information the map maker allowed his imagination to do the rest," a capricious practice that was not unusual in seventeenth- and eighteenth-century cartography. It should be noted that on the 1650 map Sanson also included a major, nonexistent mountain range just to the west of Lake Erie. But it is more likely that Sanson intentionally represented a river flowing north into Lake Erie at its midpoint. All of the *cartographic* inconsistencies that White and subsequent scholars have found in Sanson's placement of these bodies of water are resolved if he had been depicting the Cuyahoga River and its headwaters, not Lake Chautauqua. If this is the case, it is the crescent-shaped lake, not the major stream flowing from it, that requires explanation.

There is, of course, no such lake at the source of the Cuyahoga itself, yet the river is roughly hook-shaped and originates amid a series of ponds. Prior to nineteenth-century drainage of the area, low marshes and salt licks lay to the east of the river's headwaters (although the latter were in the Beaver/Shanango drainage basin), all of which may have found expression as a lake on Sanson's maps. Given the importance of salt, Native American accounts might have emphasized this region. An examination of the much later Johannes Heckewelder map reveals that the Cuyahoga's configuration and its relationship with that of the Mahoning, Allegheny, Monogahela, and Ohio rivers are quite comparable to Sanson's stream and lake and what White believed to be the headwaters of the Allegheny. Heckewelder, who was intimately familiar with the Ohio country and the lakeshore region, observed that of the streams flowing into Lake Erie west of Presque Isle, the "Cujahoga [sic] certainly stands foremost." We suggest that this major stream would be as likely to have been represented by Sanson as Chautauqua. Moreover, such a suggestion helps to explain some of the apparent inconsistencies between Sanson's maps and those of other seventeenth- and eighteenth-century colonial map makers.

An examination of other contemporary cartographic documents shows this more vividly. For this discussion, Sanson's work will be contrasted with several French maps (Bouisseau's 1643 map of New France, the undated Taunton map of Nouvell France, and Father François DuCreux's "Tabula Novae Franciae" of 1660) and three later maps (Recollect Father Louis Hennepin's 1697 map, French Royal cartographer Jacques-Nicolas Bellin's 1744 map, and the map of British colonial John Mitchell, 1755).

The French maps which preceded Sanson's were very coarse approximations indeed. On Bouisseau's map, "Lac D'erie" (which looks more like a swollen river than a lake) connects "Lac de St. Louis" (Ontario) to an oversized "Mer douce ou Lac" (Huron). "Les gens du chat" are placed to the south of Lac D'erie and to the west of the principal river that feeds it. The Taunton map, which Stothers suggests may be the "Lost Jesuit" map of 1640, depicts a more recognizable though still distorted Lake Erie connecting Ontario and Huron. The "Enrie—Nation du Chat" appears directly to the south of it and considerably inland. On both of these maps, vague and inaccurate as they are, the Erie Indians are shown as occupying lands to the south of Lake Erie. It should be noted that this area was as yet unexplored by Europeans, but these locations conform with the accounts in the *Relations*.

DuCreux's 1660 map, on the other hand, portrays the area more accurately than these previous two. Like Sanson, DuCreux placed a small lake to the south of Lake Erie and showed a stream connecting the two bodies of water. Yet he depicted the river as being much longer than did Sanson (and, in actuality, much longer than the Cuyahoga itself) and the inland lake is hardly crescent-shaped. Contrary to White's suggestion, however, these inconsistencies are not enough themselves to render his work invalid. A more telling point may be DuCreux's location of the "Natio Felium" to the west of the river several years after the Erie's defeat by the Five Nations. Yet subsequent cartographers identified the Erie throughout the remainder of the century and continued to designate the south shore of Lake Erie as the former territory of the tribe well into the next century. The *Jesuit Relations* contain accounts of Erie capture and adoption by Seneca and Onondaga into the 1660s, thus this apparent anachronism is not necessarily conclusive.

Hennepin's 1697 map showed Lake Erie on its correct axis but greatly over-sized, and placed the Erie Indians ("Erieckronois") to the south-southwest of a hook-shaped stream. White objected to this representation of "Chautauqua" be-cause it was charted "very far to the west, perhaps in the vicinity of Cleveland." Again, this geographic objection is obviated if this landmark was in fact in-tended to portray a river (and, it could easily be argued, the Cuyahoga) rather than Lake Chautauqua.

Bellin's map, which accompanied Pierre François Xavier de Charlevoix's *Histoire et Description Generale de la Nouvelle France avec le Journal Historique d'un Voyage fait par ordre du Roi dans l'Amerique Septentrionale*, annotated the south-ern shore of Lake Erie with the phrase "Ici etoiennt les ERIES qui onte ete de-truite par les Iroquois." ("Here were the ERIES who have been destroyed by the Iroquois.") In the *Journal Historique*, Charlevoix noted that Lake Erie derived its name from "an Indian nation of the Huron language which was formerly seated on its banks and who have been entirely destroyed by the Iroquoise." It is ques-tionable whether Bellin borrowed information from Charlevoix or vice versa, but in either case it should be noted that such assertions stemmed as much from geopolitical as from cartographical considerations. If Native American inform-ants were often motivated by political or diplomatic imperatives, so too were the map makers themselves.

At approximately the same time Bellin treated the southern shore of Lake Erie as the territory of the Erie Indians, "who have been destroyed" by the usurping Five Nations, the British were describing the region far differently for their own purposes. British colonial John Mitchell, who based much of his information on the travel accounts of Christopher Gist and George Croghan, noted that the re-gion along the southern shoreline of Lake Erie was "the seat of war, the mart of trade & chief Hunting Grounds of the Six Nations on the Lakes & the Ohio." He placed the "Eriez" to the east between the "Canahogue" River and an area of "Forts lately usurped by the French" (Presque Isle and Le Beouf), the "Seneka" further east, and "the Minquaas or Mingos," who some scholars speculate were remnants of the defeated Erie, immediately to the south. Mitchell also made the astounding claim that "the Six Nations have extended their Territories to the River Illinois," and that the Iroquois had "allwaies been in Alliance and Subjection to the English." In short, these colonial maps were used as much to make political claims for legitimacy, sovereignty, and control as to establish geographic accuracy.

We would like to emphasize that we are not asserting that the Erie *did* in fact occupy all of the southern shoreline of Lake Erie, but rather that the French, with the information available to them, very likely *believed* that they did. It was this judgment, evident in the *Jesuit Relations* and in later publications such as the *Journal Historique*, that gave life to the traditionally held view of Erie occupancy. Moreover, based purely upon the cartographic evidence, the historical data regarding the location of the Erie are, and likely will remain, inconclusive. The inland body of water and stream indicated in Sanson's and other cartographers' works could as easily represent the Cuyahoga River as Chautauqua Lake. Therefore, rather than the ethnohistorical sources acting as a guide for archaeological investigations, the opposite will be more nearly the case. We may be sure that the maps all contained inaccuracies and misrepresentations. Archaeological materials, however, presumably are more objective sources. It is this evidence that will help shape the interpretation of the ethnohistorical materials.

This has not been an exhaustive or thorough analysis of all the extant colonial maps. Such a detailed, comprehensive study would be of great value in charting seventeenth- and eighteenth-century ethnohistory along the moving frontier. Yet this treatment of several of these maps, albeit brief, suggests that alternative interpretations of these sources are possible and that care and consideration are necessary in utilizing them to place aboriginal populations.

With Moses Cleaveland's Surveying Party, 1796

John Milton Holley's Journal (Transcripts), MSS. 1, Western Reserve Historical Society, July 12–13, 1796, pp. 8–9.

Tuesday the 12th July in the morning we breakfasted in our camp nearby the little brook & left the packhorse men to come on after us, but when we had proceeded about a mile sent back a hand to tell the men to go round the swamp with the horses but the swamp continued and we ran on till night—here being a hemlock ridge, we were in hope the horses would be able to find us but, alas we were obliged to make a little camp of boughs strike up a fire & go to bed supperless—in the daytime I had eat raspberrys, gooseberrys wintergrew berrys & wintergrew—& in the night I began to grow sick at my Stomach & soon after vomited up everything in me—Mr. Pease too had a return of the cramps in consequence of travelling all day in the water. We all arose early in the morning with meagre looks & somewhat faint for want of eating and drinking for where we camped there was no water thus we had a little rum in the morning of the 13th we continued our course down the Pennsylvania line 200 rods through Alder Swamp till we came a mile of Oak Beach Pond & when we determined to stop & wait the coming of provisions Mr. Porter & Mr. Hall took a compass & were to travel East 20 minutes to try to find the horses track if they had passed Mrs Pease & Spafford took my compass & were to do the same to the West while I staid on the line. I made up a fire & was cleaning a spot to lie down when to my joy & surprise too I heard a voice back of us which quickly answered & found to be Joseph Landon one of the packhorsemen (and a good fellow too) coming on with a back load of provision we called Porter & Pease back as soon as possible & all partook of a most cheerful & much needed breakfast. After this was over Mr Porter Hall & Landon went to help the horses on, as they had found the swamp so large twas impossible to go around it, they were obligated to come through & they were about 3 1/2 miles behind.

John Milton Holley's Field Notes, MSS. 1, Western Reserve Historical Society, September 21–28, 1796, n. p.

On Wednesday the 21st @ 12 o'clock of Sept. 1796 we packed everything up & embarked on board the boats for Coneought in consequence of not having provision to stay any longer—we had not a mouthfull of meat when we went away—pt. of a bbl flour pt. of a bag pears 4 cheeses & some chocolate, constituted our provisions (30 in number about)—The two boats & the Bark canoe carried us—We had a fair wind that & had sailed about 8 miles when we discovered Hall & Co. on the Beach with the Cattle. We then went ashore & found by them that Tinker had arrived at Coneought with provisions—& Warren also was there, he sent on two of his men with 2 horses loaded with flour—himself & other hands waited to come with Tinker when the wind should be favorable.

This news cheered us up exceedingly & we returned to Cayahoga with much lighter hearts than we left it—'twas dark when we came to the mouth of the River & we discovered a fire lighted up on the opposite shore just as we entered the harbour Porter fired a Gun—as we passed the fire we saluted the people & found they were Indians from Grand River who had been west hunting—we eat a moutful of supper & then went to bed—Thursday the 22nd Sept. & I left Cayahoga to plot the east part of the Town with Stoddard & Spafford—The day before we started from Cayahoga we discovered a bear swimming across the Cayahoga—Porter & myself jumped into a Canoe & paddled after him, while another man with a gun went up the Shore after him—but there was such a noise a hallowing that the Bear swam back & escaped—Munson caught 2 rattlesnake which we boiled & eat—on Wensday morning the 28th Sept. I carved up on a Beech tree in the Cayahoga Town.

GEORGE W. KNEPPER

Early Migration to the Western Reserve

In late June 1799, thirty-nine-year-old David Hudson finally stood upon his Ohio lands. He had left Goshen, Connecticut, two months earlier with his eleven-year-old son, Ira, and several hired hands, including Mr. and Mrs. Thaddeus Lacey and their two children. Hudson came to the Connecticut Western Reserve to inspect and develop the lands that he and five co-proprietors had purchased from the Connecticut Land Company.

The trip had been formidable. The party proceeded by wagon to Bloomfield, New York, where Hudson stocked supplies at the home of Nathaniel Norton, one of his co-proprietors. Here he also joined company with young Benjamin Tappan, Jr., who was on his way to examine family holdings in Ravenna Township.

Leaving hired hands to drive the livestock over Indian trails to Buffalo and along the Lake Erie shore, Hudson, with Tappan and party, embarked in small boats on Lake Ontario. In six days they reached the Niagara escarpment where boats and supplies had to be moved by hand to a spot safely above the falls and rapids. Rowing, poling, and cordelling (towing by ropes) were required to move the vessels upstream to Buffalo Creek. Ice jams and headwinds postponed embarkation on Lake Erie, but once underway the tiny flotilla reached the mouth of Conneaut Creek in seven days. There a gale drove the fleet ashore, stoving in the planks of a boat carrying potatoes and other supplies. Repairs were made, then with blankets for sails, the voyagers reached the mouth of the Cuyahoga on June 10. Ten more days were required to work the boats upstream to a point near the mouth of Brandywine Creek, where one of the boats was plundered at night, presumably by Indians. Here the men driving the livestock rejoined the party and, after a search of six days, the town line was located, sleds were fashioned, a trace was cut, and the supplies dragged eight miles to the town center. Benjamin Tappan faced a similar task to reach Ravenna, although he had to clear a trace an additional eight or nine miles.

No time could be spared for self-congratulation. While some men cleared land, erected a cabin, and planted wheat, others surveyed the township into lots. A support party sent out by Nathaniel Norton assisted in these labors.

Then, after making sure supplies were adequate, Hudson, Ira, and two hired men made the long, cold autumn journey back to Bloomfield in an open boat. Leaving Ira in Bloomfield, Hudson walked on back to Goshen.

David Hudson was a "booster," one of those incorrigible optimists who could see the land as it would look after development changed it from a forest to an Eden of substantial farmsteads clustered near prosperous, well-ordered villages. He conveyed his vision to others and, in January 1800, Hudson, his wife and five children, and several neighbors started in sleighs for Bloomfield. There supplies worth two thousand dollars were loaded, and twenty-nine people set out on Lake Ontario while the livestock again was driven overland. After mind-numbing hardships, all arrived at Brandywine Creek and followed the trace to Hudson's settlement.

Order was established quickly in the new community. In 1802, the commissioners of Trumbull County, which then included all of the Reserve, authorized the name Hudson for the township. That same year a Congregational church was founded, a schoolhouse opened, and a lumber mill was built. By 1806, David Hudson was living in a frame house whose lumber was sawed in the local mill, and Heman Oviatt had opened a store. In just another twenty years, this crude frontier settlement opened Western Reserve College; Hudson's vision had materialized.

This telescoped account of one early migration to the Western Reserve reveals both typical and atypical experiences of early settlers. Hardship, improvisation, and unremitting toil are but a few of the constants of early days on the Reserve. But Hudson's experience is exceptional too. Few came to new lands in the West in parties as well organized, supported, and supplied as his. David Hudson was a remarkable leader with a knack for getting things done, and, with the exception of a handful of rowdies, his settlers pulled together. They retained their Yankee individualism alright, but perhaps this trait has been overemphasized in our histories since these folk had an equal talent for community organization and discipline.

There are numerous sketches of early settlement in the Western Reserve so it is not the intention of this essay to retell that story in all its parts. Rather we will look specifically at the early westward migration itself, touching upon other parts of the history but briefly. First, a word about how the settlers secured their lands.

The Western Reserve, retained by the state of Connecticut when she surrendered her western land claims to Congress in 1786, stretched 120 miles westward from the Pennsylvania line between the forty-first parallel and the shore of Lake Erie. The westernmost portion of this area—largely modern Huron and Erie counties—was the "sufferers' lands," or, as it was known on the Reserve, the "Firelands." Connecticut ultimately allotted these lands to citizens who suffered property losses to British raiders during the American Revolution. The rest of the land, and much of the larger portion, was sold to the Connecticut Land Company comprised of thirty-five men who paid $1,200,000 for this wilderness. In 1796 and 1797 survey crews laid out a pattern of east-west, north-south lines that crisscrossed the land from the Pennsylvania line to the Cuyahoga River. Lands west of the Cuyahoga were surveyed after 1805 when the Indians surrendered title in the Treaty of Fort Industry. The surveyed land was then proportioned among members of the land company according to the size of their investment. These men, in turn, sold lands to individuals and groups who wished either to settle or to speculate in western lands. Thus it was, for example, that David Hudson, Nathaniel Norton, Birdsey Norton, Stephen Baldwin, Benjamin Oviatt, and Theodore Parmelee became co-proprietors of Town 4, Range 10, some sixteen thousand acres. Since much of that land was swamp, the proprietors were granted an additional ten thousand acres in an "equalizing township." The price for the twenty-six thousand acres amounted to thirty-two cents per acre, a great bargain even in the Ohio wilderness.

Hudson and his associates, as we have seen, laid out lots and encouraged purchasers. With land available for $1.00 to $2.50 per acre, even a poor man, with a small down payment and a little credit, could buy a subsistence farm in the Western Reserve.

Some of the Connecticut landowners had no intention of settling in Ohio. They bought lands there solely for speculation. None of Hudson's co-proprietors ever came to the Reserve. Joshua Stow, who purchased Town 3, Range 10, was a member of the survey crews, saw the lay of the land on numerous trips west, but he returned to Connecticut to live out his life in familiar surroundings.

Since this was a Connecticut enterprise, it is natural that people from that state and from her Yankee neighbors should dominate the early settlement of the Reserve. Development of "New Connecticut" was but one phase of a large outmigration of New Englanders that had already sent thousands into newly opened lands in New York and Pennsylvania. Of these, hundreds moved on to the Western Reserve. For example, Robert B. Parkman, born in Leicester, Massachusetts, lived in New York for some years before establishing Parkman in Geauga County in 1803. The first settler of Willoughby, David Abbot, was born in Massachusetts and practiced law in Rome, New York, before migrating to the Reserve. In similar fashion, New Englanders living in northern Pennsylvania pushed on to the Reserve. This outpouring—this "Yankee Exodus" as Stewart Holbrook calls it—penetrated other areas of the west and south as well and was in his view "the most influential movement out country has known."

What caused this exodus; what brought thousands of Yankees to the Western Reserve in the early decades of the nineteenth century? Foremost among the varied reasons was the desire for economic gain. David Abbot, "anxious to make money in western lands," built a cabin at the mouth of the Chagrin River in 1797, and, in 1801, brought his wife and children to live there. In 1808, seeing better opportunity further west, he bought eighteen hundred acres near Milan and moved his family there. On a scale both great and small, this story was repeated over and over.

The search for better opportunity grew in part out of hard times in old New England. Impoverished veterans of the Revolutionary armies came west even though most were no longer young. Veterans like William Bierce, a "cardwainer" and hardscrabble farmer from the Housatonic Valley, had been paid in paper money so worthless that he gave it to his children to play with. Bierce expected better things in Nelson, Portage County, to which he migrated in 1817; but it wasn't to be. In 1820 his assets were listed as 175 acres of unimproved land, an iron plow, a hog, and a chain, total value $681.50. He died, a poor man, in 1835. Other hardships—killing frosts throughout New England in the summer of 1816 for instance—also sent farmers toward Ohio's milder climate (as it was reported).

But of course cheap land remained the primary lure. A group in Geneva, Ashtabula County, purchased 900 acres at $1.50 per acre. In nearby Windsor, some early settlers paid $3.50 per acre. These lands were good quality, hence the relatively high price. When the price became too high, sales were deferred. In Orwell Township, also in Ashtabula County, Daniel Coit and Christopher Leffingwell purchased land which they then held at a price of $5.00 an acre, high enough that it "probably accounted for the delay in . . . settlement" of Orwell, which had no permanent settler until 1815. Elsewhere in Ohio, Congress lands were for sale for $2.00 per acre, but the minimum size plot—320 acres—made it too expensive for many who could obtain smaller and cheaper lots in the Reserve and elsewhere in Ohio.

Costs to the individual buyer were often minimized by people grouping together for joint purchase of a large block of land at a price better than they could obtain through individual purchases. In 1809 residents of Granville and Blandford, Massachusetts, bought land in Portage County. Each of the thirteen members of the company agreed to move onto the land, clear five acres, and build a cabin within five years or else forfeit his right and pay a $100 penalty. All but four fulfilled the agreement. These four were replaced by substitutes and the $400 in penalty money was applied to the construction of a community building used for governmental, religious, and educational purposes.

There were as many reasons for migrating to the Reserve as there were migrants. Many young, single men like Ansel Beman, a "poor but honest" boy of nineteen years who moved to Canfield in 1806, came to the Reserve seeking opportunity and hired out to do the endless chores of an agricultural frontier. Some came to fight the devil and spread the gospel. The Reverend David Bacon founded a religious-centered community at Tallmadge, which failed when settlers refused to support his rather stringent requirements. Mrs. Betsy Austin of Trumbull County rode horseback to Bristol, Connecticut, in 1811 to persuade the Reverend Giles H. Cowles to settle in the Reserve where godlessness prevailed in some of the more isolated settlements.

Boosterism and propaganda persuaded some emigrants. Reports from the Reserve to the folks back East stressed the mild climate, rich soil, huge trees, and huge crop yields. The level loamy soil appealed to those who had struggled to farm stony hillsides in New England, and who had paid high taxes for the privilege. Stories of a radish three feet long and a pumpkin weighing over 134 pounds caused people to take notice.

"Yankee spirit" was also at work. The yen to see new lands and to start new enterprises was always a powerful lure, especially to the young and impractical. Though Yankee society had few drifters and loafers, it did have its share of escapists, seeking in the West release from some personal burden. An early settler of Ashtabula County left his family in the East and came to New Connecticut with another man's wife. In Randolph, Portage County, Nathan Muzzey was a "queer character" well known as a Yale graduate and promising young minister. He apparently was disappointed in love. "A screw became lose in his mental machinery," and he became an eccentric carpenter who carved the name "Emma Hale" on each building he constructed. He discovered a small lake in Randolph which bears his name to this day.

The New England character of early settlement on the Reserve was marked. Tiny Cleveland, not yet a village, "molded its destiny upon a foundation of New England character and culture." The term New Connecticut could be taken literally in most of Portage County, Bath, Copley, Boston, and Canfield. A strong Vermont contingent settled Hiram, Wadsworth, and parts of Geauga County. In 1873, James A. Garfield, a son of the region, spoke of townships "more thoroughly New England in character and spirit than most...towns in New England today." Settlers had preserved in the wilderness "the characteristics of New England" as it was when they left it early in the century.

Not all Yankees loved the Reserve. Many saw it once—Moses Cleaveland for example—and chose never again to venture there. Homesickness, "that dreadful malady," sent three of the first men in Ashtabula County heading for home "with the determination never to see the Reserve again." Some hated and feared the social and economic consequences of western migration. Henry Trumbull's lampoon *Western Emigration: Journal of Doctor Jeremiah Simpleton's Tour of Ohio* (Boston, 1819) severely criticized the new lands. But those who sold out their New England property and relocated in the Reserve seldom went back. Margaret Dwight, making the trip to the Reserve by wagon, despaired of the rain and a drunken wagoner who put his arm around her neck "and said something which I was too frightened to hear." She thought she knew why so few who settled the western country returned to their former homes. "It is not that the...country is so good, but because the journey is so bad."

There were two principal routes from New England to the Western Reserve in the early decades of settlement. The southern route to Pittsburgh followed Forbes' Road through Pennsylvania. From Pittsburgh the road ran along the Ohio, the Beaver, and the Mahoning rivers into the eastern portion of the Reserve. A new wagon road on the north bank of the Ohio reduced the journey by a day's time after 1805. Most using the southern route travelled by horse or ox-drawn wagon. Elijah Crosby was fairly typical; he and his family made the trip by ox-drawn covered wagon in forty days from East Haddam, Connecticut, to Ashtabula County. A well-equipped group led by John Kinsman, in 1804, had a "moving outfit" consisting of one two-horse wagon carrying the family, two four-horse wagons with household goods and supplies, one four-ox wagon, and two riding horses. Richard Iddings and his new wife crossed the route by sleigh in 1809. After negotiating four feet of snow on the mountains, they ran out of that vital material and Iddings left the sleigh, his wife, and supplies with her uncle. He then proceeded on horseback to Warren. There he hired a canoe and an assistant, paddled the Mahoning, Beaver, Ohio, and Monongahela to Brownsville where he picked up his wife and supplies. It took them twenty-one days of effort to return to Warren. Some nights they had to sleep on the river bank and several days they had nothing to eat. Many pedestrians walked the southern route; John Campbell and his friends did it in 1800, making their way through six-foot snowdrifts on the Allegheny crests.

The northern route presented alternatives. Some crossed New York on horseback, foot, wagon, or sleigh to Buffalo. There they either shipped on boats or followed the lake trail to the Reserve. Many went by land to the vicinity of Rome and then by water the rest of the way. This route involved backbreaking labor at Niagara Falls. Jonathan Hale came to Bath (Summit County) in 1810 via the land route. He objected to the "enormous price" of $1.92 charged to ferry him across the Hudson. A turnpike in eastern New York charged another 45¢ toll. He followed what later generations would call the "water-level route" to Buffalo where he shipped his goods by boat to the Cuyahoga.

As roads and other transportation improved, the time and energy required to reach Ohio was much reduced. The opening of the Erie Canal in 1825 was especially helpful. In 1842, Daniel Webster Cram went by rail from Boston to Albany, thence by canal to Buffalo, and then by lake steamer to Conneaut. By mid-century, Lucius Bierce, who migrated to Portage County in 1817, could write that the trip which formerly took months (forty to sixty days usually) "is now performed with ease in thirty-six hours." Obviously he was writing after rail connections had been completed. The "Pennsylvania System," a 363-mile combination of railroad, canal, horse car, and stage coach, opened in 1834. It cut time, but above all it saved great physical effort for travellers over the mountains.

Within the Reserve a none-too-successful effort to build roads had been underway from the earliest times. We have noted how the first people coming into an area had to cut their own roads to reach their property. Many such traces were later improved and extended to form the basis of a road system connecting the town centers and villages. Among the earliest roads of importance were the Ashtabula to Warren road built in the first years of the nineteenth century, and the road that connected Pittsburgh and Cleveland. Local farmers contracted out portions of this road. This was common practice. In 1808, three men from Deerfield "cut out and bridged" the road from Old Portage (Akron) to Range 17 west of Medina. In the Firelands the commissioners authorized the building of several east-west and north-south roads that tied the section together and connected it with the more easterly portions of the Reserve. Internal communication was aided enormously by the opening of the Akron-Cleveland stretch of the Ohio-Erie Canal in 1827. Thirteen years later, the Penn-Ohio Canal connected Akron with the Mahoning Valley and Pittsburgh. The railroad, not much of a factor in the Reserve before 1850, became the most revolutionary transportation development of all in the last half of the century.

It is appropriate to emphasize the New England character of the Western Reserve in its early days, but one must also note a considerable leavening of Yankee influence in selected portions of that region. It is hard to determine the origins of many of the Pennsylvanians, New Yorkers, and others who came early to the Reserve. Often, as we have seen, they were but transplanted Yankees. One observer had a system for spotting a Pennsylvania farm—it would have a big barn and modest house, while the Yankee farm would have a big house and a modest barn. But enough evidence remains to state with assurance that nearly every early settlement on the Reserve had a small number of non-Yankee types among the early arrivals. Some of these were squatters from Pennsylvania and Virginia (mostly the western counties of each state) who took up land illegally and then moved on or, occasionally, stayed and purchased their land when the tide of settlement reached them.

Early settlers in Deerfield came from Connecticut, Massachusetts, Pennsylvania, Virginia, Maryland, and New York. When Canfield held a militia election in 1806, the officers chosen were Philip Foust of German extraction; James McDaniel, an Irishman; and Elisha Whittlesey, a Yankee. Among the early settlers of Hudson were Irishmen named O'Brien, Lappin, and McClellan. Kinsman had several Irish settlers before 1805 as did Rootstown and many other rural townships.

Large clusters of Irish canal laborers formed at Akron and Cleveland in 1825. Akron's Irish settlement of about one hundred shanties was called "Dublin." Cleveland's Irish enclave was large enough to justify a priest. In 1829 a Cleveland newspaper reported that immigrants "were arriving at the rate of about 600 a fortnight to work on the canal." Most of them, however, must have just been passing through on their way south since the canal was already completed some forty or more miles south of Cleveland by that date.

Germans were common enough in the early days. Most of the first German settlers were native-born Americans of German extraction. After 1830, the flow of immigrants direct from the Germanies reached Ohio and the Reserve. Before 1810 Deerfield and Randolph in Portage County had many German families. St. Joseph's Catholic Church in Randolph was organized by Germans in 1829. They prospered so well in Randolph that they became the dominant element by midcentury. By 1850 Norton Township, one of the best in Summit County, was "rapidly settling with an industrious, hardy German population from Pennsylvania, who are buying out, and superceding the Anglo-Saxon race." They were paying nearly fifty dollars an acre for land that had sold for two or three dollars a generation earlier. Cleveland's Germans, direct from the old world, settled on both the west and east sides. By 1843 the city supported two German Lutheran churches and by 1846 a German-language newspaper.

The Welsh settled Paris township, Portage County, after 1831, and by 1835 had formed the Welsh Congregational church which conducted services in the

Welsh language. Near mid-century, coal mining brought the first of a sizeable Welsh contingent to the Mahoning Valley and the vicinity of Akron.

Cleveland was the area's most cosmopolitan center. To Yankee, Irish, and German stock were added English, Scots, and a surprising concentration of Manxmen who started to arrive in 1826. By 1823, Dutch immigrants were distilling gin and brandy in the village. Jews came early to Cleveland, mostly from the Germanies and the Austro-Hungarian Empire. In 1839, twenty Jews formed the Israelite Society and by 1846 there were two Jewish congregations in Cleveland. Cleveland's population in 1846 was 10,135, of whom 6,780 were native white, 1,472 German, 808 English, 632 Irish, 144 Canadian, 97 Manxmen, and 96 Scots.

Blacks in small numbers were scattered across the Reserve in the first decades of settlement. An 1810 manuscript census of Trumbull County (then much larger than the present county) shows fifty-five blacks, or as it was quaintly phrased, "all other free persons except Indians not taxed." Eleven of nineteen townships had no blacks at all, Austin had twenty, Warren fourteen, and the rest were scattered across six other townships. They represented a mere six-tenths of one percent of the population. The census of 1840 revealed that Trumbull County, now much reduced in size, had seventy "colored" persons. Only 500 resided in the whole of the Western Reserve. Cuyahoga County, with 121, had the largest concentration, and most of these resided in Cleveland where the "Colored Men's Union Society" was organized in 1839. The small college town of Oberlin in Lorain County had an unusual concentration of black residents thanks to the college's open admission policy for black students and its sympathy for the antislavery cause.

The population growth of the Western Reserve paralleled that of other developing sections of the West. Once the influx of new settlers began about 1800, there were surges and lulls in the immigrant flow; this rhythm was controlled by national conditions—war, depression, and so forth— rather than by local conditions. It is true that local conditions—quality of soil, drainage, access to markets, healthfulness—affected the distribution of newcomers within the Reserve, but it didn't keep them from coming to the area generally. As early as 1801, John Stark Edwards wrote from Mesopotamia to his sister in Connecticut, "Every part of our country is rapidly increasing in numbers. . . . Every day brings a new inhabitant; a neighbor opens a new road; raises a new house, or begins a new farm." The scripture, he says, "is fulfilled when it says 'the wilderness shall be made to blossom as the rose.'" In 1811, Ezra Kellogg, Yale graduate and early settler of Ashtabula, wrote of three to four hundred wagons in the past year bringing New Englanders into the Reserve along the Great Ridge Road. "You may well be satisfied," he writes his brother, "that this country is meeting with most unparalleled settlement."

Early growth is easiest to document in the towns. Canfield, for instance, had forty-three resident taxpayers by 1803, and the following year, sixty-three men cast ballots in a militia election. Warren, the administrative center of the Reserve until 1809, had seventeen resident taxpayers in 1801, the year of its organization. By 1838 the town marshal's census enumerated 928 whites and 10 blacks. Among them were 14 lawyers, 27 merchants and clerks, 5 doctors, 9 cabinet makers, 18 joiners, 12 saddlers, 7 hatters, 13 blacksmiths, 15 shoemakers, 2 painters, 14 tailors, 3 silversmiths, 3 tool-makers, 4 clothiers, 1 glove-maker, 3 wagon-makers, 3 coopers, 3 plasterers, 8 printers, and 7 tinners. Cleveland, with a population of 606 in 1820, ranked fourteenth in size among towns of the Reserve. By 1840, however, Cleveland was already Ohio's second largest town, and in 1850 its 17,034 persons made it more than three times the size of its nearest rival on the Reserve.

Population of Selected Cities and Towns in the Western Reserve

City or Town	1820	1850	Gain
Akron	0	3,266	3,266
Cleveland	606	17,034	16,428
Elyria	174	1,482	1,308
Madison	931	2,986	2,055
Norwalk	579	3,159	2,580
Painesville	1,257	3,128	1,871
Poland	990	2,126	1,136
Ravenna	418	2,240	1,822
Sandusky	243	5,088	4,845
Warren	340	2,957	2,617
Youngstown	1,025	2,802	1,787

Population of the Western Reserve by Counties

County	1820	1830	1840	1850
Ashtabula	7,369	14,584	23,724	28,724
Cuyahoga	6,328	10,362	26,512	47,740
Erie	——	——	12,457	18,366
Geauga	7,791	15,813	16,299	17,820
Huron	6,677	13,340	23,934	26,164
Lake	——	——	13,717	14,616
Lorain	——	5,696	18,451	25,822
Mahoning	——	——	21,712	23,645
Medina	3,090	7,560	18,360	24,406
Portage	10,093	18,792	23,107	24,361
Summit	——	——	22,469	27,364
Trumbull	15,546	26,200	38,070	30,425

In rural townships growth varied with natural conditions. Freedom Township in Portage County was not settled until 1818. By 1830 it had 342 residents and just six years later it had 841. It is difficult to gauge the growth of townships and counties because their configuration changed frequently until 1840, when the formation of Lake, Mahoning, and Summit counties completed the realignment. Some Mahoning and Summit townships lay south of the Reserve. Three of Ashland County's townships were in the Reserve, although the bulk of the county was not. One is never too certain that census figures reflect the many variations of alignment, but despite these difficulties the decennial United States census gives us a reasonable sense of population at ten-year intervals.

Population was distributed fairly well across the Reserve. Density in 1840 varied from a high of sixty-five people per square mile in Lake County to thirty-three people per square mile in Lorain County. Most counties had population densities in the range of forty-two to fifty-two persons per square mile.

It is plain that the frenetic rate of growth that marked the 1820s and 1830s slowed for most counties in the 1840–1850 decade. Except for Lake, those counties with Lake Erie ports—Ashtabula, Cuyahoga, Lorain, Erie—grew substantially in the 1840s as did Summit and Medina with their access to markets via the canal system.

By 1840, an out-migration from rural portions of the Reserve was underway. Although this population loss was more than made up by new immigration, it was nevertheless of some moment. The principal lure that had brought settlers to the Reserve—good cheap land—now lured their sons and daughters further west and north. The large farm families of the Reserve could not all be accommodated as children matured to adulthood. The extraordinary size of these families has often been described. Among the first settlers of Charlestown Township, Portage County, in 1815 was a party of four men, each with his wife and twelve children—fifty-six people in all. John Brown, resident of Hudson and other locations in the Reserve, sired so many children that several sought land in distant Kansas Territory with repercussions that were felt nationally.

Although northeastern Ohio retains to this day some visible evidences of her early origins, the Western Reserve has changed markedly from those early times. Its early migration stamped it with a Yankee character, but the meld of more recent arrivals left it with an all-American look and feel. No longer sectional in character, the Western Reserve is broadly representative of contemporary America.

THOMAS A. SMITH

The Firelands and the Settlement of Vermilion

The town of Vermilion is located at the mouth of the Vermilion River in the far northeastern corner of Erie County. Both the town and township in which the town lies are named for the river which flows through their boundaries. Both also were populated by people of New England ancestry because the lands drained by the Vermilion River were claimed at one time by the state of Connecticut.

When Connecticut ceded all its western land claims to the United States on September 11, 1786, the state reserved a generous tract of land in northern Ohio. This expanse of land contained three and one-half million acres and became known as the Connecticut Western Reserve. Instead of disposing of the land in individual pieces, the Connecticut General Assembly decided to sell the entire tract to the Connecticut Land Company. Only the Salt Spring Tract of 24,000 acres and the western twenty-six miles of the Reserve were set aside. This latter area, which includes all of Huron and Erie Counties, Ruggles Township of Ashland County, and Danbury Township (including Johnson's Island), of Ottawa County, was known as the Firelands.

The Fire Sufferers' Lands (or Fire Lands) were granted to the residents of nine Connecticut coastal towns whose property was destroyed during the Revolutionary War. The citizens of Danbury, Greenwich, Groton, Fairfield, New Haven, East Haven, New London, Norwalk, and Ridgefield suffered immensely at the hands of the British and their Hessian mercenaries. For many, the British raids resulted in a critical shortage of food, clothing, and adequate housing. Out of despair the sufferers turned to the Connecticut General Assembly for relief. From 1777 to 1787, numerous petitions were sent from the towns requesting compensation, but the insufficient financial condition of Connecticut did not permit the state magistrates to grant the sufferers immediate assistance.

Although the plight of the sufferers received modest attention from a committee of the General Assembly in May 1787, and again in 1790 and 1791, it was not until May 10, 1792, that the Assembly acted upon the committee's recommendation and "Released and quit-claimed to the sufferers..., five hundred thousand acres of land belonging to this State." In response to additional pleas from the petitioners, the governing body of Connecticut passed an act in October 1796, incorporating the sufferers under the name of "The Proprietors of the Half Million Acres of Land Lying South of Lake Erie." The following March the proprietors met at the state house in New Haven for the purpose of organizing a corporation to deal with the 1,870 claims for damages. The participants also selected a board of directors, authorized the levying of taxes to cover all expenses incurred by the corporation, and took measures to extinguish the Indian title to the lands, survey and locate the grant, and partition the area into townships.

The dawning of the nineteenth century witnessed the resolution of numerous obstacles hindering any attempt by the sufferers to settle or sell their lands in Ohio. With the passage of the Easement Act in April 1800, Congress authorized President John Adams to convey to Jonathan Trumbull, then governor of Connecticut, the United States' right and title to the lands commonly called the Connecticut Western Reserve. In return Connecticut was to relinquish its jurisdictional control over the area. Once the title issue was resolved, civil law was assured when General Arthur St. Clair, governor of the Ohio Territory, established the county of Trumbull, July 10, 1800. Five years later, July 4, 1805, the directors of the Sufferers' Land Company, through their agent William Dean, concluded the Treaty of Fort Industry, whereby representatives of the Chippewa, Ottawa, Shawnee, Pottawatami, Wyandot, Munsee, and Delaware nations surrendered their title to the lands owned by the company for $18,916. Later that year Almon Ruggles, a surveyor from Danbury, Connecticut, was engaged to survey the Firelands. As a result of an error in the marking out of the base line of the Western Reserve, Ruggles' initial survey was unacceptable. The area was resurveyed by Ruggles and Maxfield Ludlow and found to contain 500,027 acres of land. In all it took three years to complete and verify the surveys and divide the more than one-half million acres into five ranges and thirty townships.

Once the lands had been allotted to the claimants, the proprietors ordered roads opened to the Firelands. These roads were nothing more than crude trails through the wilderness.

The actual settlement of the Firelands began before the completion of the survey and the distribution of the land in 1808. Prior to this date Frenchmen were living in the area of Danbury peninsula. Jean Baptiste Flemmond, better known as John B. Flamand, was one of the earliest permanent white settlers in the area. In 1805 he established a trading post near the present location of Huron. He reportedly sold supplies to the surveying parties of Ruggles and Ludlow as well as to the early settlers in the vicinity. Organized settlement first appeared in the lake shore region of the Firelands. Because of the area's easy accessibility by water, settlers began arriving in Huron and Vermilion Townships as early as 1808. Kneeland Townsend and David Abbot laid out the first official town in the Firelands in Section Two of Milan Township. The town was platted in 1811 and named Huron after the county which had been organized in February 1809. Between 1809 and 1810, the towns of Milan, Norwalk, and Portland, later known as Sandusky, were settled. Richmond and Riley Townships in southern Huron County were the last areas to be settled in 1825.

The first white inhabitants came to the vicinity of the Vermilion River Valley between the years 1808 and 1810. The area's first settler, William Hoddy, arrived in 1808, and erected the first house in the township, a log structure which stood near the mouth of the river.

The War of 1812 caused a temporary halt in the colonization of the Firelands. Those settlers who remained in the area erected several blockhouses to protect themselves from the British and their Indian allies. After the end of hostilities between the United States and Great Britain, settlement quickly resumed. The new arrivals to the Vermilion River Valley found the area a true paradise. The valley floor and surrounding countryside teemed in white, black, and red oak, white wood, black walnut, hickory, maple, and a variety of other kinds of trees. The forests not only furnished the pioneers with excellent stands of timber, but also sheltered various types of bear, wolf, deer, wildcat, and many smaller kinds of animals. These animals furnished the inhabitants of the settlement and township with an ample source of food. The settlers used many of the pelts of the larger animals for clothing, or took them to Vermilion and exchanged them for merchandise.

Just as the forests furnished the new arrivals to the area with abundant supplies of game and lumber, the lands of the township provided them with good soil for the development of agriculture. The immigrants also found the topography of the township conducive for farming. With good soil and flat terrain, agriculture became an important industry of Vermilion Township. Most of the pioneers who settled on lands adjacent to the settlement became farmers. They cleared the land, tilled the soil, and produced wheat, corn, oats, and potatoes. At first the settlers raised what they absolutely needed, but as they began to cultivate more and more land they greatly increased their annual yield. This additional produce, mainly grain products, was taken to Vermilion where it was transshipped to various markets. Peter Cuddenback, as early as 1812, planted the first orchard. The township later became a very prominent fruit-growing area, producing apples, peaches, and grapes.

Although agriculture became the mainstay of the economy in the township, the settler took advantage of the great abundance of timber in the area by erecting numerous saw and planing mills. Job Smith built the first sawmill on La Chapelle Creek in 1819. The white oak lumber extracted from the forests surrounding Vermilion was used for the construction of lake vessels in the town. One of the reasons why shipbuilding became such an important industry in Vermilion, as well as along the entire northern shore of the Firelands, was the availability and accessibility of good stands of ship timber. The remaining lumber was used for local building needs or shipped from Vermilion harbor to other Great Lakes ports in need of this product. Some of the earliest cargoes leaving the port consisted of cord wood, staves, shingles, ship timber, and masts.

The chief source of mechanical energy used to power the mills was supplied by the Vermilion River and La Chapelle Creek. The first, which has its source in Savannah Lake, Ashland County, meanders through Huron and Lorain Counties, finally emptying into Lake Erie near the eastern boundary of the township.

The other stream, La Chapelle Creek, rises in Wakeman Township (Huron County) and flows north through Florence and Vermilion Townships into the lake. In addition to sawmills, the early settlers also built several gristmills along these streams. Almon Ruggles, the surveyor of the Firelands, constructed the first mill in 1809 along the banks of the Vermilion River for the proprietors of the land. This mill was only in operation one year before the spring floods washed it away. In 1810 he returned to the township and built a second mill, known as Ruggles' Mill, on La Chapelle Creek. Two other gristmills were erected in the township. George Sherod (earlier spelling Sherrat), who settled one mile west of the mouth of the river, built a small mill in 1809, and produced the first flour in the township the following spring. Shortly afterwards Peter Cuddenback constructed a similar mill on his farm, which was two miles from the settlement.

The second most important natural resource of the township during the pioneer period was iron ore. Local deposits of bog ore together with charcoal from the surrounding forests and limestone from nearby quarries supported a blast furnace which operated about two miles south of Vermilion at a site called Furnace Corners. The original blast furnace was very small by today's standards, approximately thirty feet high and nine feet in diameter, and was built and lined with native sandstone. In addition to the furnace, the other buildings consisted of an ironmaster's shanty, a business office and store, and a small foundry.

The early pioneers of Vermilion Township who located near the mouth of the Vermilion River found the west branch of the waterway to be an ideal location for settlement. It rose fifteen to twenty feet above the level of the river and was heavily timbered. The first settlers of Vermilion also found a wide sand beach extending from the mouth of the river west the whole length of the township and in some places forested with basswood and other trees. The site also had another distinct advantage. The river provided the inhabitants of the tiny settlement with a natural harbor. Although the depth of the river channel was approximately seven and a half feet deep, because of the lack of adequate feeder streams, the harbor could accommodate the larger vessels running on the Great Lakes in the early 1800s. The river also served as a means of supplying the early settlers with needed provisions and merchandise and for marketing their produce. This was a very important factor for all who settled in the valley, because it meant that the eastern markets, which were so highly coveted by the frontier farmer and craftsman, were no more than a few days' journey away.

The settlers of Vermilion quickly came to realize that the surrounding area lent itself beautifully to carrying on the activity of shipbuilding. The nearby forests furnished the residents of the village with a necessary supply of wood, while the precipitous slope of the west bank of the river and close proximity of the harbor provided the occupants with an ideal site for the building and launching of vessels. A finished schooner easily could be launched into the river from wooden stocks erected on the steep river bank. Captain William Austin, formerly of New London, Connecticut, launched the first vessel from the bank of the river in 1812. The launching of the schooner *Friendship* signaled the beginning of what was to become one of the town's most significant industries.

Prior to 1820, pioneer life in Vermilion, as elsewhere in the Firelands, was rugged and demanding. Everyday living was fraught with adversities and hardships of every imaginable kind. The lack of money and adequate transportation facilities meant that supplies were expensive and difficult to procure. Many of the initial immigrants to the area lived in crude log cabins which lacked the conveniences of eastern living. Fine clothing was a luxury on the frontier. The men usually wore clothes made of buckskin, while the women and children made do with coarser homemade fabrics. Death and sickness were everpresent in many forms. Cholera, the ague, and other diseases continually plagued the pioneers. Both the settlers and their cattle were subject to attacks by wild animals and rattlesnakes, and prey to the elements of nature. In order to survive in the wilderness of northern Ohio, settlers were presented with the arduous chore of clearing and tilling the land and making most of the items needed to keep body and soul together.

However, by the mid-1820s, the townspeople of Vermilion set about the task of improving their cultural surroundings as the settlement grew in size and number. On April 6, 1818, the first election was held at the residence of Almon Ruggles. The erection of the first school in 1814 and the founding of a literary society in the town in 1821 demonstrate the great value placed on education by these New England settlers. The log schoolhouse was built by the lake shore and used by Miss Susan Williams and later by Addie Harris to educate the children of the community. Boys usually attended classes only during the winter months because their help was needed on the farms. Many of the schools were run on a subscription basis and taught just reading and writing skills. The teachers often boarded with the families of their students and were paid, more often than not, in kind rather than actual cash. By 1821 some kind of educational opportunity was available in twenty-five of the thirty townships of the Firelands. In that same year, township trustees were authorized to support public education "by the laying on of taxes."

Another cultural institution attended to early in the community was religion. Before the organization of churches the religious needs of the settlers were fulfilled by weekly revival meetings. These meetings were held in the homes of the local residents, and had been an important social as well as spiritual function of the area since 1810. Eight years after the first religious meeting was held in the home of Captain William Austin, the first Congregational Church was organized in the township. In the spring of 1828 the congregation built a meeting house in the center of the township, and on May 22 of that same year installed their first pastor, the Reverend Harvey Lyon. The Congregational Church was the only organized religious denomination in the area until 1831, when five residents of the township united to form a Methodist Church.

By 1837 Vermilion had grown from a tiny settlement made up of crude shanties and log cabins into a thriving village consisting of a post office, public house, tavern, blacksmith shop, ferry, several general stores, a number of storehouses, and assorted family dwellings. With the passing of the frontier, the decade of the 1830s saw a rapid increase in the availability of different modes of transportation to meet the local needs of the town and township. Two state routes and a turnpike leading to the village were constructed during this ten-year period. In addition, the small port was rapidly developing into an economically significant trading center specializing in such products as lumber and staves, pot and pearl ash, building stone, and a wide variety of foodstuffs of which wheat was the most important. The year 1837 also witnessed the construction of permanent harbor facilities at the mouth of the river by the Army Corps of Engineers.

Vermilion's growth and development during the pioneer period was a result of a culmination of events which had begun in 1808 with the appearance of William Hoddy at the mouth of the river, and ended in the late 1830s when the township and town were involved in the political reorganization of the Firelands into Huron and Erie Counties. Throughout the years, the early settlers worked hard to make their dreams concerning the village and township come true as they transplanted and nurtured the rudimentary elements of eastern society in the wilds of northern Ohio.

JEFFREY P. BROWN

Samuel Huntington: A Connecticut Aristocrat on the Ohio Frontier

Samuel Huntington, Jr., was one of the many amibitious Americans who went west in the early nineteenth century hoping to improve their stations in life. Although most western pioneers were humble yeoman farmers, a significant number of well-to-do citizens also emigrated to the frontier in search of their fortunes. Huntington typified this latter group. Born to one of Connecticut's most prominent families, he moved to frontier Ohio, became one of the leading figures in Great Lakes politics, and headed the coalition of conservative Republicans and Federalists that broke the liberal Republican hold in the state. An aristocratic leader in a democratic society, Huntington's career illustrates the ease with which a prominent easterner could win high office in the sparsely settled West.

The Huntington clan emerged in the generation before the American Revolution as one of the most prominent families in Connecticut. One branch provided wealthy merchants and a Revolutionary War general. Another supplied Samuel Huntington, Sr., a self-taught farm boy who became a successful Norwich lawyer and served as president of the Continental Congress in 1779–81. Samuel Sr. moved at the center of American politics, and as titular head of the nation acquired responsibility for hosting foreign dignitaries. Well known in America and Europe, he capped his career by serving as governor of Connecticut from 1786 to 1796. A taciturn and soft-spoken leader, Huntington was also a confirmed Federalist.

In the early 1770s Samuel Huntington informally adopted two children from his brother, the Reverend Joseph Huntington. Samuel was childless, and Joseph a recent widower. The elder of the children, Samuel Jr., was born in 1765 and was six or seven years old when the adoption occurred. Although he always called his stepfather "uncle" and stayed in close contact with his real father, young Samuel remained forever a part of the governor's surrogate family.

The adoption meant that Huntington grew up in a family of extraordinary prominence and some affluence. In 1779–81, when he was in his mid-teens, he accompanied his stepparents to Philadelphia, where his uncle was one of the most important men in Congress. He entered Dartmouth in 1781 and later transferred to Yale, from which he graduated in 1785. He then embarked on a grand tour of Europe, a rare experience for eighteenth-century Americans. After he returned to Connecticut, Huntington studied law under his stepfather. He liked to drink and to court young ladies—habits disagreeable to the governor—but by 1791 he had settled down, joined the bar, and married a cousin, Hannah Huntington. Huntington spent the ensuing years as his stepfather's scribe, law clerk, and assistant at assembly sessions. Fully accepted as part of Connecticut's elite, he was apparently being groomed to succeed his stepfather.

This world collapsed around Huntington in 1796, when his stepfather died. Without his stepfather's support, his prospects for advancement dimmed appreciably. Increasingly,he devoted his attention to western land speculation. Huntington became one of the nineteen proprietors in the Erie Company, one of the leading land firms that coalesced into the Connecticut Land Company in 1795. The Erie group included several Huntingtons, and Samuel's interest may have been encouraged by other family members.

In the late 1790s Huntington drew increasingly closer to the Jeffersonian Republicans, and early in 1798 he publicly declared his allegiance to that party. It is at least possible that he took this step in the expectation of rising quickly in the state's minority party, but he clearly did not expect the vehement Federalist reaction that ensued. The Connecticut Land Company directors split into vociferous Federalist and Republican camps. Huntington incurred the special wrath of director Roger Newberry, whom he called "Granny" and an "old superannuated bigot." By the turn of the century Huntington wrote that the "atmosphere of Connecticut is infectuous—particularly Norwich" and that he planned to "get out of it as soon as I can." Huntington also had other reasons for emigration. He hoped to prosper as an agent for Western Reserve landholders, and several of his closest friends also planned to go west. Moreover, he was convinced that he would be politically ostracized in Connecticut. Accordingly, Huntington made a horseback tour of the Erie region in 1800, and moved permanently to Ohio in 1801. He took his wife, two young sons, and a governess, and soon after arriving paid a Cleveland builder to erect the largest block house in the new town.

By 1801, when Huntington settled in the Northwest, the territorial government was thirteen years old. The Northwest had recently reached the population level that entitled it to an assembly, and many residents expected statehood to follow shortly. The statehood movement was opposed by Governor Arthur St. Clair, an ardent Federalist who feared that statehood would end his own tenure, place the frontier in the hands of inexperienced men, and possibly send Republican senators and a representative to Washington. By 1800 St. Clair had concluded an alliance with a number of Cincinnati and Marietta politicians. Some of these men were Federalists and some Republicans, but all were united by a desire to end the political and economic domination exercised by the centrally located Scioto Valley and its chief town, Chillicothe. They feared that statehood would make Chillicothe's dominance permanent, and hence they sought either to delay statehood or to divide the territory along the Scioto, with Marietta and Cincinnati becoming the new regional capitals. Not surprisingly, the statehood movement received strong support from the Scioto assembly men, largely Virginia Republicans under the leadership of Edward Tiffin and Thomas Worthington. Since both groups had equal strength in the assembly, and both had influential friends in the East, each side looked to Connecticut's Western Reserve for decisive extra support.

Huntington could easily have landed in either camp. His general political sympathies lay with the Scioto Republicans. However, Governor St. Clair readily courted Republican support, and he had recently chosen as his personal secretary George Tod, a close friend of both Huntington and Connecticut Republican leader Gideon Granger. Tod, like Huntington, came to the Northwest as a representative of Connecticut Land Company shareholders. He was the sort of man who kept his eye firmly on the main political chance, and decided that his best prospects would come as a St. Clair ally. The governor hinted to Tod that a successful effort to divide the Northwest would delay statehood and probably leave the Reserve the dominant region in the eastern half, a hint he left "to work for itself in his mind." Huntington, who often followed Tod's lead, muted his own Jeffersonian sympathies and developed cordial relations with St. Clair. This enabled him to thwart efforts by the Company directors to promote a Federalist administration in the Western Reserve. The directors nominated officers they preferred for government posts, entrusting their list to a safe Federalist settler, John Stark Edwards, rather than to Huntington. St. Clair appointed the bulk of their nominees, but gave some of the posts to Tod's friends. Thus Huntington became justice of the peace for Trumbull County, the Reserve county, and also a lieutenant colonel in the militia. The combination of his earlier prominence, his legal background, and his new official preference quickly made Huntington the political leader of the county.

Both Huntington and Tod fully supported a territorial assembly resolution late in 1801 asking Congress to divide the Northwest along the Scioto River. They assumed that Congress would comply and that it would appoint for the eastern half, which they privately called the Erie Territory, the usual governor and three judges. These offices were the most important positions in any territory, and the men who held them could hope to move on to a governorship or United States Senate seat when statehood followed. Determined to win one of these territorial offices for Huntington, Tod wrote to Gideon Granger, the Connecticut Republican who had just become postmaster general, recommending Huntington for governor or judge in the Erie Territory. Tod had not consulted Huntington before making these nominations, but the latter was willing to hold either office. The "scheme," as Tod called it, illustrates the manner in which a competent and well-connected easterner, by his mere presence on the frontier, could seriously aspire to the highest political positions. In this case, however, Tod's plans for

Huntington went awry. Congress rejected the proposal for a division, voting instead to admit the southern portion of the Northwest—modern Ohio—as a state as soon as it drew up a constitution.

The Republican Congress that approved this statehood bill did so expecting that the new frontier state would regularly vote Republican. The growing Republican strength on the frontier rendered Tod and Huntington increasingly vulnerable. In mid-1802 a friend wrote Tod that Gideon Granger was beginning to question his Republicanism because of his ties with Governor St. Clair and that such ties could be ruinous. Huntington, in turn, recognized that his own career was in jeopardy if he continued to work with the Federalists. Thus, he ignored a request from St. Clair to speak out against statehood. Moreover, in 1802 Huntington won one of Trumbull County's seats in the state constitutional convention, defeating John S. Edwards, a Federalist. Apparently unaware that Huntington had already decided to part company with the Federalists, Tod wrote to him urging that even if he were not fully devoted to the Republican party, he allow others to "believe *you one of them*." Tod insisted that if Huntington were considered a Republican, he could easily become a supreme court justice, for other Republicans believed that he could lead the Reserve into the Republican camp. Tod emphasized his points by enclosing a letter he had written to Thomas Worthington in which he introduced Huntington as a good Republican. Already attuned to the direction in which the political winds were blowing, Huntington wrote back to Tod, assuring him that he had become a dedicated Republican and could thus support that party without embarrassment. He said that Republican leaders had already offered him a judgeship for his support, and that some spoke of higher office—possibly a United States senatorship. Huntington continued to lodge with Federalists in 1802, but his open cooperation with the Republicans at the constitutional convention startled the Federalist delegates, who had counted on his support. Huntington thereafter associated, both in public and private, almost exclusively with Republicans. He was pleased to discover that his new allies included men of talent, and that politics in the Northwest lacked the rancor found in Connecticut.

Huntington's new political affiliation was timely, for Ohio turned overwhelmingly Republican; in the first state elections Federalists put up only token candidates. Moreover, in the presidential canvass of 1804, Republican electors outpolled Federalists by a margin of about eight to one. Thus, Huntington aligned himself with the winning side, and just in time.

Ohio's early Republican leadership included Charles W. Byrd of Cincinnati, Return J. Meigs of Marietta, and a group of Scioto Valley men—Tiffin, Worthington, Nathaniel Massie, Michael Baldwin, and Elias Langham. This leadership, however, was not united. Baldwin's 1801 role in organizing Chillicothe saloon toughs into a political street mob had aroused Worthington's open contempt, while Langham and Worthington had been enemies ever since a quarrel over land-sale ethics. The brothers-in-law Byrd and Massie slowly drew away from all the Scioto Republicans, while Meigs remained virtually independent. This division left Samuel Huntington considerable room in which to maneuver.

Huntington's desire for a federal position was soon dashed. Hoping to win a federal judgeship in Ohio, he wrote to Postmaster General Granger to ask for the position. Another candidate, Charles W. Byrd, emerged at the same time. Byrd, the young territorial secretary, was related to many of the best families in Virginia and Philadelphia. Furthermore, Byrd's candidacy was supported by Thomas Worthington, the ablest of the Scioto Republicans and a Virginian with close ties to the Jefferson administration. Worthington favored Byrd at least partly because he believed that only Byrd could beat a third candidate, Cincinnati lawyer and St. Clair ally William McMillan. Huntington was helpless against this array of Virginians. He pointed out to Worthington his own services for the party in defending the new state constitution, but Worthington continued to support Byrd. By the time Granger presented Huntington's name to the president, Jefferson had decided to select Byrd. Granger could only promise Huntington to recommend him for other posts that might become available.

Huntington next set his sights on the United States Senate. He believed that he had the support of Republican leaders, and rumors quickly spread through Ohio that he and Worthington had agreed to share the two Senate seats. Although no such deal was consummated, Huntington was nevertheless surprised when he did not win a seat. The new senators were elected by Ohio's first state assembly, which convened in Chillicothe on March 1, 1803, with Huntington attending as a state senator from Trumbull County. The two houses met in joint session on April 1, one month into the session, and by secret ballot chose Worthington and Republican John Smith of Cincinnati for the Senate. Only one man, Worthington's personal enemy Michael Baldwin, later acknowledged that he had voted for Huntington. Despite his disappointment, Huntington restrained his anger. In October he wrote a letter to Senator Worthington in which he discussed a variety of political events, then also mentioned, without comment, the prevalent rumors that Worthington had broken his promise to support him. The new senator replied that these rumors were Federalist-inspired and false.

Scioto Valley Republicans quickly took control of Ohio's state government. Besides Worthington's victory, they elected Edward Tiffin governor, and through Nathaniel Massie and Michael Baldwin—the latter admittedly an enemy of his Scioto neighbors—they controlled both houses of the general assembly. There was relatively little opportunity for Yankee converts like Huntington or Return J. Meigs of Marietta (Meigs, too, was from Connecticut), but even so, Huntington played a fairly active role in the 1803 legislature. He drew up the Senate rules, headed the committee on elections, helped draw up a court system, and on several occasions served as speaker *pro tempore*. Nevertheless, he exercised little political influence. Toward the end of the session, both he and Meigs were placed on the state supreme court by joint assembly election. These were prestigious seats—George Tod lobbied to win one for Huntington, and no doubt the

Trumbull lawyer himself preferred the court to a minor role in the assembly—but they were probably dead ends politically, for they offered little power and little opportunity to become involved with the issues of the day. The Scioto Republicans were happy to shunt their allies off to these prestigious but powerless posts. By December 1803, Governor Tiffin wrote Worthington that Samuel Huntington no longer had popularity or influence, and when he later named Huntington chief justice, it was at best only a gesture.

Stymied in Ohio, both Huntington and Meigs began to look to other parts of the West. Meigs was interested in Louisiana, Huntington in Michigan. The sparsely settled region between Lakes Huron and Michigan had been an isolated part of the Northwest Territory. Its French voters had a reputation for having Federalist sympathies, and consequently in 1802 Congress had insured that Ohio would be Republican by lopping off the Michigan region and adding it to the Indiana Territory. Since Indiana did not yet have an assembly, Detroiters felt politically deprived; after two years of petitions, the government created for them another territory, called Michigan. Samuel Huntington set his sights as early as October 1803, on becoming governor of Michigan, even though that Territory was not created until a year later.

Huntington knew that if he wanted to become governor of Michigan, he needed Worthington's help. Thus, when he first wrote the senator in October 1803 about his dashed Senate hopes, he also asked who would become the governor of "Detroit." Worthington replied early in 1804 that while a bill separating Michigan from Indiana had passed the Senate, it would probably fail in the House. Furthermore, although promising to recommend Huntington to the president, Worthington said that he had already recommended Judge Meigs for the post. Huntington, in turn, told the senator that while he respected Meigs, he still wanted to be considered for the governorship. He also apparently wrote to Ohio's other senator, John Smith, who possessed little influence but could at least keep him informed on the fate of the Indiana division bill.

Huntington grew more hopeful in late 1804 when Meigs took a position in the new Louisiana Territory. He again wrote to Senator Worthington, to reaffirm his candidacy and to oppose any plans to annex Michigan to the state of Ohio. However, a new rival appeared on the scene. Solomon Sibley of Detroit, a Massachusetts native, became a candidate for the Michigan secretaryship late in 1803. Although he did not obtain this post, Sibley met with President Jefferson in January 1805 to recommend General William Hull of Massachusetts for the governorship. Huntington did not learn about Hull's candidacy for some time, and as late as February 5, 1805, in another letter of application, he mentioned Meigs as his only rival. When he finally heard that Hull was also a candidate, he hastily wrote to Worthington to remind the senator that he spoke fluent French.

Huntington's barrage of letters proved unavailing. On February 26, 1805, Worthington wrote Huntington that while he, John Smith, and Ohio Congressman Jeremiah Morrow had all recommended him, President Jefferson had chosen Hull. Worthington then recommended Huntington for one of the Michigan judgeships. The president agreed to nominate Huntington to the bench, and Worthington was confident that the Senate would approve.

The judicial appointment came as a total surprise to Huntington. Accepting it would not further his career, for he would merely be transferring laterally from one bench to another. His chances of becoming governor or going to Washington seemed much better in Ohio than in Michigan Territory, where either Hull or the new secretary, Huntington's old friend Stanley Griswold of Connecticut, would most likely hold sway. Low salaries in Michigan, plus the damage done by a fire that had recently incinerated most of Detroit, made the territory seem even less congenial. Nevertheless, Huntington weighed accepting the appointment for some time, for he feared that his refusal would doom any chances he had for holding other territorial offices. Despite his qualms, in December 1805 he formally declined the judgeship. During the next year he sponsored his friend George Tod for the vacant bench, but failed to secure the post for him.

Huntington remained on the Ohio bench, but devoted most of his attention to private business concerns in Cleveland. His neighbors chose him for minor local offices and indicated their respect by habitually dubbing him "esquire." In 1805 Huntington temporarily moved from Cleveland, perhaps because wild wolves attacked him outside his home one winter night. He operated mills and accumulated land and by 1807 he had amassed some four thousand acres along Lake Erie. During that year he returned to his large Cleveland log home, which soon doubled as both a family residence and a boarding house. Huntington remained one of the more prosperous citizens of the Reserve.

Huntington continued to take an interest in Ohio politics. Two developments gave him grounds for renewed optimism. With the Republican party, bitter infighting became a normal feature of political life. Baldwin and Langham opposed Tiffin; Massie quarreled with Tiffin; and new leaders like James Pritchard of Steubenville developed other splinter groups within the party. These divisions ended the domination of the Scioto leaders. Furthermore, the famous conflict in 1807-08 over whether the state courts could rule legislative acts unconstitutional cast most of the judges into the role of conservative defenders of order and stability. These conflicts divided the voters into two camps: one strongly Republican, Scioto-based, and supporting the legislature as the voice of the people; the other a mixture of Yankee Republicans and old-line Federalists who praised the courts and called the assembly power-hungry. The pro-court group was often in the minority. In the congressional election of 1808, for example, its candidate, Federalist Philemon Beecher, lost by a two-to-one margin. Still, the court faction enjoyed considerable influence. It made its best mark in the gubernatorial election late in 1807, when it helped Return J. Meigs win a narrow victory. Meigs's election was voided on grounds of nonresidency, but even so, the election demonstrated that a conservative Yankee Republican could carry the state.

Early in the following year, Samuel Huntington decided to run for governor himself. By this time he had achieved a solid reputation as a judicial conservative. When Daniel M'Faddon successfully sued Benjamin Rutherford for $35 in a justice of the peace court, Rutherford appealed to the state supreme court. Huntington and Associate Justice George Tod ruled that a justice of the peace could only hear cases worth less than $20. In making this decision, they voided a legislative act, which had given justices greater authority. Huntington argued that the state constitution carried over that provision of the Ordinance of 1787 which guaranteed trial by jury, and that the right to a jury was ultimately based on the federal Constitution, which promised such hearings for all cases except simple contracts under $20. This surprising extension of the United States Constitution to an Ohio law passed without notice, as popular attention focused on the fact that the court had challenged a legislative act.

Huntington's decision threw him into the maelstrom of the ongoing court-assembly struggle, making him a judicial hero to conservative voters. By April 1808, it was clear that he would be their candidate for the governor's chair that fall. Huntington's candidacy disturbed Tiffin and Worthington—the leaders of the Scioto-assembly wing of the party—especially since Worthington planned to run for the office himself. One astute Federalist, Bezaleel Wells, warned Huntington that the two hoped to persuade federal judge Charles Byrd to resign, and then get President Jefferson to appoint Huntington to his seat. As Wells put it, Huntington would be "snugly laid up in *dry dock*." Worthington himself wrote Huntington in July, expressing his deep respect and urging him to bow out of the governor's race and to try instead for the United States Senate.

Huntington ignored this advice, and by September had received public endorsements from various parts of the state. In many cases, Federalists openly avowed their support for him. He received the support of the "Federal Republicans" of Marietta—a group that also endorsed Federalist Philemon Beecher for Congress—and he won a ringing endorsement from a largely Federal gathering in Warren, Ohio. He was also supported by many anti-Worthington Republicans, including Nathaniel Massie. In the election, Huntington polled well throughout the state, while receiving his largest totals in New England-settled areas. He carried the Marietta region nearly unanimously, and in the two counties around Cincinnati he got 1,138 votes to 831 for all his opponents. Worthington and Acting Governor Thomas Kirker split the center of the state. Huntington wound up with about 45 percent of the vote, while Worthington took 34 percent and Kirker the remaining 21 percent. It is clear that Huntington's victory was partly due to Kirker's candidacy; Kirker, a Scioto Valley man and pro-assembly partisan, drew from essentially the same constituency as Worthington. But it is also clear that Huntington had forged a powerful coalition of northern Federalists and conservative Republican voters.

Although Ohio's governors had few formal powers and no veto, they had considerable influence, and thus both of the state's political factions sought Huntington's patronage. The pro-assembly Chillicothe *Scioto Gazette* complimented him on his "elegant and patriotic" inaugural address, while the neo-Federalist *Chillicothe Supporter* labeled him a "federal republican" and gave thanks for his election against the "the intrigues and base deceptions" of his rivals. At his inauguration, Huntington came down firmly on the side of the regular Republicans in foreign policy matters. He praised the moderation and firmness of Jefferson's Embargo and urged all political factions to support the president. His inaugural speech completely ignored the most controversial issue—the court-assembly struggle. Throughout his term of office, Huntington continued to sidestep this issue. Ever cautious, he sought to alienate no one, and he did not even involve himself in the exciting impeachment trial of his friend and ally, Justice George Tod. Although Tod escaped removal, the result owed nothing to the governor.

Huntington was forced to fill an important office in 1809, when Senator Edward Tiffin resigned the United States Senate seat he had held since 1807. Since Ohio's assembly was out of session, Huntington, as governor, had to appoint a temporary successor. He stunned everyone by choosing Stanley Griswold, the Connecticut Republican recently dismissed as secretary of Michigan Territory. The appointment aroused a storm of protest. Griswold had just recently moved to Ohio and thus could barely be considered a citizen of the state. Moreover, he was a bitter, arrogant, acerbic man, and completely self-centered as well. Why, then, did Huntington select him? Friendship and politics provide an explanation. The two men had been close friends in Connecticut, where Republicans were scarce, and when Griswold moved to Ohio he settled in Cleveland near the Huntingtons. One observer, perhaps biased, noted that Huntington pointed out to Federalist audiences that Griswold had been fired by Jefferson, while telling Republican gatherings that Griswold was a dedicated Republican. It is therefore reasonable to assume that Huntington hoped to make the Griswold appointment palatable to both ends of Ohio's political spectrum.

This ploy backfired. The Federalist newspapers, led by the *Supporter*, made almost no comment on the appointment, beyond apologizing for Huntington's delay in filling the seat (he waited several months after Tiffin resigned). The *Supporter* did mention, regarding Huntington, that to err was human. That newspaper rarely mentioned Huntington's name afterward, apparently because it did not know whether or not to support his policies and appointments. The regular Republicans were similarly bewildered by the Griswold appointment. Thus the *Scioto Gazette* vacillated, first condemning Griswold as a nonresident, then noting his staunch Republicanism in Connecticut and Michigan, and finally recalling that he had been removed from office by the sainted Jefferson. By summer 1809, however, the *Gazette* took a firmer stance when it called on Ohioans to decide whether Jefferson or Huntington had better judgment; and in November, the paper printed a letter asking whether Ohio did not have abler sons than Huntington. In the end, the appointment won Huntington no friends and made many enemies. Griswold was ultimately replaced by the assembly and went on to the Illinois frontier, where he remained bitter and unpleasant as always.

The major issue of Governor Huntington's term in office remained the struggle between the legislature and the courts. However, Huntington continued to avoid identification with either side. His annual message in late 1809 simply mentioned his interim appointments (including Griswold) and called for revisions in the militia laws, a plea which the assembly had already ignored once that year. Huntington did not deliver this message in person, but instead had it read by a clerk. Perhaps he hoped to benefit by Jefferson's recent examples, but it is also possible that in light of the universally criticized Griswold appointment he was reluctant to appear before the assembly. In any event, the legislature again ignored his call for militia reforms, and instead precipitated a new crisis by adopting a resolution declaring most of the state's offices vacant. This "sweeping resolution" was designed to expel all pro-court enemies from office, especially the judges, and to open up extensive patronage. The anti-court Republicans also organized Tammany Societies to marshall Republican voters to their cause. Governor Huntington played no role in either the furious debate over the resolution or the Tammany organizations.

At some point early in 1810 Huntington decided not to seek re-election. He probably concluded that he could not expect enough support within the Republican party to carry the state again. Instead, he set his sights on the United States Senate, an office filled by assembly election. This decision may explain his reluctance to oppose the assembly over the sweeping resolution. Huntington soon came to an agreement with Return J. Meigs, who was then in the Senate: Meigs was willing to resign from the Senate to run for governor, which would permit Huntington to make a bid for the vacated Senate seat. In effect, the two Yankees decided to trade offices. The trade proved to be only half successful, for although Meigs won a term as governor, Samuel Huntington lost his bid for the Senate. Thomas Worthington, still a powerful figure with many assembly friends, ran against him after being defeated by Meigs for the governorship. Huntington's men countered by sponsoring a third candidate, James Pritchard of Steubenville, hoping to drain off votes from Worthington, but this scheme failed. Worthington and Huntington were pitted head to head in several close secret ballots, and after six counts, Worthington won a narrow victory, thirty-five to thirty-one.

Bereft of office, Huntington considered leaving Ohio. He debated moving to the Mississippi frontier, where his friend Gideon Granger held large land warrants and needed an agent. However, Huntington decided to remain in Ohio, and he won a seat—representing Geauga, Ashtabula, and Cuyahoga Counties— in the 1811 assembly. When the assembly convened, he launched a campaign to become speaker of the house, but lost to Matthias Corwin, twenty-four to eighteen. Despite this loss, Huntington played an important role during this session. He authored a report recommending the impeachment of an arbitrary judge, John Thompson; by favoring the impeachment, which failed, Huntington thus seemingly placed himself on the side of those who distrusted the courts. However, he also launched an assault against the sweeping resolution, proposing an appointment that presumed it null and void. This effort to restore the older office-holding rules won support from both court partisans and those who had not benefitted from the resolution's new patronage. But even so, the appointment and thus the repeal of the sweeping resolution failed by one vote, twenty-three to twenty-four.

Thereafter, Huntington's political career declined rapidly. He considered running for Congress in 1812, but in the face of strong opposition decided against it. The legislature, dominated by his political opponents, probably drew up northern Ohio's congressional districts at least partly to divide his normal constituency and thus reduce his chances of running or winning. Huntington served as an Army district paymaster during the War of 1812, but soon fell ill, probably from cancer, and after years of agony died in June 1817 at the age of fifty.

Samuel Huntington's career illustrates several of the major themes of frontier political history. As a prominent easterner in the West, he rose rapidly to leadership, probably more quickly than he would have had he remained in Connecticut. Like other leading frontier figures, he tried to exercise influence in the nation's capital, using ties with important men there to win major appointive posts. In the new, unstable Ohio political system, his career typified the sort of personal rivalry and competition that split the dominant Republican party. With his equally typical ally and foe, Return J. Meigs, he led a coalition of northern Republicans and conservative Federalists who for a time dominated the state and thus prevented complete control by the Scioto Valley Jeffersonian Republicans. He sought offices, such as the governorship, for power and prestige rather than to pursue specific programs, and as a result his brief political tenure brought no lasting results. Finally, in his rapid changing interests in offices and goals—from "Erie" to Ohio to Michigan to Ohio to Mississippi, from the courts to the governorship, to the Senate, the assembly, and the Army—he further reflected much of the instability of politics in a newly formed frontier society. Like Meigs, Worthington, and others, Samuel Huntington exemplified the ambitious, well-educated Eastern politician transplanted to the frontier.

Additional Reading

Bush, David R. and Callender, Charles, "Anybody But the Erie." *Ohio Archaeologist* 34, 1 (1984): 31–35.

Hatcher, Harlan. *The Western Reserve.* Indianapolis, 1949.

Holbrook, Stewart. *Yankee Exodus.* Seattle, 1950.

Hunt, George T. *The Wars of the Iroquois.* Madison, 1940.

Lupold, Harry F. *The Forgotten People: The Woodland Erie.* New York, 1975.

Potter-Otto, Martha. *Ohio's Prehistoric Peoples.* Columbus, 1980.

Smith, Thomas A. *The Mapping of Ohio.* Kent, Ohio, 1977.

Thwaites, Reuben G., ed. *The Jesuit Relations and Allied Documents.* Cleveland, 1896–1901. 73 vols.

Whittlesey, Charles. *The Early History of Cleveland.* Cleveland, 1867.

PART II

The Pioneers: Town Building, Society, and the Emergence of an Economy

In the early decades of the nineteenth century, the Western Reserve wilderness was suddenly opened to an eager multitude—squatters, small farmers, town planners, speculators, businessmen, and professionals—who, in the words of frontier historian Ray Allen Billington, subdued nature and erected a civilization. The forest fell before them, the ground was opened by the industrious plowshare, a comfortable log house was raised, and the nucleus was formed for an intelligent, energetic community life.

Frederick Jackson Turner's sectional essays portrayed the United States as a mosaic of physiographic regions, each of which was distinguished by unique natural, economic, and social conditions. Even in the colonial period the American people "were entering successive different geographic provinces; they were pouring their plastic pioneer life into geographic moulds." Turner further recognized the existence of subsections within regions. He emphasized that "each region reached in the process of expansion from the coast had its frontier experience, was for a time 'the West', and when the frontier passed on to new regions, it left behind, in the older areas, memories, traditions, an inherited attitude toward life, that persisted long after the frontier had passed by."

So it was for Connecticut's Western Reserve. There is a story that relates how Ohio-born William Dean Howells once was asked the secret of his ability to present New England country life with such intense feeling and finesse. Howells replied that it was easy because his boyhood had been spent in a New England village. The name of the village was Jefferson (Ashtabula County, Ohio), a community located in the Reserve's largest farming and rural county. Villages like Jefferson, Oberlin, and Hudson were western prototypes of New England towns, with populations predominately New England in origin. I. T. Frary, in *Early Homes in Ohio* (1970), showed how the Western Reserve copied New England in the use of timber in its architecture. These structures, painted white, made a fine contrast with the deep green of the meadows and the foliage of the trees, and were usually built around a village green and a church, a copy of the New England town plan.

An early interpreter claimed: "New England is another name for conscience and conscience is a kind of immovable habit. . . . So the Western Reserve, which reflects New England, is profoundly conservative." If the qualities of the early settlers were conscience and conservatism, surely these had to be supplemented with prudence, caution, individualism, and ingenuity. Rumor had it that the farmers of Geauga County even counted their bees every night! Timothy Dwight, a president of Yale, expressed some of the negative views toward the westerners. Dwight said that the pioneers were "too idle, too talkative, too passionate, too prodigal, and too shiftless to acquire either property or character." He was glad that they had not remained in New England. Not so, said clergyman Timothy Flint. He defended the frontiersmen who came west as a "hardy, adventurous, hospitable, rough but sincere and upright race of people." One of the greatest of our "frontier" writers was Mark Twain. Perhaps the most "American" of Twain's characters is the immortal Huck Finn. Think of the frontier virtues he represents: youthfulness, honesty, common sense, equalitarianism, among others. Huck's words sum up the spirit of the literary frontier, if not the real frontier: "I recken I got to light out for the territory ahead of the rest, because Aunt Sally she's going to adopt me and sivilize [sic] me and I can't stand it." Pioneer life was really a blend of all points of view and problems. As Randolph C. Downes stated in his *History of Lake Shore Ohio*, "Life, for the most part, went on as usual and people did not sit around bemoaning their lot or rejoicing in their freedom. Life then, as now, was filled with sunshine and shadow, pleasure and pain, excitement and boredom, and mostly with just plain 'gittin along'."

Obviously, Frederick Jackson Turner's concept of frontier individualism had to be balanced by a community sense of responsibility and neighborliness. Joab Squire, pioneer settler of Florence, stated it this way: "The ten years that I lived in a log house was [sic] the happiest period of my life. . . . If one had provisions and the rest were out, it was divided up as long as it lasted. . . . We had a singleness of purpose. That was to clear away the forest and make a home for our families." Even as he lived among the stumps of his newly cut clearing, the farmer had a vision of a new order of society. Villages such as Cleveland, Akron, Warren, Youngstown, Painesville, Vermilion, Hudson, and Jefferson served as places for the exchange of goods and services. They became market centers where capital was accumulated. Roles in politics were possible since many professionals displayed a deep interest in local government. There were always pioneers with some political experience—men happy to be called "judge," "squire," or "colonel." The Reverend Joseph Badger, one of the first missionaries on the Reserve, noted in his diary: "People exceedingly stupid in regard to their external interests, but the little concern about where the county seat shall be, excites all their energies." Each town was a promotion and had its boosters.

Grace Goulder Izant's short description of the founding of Hudson introduces a most unusual and rare town builder, David Hudson. A free thinker and prosperous farmer from Goshen, Connecticut, Hudson suddenly "got religion" and with his newfound Puritan mission set off in 1799 to found a colony "based on moral and religious principles" in New Connecticut. Hudson purchased 7,000 acres of land, sight unseen, on a howling wilderness twenty-some miles southeast of Cleveland, for thirty-four cents an acre. The location of Hudson was excellent, for it was near the center of the population of the Reserve, there was little chance of illness from ague, the main roads from Cleveland to Chillicothe and east to Pittsburgh were nearby and, with time, it would be situated only five miles from the Ohio-Erie Canal. Here this onetime agnostic gave his name to a town, founded a church, established a grade school and, as "the child of his old age," chartered a college—Western Reserve College—in 1826.

Kirtland Township was an "equalizing" township used by the Connecticut Land Company to compensate for losses of those settlers or investors who received swampy or poor land throughout the Reserve. The township was named for Turhand Kirtland, general land agent and stockholder in the Connecticut Land Company. Although he owned almost two thousand acres of land in Kirtland, Turhand never took up permanent residence there. Instead, he and his family finally settled in Poland, Range 1, Township 1, in the southeastern corner of the Reserve. In 1811 Christopher Crary, from Hinsdale, Berkshire County, Massachusetts, brought his wife and nine children to the Kirtland frontier and became Kirtland's pioneer family.

Crary chose three full lots and parts of two other lots in Kirtland. He built his log cabin on a point of high ground at Peck's Corners (today Routes 6 and 306). The cabin, described by one of the Crary children years later, consisted of poles fifteen feet square covered with peeled bark. Bedsteads were two feet high above the floor in order to avoid pesty rattlesnakes. Since there were no chairs or furniture, several chests stored under the bedsteads served as tables, and the bedsteads doubled for seats. The cooking was done outside. Isolated by the Chagrin River and by the little-traveled Chillicothe Road, the Crary family's existence was tested many times, such as during the cold winter of 1812 when one of the family died, with no physician or clergyman nearby to bring relief. Christopher Crary's *Reminiscences* focuses on the conditions of pioneer life in the early years of settlement—economic self-sufficiency, living conditions and discomforts, benefits and problems of liquor, distilleries, and the temperance movement.

While David Hudson was developing the township named after him, another Connecticut man prepared for his journey westward to the Cuyahoga River Valley in Bath Township, Summit County, where he had purchased valuable farm land. His name was Jonathan Hale, and he left Glastonbury, Connecticut, on the evening of June 12, 1810. His account books show Hale to be a man of money, and his diary records a journey in June–July 1810, that covered almost 646 miles in thirty-two days on the road, at a cost of less than fifty dollars in cash. What is unique about Hale's trip is that he chose not to use the well-traveled Mohawk road west from Albany or the Bedford route in Pennsylvania. Instead, he used a shorter and better road that cut through Pennsylvania and the New York Finger Lake country to Geneva, then along the Genesee Road to Buffalo. Today the Jonathan Hale Farm and Village is a sprawling museum of the nineteenth century and owned and operated by the Western Reserve Historical Society. Hale's brick homestead was built about 1826; it and the surrounding structures, with their antiques and reproductions, remind us of a past that can be rediscovered.

During the first difficult years of settlement, every community, actually every individual farm, was self-contained. Domestic manufacturing and personal ingenuity were absolute requirements for survival. Every housewife became a manufacturer. Her instrument was the spinning wheel; she wove the woolen yarn and cotton thread into cloth which was tailored by hand into family clothing. Every family raised and grew all its own food. They killed, butchered, and preserved their own meat. In the fall, hickory nuts, chestnuts, walnuts, and butternuts were supplements to the "hog-and-hominy" diet. The tallow candle, also homemade, provided illumination for the house when the fireplace was not used.

Because many early pioneers were twenty or thirty miles from settlements, the grinding of grain was a matter of no small difficulty and labor. A pioneer had to grind with a hand-mill two hours to obtain sufficient flour or meal for one person each day. These hand-mills were known as "sweat mills," and John Doan of Cleveland described their operation: "In those days we ground corn in little hand-mills. These were two stones about two and a half feet in diameter, one above the other, the upper one being turned with a pole. The corn was poured in through a hole in the upper stone." If a larger quantity of flour was required, Doan had to make a ten-mile trip to David Abbot's mill along the Chagrin River. Sawmills and gristmills were then essential for survival, and most mill owners, such as Lemuel Punderson (Newbury), Elisha Moore (Montville), Holsey Gates (Gates Mills), and John Garrett (Garrettsville), were men of wealth who came to the Reserve with money to invest. Their mills allowed them to exercise superior social and economic power to the point of controlling local markets. The *Firelands Pioneer* referred to them as "autocrats and no appeal could be made from their decision."

Although there were small bog-iron industries, such as the Arcole Iron Company in Madison Township, the blacksmith imported the soft bar iron or cast steel he worked with from Pittsburgh or Europe. Where abundant iron and coal deposits were found in the 1830s and 1840s, men founded combined smelting and factory operations that were extensions of the smith's work. Niles, along the Mahoning River, was founded in 1806 by James Heaton, who produced the first bar of pig iron in Ohio. The factories of Niles would soon produce bar iron, stoves, kettles, horseshoes, and sheet iron. Likewise, Youngstown was another community founded near iron ore deposits. A crude smelter was erected in 1802, and in 1826 a coal mine began operations, setting Youngstown on the road to becoming a leading steel town.

On August 15, 1812, the first disaster of the War of 1812 had befallen American forces on the western frontier. General William Hull surrendered Fort Detriot to an inferior British-Canadian-Indian force. The effect of Hull's dishonorable surrender was greeted by furious anger along Ohio's lake shore; the hurt and humiliation of this defeat would not be healed until Oliver Hazard Perry's spectacular victory at Put-in-Bay on September 10, 1813. Hull's surrender opened up the Ohio frontier and the lake shore to possible British invasion. A panic ensued and most settlers west of the Cuyahoga River packed their possessions into wagons and headed east. At Milan, the inhabitants were in constant apprehension for their personal safety. They expected a British-Indian attack at any minute. Likewise, at Cleveland, able-handed men gathered to defend the village from an enemy that never appeared. Isham A. Morgan remembered that his father handed a rifle to one of his sons and admonished: "If the Indians come, you see that there is one less to go away!" Although the panic subsided as quickly as it had begun, the war years did retard immigration into the Reserve counties. The people of the Western Reserve had much to celebrate when the War of 1812 ended in December 1814. Peace would mean a return to eventual prosperity and a break with the economic isolation of the past.

After the War of 1812, Americans were led by a group of young, enthusiastic, national-minded Republicans—Henry Clay, John Quincy Adams, and John C. Calhoun—who pushed for a program of internal improvement at federal expense. Most westerners, such as Eber D. Howe, editor of the *Painesville Telegraph*, applauded such reforms. Howe used his paper to attack slavery, Masonry, and Mormonism, and to support roads, canals, and railroads, and he pushed Henry Clay for the presidency. In the Western Reserve, said Harlan Hatcher, it was critical to "get the farmers out of the mud," since most roads were all but impassable even on horseback. A minister traveling from Sandusky to Columbus in 1834 reported that his stagecoach journey took twenty-eight hours on a turnpike that was advertised as a "splendid line, equal to any in the State."

The Reserve desperately needed a way to get its farm products to market and eastern capital flowing westward if fertile farmland was going to bring its owners any livelihood. In 1825, seeing that the Erie Canal in New York was a great success, the Ohio State Legislature authorized surveys of five possible routes for the Lake Erie-Ohio River canal. The fascinating political maneuvers that led to the Cleveland-Akron-Portsmouth route are recounted in William D. Ellis's essay. Ellis shows that the salvation of the Connecticut Western Reserve suddenly rested upon the passage of a bill for the public school system in Ohio. More importantly, a Cleveland lawyer-banker-politician, Alfred Kelley, worked relentlessly to insure that the Cleveland to Akron section of the canal would get top priority. By late November 1825, about two thousand men, many being Irish immigrants, swarmed into the Cuyahoga Valley to dig the ditch and construct the forty-four locks required to lift the canal boats almost four hundred feet to reach the "summit" at Akron. As Walter Havighurst noted, Alfred Kelley drove himself to the point where the strain and exposure broke his health, "but the Ohio Canal was built within budget and on schedule." On July 4, 1827, when the Canal boats *State of Ohio* and *The Allen Trimble* floated into Cleveland from Akron and Bath, a new era dawned for Cleveland.

The canal, as we have seen, brought prosperity to the Lake Erie region and its southern shoreline ports. Many smaller communities enjoyed the economic good times—boom-and-bust periods that lasted from the 1820s until the 1870s, when Cleveland and Toledo would control a good portion of the shipping on Lake Erie. "Fairport: The Transformation of a Lake Erie Port, 1812–1870," by Harry F. Lupold, presents a case for a small port at the mouth of the Grand River that tried to survive into the twentieth century. In many ways, the Fairport story is no different than that of Sandusky, Vermilion, Huron, Ashtabula, or Conneaut. All were once competitors to Cleveland.

The economy matured and prospered throughout the Reserve in the antebellum years, and so did society, especially as more professionally educated individuals arrived. Religion is a case in point. No single church ever dominated Ohio. Instead, early Ohio became, in the words of Carl F. Wittke, "a battleground for preachers, as they engaged in the struggle of the 'isms' for the saving of souls in frontier hamlets, camp meetings and revivals." Although the New Englanders brought three sound institutions to the Reserve—the family, the school, and the church—the frontier conditions somewhat altered them. Easterners, such as Dr. Zerah Hawley, who traveled to Ashtabula County in 1820, quickly criticized westerners as godless heathens who were not as religious and community-minded as many presumed. "The greater part of the New England people in the country are pretty loose characters," concluded Dr. Thomas Robbins.

The religious enthusiasm of the Second Great Awakening, with its evangelical and revivalist overtones, spread into the Western Reserve by the 1830s, leaving in its wake splinter groups from prominent eastern religious sects as well as experimental, communitarian groups. Such were the Mormons and Shakers. Robert A. Wheeler compares Shaker and Mormon social, economic, political, and religious views and explains why the Mormons survived and the Shakers became a relic. In a complementary essay, "The First Women's Colleges," Gladys Haddad defines how women's education not only reflected their role in society, but how women's colleges also changed those traditional roles. Using Lake Erie College in Painesville (a single-sex seminary with missionary goals), Oberlin (a co-educational college with deep religious roots), and the College for Women of Western Reserve University (a "coordinate" college) as her models, Haddad concludes, "The pioneers in women's education might be surprised at the long-term outcome of their efforts, and some of them might even be pleased." Both Wheeler's and Haddad's analyses give important insights into the reform movements in religion, education, and women's rights throughout the entire nineteenth century.

What was it like for a student to attend a college in the Reserve in the nineteenth century? C. H. Cramer, in "Student Life at Western Reserve College," describes the spartan-like style and draconic rules that represented the "collegiate way." Although Cramer chose Western Reserve College of Hudson as his example, other colleges such as Oberlin and the Hiram Eclectic Institute, were not much different, with students doing whatever they could to avoid the rules and play pranks on the authorities. In order to divert student energy, said Cramer, colleges introduced a system of exercise—manual labor in workshops or farms. Western Reserve College, then called the "Yale of the West," survived from 1826 to 1882, when a wealthy Cleveland benefactor, Amasa Stone, provided a gift of $500,000, and the college moved to Cleveland, joined with its medical department established earlier in 1843, and changed its status from a college to a university.

The Medical College of Western Reserve University owed its origins to a forgotten institution in Willoughby (Chagrin, until 1834), the Willoughby Medical College of the Willoughby University of Lake Erie, a frontier college that operated from 1834 until 1847. Pioneer medicine in Ohio consisted of a mixture of science, folklore, quackery, magic and, at times, a little prayer. Treatments included bloodletting, purging, and emetics, more commonly called "bleeding, purging, and puking." If the illness did not kill the patient, the doctor's treatment might. With its founding in 1834, the Willoughby Medical School would become only the third such college west of the Alleghenies. The Willoughby Medical College gained its reputation in 1836 when Ralph Granger, a Yale graduate, became its third president. It maintained that reputation through the 1840s because of the quality of four faculty members: John Delamater, Jared Potter Kirtland, John Lang Cassels, and Horace Ackley. By 1843, these "big four" doctors on the faculty left to found the Medical Department of Western Reserve College in Cleveland; in 1847, the rest of the faculty removed to Columbus to found Starling Medical College. From 1847 to 1856, the building that housed the Medical College was used by the Willoughby Female Seminary. When fire burned the Seminary building in 1856, the Seminary moved to Painesville, where it took the name of Lake Erie Female Seminary, today Lake Erie College. Thus the Willoughby experience provided the seed from which grew three of Ohio's institutions of learning.

David Hudson:
The Howling Wilderness

In 1798, not long after David Hudson and the Nortons had acquired their New Connecticut township, the senior Hudson died. On May 3 of that year Sarah Hudson signed a quitclaim deed relinquishing to David Hudson, her stepson, her right as stipulated by her husband's will to his real estate, land, and buildings as well as her dower rights. This was "in consideration for two hundred pounds received to my satisfaction of David Hudson." When distribution of the will took place the following year, it was noted that "the widow of the deceased has given a quitclaim of all her right and title to said estate for the security of fifteen pounds to be paid her annually by David Hudson." Whether this was in addition to the two hundred pounds of the previous agreement, or instead of it, is not clear. It appeared, however, that Sarah was not to have any of her husband's property. Nothing more is heard of her until six years later when her death is recorded in Goshen.

The will's other provisions were carried out: David's sister, Kezia, received her lot of land and cash allocation; his brother Timothy's share was assigned to his heirs since he had died recently. As the old man had indicated, the rest of his land (now including the wife's third portion), the house, and barn were turned over to his son David. This inheritance plus the six hundred acres the younger David owned in Goshen made him indeed a man of substance.

It was a busy time for him. Distribution of his father's will took place on April 13, 1799, and nine days later he was to leave for the West to take possession of the township in the Reserve.

Like many of his contemporaries, David Hudson had been "contaminated," as he put it, by the publications of Thomas Paine, David Hume, and other philosophers of the French Revolution. On the eve of his departure for the Reserve, he was persuaded to attend one of the revival meetings prevalent in that area. This was at the local church, conducted by the new minister, the popular Reverend Asahel Hooker. Writing a few years later in a missionary magazine, Hudson described how he was moved in spite of himself by the exhortations of Hooker. Under the eloquence of the minister he "confessed his infidelities and blasphemies against Jesus Christ and the Gospels and was vouchsafed salvation." (In his article Hudson stated the date of the meeting was 1798, but according to church records it took place in 1799.)

In this sudden turnabout from earlier anti-Christian diatribes, David felt self-conscious and embarrassed to face his friends and neighbors. Consequently "I decided," he wrote, "to remove myself to the solitary wilds of the Connecticut Western Reserve where my former sins were unknown." There as "atonement for my transgressions" he "would found a town in that distant land." He would administer it on strict Christian principles. Maintaining it "under law and order, he would emphasize morality and promote education."

Hudson's re-conversion doubtless added a new dimension and inspiration to his enterprise in what he termed "the howling wilderness." But it did not prompt it: the idea of the undertaking and Hudson's part in it had been settled upon years before. Further, the township was acquired and Hudson's share in it established in January 1798. And four years before his "spiritual reawakening" he had bought "a one-thousandth part of the Reserve," paying $1,500 for it.

Everyone in the big Hudson house by the lake was up early. All preparations for Hudson's departure were in readiness. David Hudson was starting at dawn for that mysterious country across the mountains. He was leaving his wife and five young children. Like John Adams, who in 1778 had taken his ten-year-old son on his perilous voyage to France, Hudson was to be accompanied by his boy, Ira, who was eleven. The oldest child, Samuel, thirteen, was afflicted, probably re-tarded, although in the harsh vernacular of the day his father was to label him "crazy." We can imagine Anna, overlooking the scene from the doorway, holding baby Abigail Laura whimpering in her arms, while Timothy, who was three, clung timidly to his mother's skirts. William, ten, and Milo, a year younger, prancing about, would have envied Ira his good luck. There is no record of how Anna felt.

Hudson kept a detailed journal of his trip. This factual, unembellished record is a documentary on the settlement of Connecticut's Western Reserve. He had hired two Goshen men as helpers and en route was to engage several more, some at fifty cents a day. One of them was Joseph Darrow, an influential man who was much relied upon by Hudson. The chilly, laggard sun soon broke over the East. Ragged patches of snow, remnants of Connecticut's bitter winter, lingered in the hedgerows as the party crossed from Connecticut into New York State and headed for the Albany Road. Hudson's immediate destination was Nathaniel Norton's farm near present-day East Bloomfield in New York State's Ontario County. The stretches of fertile plain they encountered, so different from Connecticut's landscape, seemed a promise of what lay ahead in the faraway land. As they plodded on, spring overtook them. Dogwood and shadbush powdered the tall forest trees with white. Clumps of golden cowslips glowed in the marshlands, and the mud made the roads almost impassable.

Finally they turned in at Norton's gate. With Hudson and Birdsey, Nathaniel Norton was a proprietor and the third member of the "Company" controlling Reserve's Township 4. His farm was to be the launching pad and supply center for all the company's expeditions to the Ohio country even though he was never to see that land. He had bought 350 acres here in New York two years before, paying fifty cents an acre for what was once part of the vast Phelps-Gorham Tract.

Nathaniel operated a busy trading post with Birdsey, an absentee partner, who maintained his home in Goshen. Nathaniel also managed mills and a profitable distillery. Blooded livestock, offspring of herds he had driven overland from Goshen, roamed his fields. His log house was of ample size to accommodate his family and the wayfarers as well.

Hudson remained at Nathaniel's place for eleven days while he and his men collected supplies: quantities of potatoes, pork, bread, cheese, chocolate, sugar. Optimistically, bags of wheat and corn were included for crops in the new land. He gathered a variety of tools, axes, plowshares, fishing tackle, blankets, heavy shoes. One cow worth thirty dollars and another valued at twenty dollars were listed, as well as Morse's *Geography* and 31³/₄ gallons of whisky from Norton's distillery.

En route Hudson met Benjamin Tappan, who was headed for a neighboring township (the future Ravenna). They decided to join forces for part of the way. Their combined livestock was dispatched overland in the charge of their hired men. Ira went with this contingent. Their instructions were to follow "the paths of the Savages" as indicated on a crude map they were given.

As planned, Hudson and the rest of the group were to come by water via Lake Ontario and Lake Erie. The route was considered not only the most direct, but the most desirable since it avoided possible Indian encounters via land. With his supplies assembled, Hudson hurried his party to Irondequoit Bay, the Ontario port where the Genesee River empties its waters ("Jerundagut" in Hudson's journal). To his dismay he found the boats he had made provision for were unseaworthy. After sending his men back for replacements, Hudson finally got his group under way, "rowing in open boats with no power but muscles of the arm and good whiteoak oars."

They encountered continual difficulties. At Niagara they found, to their astonishment, the river choked with floating ice. Blocked also by twelve-foot sheets of ice, they were forced with the greatest effort to portage their boats around the falls. They finally reached Buffalo, and once into Lake Erie they came upon calm, clear water. But a heavy rolling swell developed, delaying them several days. Although they arrived at Conneaut with a fair wind, it shifted without warning, blowing one of the heavily loaded barges against the rocky shore where it filled quickly with water. Several days were spent trying to salvage some of the food and attempting to repair the battered craft. In a final calamity, thieves plundered one of the boats, making off with their precious supply of pork, their whisky, flour, and considerable other fare.

With food supplies dangerously low, Hudson worried that his men "faced famine." With the prospect of not enough supplies to see them through the venture, he considered turning back and abandoning the entire undertaking. Instead, after a sleepless night, he determined on a daring move: he would appropriate some of the flour in a consignment belonging to Eliphalet Austin, founder of Austinburg in the Reserve's future Ashtabula County, and promptly send payment to him there.

Finally, miraculously surviving their ordeals, on June 10 they rowed triumphantly from Lake Erie into the mouth of the Cuyahoga River. They were welcomed by Lorenzo Carter, the first settler in what was to be the city of Cleveland. From his cabin home that did duty also as an inn and trading post, Carter had been watching their approach. He helped them reassemble and provided them with a sturdy replacement for their much-weakened boat.

Hudson's map indicated he was within twenty-five miles of his township. He decided to row up the Cuyahoga with part of his equipment. The water, however, was so shallow that he was forced to disembark at Brandywine Falls (near present-day Northfield).

He was near his township, he knew. Day after day he hacked his way through the seemingly endless bogs, fighting gnats and countless other insects as he hunted for the surveyor's marker that designated it. "And all the while," he confided in his journal, "most heartily repenting ever having undertaken the expedition."

On the eve of the seventh day he stumbled on what he sought. It was June 17, 1799, the forty-eighth day since he had left Goshen. Greatly to Hudson's relief, a loud halloing and crashing of the underbrush heralded the long-overdue arrival of the men with Ira and the cattle. One can imagine the exchange of experiences that ensued. But the factual Hudson mentioned nothing of this in his journal.

A few days before, Hudson, taking time to climb out of the swamp, had found that a broad stretch of level ground lay beyond. A crude road soon was hacked out through the marsh, a rough landsled fashioned, and the oxen, straining every muscle, hauled the supplies up to the high area. The rain that had drenched them for days subsided. Like a good omen the sun burst through scudding clouds, highlighting a pleasant country of forest and plain as far as the eye could see. In their eager exploring they came upon a spring with a steady outpouring of clean, sweet water. Hoofprints indicated it was a favorite gathering place for forest animals. Hudson's chart showed he was in Great Lot 55 in the center of the township. "As darkness fell," he wrote, "I lodged here under an oak tree with grateful pleasure in resting on my own land."

His men, who had been stricken earlier with the ague, now were recovering and the all-important surveying went ahead with dispatch. The village-to-be was mapped out roughly after the plan of Connecticut towns around a central open area. The land donated and later enlarged by Hudson eventually became a typical Connecticut village green.

On a rise of ground near the spring, the towering trees were cut down, a superhuman achievement for men depending only on hand-manipulated axes and physical strength. But the forest monarchs came crashing to the earth, shattering the forest stillness. Promptly work began on building a substantial cabin with the fallen logs. Amidst the tree stumps in the clearing around this "first house in the Village" the men planted wheat and corn brought from home.

With the autumn haze creeping over the landscape and the leaves a blaze of October color, it was time for Hudson to head for home. Accompanied by Ira and one of the hired hands, he followed the same route as before, encountering even worse hazards. The hired men were left to spend the winter in the new cabin in charge of the wilderness domain. Food and generous supplies of drink were laid in, with plenty of shot to guarantee a rich supplemental diet from the abundant wild game.

Frontier Living Conditions in Kirtland

Their log houses were of the ax architecture, that tool being the only one necessary in their construction. Their general size was sixteen or eighteen feet wide by twenty-two or twenty-four feet long, inside measure. The door was in the front side, about the middle of the building. Some had a back door on the opposite side. At one end seven or eight feet of the logs were cut out about six feet high, and the opening filled with a stone wall. On this wall at each end was laid a timber sufficiently large to support the chimney to the fire chamber floor beam, about four feet from the end of the house and some two feet higher than the wall. On these timbers and wall the chimney was built with flat sticks, some two or three inches wide, laid up in clay mortar and plastered outside and in with the same. The chimney narrowed as it went up out of the peak of the roof, from six by four to three by two, giving a good light from above to the fireplace below, where it was very much needed. A wooden crane stood at one end of the fireplace, with an arm sufficiently long to reach to the other end of the fireplace. A trammel or other device was used to hang the pot or kettle, and to raise or lower it as occasion required. In the fireplace was a large back log, five or six feet long, and smaller wood could be piled on to warm the whole house and a considerable portion of outdoors above the chimney. Our cooking utensils consisted of a five-pail brass kettle, an eight-quart brass kettle, a one-pail iron pot, an iron tea-kettle, and a frying-pan with an iron handle three or four feet long. Our bread was baked in a Dutch oven out of doors. Probably we were as well off for cooking utensils as most of our neighbors. For light we had greased-paper windows by the side of the door and from the chimney above. For a buttery a few shelves in one corner of the room by the fireplace, and a chest brought from Massachusetts, had to answer. The opposite corner was occupied by a ladder for access to the chamber, until we could get lumber for stairs. For a cellar we had a trap door in the floor and a small hole dug in the ground for stowing a few vegetables out of the way of frost. Our supply of table furniture was very scant, especially of plates, from breakage on the road. We had five or six pewter plates of English manufacture; they would not do to cut on, as it scratched them; so it became the duty of the cook to cut the meat in small pieces and dish it out to us with a spoon. When Mr. Gillmore came to Chester, in 1811, he had a lathe for turning wooden bowls and plates, called trenchers. The spaces between the logs of our houses were chinked on the inside with pieces of wood and plastered on the outside with clay mortar. The building was carried up some four or five feet above the chamber floor, then each side log drawn in about three feet, each rounded as it went up to the peak. These side logs, lying horizontal, answered for rafters to lay the shingles upon, or shakes, as they were called. The shingles were about four feet long, and generally split out of white oak, the wider and thinner the better. These, if laid about three thicknesses, and weighted down with heavy poles to keep them in place, make a very good roof. The chamber was all one room, and answered for storage of corn, spinning wheels, and all the traps, barrels and household goods that were not in daily use, besides lodging-room for the young folks. The hearth, some six by eight, was of clay, pounded down hard and made smooth, five or six inches lower than the floor. When we found flat quarry stones they were laid on the clay, bringing the hearth up even with the floor. This the women folks thought a great improvement, and much more cleanly, as the hearth could be swept without raising a cloud of clay-dust. Our brooms were all splint brooms, home manufacture. The back end of the room was partitioned off into two bedrooms, originally by blankets hung up around the beds—a rack overhead, with numerous poles for drying pumpkins, and numerous pegs driven in the logs all around the room for hanging up clothing, seed corn, red peppers, dried beef, and other articles too numerous to mention.

I did not quite finish our surroundings and discomforts in my last. One great trouble was the want of light. Our two greased-paper windows gave but poor light in clear weather, and on dark and cloudy days were almost worthless. But these windows were only temporary. Our glass came from Pittsburg by wagons, and was of poor quality, thin, and much of it lost by breakage on the road. The price was very high, and much of the time it could not be obtained at any price. At night, our resource for light was the tallow dip, which would give but just light enough to make darkness visible, and we had to be very prudent in their use, as there were not beef cattle enough slaughtered to half supply the inhabitants with candles. When the candles gave out, we tied a cotton rag around a button, gathering it around the eye of the button, letting it stick up a half inch or more, set it in a saucer, filling the saucer with lard. It would take two or three lamps of this kind to make darkness visible. Our next resource for light, and perhaps the most important one, was hickory bark. We kept a supply on hand, and, by occasionally feeding the fire with this, it made a better light for half a dozen to read by than the tallow dip. . . .

. . . About the year 1819 Warren Corning, of Mentor, erected a log distillery at Kirtland Flats. It was thought to be of great benefit and a valuable acquisition; it would call in settlers, increase business, make a market for corn, enable us to obtain whisky easily without paying cash. Another great benefit would be the obtaining of yeast at the still-house better than could be made at home. Baking powder was at that day unknown. Our expectations from the distillery were fully realized but not appreciated. It made it very convenient to get good yeast. I was sent for it once, and, being naturally rather indiscreet, told my mother what I saw and the language I heard there; she concluded that she could get along with home-made yeast after that, and I was sent there no more. It made it convenient to get whisky, but did not increase our home comforts. It made a market for corn, but did not increase our cash receipts. It brought in some inhabitants, but did not improve the morals of the place. It made some business for magistrates and constables, but did not promote peace, good will, charity, or any of the graces that adorn the present age. From being a blessing, as was hoped, the still-house became an unmitigated curse. It became a resort for a score or more of hard drinkers, holding high and sometimes pugilistic carnival, while some of their families at home were suffering for the necessaries of life. I will say that those who frequented the old still-house were not all from Kirtland; each adjoining township furnished its full quota of those who congregated there, and made night, and sometimes days, hideous with their revelry. I will relate their doings for one night: A Methodist brother, whom it was thought had joined the church for a cloak to hide his thievish propensities, was caught one night with a sheep that did not belong to him. He was brought before the church and excommunicated. The still-house habitués, feeling sympathy for his lonely condition, concluded to take him back into the world, set the time, and invited him to attend, which he accordingly did. On so important an occasion there was a large attendance, and with much ceremony he was regularly taken back into the world, and given all the privileges and immunities of an unrepenting sinner. They procured a quantity of codfish, and together with this and whisky, partook of the sacrament and wound up with a kind of love-feast. They did not wash each other's feet, as some sects do, but they painted each other's eyes black, and put the head of one of their number into the arch, burning his hair off and disfiguring his face for life.

The old distillery may have been a success financially, but morally and physically it was a failure. The son of the owner, a promising young man, who bid fair to make his mark in the world, from constant use of whisky became a sot, almost mindless. Of the half dozen or more men that operated the still during its existence of thirteen or fourteen years, three of them died from the effects of their occupation and excessive use of whisky. They were all men in the prime of life, and bid fair, with prudence, to attain a good old age. A young man left the still one cold night, loaded a little too heavy. He lay down for a nap, and, when found, his feet and legs to his knees were frozen. By taking the frost out with cold water I believe his legs were saved, although in a crippled condition. An old gentleman from a neighboring town brought his jug to the still, had it filled, and started for home. He got up in the neighborhood of where Mr. Sleemin now lives, went into the bushes, lay down and died. He was not found for several days, and was too much decayed to remove. A hole was dug beside him and he was rolled in, and his jug after him, to cheer him in his lonely grave. If the spot could be found by digging, some pure whisky, near fifty years old, might be obtained, which would be valuable in these days of adulterated and poisoned liquor. It would be both interesting and profitable could we know how many years of life had been cut off and shortened by that old still-house—taking those who operated it and those who patronized it, numbering perhaps thousands during the fourteen years of its existence. But this can be known only by Him who numbers the hairs of our head. In 1833 the distillery and fixtures were to be sold, the owner, William Carrel, having died. The concern became such a nuisance that the temperance people clubbed together—ten or twelve of them—Judge Allen, of Willoughby, bidding it off for them. When sold, Captain Morse told me that he lost only seven dollars, and thought it money well laid out. I should before this have stated that the old log still was burned and replaced by a frame building.

I have before me two ancient documents—the first quoted is one of the account books kept at the Kirtland distillery. The first charge is dated December 1, 1831, and it virtually closes February 1, 1833, though there are a few charges two or three months later—covering about fourteen months. There are charges against 138 persons, and, as near as I can judge, about twenty of them consumed a pint of whisky daily. Against one man, living three and a half miles from the still, there are nineteen charges during the last twenty-eight days of January, amounting to one pint per day. Some for a time apparently used a quart a day, while others used not more than a quart a week. Some of the accounts were very sad, showing extreme poverty. One man worked by the day at 50 cents per day to the amount of $9.09; took $5.22 in whisky by the pint and quart; $3.87 went for the support of his family; 22 cents of it for a half bushel of corn meal; 44 cents for a bushel of corn meal; at another time 3 cents for three candles; 2 cents for two at another time; 37½ cents for meat; 50 cents for a hat, the balance in cash, 12½ and 25 cents at a time. There were several accounts showing poverty and destitution in which whisky was the main item. A large number of names were on the book that I did not know, but presume a large portion of them belonged in Kirtland.

The other document referred to is the constitution, by-laws and signatures of the Kirtland Temperance Society. There are 239 signatures attached to the constitution. Among the names are a dozen or fifteen that were considered hard cases, and six whose names are on the still-house book with long columns of pints, quarts and gallons under them. The book has been badly mutilated and much of it is missing, but think the first annual meeting was held October 6, 1830, at which the following votes were taken:

Voted, that no member of this society dispose of grain of any kind to a distiller of whisky.

Voted, that the executive committee be and they are hereby directed to enquire into the situation and circumstances of the distillery in this place, and whether some equally profitable and more laudable use may not be made of it.

This vote culminated in the purchase of the still by members of the society, under agreement that it should never again be used as a distillery. The officers of the society were a president, vice president, secretary, and an executive committee of eight ladies and eight gentlemen. The members of the society were closely watched, and if one violated his pledge, a committee was appointed to labor with him and if possible bring him back and induce him to make another trial. It was painful to see what a struggle it was for some of them to break off. Two or three of us went one evening to see the man who went to the still nineteen times in one month for his daily pint of whisky. He was really sick. We carried him some plums, which he ate with a relish—said they mitigated the distress at his stomach, and thought if he had some chicken's liver, something a little bitter, it would give him relief. . . .

. . . When or how the temperance society died I can only state from memory, but think that October, 1835, was our last regular meeting, and the society was overslaughed and smothered by the influx of Mormons—not that they were intemperate, for I believe they would compare very favorably in that respect with a large number of our old citizens. It was reported, however, that they consumed a barrel of wine and other liquors at the dedication of the Temple, enabling some of them to see angels, have visions, prophesy and dream dreams. But many of the temperance workers were driven away, and those that remained let the society die by default. Three of the hard drinkers returned like "the dog to his vomit."

But I firmly believe that the Kirtland temperance society, short lived as it was, did more to reclaim the drunkard, save the moderate drinker and protect the rising generation than the whole Prohibition party of Ohio has ever done or ever will do. Intemperance is a question of morals, and should no more be brought into politics than any of the crimes forbidden in the decalogue, for it is the mother and breeder of all the crimes that disgrace mankind. The Prohibition party, by bringing the moral question of temperance down into politics, have divided the temperance forces, antagonized, disgusted and paralyzed all temperance workers, and have united all liquor dealers in one solid body, who, by their great wealth, large profits and lavish use of money, hold the balance of power and can defeat any party that attempts to legislate against their interests. The elections in Iowa, Ohio, and other States last fall prove it. . . .

WILLIAM D. ELLIS

Cleveland as Canal Town

The sweeping depression of 1818 forced some settlers into bankruptcy, watching their few treasured belongings sold at sheriff sale for heartbreaking sums like these reported in the newspaper: "a handsome gig and valuable horse —$4.00. Brussels carpet and two Scotch carpets—$3.00."

A handful of leaders in Ohio and Cleveland knew that conditions would not improve until there was a way to get the settlers' surplus output to a market. The market was in the East in New York and in the South in New Orleans, but there was no viable way to get Western Reserve produce to New York. Drayage costs overland were $5 per hundred weight per hundred miles. That meant that anything Ohioans shipped east would be overpriced even before it reached Philadelphia.

Ohioans tried every conceivable way to reduce this transport cost. Some fed the corn to hogs and then packed the hogs in barrels, but it was still too heavy. Some tried droving hogs east, but they lost too much weight en route. Some tried distilling the corn and shipping it as whiskey, but it was still too heavy. Too often, also, the frontiersman consumed his own excess inventory.

Long before the Reserve was even settled, leading colonials, including Washington and Jefferson, had seen that Lake Erie could be connected to the Ohio River if one could bridge the ridge at the continental divide (at present-day Akron). Indians and white scouts had long used the canoe route from the Ohio River, upstream on the Muskingum or Scioto rivers to the Tuscarawas and up the Tuscarawas to the ridge at Akron. Then, one portaged over the centuries-old, eight-mile Portage Path from the headwaters of the Tuscarawas to the head of the bend in the Cuyahoga and then down that little river to Lake Erie.

Long before the Revolution, George Washington had recommended a slack water route between the Ohio River and Lake Erie and had even suggested the best route: "let the courses and distances be taken from the mouth of the Muskingum, and up that river to the carrying place with Cuyahoga, down the Cuyahoga to Lake Erie."

Early Ohio leadership had figured out that a linkage of navigable canals along this route would let Ohio farmers ship to New York City via the canal to Lake

Erie then east on the proposed New York-Erie Canal to the Hudson River and south on that to the city of New York. Or it would let them ship south via the canal to the Ohio River, thence down the Mississippi to New Orleans on the Gulf.

This idea was abroad in the Ohio Country long before Alfred Kelley and Dr. Long [David Long, Cleveland's first physician] arrived in Cleveland. But the concept was too big and costly beyond the dreams of frontier legislators. The attempts to pass canal legislation had smashed the political careers of many state legislators. But with the economy desperate, and with Ethan Allen Brown from southern Ohio pushing for the canal along with a dozen legislative leaders, Kelley joined the fight to get a canal bill through the rustic legislature.

The estimated costs were staggering for the times. They began at $2.5 million dollars and worked their way up to $6.5 million. The enormity of the lobbying job facing the handful of canal exponents can not be appreciated easily today when only six miles of highway costs $6.5 million. But consider these leaders were trying to sell this longest canal in history to a frontier legislature made up of many men who were personally having trouble raising $500 to make third payment on their lands and at a time when the entire annual tax income to the Ohio treasury was only $132,000.

Financing would require selling millions of dollars worth of bonds backed by the credit of the state of Ohio. But with Ohio's assets so low, frontier legislators could see mortgaging Ohio's future for a hundred years to pay for such a project. They feared it would put them in the hands of eastern bankers and foreign investors and force them to raise taxes astronomically.

Beyond this was the contentious question—what route would the canal take? Legislators whose towns were not close to any probable canal route would not support their constituency being taxed for a big ditch that went—as far as they were concerned—"from nowhere to nowhere." Milan or Sandusky people would not pay taxes for a canal terminating in Cleveland. How could a route be found acceptable to all? The legislators had killed canal-enabling acts many times before. They would do it again.

Alfred Kelley took the baton from several senior Ohio statesmen who had begun legislative work on it years before. With Micajah Williams of southern Ohio, he made a strong alliance with Governor DeWitt Clinton in New York who had waged a successful campaign for construction of the Erie Canal across New York. It was to the advantage of both states to have the two canals connect via Lake Erie. The precise and reserved Kelley also worked closely with the flamboyant, powerful Governor Ethan Allen Brown of southern Ohio, who had kept the canal flame alive, if flickering.

Since the result of this work was to be the most important single movement in lifting early Cleveland out of its depression and elevating it above neighboring settlements to become the major American city on Lake Erie, the canal genesis and its dominant Cleveland figure are a major segment of any look at the early settlement.

By 1822, when Kelley became active in promoting the canal, he was thirty-three with an intensive seasoning behind him. Precocious when he arrived at nearly age twenty-one, back in 1810, he had taken sleeping quarters in the small frame office of Judge Walworth on Superior Street nearly opposite West 6th Street, along with young Dr. Long and James Root. The building was in the heart of the village action. In it was the post office, the port collector, and the clerk of courts.

Admitted to the bar on his twenty-first birthday, November 7, 1810, he was the same day appointed county prosecutor and became the village's only work-a-day *practicing* lawman. Elected to the legislature (Ohio's youngest) in 1812, he also became president of Cleaveland Village in 1815.

Since Kelley's legal apprenticeship will become very important and will also give a picture of the early settlers, a few sample cases are germane. Kelley's first recorded case in county court, as far as we can determine, was a debt collection action on behalf of *Ralph M. Pomeroy* v. *James Leach* for two sums, $80 and $150, the debts being two years old. The case was continued one term, then settled out of court. Later on, Kelley acted for the heirs of Aaron Olmsted of East Hartford, Connecticut, against their tenants on Western Reserve lands.

Other cases of record do not necessarily involve Kelley, but help characterize early settlers. An indictment appears against Daniel Miner for selling without license "strong drink by less quantity than one quart . . . for six cents in money." The fine was twenty-five cents. Ambrose Helox was charged with selling a half yard of cotton cambric, six yards of Indian cotton cloth, and a half pound of Hyson skin tea without license to keep store. Thomas McIlrath was charged with trading a quart of whiskey for three raccoon skins without license. John Reede and Banks Finch were indicted because they "did . . . wilfully fight and box with each other at fisticuffs and did then and there strike, kick, cuff, bite, bruise, wound and ill-treat against the peace and dignity of State of Ohio."

The largest number of suits were petitions from absentee owner heirs in Connecticut for partition of their lands. There were isolated suits for theft, for divorce, and for tempting sons back from their indentured apprenticeships prematurely. Kelley would have handled all this variety, being one of only four practicing lawyers here for his first half decade.

The legal profession presents an important picture of the early settlers by recording the terms of indentured apprenticeships, which appear frequently. Fairly typical of a boy's document are these conditions: "He will cause said minor to be taught to read and write, and so much arithmetic as to include the single rule of three, and at the expiration of said time of service, to furnish said minor with a new bible and at least two suits of common wearing apparel." A girl's document might read nearly the same, but with more provision for security, thus: "be also given one feather bed and one milch cow."

As a personality, Kelley must have been one of the most complex, possessing that always interesting combination of practicality and idealism. On the one hand, he proved himself a canny financier benefiting both himself and his village and state, in the creation of banks and commercial enterprises. On the other, he was a zealous social-minded reformer pressing debtor prison reform legislation and education bills. These interests, packaged in a medium stature and lean-faced sober visage, were forwarded by a sometimes unbending honor which both intimidated and attracted men.

In 1821, an Ohio legislative committee reported once more to their colleagues on the advantages of a canal. The report covered every conceivable advantage, military, political, and commercial. The rationale was that while a barrel of flour sold for a maximum of $3.50 in Cincinnati, it would bring $8.00 in New York. The report estimated that via canals, a barrel of Ohio flour could ship to New York for $1.70, leaving a profit of $2.80. The volume of flour produced in Cincinnati alone would thus bring a profit of $364,000 to just that one city.

The leadership rested great hopes on this arithmetic, but the majority of men who learned or heard *about* this dismissed it as promotional talk. However, the legislature did authorize at least appointment of a commission to make a thorough study of all the construction problems. On this six-man study commission was Alfred Kelley. This commission had three major problems to solve: what route from Lake Erie to the Ohio River was feasible from an engineering viewpoint; what route would be popular enough to be sold to enough legislators to get an enabling act through the legislature; what would the canal along such a route cost and how would that money be raised. These were perhaps the three largest problems ever faced by an Ohio commission.

The proposed canal route needed to flow alongside rivers going in the desired direction between Lake Erie and the Ohio River to fill the canal with water; and it needed to be a route requiring the smallest possible amount of blasting through the continental divide which crossed Ohio on a southwesterly line through Akron.

While the commission's challenge was to choose a route it could successfully sell to the legislature, Kelley's problem was compounded by his need to sell the legislative commission and later the legislature on making Cleveland the northern terminus of such a canal. The challenge was severe, because in its first report the commission described favorably five desirable routes—only one terminating at Cleveland, and the other four having very positive advantages and powerful advocates, especially the proposed route bisecting the state from Sandusky to Portsmouth.

The intense wrangling which began in the legislature over which of these routes was best did not indicate probable passage of the canal bill because the wrangling was only among those whose constituents had a lot to gain by one or the other of the routes. The majority of legislators and constituents were either indifferent or opposed to any canal and the tremendous cost.

Eventually, through a dramatic political alliance, enough votes were gained to at least authorize the commission to do a more detailed comparative study of the five routes, complete with cost estimates, a recommended choice of route, and sound evidence that capital could be raised. The same act designated Kelley of northern Ohio and Micajah Williams of southern Ohio as *acting commissioners* to actually take charge of the surveying in the South and North respectively; and it authorized hiring a professional engineer to assist. Thus when the engineer (Geddes of New York's Erie Canal) surveyed the potential northern routes, he was in the company of Kelley, whose preference for the Cleveland-Cuyahoga River–Akron-Portsmouth route certainly was made known to Geddes early and often. Kelley, not of unusually robust health and totally unused to the rigors of the field, trudged with Geddes through the swamps of all the routes under study during an exhausting year.

When the commission reconvened to prepare a thirty-three page recommendation to the legislature, it proposed the Cleveland-Akron-Portsmouth route. This immediately threw the legislature into a sectional squabble. Powerful Columbus and Delaware and Cincinnati representatives were especially vociferous in opposition.

Micajah Williams, a brilliant, genial politician who worked well with sober Kelley, wrote to Ethan Allen Brown, who had kept the canal alive for years and had just left the Ohio governorship to become a U.S. senator, "Kelly [his spelling] is charged with partiality for Cleaveland—and I am charged with—I cannot tell you what—but the Sovereigns are not satisfied."

A reexamination of the route was demanded. Senator Brown traveled to New York and procured a disinterested, experienced engineer, David S. Bates, for that purpose. He also tested the money markets to judge the private financing potential, feeling that the weight of his senatorial voice would be persuasive. His New York money overtures were not enthusiastically received at that time, though he did not generally relay this news.

Engineer Bates's re-audit confirmed the proposed route. However, Kelley and Williams were still in trouble trying to sell Cleveland as the northern terminus. They lobbied their colleagues intensively and proposed several concessions, but the vote count was not adding up in their favor.

The canal proponents now began a fascinating political move, not to be credited to Kelley alone, for it was begun shortly before Kelley was on the commission, in fact it was used to pass the authorization of that first commission to which Kelley was appointed; but now Kelley worked hard at developing that alliance.

The other major effort trying to work its way into law these past ten years was a bill for establishing Ohio schools. This movement was having, if anything, even harder sledding. Frontiersmen concerned with survival had no time, patience, or tax-tolerance for anything so intangible as education benefits. They were in fact plundering the existing education provision established by the Ordinance of 1787 and ensuing federal grants.

The Connecticut Western Reserve was established to finance a school system for Connecticut—not for Ohio. By an interesting turn, the salvation of the Connecticut Western Reserve might suddenly depend upon the success of *Ohio* schools, if Kelley and the commissioners could arrange a special trade.

The voters who favored the canal were thickest in central and western Ohio where canals offered the only possiblity of getting produce to market. These same sparse settlements, still concerned with survival, were opposed to the nicety and costs of compulsory education. Conversely, opposition and indifference to canals came from the more populous southeastern Ohioans who had fair access to Ohio River transportation and some crude trail roads. These same southeasterners were the only ones in Ohio far enough along to begin caring about education.

While the canal group had a nucleus of tough, determined, shrewd leadership, the battle for state education laws also had been led for years by three aging lions. Beetle-browed, granite-faced Ephraim Cutler of Washington County had begun the fight by getting the education lands for each township written into the Ordinance of 1787, and he fought the despoilation of these provisions. Brilliant Caleb Atwater of Circleville drafted law after law which went down to defeat. Tough Cincinnati lawyer Nathan Guilford spent most of his effort campaigning and lobbying for formal establishment of tax-supported Ohio schools. What all of them wanted by 1825 was a comprehensive law establishing a tax to supplement the school land revenues; school districting rules enabling an area with twelve to sixty families to begin formal school, complete with a school committee and tax collector and clerk with approval of two-thirds of the voters, and including the right to assess citizens; and a state superintendent to oversee this.

The campaign to get this far had comprised many smaller battles. One battle which was waged over and over was the massive robbery of the school lands by frontiersmen.

The Ordinance of 1787, with amendments, had established that in government lands, Section 16 of each township must be set aside for the support of education. The idea was not to build the township school on Section 16, but to rent or leave that section and earmark the revenue for support of education.

In practice, the township trustees would habitually lease these school lands to their friends or themselves at pitifully small rentals. One state senator rented seven of these sections. They would default even on these small rents while exploiting the resources on the lands and defaulting on the improvements the ordinance required them to make on these lands (clearing, planting, road building). This breach of trust enraged the education advocates, but they were largely crying in the wind, gaining only small reforms in the legislature when their votes were pivotal in some other close contest.

Now, however, crusty old Ephraim Cutler listened to a proposal by Kelley and Williams. The canal leadership would undertake to swing all the pro-canal votes behind the education bill if Cutler, Guilford, and Atwater would deliver the education legislators' votes to the canal bill. Cutler had been disappointed before. The school men could probably mobilize their people behind the canal because ultimately the canal costs would be borne by private investor-bond holders—but could canal leadership really deliver votes which would cost their constituents a tax, a tax which would ultimately outrun the cost of municipal government?

Guarded negotiations proceeded over long weeks. Kelley came back with an exciting modification. It would probably be many years before the school lands would really produce substantial revenues. What if permission could be obtained to sell some school lands for cash and invest the dollars in canal bonds? Then perhaps some school lands could be traded for lands adjacent to the canal where land values would appreciate faster.

The school men continued to consider, examining the probability of getting permission to convert school lands to canal bonds, and the probability of canal success.

Ultimately, the school men, disillusioned by past experience, felt that although the deal looked good, there was strong possibility that they could deliver school votes to the canal, but the canal men must see that the school tax measure *preceded* the canal bill on the legislative docket. If the school bill passed, the school men would deliver their votes to the canal.

While this oversimplifies a trade negotiated over many hours and months, the outcome was that in a space of forty-eight hours on February 3 and 4, 1825, possibly the two most sweeping movements in Ohio pioneer history were launched: a tax revolution providing for formal statewide education, and the then largest canal system in the world.

Ground breaking began July 4, 1825, from Newark, Ohio, digging north. Micajah Williams was in charge of the southern leg, Kelley of the north. Senator Brown must be credited with the fund raising.

Kelley suffered further criticism for rushing into construction from Cleveland south to Akron. His reason was urgent. From the moment of passage of the Canal Act, the opposition began attempting to nullify it, especially the two powerful rivals of Cleveland—Sandusky and Warren. Both towns held opposition meetings. Warren, the first unofficial capital of northern Ohio and the seat of powerful Simon Perkins, raised funds to place advertisements in New York papers timed to coincide with Senator Brown's big New York trip to attract New York investment money for the canal. These ads warned potential investors against Ohio canal bonds because Trumbull County citizens were refusing to pay taxes if any part of their tax dollars were to be used to pay canal bond interest.

Kelley wanted to get so far along that the canal couldn't be stopped; but Ohioans accused him of favoring his home town by starting at Cleveland. Clevelanders would get first benefit.

If there was a bit of truth in that, it must be admitted there was strong logic in Kelley's wanting the Cleveland-Akron leg finished quickly. A public, not much enchanted with the canal anyway, would soon be clamoring for financial results. The quickest financial benefit would come from the Cleveland-Akron leg, even if the rest of the canal construction lagged; Ohio would ship overland to Akron, then down the canal to Cleveland, transship by schooner to Buffalo, thence over New York's Erie Canal to the Hudson and down that to the big New York City market.

Kelley ignored bitter criticism and drove the canal construction relentlessly. The work was let to competitive bidding contractors, each contract being for a mile or two or for a lock or aqueduct or bridge.

Kelley drove himself as hard as he drove his contractors, and he was considered ruthless in holding contractors to the specifications, which were fairly exacting: four-foot depth of water with drainage fall of one inch per mile; width at water line forty feet, at bottom twenty-six feet; tow path to be level and packed down, and to include no stumps which would rot and cause the path to settle.

Kelley's section had the largest number of locks, forty-four from Cleveland to Akron to lift the boats up 395 feet.

In fair weather and foul, Kelley was out on the canal right-of-way seeing that contractors were doing the job right. He earned their grudging respect by making them tear out berms and tow paths they had filled with old stumps, by making them regrade if the fall wasn't an inch per mile, by making them stone-face the canal banks if erosion destroyed the face. He caused contractors to reface the locks if the cement mortar didn't resist his iron prod.

Contractors who found Kelley too tough did not bid on a second section in the North, but moved south for their next contract. On the other hand, good contractors stayed on the northern section because another aspect of Kelley's style of operation was prompt payment once a contractor's work passed inspection. A contractor could submit his bill at the completion of separate phases of the work: clearing, rough excavation, canal prism formation, completion of tow path and berm. Additionally, Kelley would make himself immediately available to inspect any phase of any contractor's work so the contractor was not held up.

The contractors also were impressed with how quickly Kelley mastered the engineering phase of the work, with a true appreciation of their problems. This understanding was especially necessary on the northern section for reason. Kelley had pushed for such an early start that he did not have advantage of the experienced contractors and canal workmen who would be increasingly available coming off New York's Erie Canal job to work on other parts of Ohio's multi-fingered canal system (ultimately over nine hundred miles). Kelley received bids from local businessmen who hastily formed themselves into contracting companies to build the canal, hiring farmer-settlers as workmen. While many of these were excellent, others got into the middle of the work and struck problems they couldn't handle: gravelly soil that wouldn't hold the water; clay soil they couldn't excavate at the price they had bid; rock that wouldn't cut into blocks for canal locks. The greatest problem of all was the miasmic ague—the fever and chills which had plagued early settlers here. Now they were working calf deep in the muck during driving rains and burning heat.

From the ranks of two thousand men and one thousand horses working the canal from Cleveland to Akron in 1825 and 1826, men were dropping in their tracks with ague. Many quit. Turnover was high. Kelley and his division engineers had to help contractors recruit men. Not yet had the wiry, enduring Irish come in large numbers off the Erie to take over the Ohio Canal work. They would later come through Cleveland to travel south to work other divisions of the Ohio and Erie Canal and the Ohio and Maumee Canal in western Ohio. And they would leave an Irish heritage in Cleveland.

If there was a fault in Kelley's style of operation it was his failure to delegate enough of the responsibility and decisions to his division engineers. As a result his health began to fail under the pressure he put upon himself. Senator Brown and the able Micajah Williams urged him to spare himself, but he hadn't that one ability.

Despite this, he soon found himself in overall charge of the canal as Williams and Brown accepted other posts. One of the most remarkable tributes to his managerial skill and integrity was that when his enemies demanded a state audit of the largest project in then Ohio history, the audit confirmed Kelley's figures to the penny and the general assembly passed a resolution of tribute to him. No corruption or financial mismanagement touched this project.

The greatest evidence of Kelley's growing national stature occurred when enemies of the canal caused the state of Ohio to officially repudiate its obligation to bond holders. Kelley organized a group of prominent western businessmen with himself in the center, pledging their present and future personal fortunes to paying interest on the bonds (of a certain issue). On the strength of this, New York brokerages continued offering bonds.

HARRY F. LUPOLD

Fairport: The Transformation of a Lake Erie Port, 1812–1870

Dwight Boyer, the late storyteller of the Great Lakes and *Plain Dealer* reporter, believed formal historians have not done justice to the truth and drama surrounding these "Seas of Sweet Water." Boyer once concluded: "It is the firm belief in the east, from whence most publications originate and where history is written, rewritten or totally ignored, that the Great Lakes are some sort of vague midwestern recreational facility." Particularly shortchanged by historians have been the smaller lake ports along the southern shore of Lake Erie. One of these locations, Fairport, had a favorable harbor which throughout the nineteenth century served as a port of entry for Western Reserve pioneers, as well as a port for ships carrying immigrants westward. Ships could always put in to Fairport's friendly harbor when violent storms struck Lake Erie.

Fairport is located at the mouth of the Grand River, twenty-eight miles northeast by east of Cleveland. Moses Cleaveland, leader of the Connecticut Land Company's surveying party, described the Grand River on August 5, 1796: "The Grand River is about twice as large as the Ashtabula, and will afford good navigation for small vessels and boats. The land on which we went is as good as I ever seen in any country. On this river is an Indian corn, etc., growing luxuriantly."

The Erie Indians had long recognized the economic and military importance of the Grand or Geauga River. They used the mouth of this river—as they did the Chagrin, Cuyahoga, and Ashtabula—as a seasonal gathering place, and they located their villages along its banks. The Fairport Village site was excavated by Richard G. Morgan and Robert M. Goslin of the Ohio State Museum in 1937. Assisted by Elijah H. Brown, principal of Harding High School and a field force of his students, they uncovered 1,950 artifacts, 11,603 potsherds, and hundreds of animal and bird bones. These investigators concluded that the village was established toward the close of the sixteenth century by the Erie Indians and occupied by them up to the middle of the seventeenth century, when they were destroyed in a ferocious war with the Iroquois.

The New England pioneers, like the Indians before them, chose to locate a number of their estates and villages along the Grand River for all the same natural and economic advantages. One of the first of these emigrants was John Walworth from Aurora, New York. Walworth moved his family and the family of a hired hand, John Miller, to his 2,000 acres of land in the present township of Painesville, a mile east of the mouth of the Grand River. The Walworths, in 1800, had to live in a tent for several weeks until their cabin was completed, "during which time the sun was not seen." In 1805, President Thomas Jefferson appointed Walworth collector of customs for Cleveland and, later in that same year, Walworth was made postmaster for Cleveland. To meet his public responsibilities Walworth removed to Cleveland in 1806, after exchanging most of his Grand River holdings with future governor Samuel Huntington, who held a 300-acre tract in Cleveland. Huntington would develop Walworth's excellent lands and improve his estate, "Blooming Grove."

In 1800, there was no Painesville or Fairport. Originally called Oak Openings and then Champion, Painesville comprised about eighty acres of the present city at the junction of Old State Road (State Street) and the Erie-Cleveland Road (Route 20). It did not extend to the Grand River. The two men who developed the area north of Painesville near the mouth of the Grand River were Abraham Skinner, agent of General Henry Champion, and Eleazer Paine, nephew of General Edward Paine. Skinner and Paine laid out the village of New Market, a speculative venture and the first such planned village east of Cleveland. Captain Skinner sold chickens, apples, vinegar, cider, potatoes, beef, tea, corn, whiskey, wheat, flour, pork, tobacco, brandy, wood, and bitters from his landing on the Grand River. Unfortunately for their partnership, Paine died in 1804.

Grandon became the last of the early settlements along the Grand River near the Lake; it was situated on land deeded in 1798 to Samuel Fowler by the Connecticut Land Company. Here the future site of Fairport was laid out in 1812 by its cofounders Abraham Skinner, Samuel Huntington, Seymour and Calvin Austin, and Simon Perkins. William Darby, a traveler through the area in 1818, wrote in his journal: "Grand River is a stream of some consequence.... It is about 70 yards wide at the mouth, with seven foot water on the bar near the entrance into the land. The east bank rises to the height of thirty or forty feet affording a very handsome site for a village. The harbor is excellent for such vessels whose whole draft of water will admit entrance." Darby might have exaggerated slightly, since prior to 1825 the mouth of the Grand River was obstructed by a sand bar so hard and dry that in the summer months a roadway was used there to cross the river.

In the early years, before harbor improvements were initiated, Fairport was an embarkation point for pioneers who were moving to the interior of Geauga County (Lake County after 1840). For instance, we have this record of the Thomas Umberfield family who were en route to Burton Township in 1798:

> They landed at the mouth of Grand River, on whose banks no tree had been cut, or cabin or tent of civilized men erected. Here a frail cabin of bark was constructed to

shelter the women and children and store the goods. . . .Having provided a shelter for the families, the men blazed a road to Burton. . .on which they transported their goods and families to their intended homes in the homeless woods.

As the economy of Ohio matured by the decade of the 1820s, Lake Erie ports such as Conneaut, Ashtabula, Cleveland, Huron, Vermillion (spelled with two l's at this period in history), Sandusky, and, of course, Fairport all clamored for some way to get their harbors improved. This was essential so that the products of Ohio's farms could reach the eastern markets and badly needed cash could flow back to Ohio. Steam navigation on Lake Erie commenced in 1818 with the launching of the steamboat *Walk-in-the-Water*, near Buffalo, New York. On May 7, 1823, the steamboat *Superior* entered Fairport harbor, and from May 28 to June 2, 1823, a total of nine schooners and one steamboat visited Fairport. The changing technology of lake vessels demanded harbor improvements.

In October 1825, the steamboat *Pioneer* went ashore just west of the harbor entrance. This accident to the *Pioneer* encouraged the people of Fairport to circulate a petition asking Congress for an appropriation for the construction of piers in the harbor. The Western Reserve's representative to Congress, Elisha Whittlesey of Canfield, brought the issue before Congress. Internal improvements at federal expense was greatly debated in the 1820s, particularly because many members of Congress and even some presidents doubted the constitutionality of such expenditures. But, in 1825, an appropriation of $1,000 was made and, in the next session of Congress, the appropriation was increased to $4,000. The work on the pier began in 1827 and was completed in 1831. Fairport had received one of the first appropriations for an interior harbor on Lake Erie.

By 1844, after a total expenditure of $16,000, the piers extended into the lake a distance of 480 yards and admitted vessels drawing twelve feet of water, a greater depth than was expected. A setback to further improvements came, however, in 1846, when President James K. Polk vetoed a River and Harbor Bill, stating:

Some of the objects of the appropriations contained in this bill, are local in their character and lie within the limits of a single state; and though in the language of the bill they are called harbors, they are not connected with foreign commerce, nor are they places of refuge or shelter for our navy or commercial marine on the ocean or lake shores.

Public reaction to the veto was strong and immediate; it resulted in the River and Harbor Convention in Chicago on July 5, 1847. Samuel Butler, keeper of Fairport's first lighthouse and local abolitionist, was among the fifteen regional delegates at the 2,300-delegate, nineteen-state conference. Polk's mind could not be changed, but the delegates protested to Congress, and future appropriations for local interior harbors were increased.

The next step for Fairport's harbor improvements was the movement for a suitable lighthouse. Many lighthouse proposals along Lake Erie were not funded, and many ports had to depend on temporary locally made devices. At Ashtabula, for instance, the first lighthouse was built in 1834–35 on a crib about twelve feet east of the east pier and some two hundred feet from the beach. "Prior to the building of the first beacon light the only guide a vessel had to the harbor at night was a lantern hanging from the end of a pole on the end of the pier," said Moina W. Large. Vermillion badly needed a beacon to improve harbor utilization. The local citizens had furnished their own light in 1838, and in 1847 they began to build a suitable temporary light, since the federal government had excluded funds for such a lighthouse as well as repairs to Vermillion's piers.

On March 26, 1825, the *Painesville Telegraph* published an announcement which asked for bids on the lighthouse and the keeper's dwelling. The proposal stated that the lighthouse and dwelling must be constructed of stone or hard brick. The tower was to be thirty feet from the ground, while the top of the tower was to hold an octagonal-shaped iron lantern, each side of which would contain eighteen lights. The keeper's house was to be two stories high, with a "cellar under the whole of the house." A contract was subsequently drawn up between the noted architect Jonathan Goldsmith; Hiram Wood for the contractors; and Jairus Thayer, who represented the federal government. A misunderstanding arose when the contractors understood that their agreement did not include a cellar for the keeper's dwelling. As a result, Goldsmith and Wood informed A. W. Walworth, collector of customs at Cleveland, that they would construct said cellar for $174.30. Walworth objected to the price as being too high but, nevertheless, relented and accepted it. A new foundation had to be added to the original lighthouse in 1835, and a new stone structure replaced the wooden beacon in 1871. It warned ships on Lake Erie until 1925 when it was replaced by the present lighthouse.

Interestingly, Jonathan Goldsmith, in 1841, sought the position of lighthouse keeper for the beacon he himself had built. This fact was disclosed in a letter from Congressman Joshua Giddings to General L. Diller who was acting on Goldsmith's behalf. Goldsmith did not get the appointment, and Giddings disclosed a rare view of the use of congressional patronage when he wrote that the lighthouse keepers on Lake Erie would be appointed by the collector at Cleveland:

> It would give me pleasure to aid your friend, Mr. Goldsmith, but I have laid down a rule for my own guidance from which I do not like to depart. That is to lay all papers on the subject of appointments before the proper officers and if inquired as to character of the applicant or of those who sign his application frankly to state all I know upon the subject and then leave the matter to rest and place the responsibility upon the officer making the appointment.

By 1837, Fairport was the center of a vibrant and spacious market. This economic development began in the harbor area. The early commerce of the port consisted mainly of the forwarding trade. Warehouses were built and freight was received on a consignment basis. Alvah Cable constructed his warehouse on

Water Street in the 1820s. Shortly thereafter Dexter Knight operated a warehouse on the corner of Water Street and Fourth Street. According to advertisements in the *Painesville Republican,* Cable and Gregory traded and sold readymade clothing, boots, crockery, groceries, hardware, and provender for ships. Their imports also included fine tobacco, Holland gin, St. Croix rum, Java coffee, and sugar. Much of their business was in trade of goods; cash was offered for meat, dairy products, eggs, and pickles.

A shipping report that appeared in the *Painesville Telegraph* in 1836 showed that the price of passage on the lake was pretty uniform among all ships. There are two kinds of passage, cabin and steerage, differing in accommodations and prices. A cabin passage included meals and lodging as well as all the privileges of the vessel. A traveler in steerage carried his own food or paid extra for his meals and slept on deck or in a forward cabin. Most emigrants heading west preferred the deck passage. Typical rates from Buffalo to different ports on the lake included:

	Cabin	Steerage
Buffalo to Erie	$4.00	$2.00
Buffalo to Cleveland	$6.00	$2.50
Buffalo to Detroit	$8.00	$3.00

Shipbuilding was an important industry for many of the lake ports. Vermillion's fame was due to shipbuilding. For thirty-two years (1809–41), nine vessels were launched from the west bank of the Vermillion River. Capt. William Austin, a sea and lake captain, built and sailed the first sailing vessel to leave Vermillion, the 32-ton schooner *Friendship.* Conneaut, thirteen miles east of Ashtabula harbor and a short distance to the Ohio-Pennsylvania border, also had a shipbuilding industry by 1830. Shipbuilding commenced in Fairport in 1826 with the construction of the 120-ton schooner, *United States.* Fairport remained an important shipbuilding center until the end of the century. The peak of activity was reached in 1866–67 when ten vessels left the Fairport yards. Vessels, including schooners, steamers, scows, and tugs, built at Fairport between 1826 and 1895 totaled thirty-three. During the same period, nearby Richmond, on the west bank of the Grand River, built five vessels, while Madison, at the mouth of Arcole Creek and just east of Fairport, constructed five schooners.

The prosperity along the Lake Shore naturally attracted speculators. In Vermillion, for instance, thirty men from Huron County joined together and invested their money in the sale of that town's real estate. Thus in 1837 they helped prepare the way for Vermillion's "Golden Age" from 1842 to 1860. In Huron and Milan, the Milan Canal Company was chartered on January 24, 1827. This canal cost $23,392 to construct over a period of six years. It was completed on July 4, 1839, and ushered in a period of brief prosperity for both Huron and Milan. Thomas Richmond, a salt merchant from Syracuse, New York, purchased a tract of land, sight unseen, across the river from Fairport. Richmond believed that the Grand River area would become a great commercial center for the Midwest, since he expected that a north-south Ohio canal would terminate there. The village of Richmond grew spectacularly and, by 1835, housed 2,000 persons. Richmond established a storage and shipbuilding business, and another boomtown was born, an unforeseen rival to Fairport. But Richmond's enterprise did not last long—by 1840 he was finished. Not only had the canal terminus on Lake Erie gone to Cleveland, but the Panic of 1837 left Richmond, the proprietor, $35,000 in debt. The town of Richmond eventually entered the twentieth century as the community of Grand River.

The golden years for Fairport as a lake port were the years from 1842 to 1852. Henry Howe visited the flourishing county seat of Lake County, Painesville, in 1846, and reported: "Painesville is one of the most beautiful villages in the west: it is somewhat scattered, leaving ample room for the cultivation of gardens, ornamental trees and shrubbery. A handsome public square of several acres, adorned with young trees, is laid out near the center of the town, on which face some public buildings and private mansions." Painesville owed its importance to its location in the center of a rich agricultural area and on the main mail road from Buffalo to Detroit. Two miles north on the lake was Fairport, considered by many "the finest and most spacious harbor on the south shore of Lake Erie, constructed by the United States." Fairport was a "regular place of landing and embarkation for passengers between the western country and the state of New York." Already in 1841, near Painesville was a thriving bog iron industry at Madison Dock (Ellensbury), representing a considerable investment for that period in iron manufacturing.

But Fairport's prosperity may not have been unique since the records indicate that the decade of the 1840s seemed to benefit the economic progress of many of Lake Erie's ports. Vermillion, for example, enjoyed considerable prosperity from 1842 to 1860 due to the iron, lumber, and stone industries of the adjacent area. Agriculture (grains, flour, bacon, ham, butter, cheese, fruit) also aided Vermillion's commercial growth. Yet her export total did not equal those of Toledo, Sandusky, Huron, and Cleveland. Another port, Huron, enjoyed a temporary boom with the Milan Canal Company. Fourteen warehouses lined the Huron River along the canal basin in Milan. Shipments of wheat totaled 917,800 bushels in 1847, while total exports in that year were $1,250,000. By the 1850s, Sandusky was considered by many to be the most important port on the southern shore of Lake Erie, possessing the only connection by rail with the Ohio River. Here lumber was available for manufacture into wood products; commercial fishing on the Lake was started; an ice industry and limestone quarries added to the commercial enterprise; and in the 1850s grapes were planted on the islands. In 1849, Sandusky's population numbered 5,667, but many fled the area with the cholera epidemics of that year—and of 1852 and 1854. Ashtabula investors also enjoyed a small boom in 1851 when exports totaled $442,389, while imports showed a trade worth $419,105.

A line of stages from Wellsville via Warren to Fairport was placed into operation in 1845. Triweekly trips were made, over the Painesville and Warren plank road, which extended from Fairport to Bloomfield and there connected with the

Warren pike. Although a busy thoroughfare for several years, it was discontinued as a toll road in the late fifties. Travelers, lake sailors, local stevedores, and Fairport citizens could socialize at four hotels—one, the largest, situated on the south corner of Water and Second Streets, was operated by Phineas Root. In the years 1830 to 1852, when the first railroad came, Ashtabula also had a regular line of stages plying between the harbor and Wellsville on the Ohio River. The less than one hundred mile route was covered in a scheduled time of twenty hours for a fare of $4.00. One report suggests that over one thousand travelers and emigrants were transferred from boat to stage as early as 1832. In Vermillion, two state routes and a turnpike built earlier allowed the merchants to service the backcountry.

The zenith of prosperity for Fairport as a Lake Shore port was reached in 1847. The custom records for that year indicated the following business:

Exports	$462,028	
Exports, 1846	309,477	
Increase	$152,551	
Imports	$529,421	
Steamboats Arrived and departed		2,150
Vessels Arrived and departed		836
Total		2,986

The most important exports included $67,867 worth of cheese (1,131,107 pounds), $52,850 worth of corn, rye, and barley, and $38,790 worth of wool. Imports, in value, included $493,733 in general merchandise, $5,802 in salt, and $4,950 worth of whiskey (550 barrels).

One of the most successful of Fairport's entrepreneurs was Jonathan Ford Card, who operated a ship chandlery and furnished groceries, produce, and lumber to the vessels. Business was so good that after two years, in 1847, Card built a large warehouse near the government pier. Card also speculated in land. For instance, he purchased 260 acres of timberland at $10.50 per acre on the headlands. He cleared the timber, cut some fine white oak staves, and made enough profit from the sale to pay for the land, which he then proceeded to sell for $11.00 per acre. With ingenious Yankee know-how, Card turned a nifty profit on most of his ventures. By 1852, he netted $2,500 yearly. Card purchased the brick dwelling on the southeast corner of Plum and Third Streets, the former mansion of Ralph Granger, Lake County lawyer and politician. He described this period (1847–53) of his life: "This house was a better one than I had ever lived in before or since. The lot contained about five acres, beautiful shade trees, both native and imported, fine vegetable gardens, good barn, large ice house. . . . I may safely say that the happiest six years of my life were spent right there."

Later in life Card recalled that land sales around Fairport were made by the foot, instead of by the acre as formerly. He once purchased thirty-two rods on High Street in 1835, from Colonel Storrs for $3,200, which he sold six weeks later for $25 per front foot, clearing over $11,000 net profit. When the Lake Shore Railroad neared completion in 1853, however, Card shrewdly sold his business and moved to Buffalo. Could he, by chance, have anticipated the end of the economic boom for Fairport?

As Thomas A. Smith has so wisely observed: "Ports such as Vermillion, which continued to rely on local produce for much of their commerce, began to be passed over by the new industrial age." The prosperity of the 1840s and 1850s gradually disappeared by 1870. The loss of the proposed Vermillion and Ashland Railroad, the federal government's refusal to provide funds for the harbor, the removal of Alva Bradley and Ahira Cobb, Great Lakes merchants, who relocated in Cleveland, and the exhaustion of local deposits of bog iron and secondary stands of timber all led to the end of Vermillion's "Golden Age." Sometimes natural disasters hurt, such as Ashtabula's flood of 1878.

So it was for Fairport. The Lake Shore Railroad, which bypassed Fairport, and the construction of a canal from the Ohio River to Cleveland rather than to Fairport hurt the village's commerce and local trade. But it was different in the capital city of the Western Reserve, Cleveland; in Akron, Warren, and Youngstown; and to a lesser degree at Sandusky and Ashtabula, and later, Lorain. These towns were destined to become the manufacturing, commercial, banking, and shipping centers of the Reserve. The industrial revolution meant that Lake Shore Ohio would play a more diversified role: it would service the railroad industry, become a shipbuilding center, supply and transfer iron ore and coal, become the oil refining center, and dominate the machine tool industry.

The new industrial order of the post-bellum years transformed the economy of Fairport. In the 1870s, the village of about eight hundred inhabitants still survived, with a fish packing establishment where large quantities of black bass, whitefish, pickerel, and pike, caught in the lake, were frozen and shipped to various markets. A great number of sturgeon were also caught. The sturgeon eggs were removed and shipped to Hamburg, Germany, where they found a ready and profitable market for the manufacture of caviar.

In 1860, the population of the village numbered 878 with 325 families and 339 dwellings. In 1870, the population decreased with a total number of 261 families and 277 dwellings in the community. Yet in many ways Fairport represented a typical nineteenth-century American village, retaining some of its New England origins. But the industrial revolution also changed the demography of Fairport, for in 1872 a number of Finnish people arrived from Finland's Vaasa Province, an area of Finland known for its rich farmlands with a terrain similar to northeastern Ohio. By 1887, Fairport's Finnish population consisted of almost two hundred. The Finns were soon joined by Hungarians, Slovaks, and some southern whites. The industrial revolution and the demands of the new economy along the Lake Shore had led to the development of a melting pot population, and tiny Fairport entered the twentieth century, a changed but proud Western Reserve village, still struggling to maintain its unique identity.

Eastern Criticism of Frontier Religion

In a few towns on the Reserve, clergymen are settled for four or six months in the year, and the remainder of the time they ride as missionaries, through the townships which lie contiguous to them. In a very small number of towns, ministers are settled for the whole year.

These remarks apply to Presbyterians and Episcopalians. The other preachers are illiterate Baptist elders and still more illiterate itinerant Methodists. From this view of the subject it will easily be seen that the situation of the inhabitants of this country is most deplorable with regard to religious privileges.

It may further be remarked that many families are without the Word of God, and are groping in almost heathenish darkness, and are unable to procure the word of life to make them wise unto salvation. This is not all; at least eleven months in twelve, the great body of the people have no better oral instruction than what they receive from the most uninformed and fanatical Methodist preachers, who are the most extravagant ranters of which anyone can form an idea, who bawl forth one of their incoherent rhapsodies in one township in the morning, in another township in the afternoon, and a third in a third place in the evening. Thus they run through the country, "leading captive at their will, silly women," and men equally unwise....

Their sermons are without plan or system, beginning with *ignorance* and ending in *nonsense*, interlarded with something nearly approaching blasphemy in many cases....

...Missionaries are, as appears to me, almost as much needed here as in the Islands of the Seas; and as these people are our brethren according to the flesh, there appears to be a duty incumbent on those who possess the means, an *urgent necessity*, to send them well-instructed teachers who may lead them in the way of Heaven.

This state (with the exception of a few towns) is still thinly settled, many townships remaining in the same situation, or nearly so, as they were when possessed by the savages of the forest.

ROBERT A. WHEELER

Shakers and Mormons in the Early Western Reserve: A Contrast in Life Styles

In 1835 the *Painesville Telegraph* spoke for many residents of the Western Reserve when it expressed both appreciation for and apprehension of religious sects:

> No other country on earth can boast of such varied forms of religious sects and such palpable departures from primitive simplicity and purity of the Gospel, as this country. We would not forge chains nor bind fetters around any human mind, but we would gladly see public sentiment frown upon those mental hallucinations which disgrace Christian lands, and shun communion with those preposterous forms of worship, which are merely solemn mockeries of Religion! (April 3, 1835)

The dilemma suggested by the editorial was not easy to resolve. The region was located just west of the "burned-over" district of New York, an area constantly swept by the fires of successive revivals, which often spread into the Reserve before 1860. Residents constantly heard of splinter groups from prominent sects like the Baptists and the Methodists, of extensions of eastern religious communities, and of totally new groups. In fact, since the numbers and approaches seemed endless, the turmoil of the era is characterized as "freedom's ferment."

Two of the most controversial groups in the nation left their stamp on the Western Reserve: the Shakers and the Mormons. While they were remarkably different in style, both came from similar traditions and stirred up their own brands of sympathy and antipathy. Both would last over fifty years and thereby outlive many other contemporary rivals. Both would influence the Reserve beyond their combined numbers, which never totaled more than seven hundred before 1860. By comparing the Shakers and the Mormons, a hint of the difficulties encountered in establishing a new sect in the area can be examined.

If we use the analogy of the life cycle of a person, it is easy to see some of the important similarities and differences between the two groups. During the 1820s the Western Reserve itself was still in its early years. Like many youngsters, it was learning its strengths and weaknesses and was particularly vulnerable to suggestion.

Religious enthusiasm fascinated residents as it spilled into northeastern Ohio not only from New York but also from the southern part of the state. The Ohio River basin was older and experienced part of the Cane Ridge (Kentucky) revival, which began a religious period called the Second Great Awakening. The Awakening directed religion for many frontier Americans in 1800 away from intellectual arguments toward immediate, emotional involvement with a God who was always present and willing to help. Emphasis was placed on rebirth of the believers. In large camp meetings their spirits were "awakened" to the life exemplified by Jesus Christ. They were encouraged by powerful, itinerant ministers who preached a sincere, direct Christianity based on a literal interpretation of the Bible.

Most meetings were held in the countryside. In the early 1830s a typical camp meeting was held in Newburgh township, three miles from Cleveland. The *Cleveland Herald* wrote, "Preachers and members of the neighboring circuits together with all who feel an interest in the religion of Jesus are invited...N.B. Pasturage can be had near the camp ground. There will also be a boarding tent kept for the entertainment of strangers and others" (June 5, 1852).

Many of the "regenerated" converts firmly believed America was the land of biblical promise, Zion, and that the promised second coming of Christ was near. Each sect spurred by the Awakening felt it would have a special place in the world after Christ returned, so while they were optimistic about the second coming, they often insisted their ideas were the only true way to salvation.

As stated earlier, the Shakers and the Mormons both confronted an unsettled, experimental period in the infancy of the Western Reserve. The Shaker sect was not in its infancy, however. "The United Society of Believers in Christ's Second Appearing," as the sect was officially named, was formed in England in the 1750s, and by the 1770s Ann Lee Stanley had emerged as the leader.

Mother Ann and her followers practiced an early form of simple Christianity. As they worshipped, their bodies trembled, reflecting the infusion of spiritual presence. The trembling caused detractors to call them "Shaking Quakers" or Shakers. In contrast, sect members referred to each other as brother or sister, and to the group as "the brethern" or "the believers."

Ann Lee had a vision which led her to bring her small group of eight to America in 1774, the eve of the American Revolution. In part because they were English, the group was on occasion persecuted and jailed as traitors. Such treatment contributed to Ann Lee's death in 1784. The sect, however, did not expire like so many which had lost a charismatic leader, since Joseph Meacham and Lucy Wright carried on her work. They managed to establish eighteen permanent communities by 1830. Generally the Shakers made converts by following on the heels of revivals and convincing some of the newly regenerated to join them. By the time the North Union community in present-day Shaker

Heights was established in 1822, the faith was over a half century old and had weathered the death of its leader and the persecution of a generation of its members. The United Society had learned to form communes partially separated from the world and protected from constant threats.

Since the Shaker movement was middle-aged when it came to the Western Reserve, it had a decided advantage over the Mormons, who arrived shortly after their founding. Joseph Smith, Jr., the founder, had moved with his family from Vermont to upstate New York in 1815, when Joseph was ten. During his teenage years, the youth became involved in several revivals.

In 1820 he had the first in a series of visions which led him to a buried set of golden tablets, which he translated into English and published as the *Book of Mormon* in the spring of 1830. Public notice of these events reached the Western Reserve as early as November 1830, when the *Painesville Telegraph* reported missionaries in the vicinity. Two men from nearby Kirtland were converted and returned to New York to visit Smith.

Within weeks the prophet had a vision that his church should be located in Kirtland. He arrived in February to begin the mission. Over the next several years Smith had other revelations which defined more precisely the structure and content of church doctrine and practice. Since the faith was not completely formulated but was one of many available in the area, the Mormons were subject to a great deal of ridicule and persecution at the hands of local residents who felt Mormonism was a preposterous form of worship as did the writer for the *Painesville Telegraph*. However, the Mormons were determined to persevere. Unlike the Shakers, the local Mormon community represented their whole church at the time. If it dissolved, so would the entire movement, whereas if the Shakers failed at North Union, seventeen other communities would carry on.

Occasionally, these stages of development were less important than the prevalent religious atmosphere of the Western Reserve. During the Second Great Awakening, spiritual visions were a frequent occurrence and sign of the times. Both the Shakers and Mormons relied on spiritual visits, visions, and other signs to govern their actions. They believed messengers, sometimes angels, were sent by God to guide them. We already know, for instance, that Joseph Smith determined Kirtland was Zion by this method.

The Shakers were established in the region under similar circumstances. Ralph Russell had visited Union Village in southern Ohio to see what the group there practiced. He was told he should return to Warrensville township and wait. In March 1822, two Union Village leaders sent to help Russell form the northern branch, found he had seen "a strong, clear ray of light that proceeded from Union Village, in a perfectly straight, horizontal line until it reached a spot near his dwelling." Therefore, the North Union community took shape on his farm in the present Shaker Lakes area. Other spiritual manifestations continued to guide, educate—and confuse—followers of both groups. For instance, when the temple in Kirtland was dedicated the Mormons saw it filled with angels with a pillar of fire resting upon it.

But there were also "false spirits" (as Joseph Smith called them) too. Perhaps one was "a negro generally known as Black Pete, who became a revelator..., Black Pete got sight of one of those revelations carried by a black angel, he started after it, and ran off a steep wash bank twenty-five feet high, passed through a tree top into the Chagrin River below." (Pete was not hurt.) He was probably not a Mormon, but just one of the many drawn by the speaking in tongues, healing powers, and casting out devils practiced in Kirtland. Even though Joseph Smith often used some spiritual methods to direct missionaries and set policy, he himself was able to distinguish between false and true use of these tools. Sometime in the mid-1830s Smith discovered "a Shaker spirit was on the point of being introduced...but the spirit was rebuked and put down and those who did not submit to rule and good order were disfellowshipped." Smith's strong negative reaction demonstrates the threat the two groups posed to each other—partially because they were so similar.

While it is impossible to tell exactly what Smith objected to, it is possible to judge the depths of Shaker contact with the spiritual world. The Shakers used mediums within the group to communicate with it and recorded these transactions in "The Book of Revelations containing letters from the Spiritual World."

Spiritual visitations were particularly heavy from 1838 to 1845 at North Union. In the late afternoon on July 29, 1841, "three young sisters were powerfully exercised in body and all went into vision together. They continued exercising and talking and spoke of seeing several Sisters who had formerly deceased. Here they gathered flowers. They spoke of seeing a great number of spirits dressed in white with gold bands on their heads." One of the by-products of these visits was a series of spiritual drawings which were presented to specific people as rewards. The drawings were not done automatically during a vision but by those who listened to the experience later. Perhaps the most outstanding occurrence of the entire era happened on New Year's Day 1843, when the community was closed to outsiders (contrary to normal practice) because "The Holy Savior made his visit to North Union in a remarkable manner...he gave a sketch of his life [and] was attended by many bright and holy angels."

In addition to religious practices, Shakers and Mormons can be compared in terms of their economic, political, and social organization. These forms determined how they survived as units, how and when they came into contact with nonbelievers, and how they were treated.

The North Union Shakers were not typical of other Shaker communities because many were not farmers. The problem was that each of the 1,366 acres of land they owned had a heavy clay base requiring one hundred loads of sand to prepare for farming, and even then it did not produce very well. Undaunted, the society moved into two other areas: dairy farming, the mainstay of the entire region, and manufacturing. Between the formal creation of the community in 1828 and the year 1860, the "Millennium Church of United Believers," as the North Union group called itself, created the Shaker Lakes and used them to power a woolen mill, a saw mill, a grist mill, and a tannery. They also produced brooms and buckets. In all these endeavors their goal was to work slowly and achieve perfect products. Consequently, their products were known for their simple, sturdy construction and utility. Devotion to the success of these goods was helped by the communistic nature of the settlement, which required members to give all property to the group when they joined. Hence individual success was included in group success.

Innovation was one of the elements in Shaker achievement. At North Union one of the members invented a special alloy, and the dairymen were some of the first in the Reserve to import thoroughbred stock. The reputation built by the hard-working brothers and sisters assured quick sales each time enough merchandise had been produced and taken by wagon into Cleveland. In fact, a study of their account books indicates until well after the Civil War the North Union enterprises always showed a profit. The longevity of the entire faith, and of those in the Western Reserve in particular, is due in part to their ability to supply superior examples of products needed by the community.

In some ways the "Believers" used their facilities to help improve relations with the surrounding inhabitants. The *Ohio Farmer and Mechanic's Assistant* sent a reporter to North Union in June 1853. He marveled at the efficient use of water. As he described it, after powering the saw mill: "a spout conveys the water to a large trough near the sheep fold. . .the sheep are here caught and plunged into it, half a dozen at a time. The men who wash them, of course, stand outside, and wet no part of their body except their arms" (June 23, 1853). The reporter casually added, "the whole neighborhood goes there to wash their sheep." By letting neighbors use their superior facilities, they built up respect and confidence in the outside community. A further expression of the sect's good public relations was the policy of always paying cash, which kept it from trouble with civil authorities. Obviously, consistent profits allowed them to continue this policy, which gave them excellent bargaining power with retailers.

The Mormons began their economic life in the area much like the Shakers, for some of the early converts had given all their property to the group. But the communal ideal was dead by 1834. Since Kirtland was settled before the arrival of Smith, the Mormons could not isolate themselves and were, therefore, more visible and subject to ridicule. While most Mormons spent their time building the temple, those who sought work in the community were denied it.

This attitude made it difficult for the newly renamed (1834) Church of Jesus Christ of Latter Day Saints to finance their programs. The church was opposed to a national bank and therefore, in 1836, the leadership decided it could make a political statement and improve its financial position by forming a bank of its own. Their application in the name of the Kirtland Safety Society Bank Company was denied by the state along with several others. This did not stop the Mormon attempt, however. Smith simply had "anti" printed before the word bank and "ing" after it on the currency making the new organization an "anti-banking" company, and therefore, not in need of a license.

Although there was little capital, Smith had hopes the company would spread throughout the region and eventually the nation. These aspirations led him to have thousands of notes printed. (In the 1830s each bank had its own currency.) Suddenly, the believers, who numbered several hundred in Kirtland, had wads of money. It seems Smith himself was caught up in the prosperity, for he purchased large quantities of goods on credit backed up by the company. Some wary merchants refused to accept the bills, but others gladly accepted them.

Unfortunately, new funds did not flow into the company coffers to back up the notes. Confidence in them declined as local people found they were not worth the notes' face value. Then, too, others called in debts and found the same weak financial position.

In 1837, some of the leaders of the bank, including Joseph Smith, withdrew from the company and it virtually collapsed in the nationwide bank panic of that year. While its failure had more to do with national problems, the immediate result was the departure of six of the sect's twelve leaders because of the deceptive way in which the prophet handled the affair. Smith himself went on a mission shortly thereafter. Detractors suggested the scandal was one of the reasons Smith permanently left Kirtland in early 1838. A notice appeared over a decade later in a Western Reserve paper which shows the haste with which the departure was made from the region: "The Mormons it is stated, had a large quantity of unsigned [therefore, not negotiable] bills of the old Kirtland Bank. They have now been signed and issued. They are redeemable at Salt Lake, where sufficient uncoined gold has been deposited for that purpose." Needless to say, the economic organization and policies of the Latter Day Saints differed markedly from those of the Shakers; while the Shakers paid cash, the Mormons made their own.

The social and political differences between the two groups were also significant. The Latter Day Saints believed they had to be involved in the world, whereas the Shakers had relatively little contact with their neighbors. These attitudes were also true of the political structure and beliefs of both sects. Internally the North Union Shakers lived in large communal groups called families. The three groups at North Union were called the Center, Mill, and East Families. Each had its own economic structure which was governed by a simple hierarchy.

The sect believed in separation and equality of the sexes and the large dormitory-like dwellings had separate facilities for the men and women. At the head of each of the families, which averaged fifty members, was an elder and an eldress who jointly made decisions affecting the unit. Above these leaders was a group of trustees who managed the entire community. Some of the decisions seem to have been guided by inspirations, but most were made through consultation with all the members. Relative equality existed within the families when decisions were made. When it came to political participation in the world outside North Union, the commune paid its taxes, but members did not vote in local elections. If they had joined the political process, they could have been influential in Warrensville because of the high number of adult males (voters) they counted as members. However, they left these decisions to the "worldly people."

As one might expect, the Latter Day Saints had a highly structured internal organization controlled by Joseph and the apostles, aides selected by Smith to lead the members. Most of the decisions made at Kirtland seem to have been either revelations or prophecies from Smith. Therefore, little actual direction was done by subordinates.

Unlike the Shakers, the Mormons were active in politics, much to the chagrin of local leaders. In national politics Smith supported Andrew Jackson, which outraged E. B. Howe, editor of the Painesville newspaper. Howe was upset by what he saw as a conspiracy to control Kirtland government. He stated in 1835 the Mormons "now carry nearly a majority of this township, and every man votes as directed by the prophet." Before a recent town election, Howe asserted, the Latter Day Saints planned to combine with the Jacksonians to control the spoils of victory, but the Mormons ran an entire Mormon ticket "which they calculated to smuggle in, independent of the 'democrats'. . . . This caused the citizens to rally and make an effort, which by a small majority, saved the township from being governed by revelation for the year to come" (*Painesville Telegraph*, April 17, 1835). The fear was the Mormons would win the election handily. The church did gain members quickly which definitely created jealousy and would have given the group the numbers to take over the government of Kirtland. The Mormons were seen as a threat because they were active, politically astute, and expanding quickly, while the Shakers were none of these.

Shaker social organization set the sect apart from any contemporary groups. Two ideas defined their structure. First, they believed there were two orders in the world: the "Adamic," an order including most people whose purpose was to procreate; and the order of Shakers themselves, the spiritual order, which was celibate, for it strived for perfection. As one contemporary described their lives in 1831, "They are from common stock, and rank marriage among the works of the flesh—They are plain in their apparel, and assume the aspect of friars and nuns of the Catholic superstition" (*Painesville Telegraph*, March 8, 1831).

Second, most of the cohesiveness achieved by the group resulted from the intensive regimen it practiced. Each weekday they rose early, immediately prayed, then cleaned up, silently ate breakfast, and went to the day's chores. After work, the families often held religious meetings. As you read the accounts of their lives, you have the impression these people were intensely devout and that the meetings provided an emotional release for this devotion. The level of the intensity governed not only religious practices but every facet of life.

We can describe the typical member at North Union because federal and communal records exist. The ratio of men and women and the differences in their ages are striking. At mid-century there were a total of 165 Shakers—90 women and 75 men. Not only were there more women, but they were distinctly younger averaging twenty-four as opposed to thirty-nine years for the men. In fact, forty percent of all women at North Union were between ten and nineteen. Of course, most of the members were white, but several black women did live with the group at North Union, a further testimony to the group's liberal attitudes.

Shaker interaction with the outside world offers one possible explanation for the large number of young females in the community. The sect performed a valuable service for the neighborhood by taking in orphans and physically handicapped children, for there were no formal orphanages in the Reserve. The Shakers fed, clothed, and educated the children at their own expense in exchange for their labor at community tasks. When the children reached eighteen, they could choose to leave or to sign the covenant. In addition to taking in children, several sources mention their support of indigents over the winter and some lake men who could find no other place to stay. At any rate, North Union was a charitable organization which benefited the area without creating a burden.

In some ways the Shakers allowed a surprising amount of contact with the world. For instance, during most of the period they opened their services to the public, presumably in hopes of obtaining converts. The most unexpected form of contact was suggested by a newspaper reporter in the early 1850s: "If any of our city people who are pressed to death with business, bound up with heat and suffocated with dust, wish a little relief, we would advise them to make up a party and visit the Quaker village going up by Euclid and returning by Kinsman. To avoid the heat let them start early and return late. The table fare at North Union is most delicious." In other words, escape the city, relax, and eat at the Shaker village.

Ironically, the Shaker belief in the importance of each human being meant that they were pacifists and therefore ran up against the federal government. In 1862 George Ingels, a member of North Union, was drafted into the Union army. Quickly the national leaders of the sect went to Washington. They convinced President Lincoln to give Ingels a reprieve and submitted successful petitions which made all Shakers conscientious objectors.

By contrast, the Latter Day Saints were certainly not pacifists. They were constantly on the defensive because of their zeal and the outlandish views they held according to contemporary standards. While the major Mormon settlement was at Kirtland, Joseph Smith led a number of missions to the West where armed confrontations occurred. One local newspaper labelled him "general" because of these actions.

Like the Shakers, the Mormons also opened their ceremonies to the public. Judge John Barr, one-time sheriff of Cuyahoga County, attended a service in 1830 as an observer. He noted the preaching continued for a long time, but when Smith asked for people to come forth and be immersed, only an old man "by the name of Cohoon, who occasionally joined the Shakers and lived on the country generally" was baptised. Converts were more numerous at other times, and over a period of time, there were many converts. Contact between the two religious groups also continued.

The Kirtland sect did take their message away from the temple and into the communities. Small groups of followers sprang up in Mentor, Chippewa, Elyria, Chardon, and Mayfield. Meetings were held throughout the region. In May 1836, the *Cleveland Herald* carried an advertisement which said there had been many "misrepresentations" which had prejudiced the public against the Mormons. They invited the public to a sermon at the Court House in order to clear up false ideas. On another occasion, leaders had held a similar meeting in Masonic Hall in Cleveland which ended in an attack as part of the audience "began to blow out the candles and throw inkstands and books, etc., at the speaker." Tolerance of different customs and beliefs, it would seem, were not automatically found in the Western Reserve.

It is possible to estimate the nature of the Mormon society even though we can not do so as exactly as we can for the Shakers. Social interaction was based on the individual family unit. Since polygamy was not yet a doctrinal practice, this was not a source of irritation with the surrounding community. Economically, we know that many of the converts were poor and we can speculate that much of the cohesiveness achieved by the group was the product of constant persecution. When Smith left Kirtland for the last time in January 1838, he left behind five hundred of the "poorer" members who were eventually able to follow in July.

While the number of converts who left Kirtland impressed local residents, the number which passed through the Reserve after the headquarters had moved to Illinois was more astounding. An article on July 7, 1841, in the *Cleveland Herald* reported a "train of seventeen wagons...passed our office yesterday containing 100 Mormons, big and little bound for the promised land,...a party of the singular sect in eleven wagons passed through our city a few days previous."

The ultimate reason for the departure of the sect was the revelation that Zion was further west, but the treatment members received in the Western Reserve and the failure of the Kirtland Safety Society Anti-Banking Company were the more immediate propelling forces.

Although the Shakers never were forced to leave North Union, they too were disliked by a portion of the residents. When the community was first formed a meeting was held to present its major ideas. As one of the Shakers spoke some said, "They're like people shooting arrows against a stone wall, they make a great clattering but they effect nothing." As the meeting became more rowdy, a justice of the peace who was there had to call for order. The sect was harassed during the next fifty years. In the early 1850s, for instance, outsiders were not permitted to attend worship for more than a year because "too many young men from the city visited them to make sport." The believers were particularly susceptible to this kind of treatment for they were nonviolent.

There were some real fears of the Shakers because their reclusive lifestyle made them somewhat mysterious. You will recall they were equated to Catholic priests and nuns in a time period when the Roman Catholic church was thought to be secretive and dangerous. A lawsuit accused the North Union community of not paying for the work of a handicapped woman, Mary Ann Calder. Testimony was produced that the Shakers forced people to sign their covenant, held them in bondage, and were immoral. Further, the group was said to be a threat to the institution of marriage because it taught marriage was unacceptable.

To defend the group from these charges, the believers cited the charitable work they did. The contract each adult was required to sign was also produced in court and pronounced legal. In his discussion, the Shaker lawyer stated they were an example to all Christians because they were closer to the primitive church than other sects, for they held property in common. The attorney also indicated he had been their counsel for twenty-one years and had never heard of any immoral conduct. The jury verdict was in favor of the commune. "It is surprising the effect this trial has had on the minds of the people in Cleveland. They saw it has given them a favorable opinion of the people [Shakers] and they know more than they did before." While minor problems continued, the community at large accepted Shakers, partially because of this public airing of the issues.

Public reaction to the Latter Day Saints, on the other hand, was generally negative. As the newspaper office nearest Kirtland and reporting strong local feeling, the *Painesville Telegraph* was especially sensitive to Mormon activity— real or imagined. A series of fears helped increase the intensity of feeling. Many people thought Smith was a false prophet who was leading unsuspecting people away from a true faith. E. B. Howe, editor of the *Painesville Telegraph*, was so convinced of the "sham" he wrote *Mormonism Unvailed* [sic] in 1834. Howe accused Smith of holding prayer meetings nearly every night and subjecting young men and women to virtual delirium before they converted. The healing power of the prophet was also questioned.

According to Howe's paper, a Mormon convert, Warren Doty, was convinced he would live a thousand years, so when he became ill he refused to be treated by a doctor. Finally when his Mormon friends allowed a doctor to see him he found Doty was too close to death to save.

Words of these dangerous events traveled quickly. In 1832 Smith was visiting some followers in Hiram when a mob dragged him from the house, stripped, and tarred and feathered him. The Mormons reacted differently to attacks than the Shakers—they armed. From that time on Smith and his house were always guarded. In fact, as Smith was leaving the Western Reserve for the last time in early 1837 he passed through Cleveland where "tar and feathers were prepared for our backs but the Lord delivered us."

Adversity seemed to reinforce the determination of the prophet and his followers. As they moved west the *Cleveland Herald* reported the persecution of the Mormons in Missouri in 1833 by saying it was unfortunate because "it will eventually be a means of building up the delusion" because sympathy would result. Surely many people were more tolerant and not outraged or felt their values threatened by the Mormons, but few of their views were made public. Even after the Saints left the Reserve, a meeting was called in Cleveland at the "Musical Hall" on the "dangers and absurdities of Mormonism and the knavery and treasonable designs of its leaders." Apparently the fear remained.

In 1839 only a few Latter Day Saints remained in the region and the temple was sold to pay debts. Subsequently it became a school and finally, in 1880, it became the property of one of the Mormon groups to emerge after the 1844 death of Joseph Smith.

The significance of the Mormons and Shakers in the Western Reserve can be measured in several ways. First, for a minority of residents, both provided an all-encompassing solution to the turmoil of the day. Both groups demanded total commitment for full membership. That membership conferred something few people then had—relative certainty of salvation. Shaker communal life was exacting but spiritual rewards were impressive. Mormon life was virtually communal because of the determined work needed to complete the temple and the intense persecution its members endured. It should be added that after leaving Kirtland, the Mormons learned a Shaker lesson—they formed their own separate community in Nauvoo, Illinois.

From another perspective the two sects gave the Reserve a chance to find its level of toleration. The area accepted unobtrusive, nonviolent communes with charitable goals, as had the rest of the country, but virtually headed the list of areas which found the Mormon's public preaching, political involvement, and financial policies intrusive and dangerous. If the Mormons had been more withdrawn, they probably would have been spared the persecution, but it was not in their nature.

By 1860 the revival fervor had subsided in Ohio, or rather had been replaced by the fervor of the coming civil war. The North Union community prospered but its numbers began to decline dramatically after 1875. A lack of converts and a decline in the demand for its products doomed it. In 1889 the assets were sold and the remaining members went to other Shaker villages.

The Mormons, in 1860, were split into a number of groups. One group of the Reorganized Church of Jesus Christ of Latter Day Saints reclaimed the Kirtland temple after a legal battle in 1880. Another group was led to Utah by Brigham Young. Both groups were later factions of the original 1830s group in the Western Reserve. Of course, the followers of Joseph Smith, Jr., are still very active today, perhaps helped along by the converts from the Western Reserve and unfortunately, by the persecution they received here as well.

Both the Shakers and the Mormons were remarkably successful. The Shakers lasted well over a century and a half, and the Mormons have already compiled a similar record.

Why did the Mormons ultimately survive and the Shakers fail to expand? The communal life of the Shakers required strict observance of religious ideals which included suppression of personal individuality. Perhaps if North Union had been located in more rural surroundings, the communal image would have persevered.

severed. In the Western Reserve, however, it was too close to the developing might of the region, Cleveland. Those Shaker communities which did survive the longest were farthest away from the competition of the "new" age. The attractions of city life and the possibilities of individual success were tempting. Furthermore, with the increased volume and lower prices of machine-made goods, the hand-crafted Shaker products were no longer fashionable or competitively priced for the rest of the world. The Shakers could not keep up with the changing world.

The Mormons were more flexible. Because they were involved in local affairs, they adapted to the lifestyle of the period. It was their zeal, not their lifestyle, which made them threatening. Unlike the Shakers, individualism was encouraged and, therefore, the Mormons were able to adapt to the twentieth century.

Finally, then, the Latter Day Saints still exist because their solution to the religious questioning of the 1820s was just that—a religious solution without the specific social, economic, and political ideas which eventually made the Shaker sect a relic.

GLADYS HADDAD

The First Women's Colleges

At the age of seventy-seven Freud asked in despair, "What do women want?" In the early nineteenth century, in the United States, one answer might have been: higher education. At that time, for a variety of reasons, colleges or universities admitted only men. It was thought that women were physically and mentally too weak to stand the rigors of college study, and also "that such training would raise woman above the duties of her 'station.'" Of course, among upperclass families in England and on the Continent could be found many highly educated women who were instructed by private tutors. But for the middle classes who shaped America's institutions, a female was viewed, as far as educational opportunities were concerned, as either daughter, sister, wife, or mother— all roles tied to home and family and not requiring college training.

One common perception elevated woman to an angelic creature, fragile and ethereal; another honored her as the Mother, guardian of civilization, divinely entrusted with the rearing of sons who went out and conducted the business of the world. Though these perceptions were used in part to deny higher education to women for years, women's roles as mothers and teachers ultimately provided the justification for admitting them to colleges in this country.

Three colleges for women in northern Ohio furnish an excellent illustration of how higher education for women got its start in America: Lake Erie College in Painesville, a "daughter" of Mount Holyoke, based on the single-sex seminary model embodying missionary ideals; Oberlin, the country's first coeducational college, a frontier experiment with profound religious underpinnings; and the College for Women of Western Reserve University, a "coordinate" college established alongside the men's college for the daughters of prosperous Clevelanders.

SEMINARIES FOR WOMEN

The pioneers of women's education were the leaders of the female seminary movement, which, at its height from 1830 to 1860, reflected the ideology that women should use their rational powers within a limited sphere to manage the home and educate children and to spread the word of Christianity. The seminaries, the first institutions to provide education for women beyond the rudimentary level, and the dominant agencies for female instruction for three-quarters of the nineteenth century, sought to prepare women to be better wives, mothers, teachers, and missionaries. The period's most notable educators—Emma Willard, Catharine Beecher, and Mary Lyon—exemplified the qualities of "true womanhood" in their educational designs. Mary Lyon, whose life spanned the first half of the century, established the Mount Holyoke Female Seminary at South Hadley, Massachusetts, in 1837, which served as a model for the education of women throughout the world—to it the development of women's education in the Western Reserve can be traced.

Mount Holyoke taught that the life of a missionary was one committed to material self-denial, teaching from a sense of duty, a general benevolence, and a readiness to answer where Providence should point out the post of duty, in this country or abroad. Mount Holyoke and other seminaries fulfilled their mission to teach women with curricular programs that ranged from a modest advancement in the basics, with an emphasis upon ornamental "female" accomplishments (e.g., needlework) to an emulation of men's colleges with an education that approached a classical curriculum. Still, the curricula of these seminaries did not equal those offered by men's colleges, and the female seminaries did not qualify as degree-granting institutions (graduates received diplomas). Some, like Mount Holyoke, a classically based institution, progressed to that point later in the century. Many other female seminaries emphasized teacher training and evolved into normal schools. In fact, one of Mount Holyoke's biggest contributions at that time was preparation of disciplined female educators.

In the spring of 1847, Mount Holyoke graduate Roxena B. Tenney came to the Western Reserve to be principal of the Willoughby Female Seminary. She later wrote: "The trustees of a medical college in Willoughby, Ohio, applied to Miss Lyon to send them a teacher to establish a seminary for young ladies in Willoughby. The College faculty had disbanded and left a good building for that purpose. She recommended my humble self and I commenced working March 1847, in a town of only forty families with fourteen pupils."

The Willoughby Female Seminary, Mount Holyoke's "first god-child in the West," was the Western Reserve's only single-sex institution of higher education for women until 1856, when a fire brought it to an end. After a brief interval, that same year the school was reorganized "on the Holyoke plan," fifteen miles east of its former location, as the Lake Erie Female Seminary in Painesville. The missionary ideology espoused by Mary Lyon was integral to the development of both schools. Both schools replicated the course, methods of instruction, discipline, and general regulations of Mount Holyoke. The teachers were Mount Holyoke graduates intent upon an institutional mission to provide "the most thorough mental, moral and social discipline, the acquisition of sound knowledge and of pure evangelical principles." It was the aim of the trustees "to present the young ladies of the west, full facilities for obtaining a thorough and finished education."

Buildings for the accommodation of school and boarders were to be furnished by voluntary contributions and placed free from encumbrance in the hands of trustees, "who should be men of enlarged views and Christian benevolence." The teachers secured should possess a missionary spirit that moved them to "labor faithfully and cheerfully, receiving only a moderate salary." The style of living was to be neat, plain, and simple. The domestic work of "the family" was to be performed by members of the school. Board and tuition was to be placed "at cost, or as low as may be, and still cover the common expenses." The whole plan was to be conducted on the principles of "missionary operations," with surplus income placed in the treasury for operating expenses.

Following the laying of the Seminary's cornerstone on July 4, 1857, a commemorative editorial appeared in the *Painesville Telegraph*: "It is quite a modern idea, this, that Girls are capable of any considerable intellectual improvement . . . . In this Lake Erie Seminary it is proposed to give young ladies the opportunity for securing as good an education in every way, as the best colleges of the land are furnishing young men." Hailing the dawn of women's abilities, the editorial made clear the secondary role to which women still were to be relegated: "The Women of the Republic—the Mothers of our future men—every Patriot and Philanthropist must rejoice at all these efforts for the development and strengthening of their highest and noblest nature. The great interests of civilization will be safe when in the hands of the sons of educated mothers."

On September 13, 1859, Lake Erie Female Seminary, "designed to furnish young ladies all the requisite facilities for a thorough education at a greatly reduced expense," opened to enroll 127 who met the minimum age requirement of fifteen for admission. Within a few days they were examined for their knowledge of English grammar, modern geography, American history, arithmetic, philosophy, and Latin, which determined admission to the Junior class, and in the studies of the Middle and Senior classes for those seeking advanced standing. Students were given a probationary period of a few weeks duration in order to make an assessment of their fitness "in maturity of character and mental discipline" to carry out a year's work. Another review took place at the end of the year to determine continuance at the Seminary.

Prospective students were expected to be present the first day of the term and prepared to commence their examinations. Students furnished their own linens, blankets, and table service, specifically a dessert spoon and teaspoon. Clothing suggested for Painesville's climate included flannels, warm stockings, thick shoes, overshoes, and an umbrella. Students were asked to bring an English dictionary, Latin lexicon, an ancient and modern Atlas and Bible, Bible dictionary, and standard hymn book. The academic year was arranged in three terms—fall, winter, and summer—and concluded with public examinations and exercises held during "Anniversary Week" in early July. An account of this event was provided by teacher Ellen Wright, recording in the Seminary *Journal*: "The Examinations began Tuesday afternoon before a very pleasant company of visitors. About the middle of the afternoon the class in calisthenics went through various figures . . . gracefully accomplished. The success of the young ladies during examination...and the music was pronounced almost as good as that at Holyoke."

On Wednesday and Thursday, throngs of visitors came to the seminary to hear oral recitations and compositions by students in history, geography, mathematics, science, literature, Latin, philosophy, and religion, alternating with musical and athletic performances. Just before noon on Thursday, the procession formed for the graduation exercises held outdoors in the sylvan setting of the grove. There the graduates, dressed in white, received diplomas and heard ministers' prayers and addresses by educators.

Under the principalship of Lydia Sessions from 1859 to 1866, enrollment reached 150, and the Seminary graduated between six and twelve each year. In the winter of 1866, Miss Sessions resigned to marry William W. Woodworth, pastor of the Congregational Church in Painesville. The teachers shared the government of the school until September, when Anna C. Edwards of Mount Holyoke was appointed principal. After two years, she was succeeded by Mary Evans, also of Mount Holyoke, who served the school for forty-one years, retiring in 1909.

In the fifteen years from its start in 1859, Lake Erie Female Seminary enrolled 1,800 students, the majority from Ohio, Pennsylvania, New York, Illinois, and Michigan, although twenty-eight states were represented. Only 140, or 8 percent, graduated; of these, 37 became teachers and missionaries. The low proportion of students finishing the course of study was attributed to rising admission requirements, the availability of public high schools, the opening of other college doors for women, the Civil War, and financial depression. Many young women of traditional outlook viewed the seminary as a brief, terminal educational experience that enhanced their marketability as marriage partners. In its first forty years Lake Erie Seminary gradually expanded its course of study, reaching a standard that in 1898 qualified its graduates for a college degree rather than a seminary diploma. In that year the name of the institution was changed to Lake Erie College and Seminary, and in 1908 to Lake Erie College.

COEDUCATION

In 1835 Alexis de Tocqueville wrote, "Americans send priests out into the new states of the West and establish schools and churches there." The effort to Christianize the West arose from deep religious convictions as well as from a pragmatic interest in furthering law and order. Pastor John Jay Shipherd heard the call in Vermont to go forth into the "unplowed spiritual fields" of what was to New England the West—Ohio. In October 1830 he arrived at the frontier settlement of Elyria in Lorain County, Ohio, twenty miles west of Cleveland. Within three years he was joined by former Vermont academy classmate, Philo Penfield Stewart, with whom he talked, read, prayed, and eventually decided upon a plan for the Oberlin colony and school.

Shipherd conceived of a new colony of dedicated souls in the virgin forest far from the taint of established and sin-infected towns. The whole enterprise would be devoted not to worldly ends but to the salvation of men's souls. When the settlement was firmly established, a school would be founded which would serve, by educating missionaries and teachers, as an evangelical agency to create new colonies, churches, and schools. A manual labor system was to be employed whereby students worked on the college farm, workshop, or boarding house to defray costs.

On December 3, 1833, the school opened with twenty children enrolled in the "infant school" (primary school) and forty "young gentlemen & ladies" in the academic or preparatory school. On February 28, 1834, the Oberlin Collegiate Institute was granted its charter by the Ohio Legislature "to confer on those whom they may deem worthy, such honors and degrees as are usually conferred in similar institutions." The Institute was dedicated to provide "the most useful education at the least expense of health, time and money" and designed to "extend the benefit of such education to both sexes" to thoroughly qualify them as Christian teachers, "both for the pulpit and the schools." A prominent objective was "the elevation of female character, by bringing within the reach of the misjudged and neglected sex, all the instructive privileges which hitherto have unreasonably distinguished the leading sex from theirs."

The Collegiate Department offered "as extensive and thorough a course of instruction as other colleges." The Female Department "furnished instruction in the useful branches taught in the best Female Seminaries," but was not of college grade. Women, however, were eligible for "all the instructive privileges" of the institution and attended classes in every department. For the first time, male college students shared their classrooms and instruction with women. In 1837, four women presented themselves as qualified for entrance into the regular course of the Collegiate Department. They had prepared themselves by taking subjects at Oberlin with men qualifying for the college course. They were the first women in history to matriculate for a regular college course. Thus, true college education for women began as coeducation.

In Oberlin's early days, because academies preparing for college were exceedingly rare in the West, a preparatory department was a necessity, providing instruction in geography, mathematics, elementary Latin and Greek, English, history, and religion. For those interested in the college course, Latin and Greek were required; those taking the teacher's course followed the English curriculum. Histories of Greece, Rome, England, and the United States were required of both.

The preparatory studies for women entering the ladies' course were lighter and more elementary. History, Greek, and Latin were not included. Their preparatory work was not secondary education at all. Hence the ladies' course itself became partly secondary, and the women in it took many classes with male preparatory students in English grammar, history, geography, and the Bible. The ladies' course was heavily weighted toward religion, important presumably for prospective wives and mothers destined for work in missionary and teaching endeavors. Women who wanted to pursue the classical college course took Latin and Greek with men in the preparatory classes to qualify themselves.

In 1850, when the Oberlin Collegiate Institute was renamed Oberlin College, some thought the title misrepresentative, since the College was only part of the institution, accounting for only 69 of the 500 students enrolled there. The majority had always been in the Preparatory and Female Departments. Between 1833 and 1866, over 11,000 students—6,500 males and 4,800 females—the sons and daughters of farmers with pious intentions, poor preparation, and little money moved through Oberlin. The majority at first came from New England and New York, a trend which reversed itself over a thirty-year period as more of the student body was drawn from the Western Reserve.

Oberlin's founders educated women for what was considered their proper sphere. The first Oberlin faculty included Dr. James Dascomb, professor in sciences, and his wife, Marianne Parker Dascomb, first principal of the Female Department. She was a graduate of Ipswich Seminary who had studied with Mary Lyon prior to the Mount Holyoke enterprise. A frontier wife and educated woman, Marianne Dascomb provided an attractive model for the school's women students. The ideal of evangelical womanhood dominated the imaginations of Oberlin's females. For them the frontier represented an opportunity for spiritual and benevolent activity as wives, teachers, or missionaries.

Oberlin was founded when the place and time were right for bringing the sexes together. Interest in education was high. On the frontier, society was in a fluid state; ideas and customs were not fixed. Experiments could be attempted that in the traditional East would have been doomed at birth. Oberlin's co-founder Philo Stewart wrote: "There are many in the Eastern states who are determined that everything at the West shall be modeled after the tradition of the fathers. But let us inquire what kind of institutions are needed in the West."

Many small denominational colleges followed the pattern of Oberlin in the next three decades, and the passage of the Morrill Act in 1862 created land-grant colleges and universities to which women were admitted on the same terms as men. Coeducation became the rule in the Western states and in the new universities of the East, such as Cornell, which admitted women in 1872.

COORDINATE EDUCATION

In the meantime, controversy continued to surround the education of women; they still needed to prove that they were intellectually, physically, and emotionally capable of meeting the demands of higher education. The founding of Vassar in 1859 and Smith and Wellesley in 1870 marked the first attempts to provide a collegiate education for women similar to that for men, one distinguished at the outset by the classical curriculum and its award for completion, the baccalaureate degree.

When efforts to secure admission of women to Harvard and other universities failed, a new arrangement became popular: the coordinate college, a division for the education of women affiliated with a college or university for men. In 1879, the "Society for Collegiate Instruction of Women" was formed; at first called the

"Harvard Annex," it was named Radcliffe College in 1883. It was joined by other coordinate colleges, including Barnard at Columbia in 1883, Sophie Newcomb at Tulane in 1887, and Pembroke at Brown in 1891.

During the nineteenth century, Western Reserve University progressed from a single-sex, all male institution, to a coeducational school, to a coordinate arrangement with a women's college parallel to the men's college.

David Hudson, founder of Western Reserve College, was a prosperous Connecticut farmer infused with a Puritan sense of mission. He sought an opportunity to express his faith through good works. A purchase of 7,000 acres of land in Connecticut's Western Reserve in northern Ohio led him West, where in 1800 he started a colony based upon high moral and religious principles. In the wilderness twenty-three miles southeast of Cleveland, Hudson established the town which took his name. He founded its church, grade school, and, in 1826, a college for the purpose of educating ministers.

It was well past the century's halfway point when Western Reserve College offered education for women. In 1871, a young woman from the town of Hudson approached President Carroll Cutler with a request to study at the College. Unable to afford to attend school away from her home, she wished "to pursue certain studies and recite in the classes of certain professors." Cutler, who was an advocate of advanced education for women, acted unilaterally and astonished both trustees and faculty by announcing that "women would be admitted to all the privileges of the College on the same conditions as men." It was a policy that during the next seventeen years would allow forty-three women to matriculate and nineteen to graduate.

In 1882, as a result of a gift of $500,000 from Cleveland millionaire Amasa Stone, Western Reserve moved from Hudson to Cleveland and changed its status from a college to a university. Stone's gift carried other conditions: control of the board of trustees, supervision of building construction, and selection of the College name—Adelbert—in memory of his son, victim of a drowning accident while a student at Yale.

At the time of the move from Hudson, the college had a faculty of eight and a student body of seventy-five, five of whom were women. By 1884, two years after the move to Cleveland, Professor Edward Morley asked if "the proper time had come to ask whether the college is committed to the education of women in the same classes with men" or was "looking towards the establishment of a parallel or annex course of instruction for young women." President Cutler argued that he was not only opposed to turning out the women, but that he considered their presence in the College in all respects good and desirable. In 1887 the faculty had increased by one, and enrollment decreased to sixty-five, sixteen of whom were women. In Cleveland in the 1880s, the number of women graduating from high school was twice that of men. Young men left home to attend college; young women remained nearby. Coeducation in private and public colleges was thriving in Ohio and other parts of the country. Clearly, the growing number of women seeking education at Western Reserve challenged an "institution modeled after New England ideals, in close touch with Yale College."

President Cutler resigned early in 1886, in part because of the coeducation controversy. Hiram C. Haydn was elected president of Western Reserve University but retained his position as pastor of Cleveland's Presbyterian Old Stone Church. Haydn announced at his inauguration on January 24, 1888, that women would no longer be admitted to the college. This was not intended as an indictment of coeducation, he maintained, but the current situation called for an institution which furnished young men the advantages they were seeking elsewhere "in colleges for men only." There was an earnest suggestion for "founding a College for young women in proximity to our own, and in every respect equal to it in its course of instruction."

"What Shall We Do With Our Daughters?" was the rhetorical question Dr. Haydn put to his congregation at the Old Stone Church almost three months after he suggested the creation of a women's college to replace coeducation. "It is a matter of immediate interest whether our city is to have a college for women," he said. "I know of nothing in the way but the cost of it." His parishioners were among Cleveland's wealthiest families, and it was to them that he made his appeal for the endowments to sustain the college for women. He was particularly successful with women who had male models of giving within their families. Of these, Flora Stone Mather was foremost.

Flora, the youngest child of Amasa and Julia Gleason Stone, was born in 1852, two years after the family that included Adelbert and Clara came from Massachusetts to settle in Cleveland. She was reared in a home on Euclid Avenue's millionaires' row and educated at the Cleveland Academy, one of several secondary level schools established in Cleveland by Linda Guilford, a graduate of Mount Holyoke under Mary Lyon. In 1881 Flora Stone and Samuel Mather, longtime friends and neighbors, were married, uniting two of Cleveland's wealthiest families.

Flora Stone Mather's many gifts to Western Reserve University included $50,000 to endow its first chair of history in the name of Hiram C. Haydn. Contributions from her family enabled the College for Women to open in rented quarters at the southeast corner of Euclid Avenue and Adelbert in 1888.

Haydn established an Advisory Council of local women, appointed by the board of trustees, which had ultimate responsibilities for the educational and social conditions of the College for Women. The Council began to build the library and to furnish the first classrooms of the new college with their own pictures, furniture, and curtains.

In honor of Linda Guilford, Mrs. Mather contributed $75,000 for building and endowing the College's first dormitory in 1892. Called Guilford Cottage, it was given "in grateful loving acknowledgment of the debt which this community owes to her" who had established reputable instructional programs in several academies and seminaries in Cleveland. At the dedication of the building named for her, Linda Guilford cited the opportunity for women enrolled in a college course as "keeping step with their brothers along the paths of higher learning."

While women's opportunities for becoming educated grew during the century, the roles in which this education could be applied remained essentially the same—wife, mother, and teacher. Nevertheless, the expanding number of educated women undoubtedly led to women's suffrage in 1920 and to the ever increasing importance of women in business and public life. The pioneers in women's education might be surprised at the long-term outcome of their efforts, and some of them might even be pleased.

C. H. CRAMER

Student Life at
Western Reserve College

In the nineteenth century educators believed that something beyond a library and a faculty and students was necessary to make a viable college. The additional factor, borrowed from the practice of English institutions, was known as "the collegiate way"; it meant complete devotion to the residential scheme of things in quiet rural settings, dependent on dormitories and dining halls—and governed paternalistically. Adherents of the "collegiate way" became misty-eyed over the college as "a large family, sleeping, eating, studying, and worshipping together under one roof." They exulted over the beneficial influence that classmates exerted on one another and over the opportunities presented to inculcate religious principles and orientation. In practice the "collegiate way" often worked hardships on both the student body and the college. The students had to submit to living conditions that were Spartan, and to observe rules of conduct that were Draconian. Some colleges suffered because their administrators came to think that the extracurricular "collegiate way" was more important than the curriculum; this lowered academic standards by providing a rationale for de-emphasis of the intellectual side of the college experience.

Dormitory life was inexpensive and rugged and required; students might be permitted to room in a private house, but had to pay room rent to the college as well if there were a single vacancy in the dormitories. In the early days in Hudson four to six dollars paid for an entire year's room rent—but the accommodations presented the most primitive of furniture, little heat in the dead of winter, and no plumbing. There were outhouses. There was a nearby creek where ablutions could be accomplished in the warmer months. In winter, bathing—such as it was—was attempted at the college pump. At this fountain, naked students, standing ankle-deep in snow, sloshed pails of water on each other, covering the bodily surface from crown to heel in a major test of endurance. Regulations obviously restricted this municipal bathing to hours after dark lest the women of Hudson village be shocked by a startling exposure to college life.

Before central heating was introduced in the late nineteenth century, students paid for their fuel. In the early days they bought logs which were chopped and hauled to dormitory rooms that had a fireplace or wood-burning stove. Coal stoves were introduced in Hudson around 1850. Students bought coal which was placed in individual coal bins near each dormitory. In theory they were expected to carry it from their own coal bins to their own rooms. In practice students manifested a remarkable inability to identify their own coal bins and helped themselves to fuel from neighboring ones. This impasse was solved by turning a closet in each room into a coal bin; each student bought a ton of coal and carried it to his own closet for safekeeping. College authorities convinced themselves that this procedure provided needed exercise and was conducive to good health.

For food the student could either eat at the college or in a private home, which charged more. In 1831 Reserve charged seventy-five cents a week for the standard menu and a dollar if the boarder desired the luxury of tea and coffee. (Oberlin considered these beverages sinful and refused to serve them.) No educational institution has ever succeeded in satisfying the majority of its students with the quality of its cuisine. Many have given up, consigning their students to local facilities or leasing the college dining hall to an entrepreneur possessed with both courage and patience. At Harvard in 1822 a student made the following entry in his diary: "Goose for dinner. Said to have migrated to this country with our ancestors." At the University of North Dakota it was a member of the faculty who was disgruntled about the fare in the commons. The president complained to the trustees that an instructor of English regularly, and with complete deliberation, began to eat before he had asked the blessing. She defended herself with the gratuitous comment that the food was as bad before as after the blessing. The trustees solved the problem by dismissing both of them. At Western Reserve student publications were caustic about all eating establishments, whether they were operated under college or private auspices. One refectory had the motto:

> Heaven sends us good meat,
> But the Devil sends cooks.

Its members were dubbed "Hash House Victims." There were stock jokes about the "grub." One concerned Shadow Soup: "They fill a kettle full of water; then they hang up a chicken in the sun where its shadow falls on the kettle; then they heat the water, and here it is." A student glares at dessert and shouts: "Take it away! That ain't watermelon—it's nuthin' but a sliver of punkin' tryin' to blush because it's so small!" Breakfast was largely oatmeal and crackers; students grabbed crackers by the handful and crushed them over the oatmeal. Said one: "It's so you can eat the damn stuff without seeing it."

Living conditions left something to be desired in comfort and refinement. In addition, the student's movements during the day were regulated with care and precision. Because few of them had watches and the institution could not afford numerous clocks in conspicuous places, the schedule was regulated by the college bell. Students followed Franklin's counsel about early to bed and early to rise, in part because candles did not provide illumination that was either safe or satisfactory before the kerosine lamp came into use after the Civil War. The clanging of the morning bell was at five in summer and six in winter. Students dressed in their cold rooms, carried out the slop jars to the college trough, and drew fresh water from the pump—unless it was frozen.

The curfew tolled at 9:00 p.m.; in between the bell rang for meals, prayers, study, and classes. Students regarded the device as an instrument of torture and made every effort to destroy it by stealing the rope or the clapper—and even the bell itself. In the 1840s at Yale, Leonard Case, Jr., who would establish a prominent school in Cleveland, was involved in the classical course and was hardly pleased with the regimen:

> Monday, six o'clock in the morning, a bell rings—and out I tumble (most unwillingly to be sure)—rings for five minutes—stops five—then tolls five, at the end of which if you are not there, down goes a tardy mark. Then someone on the Faculty reads a Chapter and the President gives a lengthy prayer, after which we "scud" for the recitation room . . . . Well! recitation until seven, than half an hour to ourselves. Half past seven—breakfast—toast and coffee. Eight until eleven—study. Eleven—recitations. Twelve until one—to ourselves. One—dinner—beef and cold water. Two till four—study. Four—recitation. Five—bell rings again three minutes—stops three and tolls three—then we "scratch" for Chapel . . .; then supper—bread, butter and tea—after which we get our lessons and do what we please till six next morning. . . . I have sat up at my lessons until two o'clock every morning and once or twice till three. There is no getting off—the lessons must be recited at six and I must recite or flunk, which doesn't agree with my stomach.

At Western Reserve College the "Rules of Order" went on and on. No student was allowed to hire a horse or carriage, or leave town without permission, nor could he attend "assemblies for dancing or similar amusement, or to call for entertainment at public houses for purposes of conviviality." "Spiritous or vinous liquors" were prohibited—as was playing at cards, dice, or checkers—with or without a wager. In 1850 the faculty decreed that if any undergraduate entered "into the marriage relation, his connection with the College shall thereby cease." In the 1830s one student tried both Western Reserve and Oberlin Colleges, and left both. His explanation: "I left Hudson, because I had to make too many bows, and Oberlin, because I could not get enough to eat." He was referring to the rule at Reserve which enjoined all students to lift their hats to the professors if they chanced to pass them, and to rise whenever a member of the faculty entered the classroom. The lack of food at Oberlin was a commentary on the "Graham System," which had been adopted there and in other colleges. It was a dietetic reform, advocated by a minister who thought a vegetable diet and coarsely ground whole wheat flour would serve as a cure for intemperance.

Attendance at numerous religious services was *de rigueur* because the trustees regarded the spiritual prosperity of the college greater in importance than its economic solvency. At Western Reserve there were daily morning and evening prayers plus, in the early decades, three services on Sunday—each two hours in length. This followed the practice at Yale where the laws required the president to "constantly" pray in the college every morning—and also enjoined him to visit student chambers after nine o'clock in the evening to ascertain whether they were there, and, if so, were they applying themselves to their studies. Everywhere, the Sabbath was the New England one, which began at sundown on Saturday and continued throughout the next day. On Saturday evening the student could attend a religious meeting or stay in his room. On Sunday, between the long services, students were not permitted to "walk abroad" for exercise or diversion—nor could they visit the room of another student or receive visitors. In their own rooms there was to be no studying on the Lord's day; instead the time was to be spent in meditation, the reading of religious books, and the singing of psalms. President Cutler commented later that all this "made the day a weariness...not a day of *rest*."

For the student, violation of these myriad regulations and decrees could result in fines, "marks," rustication, or expulsion. At Reserve a student who napped in class or chapel was fined twelve and a half cents. At Harvard the penalty was five shillings if the student lied or made "tumultuous or indecent noise in town or the College yard," and twenty shillings for playing at cards or dice. In every institution a student could achieve a "mark" or demerit for a number of delinquencies, including absence from regularly scheduled meetings of various kinds. This presented an awesome potential for the accumulation of "marks" because at Reserve in 1867 there were 3,614 in all—2,212 recitations and lectures, 1,344 religious exercises, 45 examinations, and 13 rhetorical exercises.

If the student accumulated enough demerits (usually fifteen) or was involved in a single example of gross misconduct, he was turned over to the faculty for action. This could result in a reprimand, expulsion, or rustication. If the culprit was thought to be beyond hope, he was expelled. In such cases the minutes of the faculty carried a laconic verdict: "Voted, that the father of G. L. Mills be informed of certain irregularities in his son and advised to take him away." If there was hope of redemption and improvement the student was rusticated. This was a term and a practice inherited from English colleges; the student was sent to some individual, usually a minister, in a small village safely removed from the diversions of the campus, where he continued his studies with assignments heavier than those given in the college. Rustication lasted at least a month and meant double expenses for the student; he paid a fee and cost-of-living expenses to his tutor, but received no reduction in college tuition or room rent for the term involved.

In spite of all these sanctions and controls the normal animal spirits of young men sometimes inclined them to activity that shocked their elders. At Yale James Fenimore Cooper—a future novelist of some note—was expelled after a series of escapades: involvement in a major donnybrook, teaching a donkey to sit majestically in a professor's chair, and finally, blowing open a classmate's door with a blast of gunpowder. At Harvard the conservative John Adams, who loved to hunt, was dismayed that he could not keep a gun in his room, along with the axe. Seventy-five years later President Josiah Quincy would suspend all Harvard sophomores for a year because of "window-smashing, bonfires. . .and other riotous behaviour." At Western Reserve there was a variety of violations of the code, varying from peccadillos to the monstrous; on these the minutes of the faculty make interesting reading. Some pranks required great physical effort. Freshmen carried a number of tombstones from a neighboring cemetery, an enervating exercise, and placed them with tender loving care and precision on the lawn of a professor who was in disfavor. A psychiatrist might conclude that symbolically the first-year students wanted to bury their professor and were making an attempt to show their fairness by giving him a choice of tombstones. On at least two occasions wagons were hoisted to a position on top of the observatory. The college backhouse was a favorite target; on one occasion the faculty found that five students "did, by previous concert, clandestinely close the college backhouse by rolling logs against the door" but "in consideration of their having had some provocation to the act, the instructors request them only to replace the building in its former position—which request was complied with."

Some capers had a modern ring. There was the practice of breathing ether. The faculty asked the president to announce at chapel that "it is regarded as a species of intoxication and will be treated accordingly." There were streakers. During a heavy shower students were seen about the buildings in a semi-nude condition, making "savage noises." They were informed that the faculty regarded such conduct with "strong disapprobation."

Students resorted to manifold devices to escape classes and to show their disdain for the numerous religious services. They stuffed newspapers into the chimney or stovepipe, which resulted in the heating device smoking so much, the professor had to dismiss the class. On occasion they "egressed from windows" and had to be cautioned against a repetition of the act. In winter, morning prayers were held as soon as one could see to read, with the result that they were often not conducive to piety. Missiles, which included prayer books, flew through the dark. At Miami, President Robert Bishop always prayed with one eye open; he was known to "take a flying leap from the platform, clutch a troublemaker, and return to his post without a pause in supplication." In these operations, because the students sat quietly or slumbered, the only participants who got any exercise were the presidents. At Hudson students were censured for sharpening pencils at morning prayers, and for reading novels during church services on the Sabbath. Once they broke into the prayer room and tied a horse there, with the Bible positioned before him as if he were reading from it. Ultimately four students were suspended for the remainder of the term for participation in this escapade. On another occasion a student was censured for making too much noise during the New England Sabbath, when musical students were restricted to the singing of psalms. The minutes of the faculty noted that "Pierce of the Junior Class was detected in blowing a horn on Saturday night, and on deliberation it was resolved that he be called before the Faculty, acknowledge his offence, give a pledge of future good behaviour, and receive a second warning—which was accordingly done." This was embarrassing to the president of Western Reserve College; the "Pierce" who was desecrating the Sabbath was his son.

In order to divert this excess energy into safer channels, dozens of colleges, including Western Reserve, introduced a unique system of exercise—through manual labor in workshops or farms. There was national agitation for the innovation—a Society for Promoting Manual Labor in Literary Institutions was founded in 1831. It contended that "the plough, the hoe, the spade, the shovel, the axe, and the scythe, fall into the same hands that Virgil, Cicero, and the sages of Greece...have occupied." The society's most successful propagandist was Theodore Weld, the reformer who exerted so much influence on President Storrs and Professors Elizur Wright and Beriah Green during the crisis over slavery in the early 1830s. When he was studying for the ministry at Oneida Institute, Weld had risen at three-thirty in the morning to serve as "monitor of the milking class." He arose extra early to supervise the milking of thirty cows and to ensure the delivery by wagon to Utica by daybreak. Later, as agent of the society, he "became a living, breathing, and eloquently speaking exhibit of the results of manual labor- with-study." In one year he delivered over two hundred lectures on the virtues of manual labor and temperance, and traveled more than forty-five hundred miles, half of it on horseback or afoot. It was exhausting and dangerous work. In Ohio, near Columbus, his stage was carried downstream by high water at a ford. Weld nearly drowned; he claimed that his subsequent recovery from the exposure was due to a physique that had been strengthened by hard work.

Advocates of manual labor used three arguments to support their system—they were based on morality, health and dignity, and financial gain. The Puritan influence was strong; it was considered both a waste and a sin to expend bodily energies in play that might otherwise yield potatoes or furniture. William Paley, an English theologian of the eighteenth century, contended that if a young man had an itch to do something, he could jolly well plant a garden. Some also argued that games in themselves were bad because they were frivolous diversions that gave pleasure. In that era any seeking of pleasure, except through religious contemplation, was considered sinful by college authorities. Others contended that games lacked the dignity and stateliness expected from academicians. At Princeton the faculty forbade shinny and hockey on the grounds that they were "low and unbecoming gentlemen and scholars." At Rensselaer Polytechnic Institute an official announcement in the 1820s declared that "such exercise as running, jumping, climbing, scuffling, and the like are calculated to detract from that dignity of deportment which becomes a man of science." Young men on farms had obviously been expected to work, not play. In 1875 the chancellor of Syracuse University was alarmed about over-emphasis on athletics; he snorted, "As well might the Methodist, Presbyterian, and Baptist ministers of New York City select a crew to exhibit their prowess in a boat race on the Hudson."

On the question of health the protagonists of physical labor quoted Benjamin Rush, the eminent physician and signer of the Declaration of Independence. He had been concerned about the great incidence of tuberculosis and gastrointestinal disorders among college students and thought hard exercise would alleviate them. Francis Parkman, the distinguished American historian in the nineteenth century who suffered from ill health and in spite of it endured journeys up and down the challenging Oregon trail, was worried about pale students glued to their desks. He thought they ought to unglue themselves and spend some time in the saddle, with a rifle as their companion. At Western Reserve it was claimed, extravagantly, that "not a pale face was to be seen among them, nor an emaciated form."

On the economic side it was argued that both colleges and students would profit; unfortunately this ideal never worked out in practice. It was assumed that young college men, like the monks of the Middle Ages, might earn their livelihood by laboring on the farm or in the shop for two or three hours a day—and because of the exhilaration of this exercise would be able to study all the better. Unfortunately, few students made enough money to pay even a portion of their expenses. Those with no mechanical ability were paid nothing; those who approached the status of apprentices might be paid as much as three to five dollars a month—enough to pay their board—for their hours of so-called "recreation." Western Reserve College was careful to stress physical and mental health, rather than the amassing of money, as the major reason for introducing the program. In 1834 it cautioned parents against the expectation of too much pecuniary aid to their sons from manual labor. It admonished them that "the grand design of the manual labor system is the preservation of the health of the student; pecuniary support is to be considered as altogether secondary and of minor importance."

If students gained little or nothing from the operation, the colleges lost steadily and most of the programs were killed by the Panic of 1837. Western Reserve College stubbornly continued its workshops until the 1850s, and the losses incurred during this long period constituted one of the reasons for the financial debacle of the Pierce administration.

In Hudson the trustees decreed that students were to work in the shops for a minimum of two hours a day, either in the morning or late afternoon. They produced a variety of products: wagons, tables, bedstead, coffins, wooden sap buckets, and barrels. The barrels were sold to the neighboring distilleries; this was paradoxical because Weld had combined manual labor with temperance, and college rules forbade any use of intoxicants by students. In its advertisements, Western Reserve College claimed all of these products were "made to order promptly and guaranteed to give satisfaction"—perhaps an inappropriate claim for the coffins. In actual practice the products were seldom produced on time and turned out to be crude, ill-jointed, rickety, and very hard to sell. The manual-labor experiment was as complete a failure as can be found in the history of the college; it was also the one that caused the most friction between the college and its students, lasting for a quarter of a century. Blame for the failure can be placed on both.

As far as the college was concerned, an evil, smirking fate beset the entire enterprise. There was trouble with machinery, superintendents, fire, and students.

Shops were built and equipped with machinery, including a steam engine which cost an amount that was enormous for a struggling college. When the engine arrived from Pittsburgh, it would not run. For more than a year committees of the faculty and of the trustees, plus an "expert" from Cleveland tinkered with it; the engine remained silent. Ultimately a student mastered the difficulty and the engine became operational; ironically his knowledge of, and interest in, engines turned out to be his only virtue, and he had to be dismissed from the college.

The trustees had great difficulty in finding competent superintendents for the workshops, and if they succeeded it was difficult to keep them for any length of time because of the exasperation of the job. In the summer of 1832 the position was again vacant and the trustees were determined to fill it—they did, in full measure. A subscription agent was sent to the East to raise funds during the summer months. The trustees authorized him to be on the lookout for a suitable superintendent. His reconnaissance was successful, and he hired one. In the meantime the trustees had found another in Hudson who seemed to be a likely candidate; they hired him. Both superintendents appeared at the college, eager for duty, during the first week of the fall term. In the early summer the trustees had no superintendent, and now they had one too many. A heated discussion followed on guilt; which party had exceeded instructions? This controversy was never resolved for understandable reasons. Representatives of the college, separated by time and space, had done their level best—which turned out to be much too productive. Ultimately the trustees had to decide which superintendent should stay. After much deliberation, the candidate from the East returned home, mollified by the payment of a sum sufficient to "reimburse him for his expenses and his injured feelings." It was twenty dollars!

In 1844 two of the shops in Hudson burned to the ground. In view of the cordial dislike of students for the manual-labor program, there was some speculation as to whether the conflagration was accidental or had been carefully planned. There is no evidence of conspiracy. In actuality the burning of college shops was not infrequent because of the inflammable litter left by woodworking. In Hudson the fire broke out in the carpenter shop. The weather had been cold and there was a hot fire in a stove in the building. The conflagration was hardly surprising.

The kindest comment on student participation in the project is to say that most of them were disinclined to manual labor. Few had any initial knowledge of the use of tools, and the majority had no desire to learn. They badgered the faculty with applications for excuses on every conceivable ground, some highly imaginative. Enough waivers were granted that an invidious distinction was established between workers and nonworkers. Superintendents found the short work period inefficient and exasperating; all workmen came at one time, overtaxing the accommodations—although during the greater part of the day all equipment was idle. Students compounded the aggravation by shortening still further the already abbreviated work periods. They overslept and arrived late for the morning shift, but left promptly for the required morning prayers.

At this point in time no one can be certain of the exact economic cost of the manual labor system. When it was finally abandoned in the early 1850s, the trustees knew that they had lost about ten thousand hard-to-come-by dollars—simply because they had to pay for shops, tools, the steam engine, and compensation to superintendents and students—while the sale of manufactured articles hardly paid for the materials in them. In 1854 President Pierce sadly concluded, "an experiment was tried that will not need to be repeated."

Additional Reading

A Memoir of Rev. Joseph Badger. Hudson, Ohio, 1851.

Buley, R. C. *The Old Northwest.* 2 vols. Bloomington, 1962.

Conlin, Mary Lou. *Simon Perkins of the Western Reserve.* Cleveland, 1968.

Cramer, C. H. *Case Western Reserve.* Boston, 1976.

Dittrick, Howard, ed. *Pioneer Medicine in the Western Reserve.* Cleveland, 1932.

Downes, Randolph C. *History of Lake Shore Ohio.* 3 vols. New York, 1952.

Ellis, William D. *Early Settlers of Cleveland.* Cleveland, 1976.

Howe, Eber D. *Autobiography.* Painesville, Ohio, 1878.

Howe, Henry. *Historical Collections of Ohio.* 2 vols. Columbus, 1888.

Hitchcock, Elizabeth G. *Jonathan Goldsmith.* Cleveland, 1980.

Izant, Grace Goulder. *Hudson's Heritage.* Kent, Ohio, 1985.

Lupold, Harry F. *The Latch String is Out.* Mentor, Ohio, 1974.

Parkin, Max H. *Conflict in Kirtland.* Master's thesis, Brigham Young University, 1966.

Prusha, Anne. *A History of Kirtland, Ohio.* Mentor, Ohio, 1982.

Rose, William G. *Cleveland: The Making of a City.* Cleveland, 1950.

Smith, Thomas A. *Oulanie Thepy: The Golden Age of Harbour Town, Vermillion 1837–1879.* Bowling Green, Ohio, 1973.

Upton, Harriet T. *History of the Western Reserve.* 3 vols. Chicago, 1910.

PART III

The Transition Years:
Slavery, the Civil War, and the
Reserve in National Politics, 1850–1880

Agriculture, the stagecoach, and the Ohio Canal gave many Western Reserve villages a healthy beginning, and, for several decades, a promising future. From 1820 to 1850 canal water and power had increased the wealth and population of Ohio and established the cities of Cleveland and Akron on the Reserve. And many of the men who labored on the canal, such as the Irish and the Germans, remained to add diversity to the Reserve's population.

Strategically located on the lake and canal, Cleveland was a terminal for freight shipments of farm, mine, and factory products. Railroad building was in the news from 1850, when rails of iron joined Cincinnati and Columbus to Cleveland and later Youngstown, Pittsburgh, Erie, and Buffalo.

Railroads developed rapidly, stimulating manufacturing and revolutionizing transportation and communication. Trails of commerce shifted; the move to cities increased. The days of stagecoach travel diminished, stage roads and turnpikes decayed, stage stopover taverns and inns suffered, and villages declined. Canal passenger and freight traffic succumbed to cheaper, faster year-round accessibility of railroad competition. Small canals, like the seven-mile waterway from Milan to Huron in the Firelands, particularly could not meet this competition from the steam age.

In 1855 the opening of the Sault Ste. Marie Canal signalled the dawn of the industrial era for the Western Reserve, as trade shifted to the lower lakes bringing natural resources within reach. Rich iron ore deposits from the north, vast coal fields to the south, untapped reserves of petroleum to the east, and limestone along the lake shore were the resources that, combined with capital, labor, management, improved transportation, and ready markets, outlined Cleveland's future as an industrial center.

The unification of the North east and west of the Alleghenies had profound meaning in the approaching crisis of the Civil War. Newspapers aided by the telegraph and train provided rapid communication as they hustled to compete for the newsworthy topics of the time—slavery, morality, temperance, equal rights, religion, and politics.

The Western Reserve of the antebellum period was populated by those heirs of industrious, pious New Englanders responsible for its settlement. A fertile ground for reform by 1850, the crusade against Negro slavery commanded the attention of the entire community. Ferment between the North and the South was manifested in increased traffic of escaping slaves over the Underground Railroad north of the Mason-Dixon line. Ohio had many escape routes connecting the Ohio River with Lake Erie. Barns, sheds, and farmhouses of friendly abolitionists and free Negroes constituted the stations of the railway. Escaped slaves were smuggled from station to station in the dark of night by conductors in defiance of the Fugitive Slave Act of 1850.

David Hudson, pioneer community builder, was a station master, as was nearby resident Owen Brown, father of John Brown, fiery foe of slavery. Ashtabula, Painesville, Sandusky, Lorain, Vermilion and Oberlin, seat of the famous Oberlin Wellington Rescue, were gateways to safety. Cleveland was an embarkation point for Canada, hence a center for professional slave hunters. Harry Lupold, in "1820–1860 Anti-Slavery Activities in a Western Reserve County," selected eastern Lake County as a focus for a case study in which he traces the development of the slavery issue from a political perspective. In a companion piece that shifts geographically west, "Oberlin-Wellington Rescue Cases," Elroy M. Avery captures the emotional tenor of the times.

On March 27, 1852, the flames of the slavery controversy were fanned when Cleveland publisher Jewett, Proctor and Worthington announced its publication of *Uncle Tom's Cabin or Life Among the Lowly* by Harriet Beecher Stowe. The city's *Daily True Democrat* hailed it as "the most beautiful, truthful and valuable book ever written or published by an American."

Seven years later on October 16, 1859, John Brown, nineteenth-century Calvinist son of the Western Reserve, whose "failure scarred life," his biographer suggests, contributed to his revolutionary act, heard God's call,

> "I saw Thee when Thou did display
> The black man and his lord
> To bid me free the one, and slay
> The other with the sword."

John Brown's Prayer
John Brown's Body
Stephen Vincent Benét

For ten days in the spring of 1859, before the autumn assault, Bertram Wyatt-Brown described the presence of John Brown in Cleveland where, although there was "a price on his head" for the Kansas carnage, he was never turned in: "The city was in the throes of excitement and indignation over the Oberlin-Wellington Fugitive Rescue Case. The protest rally for the defendants at which [Joshua] Giddings spoke to 10,000 Clevelanders in Public Square provided the cover and sympathy that Brown needed." When John Brown and his followers, five of them black,

"reached the Maryland bridge of Harper's Ferry
That Sunday night. There were twenty-two in all,
Nineteen were under thirty, three not twenty-one."

The tale of Harper's Ferry
John Brown's Body

His plan was to follow the Harpers Ferry attack with others on a drive through the South, igniting a chain of rebellions. Even if this raid failed, Brown argued, it would cause a sectional blow-up in which slavery would be destroyed. Brown's biographer, Stephen B. Oates continues:

He was prophetic. In southern eyes he was. . . a Yankee abolitionist sent by the "Black" Republican party to drown the south in rivers of blood. Because it linked southern fears of slave revolts with southern apprehension about the Republican party, Brown's raid polarized the country as no other event had done, setting in motion a spiral of accusation and counteraccusation that bore the country irreversibly toward the Civil War.

On December 2, 1859, the day of Brown's execution by hanging in Charles Town, Virginia, flags flew at half-mast and bells tolled the two o'clock hour in Cleveland. Ministers hailed the martyr and instructed people to "baptise themselves in his spirit and stand upon a foundation of adamant and unalterable hostility to slavery."

At four o'clock in the afternoon of February 15, 1861, a thundering cannon announced and welcomed the arrival of President-elect Abraham Lincoln by train at Cleveland's Euclid Street Station. Against a cacophony of shrieking whistles and ringing church bells, throngs of people moved toward the Public Square. Carrying his stovepipe hat, the gaunt man in black rode down flag-draped Euclid Street in a cold drizzling rain, in an open barouche drawn by four white horses accompanied by an array of military companies and carriages bearing public officials. From the balcony of the Weddell House he addressed thousands assembled to greet him on his way to Washington, appealing for their devotion to the Constitution and the Union and for their loyalty to "the good old ship." The next morning a military escort conducted Lincoln and his party to the Union Depot for the next leg of his journey.

The train stopped in Painesville, and a teacher at the Lake Erie Female Seminary recorded that the young ladies of that institution "were all on tiptoe, to see a real true President of these United States":

A large number of enthusiastic people from Painesville and vicinity had gathered around the platform which had been erected near the depot. We had not waited long before the expected train with its precious freight came in sight; the Band immediately struck up "Hail Columbia." We had a fine view of Mr. Lincoln as he stepped from the car to the platform and addressed the assembly and we were all pleased to find that he is much more interesting in his appearance than his pictures represent him.

Abraham Lincoln, sixteenth president of the United States, was inaugurated on March 4, 1861. In the view of the war-mongering Democratic *Cleveland Plain Dealer*, the event in effect signalled the beginning of the "irrepressible conflict." One month later *Plain Dealer* editorials set the stage for the April 12, 1861, attack on Fort Sumter. President Lincoln called for volunteers, and to the wistful refrain of "The Girl I Left Behind Me" and the measured cadence of "Tramp, Tramp, Tramp the Boys are Marching," mobilization commenced.

In "Cleveland During the Civil War," Kenneth E. Davison delineates the city's contribution to the war effort in a review of its military and political response. The city's strategic location suggested the possibility of a Confederate invasion from Canada. Davison states, "War did come close to Cleveland in November 1863 when Canadian refugees and Confederates plotted to free war prisoners on Johnson's Island in Sandusky Bay." The outcome of this "invasion" is discussed as part of the comprehensive and compelling narrative by Edward T. Downer in "Johnson's Island" that places the Civil War in closer proximity than most imagined.

On April 9, 1865, Lee surrendered to Grant at Appomattox. The news of the cessation of hostilities reached Cleveland by telegraph on the morning of April 10. People celebrated wildly, raising the Union flag and banners amidst band playing and impromptu parades. On the morning of April 15 another telegram reached Cleveland stating that a shot fired by John Wilkes Booth in Washington's Ford Theater the night before had claimed the life of President Lincoln. A day of mourning was proclaimed as flags were lowered and churches and public buildings were draped in black.

The late-president's train passed through Cleveland on its way to the final destination in Springfield, Illinois. On April 28, artillery saluted the dawn as thousands of mourners awaited the arrival of the Lincoln funeral train at the Euclid Street Station. In the last black-draped car lay the mortal remains of the martyred president.

Cannon roared, a military band played a solemn dirge, and the coffin was raised and placed on the hearse drawn by six white horses. The procession of six thousand men moved slowly toward the Public Square where a canopied pavillion had been erected. The coffin was placed on a low catafalque banked with white flowers arranged by Cleveland's women. Throughout the day and evening one hundred thousand people looked for the last time upon the face of the Great Emancipator, while thousands waited in the wind-and rain-lashed night until ten o'clock, when the coffin was escorted back to the train. At midnight the slow, sad journey west resumed.

Cleveland made a significant contribution to the Union effort in goods and human resources. The most important events, however, occurring in Civil War Cleveland involved economic development. Primarily a commercial center in 1860, the Civil War made Cleveland an industrial center. With its favorable geographical location and resources, railroads and shipping, capital and labor, Cleveland's economy prospered.

Cleveland's shipyards, renowned for craftsmanship, met the increased war demands for ships and built many of the freight and passenger vessels constructed in the region. By 1865 eight railroads and four steamship lines radiated from Cleveland. New passenger and freight depots were built to handle the traffic through the city as the war demands for materials, supplies, and personnel accelerated.

The growth of industry was attributed to the availability of three essential raw materials—iron ore from Lake Superior, limestone from Ohio quarries, and coal from northeastern Ohio, western Pennsylvania, and West Virginia. Just before the war, oil was discovered in western Pennsylvania. John D. Rockefeller, who made his initial capital as a Cleveland commission merchant, turned to oil, and, with Henry Flagler, founded the Standard Oil Company in 1870 in Cleveland.

Iron and oil changed Cleveland's economy during the Civil War as local investors and businessmen realized that natural resources and good railroad transportation offered greater economic opportunities than a continued emphasis on commerce. Chronicler of the Western Reserve Harlan Hatcher, in "Building the Railroads," traces the development of transportation networks and the regional implications to illustrate the significance for the shift in Cleveland's economic base and the creation of new wealth.

"Have you seen Euclid Avenue?" a visitor to Cleveland was asked. Originally Euclid Road, it was the most popular route from Cleveland to Buffalo, and in 1832 it was declared a public highway by the Ohio Legislature. Then Euclid Street or "Prosperity Row," it grew to reflect Cleveland's wealth as the scions of banking, industry, transportation, and communication built their resplendent residences and surrounded them with formally landscaped acreages—Samuel Mather, Henry Chisholm, Amasa Stone, Jeptha Wade, John D. Rockefeller. In 1870, officially named Euclid Avenue, it had achieved the ultimate status, although more often and accurately perhaps it was called "Millionaires' Row."

Exemplifying the Western Reserve's transition years was James A. Garfield, who at the age of seventeen in the summer of 1848 spent two months working aboard a Pennsylvania and Ohio canal boat. Leaving Cleveland with a fifty-two-ton load of copper ore, they unloaded at Pittsburgh twelve days later. Returning, they took on sixty tons of coal at Youngstown, unloading at Cleveland four days later. Young Garfield's job was to make the locks ready, see the boat through, trim the lamps, and serve as general handyman.

In the antebellum years Garfield was an elected state representative and then a member of the Ohio Senate when he volunteered for the Union Army. At Lincoln's request, he resigned the promise of a brilliant military career in 1863 to take a Republican seat in Congress representing Ohio's nineteenth district. While a member of Congress, James A. Garfield, Western Reserve born and bred, purchased Lawnfield, one hundred and sixty acres in Mentor, Ohio, on which stood a small white farmhouse. Here, he said, "my boys can learn to work, . . . I can myself have some exercise . . . and touch the earth and get some strength from it." In "Garfield's Front Porch Campaign: The Mentor Scene,"

Frederick D. Williams resumes the narrative following the June 8, 1880, nomination of Garfield as the Republican candidate for the presidency and his innovative contribution to presidential political campaigning.

It was the autumn of 1880 when emissaries from the Lake Erie Female Seminary travelled west on Mentor Avenue to Lawnfield, the home of newly elected president of the United States and their neighbor, James A. Garfield. It was not a first meeting, for General and Mrs. Garfield had spent a Saturday evening earlier in the fall visiting at the Seminary. It was November, and knowing that the nineteenth was the General's birthday, Lake Erie's representatives extended an invitation to celebrate it with a tea at the Seminary. When his availability was certain for the eighteenth, a birthday eve celebration was planned. The Seminary commenced activities of preparedness on a grand scale commensurate with the stature of its guest. Rooms were festooned with garlands of evergreens, and mottoes cut from individual letters were hung that read: "Honor" and "To the Teacher—Hiram; To the Soldier—Chickamauga; To the Statesman—1859-1880." Flowers and plants were arranged in the drawing room and on its tables. The students wore badges of red, white, and blue grosgrain ribbon with the dates 1831, the year of Garfield's birth, and 1880, to commemorate the occasion. When the Garfields arrived by sleigh at six o'clock, their welcome began at the sight of the Seminary, fully illuminated from its basement to tower. Trustees and friends of the College along with teachers and senior-class students received the guests in the drawing room. The party moved to the dining room where the students stood in rank and sang while the Garfields took their places. The supper of scalloped oysters, ham salad, biscuits, Graham bread, coffee, and cake was served by the students and was followed by their performances in gymnastics and music. When the Garfields departed at evening's end, red and blue lights were thrown over the building and grounds, and, with the whiteness of the snow, completed the national colors. A note arrived the next day addressed to Mary Evans, principal of the Lake Erie Female Seminary. Its words of appreciation contained a prophetic note:

Dear Miss Evans:

Please accept for yourself and express to your associate teachers and to the young ladies of your Seminary, my heartfelt thanks for the very kind reception you gave me last evening.

I can hardly expect that any other birthday of my life will come to me with such a bright and beautiful welcome. The exercises, the decoration, the whole evening brought back very vivid memories of my teacher life and I enjoyed again the pleasure of seeing the hand of hopeful happy youth offering me its helpful blessings.

Mrs. Garfield joins me in thanking you all for your kindness.

Very truly yours,

James A. Garfield

In a tragic turn of events, Garfield, after four months as president, was the victim of an assassin's bullet. He died in September 1881. His November birthday celebration at Lake Erie Female Seminary was in fact his last. Its aftermath constitutes Garfield biographer Allan Peskin's "The Funeral of the Century," in which, for the second time within the decades of the transition years, a president is assassinated. The Western Reserve grieved for one of its own and gave to him a final resting place.

HARRY F. LUPOLD

1820–1860 Anti-Slavery Activities in a Western Reserve County

From 1820 to 1860, the counties bordering on Lake Erie, known as the Western Reserve, entered a politically divisive period when national issues relating to the extension of slavery, the annexation of Texas to the United States, the war with Mexico, and the increasing power of the slave oligarchy involved people in heated debate and often in violent actions. These issues swept with destructive force through both the Whig and Democratic parties in the Reserve.

The anti-slavery movement in Ohio and the Western Reserve showed a lack of unity from its inception. The degrees of intensity included: (1) the extreme radical element (abolitionists), which was especially strong among the emigrants from New England in the northeastern part of the state; (2) the Liberty party, which advocated the gradual emancipation of the slaves and their colonization to Africa; (3) the Free-Soil party, which was against the spread of slavery; (4) the abolition element in the Whig party; and (5) the liberty and free-soil elements drawn from the Democratic party.

Very few blacks were found in the Western Reserve prior to 1850. Blacks were certainly not numerous enough in any Reserve community to excite racial hostility. However, in the decade 1850 to 1860, there was a 45 percent increase in the black population of Ohio. The number of blacks in Geauga County, and then Lake County, the subject of this paper, can be observed in these totals:

	1820	1830	1840	1850	1860
Geauga County	6	21	3	7	7
Lake County	—	—	21	38	36
Total (Reserve)	167	184	591	1,321	2,082

Lake County, Ohio, was born on March 6, 1840. Carved out of Geauga County (formed in 1806), its eight townships had a population of 13,719. The black population of the county was only 21. The anti-slavery activity that characterized Lake County politics from 1840 to 1860 actually began much earlier, in

the 1830s, when Leroy, Concord, Mentor, Perry, Kirtland, Willoughby, Painesville, and Madison Townships were still a part of Geauga County.

Propagandists for the anti-slavery cause came to Geauga County in the 1830s.
They were not always well received. One of the leading abolitionists, Theodore
Dwight Weld, arrived in the area in 1835. Silas Pepoon, Sr., wrote a letter in the
Geauga Democrat, which had originally been written to the *Painesville Telegraph*,
that Weld spoke at the Chardon Court House but was interrupted by a "proslav-
ery mob." Weld had to move to a private building by the square in order to finish
his speech. From Chardon, Weld went to Painesville. Here, he lectured in the
Congregational Church and infuriated those who opposed him. The white walls
on either side of the pulpit were defaced after the lecture. These pictures of "his
Satanic majesty" were hard to erase, and they confronted the horror-stricken audience who attended the lecture the next evening. A black smudge remained on
the walls for many years. Eber D. Howe said that the town council, composed of
P. P. Sanford, mayor, and William L. Perkins, J. H. Paine, Addison Hills, Milo
Harris, Edwin Palmer, and David Hull, passed a resolution, not mandatory, that
Mr. Weld discontinue his lectures in Painesville. Weld's next stop was Madison,
where he gave three lectures "to full houses on the relations of the Bible to slavery." Once again the town authorities passed resolutions advising him to leave
this place. But Weld refused to leave Madison.

Another abolitionist who visited Geauga County was J. W. Alvord, a member
of the American Anti-Slavery Society. Alvord visited Willoughby and left these
impressions in a letter to Elizur Wright of the Society: "My next place was at
Willoughby, a large village, nineteen miles from Cleveland, with a medical college, &c. Found many opposed to me, and but few abolitionist, not more than
two or three." Alvord's second lecture was interrupted by "boisterous fellows"
who were sent in to break up the meeting. Alvord believed that many of his enemies were brought in from the countryside since he concluded that a majority of
the village favored free discussion. Antagonized, his opponents formed a mob
and invaded his bed chamber and forced him to leave town with a pledge he
would never speak in Willoughby again. Alvord was nearly tarred and feathered
because he refused to give the pledge that the mob demanded. The *Telegraph*
reported that three or four hundred people met at the College in Willoughby to
discuss the propriety of permitting certain abolition lectures by Mr. Alvord.
Their resolution requested Alvord to withdraw from the village: "that we view
with feelings of indignation mingled with regret the arrival in this place of a dis-
semination of doctrines alike injurous to the interests of the black population
and subversive to the harmony of the union."

By 1840, however, Lake County began to show signs of a political unrest that
was not normally a part of the Whig-Democratic rivalry. Lake Shore, Ohio,
which included Lake County, became the anti-slavery center of Ohio from 1848
to 1853. But the kind of abolition that the average Lake Shore Ohioan wanted,
said Randolph C. Downes, was not the Garrison-Brown-Liberty kind. Instead,

they favored abolition promoted by Southerners in the South that would keep the blacks from moving to the North. The Underground Railroad seemed to operate with that philosophy—that is, send the blacks to the next station and then on to Canada. Lake County Whigs also opposed the expansion of slavery as a means of Southern minority domination of the North. Whig papers, for instance, viewed the annexation of Texas in 1845 as a Southern plot to expand the slave interests.

The annexation of Texas, the Mexican War, and the slave question turned Lake County Whigs, who viewed Congressman Joshua R. Giddings (Jefferson, Ohio), a bitter critic of the slave power, as their hero, to support the Free-Soil party by 1848. Free-Soil voting strength in Lake County rose from 904 votes in the election of 1848 to a high of 1,111 votes in the election of 1852. In all elections from 1848 to 1853, the Free-Soilers out-voted the Whigs and Democrats in Lake County.

A compromise was hammered out in 1850 that temporarily calmed the passions in both sections, but the entire settlement depended on the North's enforcement of the new and stricter Fugitive Slave Law. It was clear from the beginning that this was a law that Lake Countians would not obey. On October 19, 1850, a mass meeting in Painesville went so far as to recommend nullification of the law, and vigilance committees were formed in the different townships to keep watch for slave catchers. The Fugitive Slave Law was denounced in speeches and resolutions as unconstitutional. At a meeting in Painesville, April 25, 1859, this resolution was adopted:

> The Fugitive Slave Law is not only clearly unconstitutional, but is also so repugnant to every principle of Justice and Humanity that no Constitution or Compact can make it binding; and so derogatory to the moral sense and self respect of a free and honorable people, that it deserves no argument, but only execration and contempt.

If any one activity described the attitudes and mysteries of Lake County's antislavery activities, it was the participation of its citizens in the Underground Railroad. These activities, done secretly, violated the Constitution and the Fugitive Slave Laws of the United States, since these laws provided for the restoration of escaped slaves to their masters. The Underground Railroad became a source of continued agitation in Ohio. Every rescue case made converts to the anti-slavery cause. Wilbur H. Siebert estimated the number of underground workers in Ohio at 1,540, compared to 1,670 workers in other states. Of these Ohio workers, 100 were black.

Four underground routes converged at Concord, on the line to Painesville and Fairport. Several miles northeast of Painesville was "Nigger Hollow," where fugitives were hidden before the trip to Fairport. Eber D. Howe, editor of the *Telegraph*, once lived near here and aided fugitives as they were transferred to Fairport for shipment to Canada. If slave catchers were in the area, blacks would be secreted out of "Nigger Hollow" and taken to Ashtabula Harbor. Fairport's keeper of the lighthouse was one of the first abolitionists in the county. Samuel Butler settled in Fairport in 1816 and later built Eagle Tavern near the Lake Shore. Many slaves waited here, and in his warehouse on the docks, before boarding vessels for Canada. Butler often took his passengers to the steamboat of an anti-slavery captain anchored at the Grand River. There were times when he loaded his own scow and took fugitives across the lake. Another Fairport abolitionist was Phineas Root, who put up the Steamboat Hotel at the foot of lighthouse hill.

Seth Marshall, a hardware store owner, and Uri Seeley, a farmer, were two of Painesville's notorious abolitionists who aided the fugitives during their stay in the area. At night, the slaves found shelter in Seth Marshall's barn. He and his wife often had as many as twenty-five "guests" for breakfast. A covered wagon usually conveyed the fugitives from Painesville to Fairport at night. A story has it that on one occasion a deputy sheriff arrived unexpectedly at Seth's Bank Street home, and he only had time to tell the fugitives to crawl into a load of hay standing up in the barn. In the presence of the officer, Marshall calmly hitched up his team and drove the wagon around the streets of Painesville until the officer was no longer suspicious. Very prominent in the anti-slavery movement, Seeley worked with Benjamin Wade and Joshua Giddings, of Jefferson, two of Ohio's outstanding anti-slavery congressional leaders. Seeley became a member of the first National Anti-Slavery Convention, and later became a delegate to the Free-Soil Convention. The first representative of the abolition element in the state legislature from Lake and Ashtabula Counties, his home became a station on the Underground Railroad.

Various county newspapers boasted that blacks were free from capture in the Western Reserve. In Painesville, the *Telegraph* bragged: "The U.G.R.R.—The travel on this line is constant and increasing. Last Monday night some six or seven thousand dollars worth of passengers passed over on the underground track not a thousand miles from these parts."

Unionville was a station on the Underground Railroad. The Old Tavern there had secret closets, peek-holes, and tunnels in the basement. A slave-catching adventure took place outside the Tavern at the corners in 1841. It involved the rescue of an escaped Kentucky slave, Milton Clarke, who was saved by abolitionists after an angry crowd of Lake County and Ashtabula County citizens gave two Kentucky slave catchers a hard time. Milton Clarke's brother, Lewis, who was also present and being pursued, became the model for "Harris" in Harriet Beecher Stowe's *Uncle Tom's Cabin*. After the return of the two slave catchers to Kentucky, one of them (named McGowen) wrote a letter back to General J. H. Paine, an abolitionist defender of Milton Clarke: "Jim Paine, you dam [sic] black abolitionist, if you come to Kentucky I'm good for your scalp, if I meet you in hell." Another slave catcher, one Anderson Jennings of Maysville, Kentucky, visited Cleveland, Sandusky, Elyria, and Painesville. In Painesville, he and his party were ordered to leave the town in twenty minutes. Jennings said of Painesville: "Never see so many niggers and abolitionists in any one place in my life!

They gave us twenty minutes to leave, and they wouldn't allow us that. There was a crowd of fifty or sixty, armed. Might as well try to hunt the devil there as to hunt a nigger."

Although Lake Countians were free-soil advocates who supported the Underground Railroad, it does not follow that they necessarily believed blacks were equal to whites. On the contrary, many were white supremists who accepted the argument that blacks were naturally inferior to whites. But then this attitude probably prevailed throughout the North and is one that Lincoln even espoused. The object of the Underground Railroad was not to get blacks to settle in the Reserve, but to pass them on to Canada quietly and quickly. Of the nearly 40,000 blacks who passed through the Reserve, only 2,082 resided there in 1860 before hostilities began between the North and the South. One story circulated that it was the custom of Rev. Jonathan Winchester, of the Madison Central Congregational Church, to kiss the bride when he officiated at weddings. A committee of church members visited him about the practice. One member of the committee, a deacon and pro-slavery man, asked: "Suppose you were to marry a colored couple, would you kiss the bride?" "Well," said the parson, "in such a case I believe I should delegate the duty to my deacons."

Oberlin-Wellington Rescue Cases, 1858–1859

In 1858, events in Kansas aroused the North to feverish excitement and, on the twelfth of March, the anti-Lecompton Democrats of Cleveland held in Melodeon Hall a meeting that was addressed by Frederick P. Stanton, lately the secretary and acting-governor of "Bleeding Kansas." Mr. Stanton had resigned his office on account of the presidential policy, especially as it related to the fraudulent returns of the vote by which the notorious Lecompton state constitution had been "adopted." James M. Coffinberry was chairman of the meeting, and Dan P. Rhodes, Jabez W. Fitch, and John H. Farley were among the vice presidents. One of the resolutions adopted declared "that the Lecompton constitution, in view of its parentage and history, is unworthy of the consideration of the president and congress." It is not on record that President Buchanan enjoyed this practical repudiation by these honest Democrats who had lately voted for him. The iniquities of the Fugitive Slave Law also piled their burden on the conscience of New Connecticut and paved the way for stirring events in Cleveland and its environs. In 1859, the trial of the Oberlin-Wellington rescue cases in the United States court in Cleveland created great excitement in the city and elsewhere. At that time, Oberlin, Ohio, had a population of about three thousand, exclusive of the twelve hundred or more students at the college, which drew no restrictions on the line of color, sex, or creed. The collegiate advantages thus offered brought to the town many free blacks, and the public sentiment thus announced made Oberlin a haven of refuge for enterprising runaway slaves, some of whom had the courage to remain. Here, in September 1858, a slave catcher found John Price, who had escaped from slavery in Kentucky. John was decoyed from the town, seized, and taken to Wellington nine miles away and on the railway between Cleveland and Columbus. The slave catcher was intending to take John before the United States commissioner at Columbus. News of the abduction floated into Oberlin and "was all over town in a flash." From shops, stores, and offices, men rushed into the streets, took the first vehicles found, and drove rapidly toward Wellington. Some of the students started on foot and had a lively race to beat their professors who went by any transportation that could be obtained. The minute men increased in numbers on the way and were further reinforced at Wellington. The four kidnappers with their victim were behind the closed door of an upper room of the village hotel, awaiting the arrival of the train to take them to Columbus. The excited crowd surrounded the hotel; the train came and went. While the prudent were parleying and the calm were discussing plans, the door was forced, John was taken down to the street and driven out into the country before many of the rescuers understood what was being done. The citizens of Oberlin, having made good their boast that a slave should never be taken from their town, quietly returned to their homes. For several days, John was secreted in the house of James H. Fairchild, professor of moral philosophy and theology, and, subsequently, the president of the college. John was finally shipped in safety to the free land across Lake Erie.

For participation in this rescue, twenty-four residents of Oberlin and thirteen of Wellington were indicted (December 7, 1858) under the provisions of an act of 1850, and arraigned before the United States district court at Cleveland. No more respectable prisoners than these ever pleaded "not guilty." They were dismissed upon their own recognizance to appear for trial in the following March. In March, the trial was deferred another month. Four eminent attorneys, Rufus P. Spalding, Franklin T. Backus, Albert G. Riddle, and Seneca O. Griswold, volunteered their services for the defense without fees. The district attorney, George W. Belden, was aided by an able associate, and both sides put forth extraordinary efforts. The prosecution had the sympathy of the judge—the defense, that of the community. The first to be brought to trial (April 7, 1859) was Simeon Bushnell. The evidence was clear, the law was plain, and the verdict was "guilty." The prisoner was sentenced to pay a fine of six hundred dollars and costs and to be imprisoned in the county jail for sixty days. At the end of the Bushnell trial, the court made a ruling so unfair that the others who had been indicted refused to continue their words of honor to appear in court when wanted. The ruling was subsequently recalled and the prisoners notified that their recognizances would be accepted as before. Declining to renew their recognizances or to give bail, the indicted men became real prisoners. From the middle of April to July, the Cleveland jail was the center of an intense and widespread interest. "It was a self-imposed martyrdom; but the fact could not be ignored that these respectable people were in prison, and the preaching on Sunday of Professor Peck from the jail-yard produced a remarkable sensation."

The second person to be tried was Charles Langston, a black man. He was found guilty. Before receiving sentence, Langston took advantage of the opportunity generally given and made an eloquent speech, a pathetic description of the Negro's disabilities, and a claim that he had not been tried by his peers. When he took his seat, the courtroom rang with applause and the court fixed the sentence—a hundred dollars fine and twenty days imprisonment. At the close of Langston's trial, and when the remaining cases were about to be continued from the middle of May to the July term, three of the Wellington prisoners entered a plea of *nolo contendere* and were sentenced each to pay a fine of twenty dollars and a cost of prosecution and to remain in jail twenty-four hours. When "Father

Gillette," an old man from Wellington, was entreated thus to leave the jail he replied: "Not until I have shrunk small enough to slip through that keyhole." Continuance in jail had become a point of honor.

In the recess of the United States court at Cleveland, Bushnell and Langston were taken, on a writ of habeas corpus, before the judges of the supreme court of Ohio. The case was ably argued for a week, the attorney general of the state appearing as counsel for the prisoners. The court divided three against two, and the prisoners were remanded. The vote of one man had turned the scale; had it been turned the other way, Ohio might have been brought into armed conflict with the national government and in defense of state rights. "Had the party of freedom throughout the North then rallied, as seemed probable, the war might have come in 1859 instead of 1861, with a secession of the northern instead of the southern states." Dazzling speculation!

The interest excited by these trials was deep and widespread. Public meetings were held in all parts of the Western Reserve, and an immense mass convention of the opponents of the Fugitive Slave Law was held (May 24, 1859) in Cleveland. Delegations came from many counties of northern Ohio. They came "by trainload and wagonload. There were multitudes of bands and banners. A vast parade formed and marched by the prison yard cheering the martyrs." A large platform was built in the Public Square so near to the high fence around the jail that speakers could address the crowd from one side of the fence or the other as occasion required. From the inside of the fence, speeches that were free from any attempt to move the passions of the crowd were made by Langston, Professor Peck, Superintendent Fitch, and other prisoners. On the other side of the fence, there was more fire. Cassius M. Clay of Kentucky wrote: "Are you ready to fight? If you have got your sentiments up to that manly pitch, I am with you through to the end. But if not, I'll have none of your conventions." Joshua R. Giddings, the president of the convention, was radical, almost revolutionary. Governor Salmon P. Chase advised patience and dependence upon legal and constitutional agencies, affirming, however, that when his time came and his duty was plain, the governor of Ohio would meet it as a man. Speeches were also made by Daniel R. Tilden, Rufus P. Spalding, and others. The resolutions that were adopted had something of the tone of a state-rights convention, but the crowds that had assembled to denounce one law were not there to break another.

Meantime, the men behind the walls of the Cuyahoga County jail were doing propaganda work, writing to the newspapers, issuing pamphlets, and advising the preachers of the North to make sermons on the case. The fire they started extended throughout all the states in the North. The railways carried relatives and friends to Cleveland at reduced rates, and the prisoners were bountifully supplied with all the delicacies of the market by the sympathizing public. Sheriff Wightman and the jailor treated the prisoners as guests and friends rather than as criminals. Prisoner Fitch's Oberlin Sunday school decided to pay a visit to the Cuyahoga jail to see their superintendent instead of having their usual picnic. When hopes of a speedy release vanished, the prisoners secured the tools of their several callings, and soon the jailyard was a busy hive of industry. The professors and students read Latin and Greek and metaphysics, keeping up with their classwork at college, and sending to the outside world stirring anti-slavery epistles. A printing office was established and *The Rescuer* issued. Religious exercises formed a considerable part of the daily life of this remarkable penal colony.

In the meantime, the grand jury of Lorain County, in which were Oberlin and Wellington, indicted the four men who had abducted the black man in violation of the Ohio laws against kidnappers. The penalty for this offense was imprisonment for three years in the penitentiary, "and if there was any one fact in the matter more certain than another, it was that if the indicted men should fall into the clutches of the Lorain County court they would serve the last hour allowed by the law." When, at the end of the second trial, counsel for the defense moved to take up the third case, the United States district attorney indignantly explained that his four witnesses were in the custody of the Lorain County court, and that he was obliged to ask for a continuance to the sixth of July. After a skillful and amusing display of thrust and parry between the officials of the United States district court and those of the Lorain County court, in which the latter scored the more points, it became evident that the kidnappers must stand trial with a certainty of conviction, or leave the state and thus abandon the cases against the untried rescuers. The outcome appears in the following paragraph from the *Cleveland Leader* (July 7, 1859):

> Considerable excitement was created in this city by the announcement that a proposition had been made by the Kentucky kidnappers to have mutual nolles entered in their own case and the case of the Oberlin rescuers. The consequence was the most intense anxiety among men, both Black Republicans and Yellow Democrats, to learn the upshot of the whole matter. The negotiations between Judge Belden and the kidnappers on the one side, and the authorities of Lorain (holding the kidnappers) on the other (the Oberlinites refusing to be parties), were consummated yesterday when Marshal Johnson called at the jail and announced to the rescue prisoners that they were free. The news spread rapidly that the government officials had caved. Hundreds immediately called on the rescuers to tender their congratulations at this signal triumph of the Higher Lawites. In the afternoon, about five o'clock, one hundred guns were fired, and several hundreds of our citizens gathered at the jail to escort the rescuers to the depot.

On the other side, the *Cleveland Plain Dealer* said: "So the government has been beaten at last, with law, justice and facts all on its side; and Oberlin, with its rebellious higher-law creed, is triumphant."

At Oberlin the whole community met the rescuers with music and cheers and prayers. A few days later, Bushnell, who had served out his sentence, returned to Oberlin and was received as a conquering hero.

Lincoln and Rumors of War
Cleveland Plain Dealer
March 4, 1861
April 5, 1861
April 6, 1861
April 8, 1861

MARCH 4, 1861

Washington in Commotion

The Federal Capital is rocking with excitement and undergoing a fearful ordeal today. The so long predicted crisis, has really come. The "Irrepressible Conflict" is upon us, and the country is shaken with fears and rent with divisions, all for the "poor negro." Last night Lincoln announced his Cabinet complete and laid before his Premier his forthcoming Inaugural which was adopted with slight alterations. The telegraph represents it as short, but big with portents, as it adopts the coercion and force policy. The closing scenes in Congress point the same way, and war, devastating civil war involving the whole country seems inevitable,—all for the "poor negro." The Cabinet at present seems likely to stand as follows:

Secretary of State—Mr. Seward, of New York.
Secretary of Treasury—Mr. Chase, of Ohio.
Secretary of War—Montgomery Blair, of Md.
Secretary of Navy—Caleb B. Smith, of Indiana.
Secretary of Interior—Mr. Cameron, of Penn.
Paymaster-General—Gideon Welles, of Conn.
Attorney-General—Edward Bates, of Missouri.

This is a War Cabinet, an irrepressible, Chicago Platform Cabinet, and with Lincoln at its head is made up of *six Presidential and Vice Presidential candidates,* each and all of whom were actually voted for at the Chicago Convention. It is emphatically a Wigwam combination of uncompromising Politicians, and irrepressible Black Republicans, bound to carry out a party platform even to the ruin of the country.

The Inaugural today will probably culminate affairs and give notice to all the border conservative States to quit the Union and prepare for war!...

Ethridge, of Tennessee, a Union man and one of the many high-toned Southern gentlemen who have been *talked* of for a place in this Wigwam Cabinet, declares the sentiment which will actuate the Union men in the coming crisis as follows:

> But, sir, if, in an evil hour, led on by rash, inconsiderate, and extreme men, you should attempt, under any pretext, however plausible, to subjugate her, (i.e., South Carolina), or one of her sister States of the South, by force of arms, "At once there'll rise so fierce a yell, As all the fiends from Heaven that fell, Had pealed the banner cry of hell." And she will stand the dread arbitrament of the sword. This, in my opinion, is her position; and in this position, I am proud to say, I concur with my whole heart; but, sir, whatever may be her choice or her fate in this dark hour, I, as one of her sons, will abide it; and, in the language of Ruth to Naomi, say to her: "Whither thou goest I will go; where thou lodgest I will lodge; thy people shall be my people, and thy God my God."

APRIL 5, 1861

Wars and Rumors of Wars

Will there be a fight? That is what everybody is wishing to know. We answer there will be fighting and civil war in its worst forms if there is any pluck in the Administration. There is plenty of pluck on the other side. There is no back out there. The Cotton Confederacy has demanded the evacuation of Fort Sumter, Fort Pickens and all the other Forts now in possession of this Government lying on the Cotton coasts. These Forts it is true were built at great expense from the Treasury of the common people for the defense of our common country. They were considered necessary to the defence of our coast against a foreign enemy. Louisiana, Florida and Texas were acquired mainly on the plea of carrying out the Monroe doctrine, that no foreigner should have military possession of any part of the country. But President Lincoln and President Monroe are two very different individuals. Monroe did not hesitate to declare this doctrine in the face of all the Powers of Europe and to enforce it too, although the Government was then in its infancy. Now, with an unconquerable army and our gallant navy at his command, he abandons Fort Sumter, because it is considered "*impolitic*" to hold it, and he will have to surrender Fort Pickens because he can not help it. Look to the telegraph.

APRIL 6, 1861

Will There Be War?

That is the great question which now agitates the American people from Maine to California. The ingredients necessary for a fight are parties and pluck. There is no want of parties in this case, no want of pluck so far as the Secessionists are concerned, but there must be pluck on both sides to ensure a fight. There is the rub. Now, we have no doubt the Administration policy is this,—*Divide the Republic with as little fighting as possible.* Some fighting will be necessary to convince the people of the necessity of the measure. That fighting will be done and no more. It will be done, not with a view of reuniting the Republic, but of demonstrating the necessity for two republics, slave and free. This is Chase's idea, and in accordance with Lincoln's celebrated declaration that slave and free States could not exist in the Union together.

The President and his advisers are Sectional men. They have obtained their present position by being such. The records of their lives are Sectional and they cannot become National now, without stultifying themselves and losing cast with the party that placed them in power. They never can be anything but Sectional men, Black Republicans, and therefore go for a Black Republican Republic, over which they and their posterity hope to rule.

Depend upon it, this is the policy of the powers that be. The country is sold. The Union is to be divided, and in less than one year the leading men of the Republican Party will advocate it as a political necessity.

Look to Washington!

APRIL 8, 1861

Chicago Fugitives on the Chicago Platform

The Republican Marshal of Illinois has opened his official labors by catching a whole family of fugitives in Chicago and sending them at the rate of a mile a minute, South, all in accordance with the Chicago Platform. Thus the Republicans do with vigor and alacrity just what they hazarded their lives and liberty to prevent the Democratic federal officers from doing. Before taken out of Cleveland, or the fugitive family out of Chicago, but now the U.S. Commissioner at Springfield, Illinois, promptly sends back a whole family. Thus from the very home of Old Abe Lincoln comes the cry of the enforcement of the laws. Who says the Union isn't worth preserving?

Hundreds of fugitive slaves in Chicago, who have made their home there in perfect security, as they fancied, during the Democratic Administration of the Federal Government, have taken to flight, now that the Republicans have commenced the enforcement of the laws, like a flock of black birds at the discharge of a gun. It is suddenly discovered that fugitive slaves can be captured in Chicago in accordance with the Chicago Platform. The negroes were in a high state of excitement, after the Fugitives had been captured, and attempted to massacre one whom they accused of being a traitor, but the police interfered, and beat some of the most excitable of the colored rioters, and captured others who will be held for trial.

KENNETH E. DAVISON

Cleveland During the Civil War

Cleveland's role in the Civil War was a vital part of Ohio's contribution to the war effort. The city not only exceeded its quota of men for the army, but also served as a base for training troops and a center for the collection and distribution of war supplies. After the evacuation of Fort Moultrie on December 26, 1860, a mass meeting at the old Atheneum Hall unanimously adopted resolutions calling upon the state legislature to take measures for the immediate organization of the state militia. Without waiting for state action, several new companies were organized and regular training inaugurated. The fall of Fort Sumter on April 13, 1861, created great excitement in Cleveland. People gathered in meeting halls and on street corners to discuss the solemn news, and the armory was crowded with young men anxious to enlist in response to President Lincoln's call for seventy thousand volunteers.

The Cleveland Grays were the first volunteers to leave the city for the war zone. Mustered into service as Company D, First Ohio Volunteer Infantry on April 16, 1861, they left two days later for Camp Dennison at Cincinnati for an initial three months' service. A few Cleveland business firms offered to continue the salaries of their clerks who enlisted in the Grays. Upon their return, August 2, 1861, they were feted at the Weddell House and many re-enlisted for three years as Company E when Lincoln issued a second call for volunteers.

On April 22, six companies of Cleveland artillery, commanded by Colonel James Barnett, left for Columbus with six guns and caissons. The Hibernian Guards, the Zouave Light Guards, and the Sprague Cadets, all local infantry units, were the next Clevelanders to enter the service, where they quickly lost their identity among larger units. The Civil War laid a heavy hand upon Cleveland manpower. Roughly two-thirds of the city's available men eventually joined the service.

Cleveland took on a military air as recruits arrived at Camp Taylor, hastily established for preliminary training on the county fairgrounds, April 22, 1861. Camp Wood was established in July and Camp Cleveland in August. Camp Wade was moved to the county fairgrounds on October 22, 1861, and merged with Camp Taylor. Camp Brown served as quarters for German regiments until

1863. Thousands of recruits were trained in these Cleveland military posts. Meanwhile, home guards drilled to ensure the safety of the city. Living conditions in the improvised camps were poor at first, but steadily improved as the women of Cleveland collected bedding and mattresses.

Exactly how many Cleveland men served in the armed forces during the Civil War is difficult to determine because they were absorbed into many regiments along with men from the rest of Cuyahoga County and the state of Ohio. Even the Ohio statistics are a matter of dispute. The figure most often cited is that given by Whitelaw Reid, based in turn upon the authority of the United States provost marshall general in his final report to the War Department. Reid put the number of Ohioans in the Civil War service at 310,654, which exceeds Ohio's total wartime quota by 4,332. He did not count re-enlistments, those who enlisted from other states, or those who paid commutation money to escape the draft. By any count, Ohio ranked third among the states, after New York and Pennsylvania, in the number of men furnished for military service, and first among the northern states in proportion to population. The Ohio military contribution involved 230 regiments, 26 independent batteries of artillery, and 5 independent companies of sharpshooters. Ohio troops were called for terms of service lasting three months, one hundred days, six months, one year, or three years. Ohio's Civil War losses totaled 35,475, or nearly 10 percent of all deaths in the Union forces.

Cuyahoga County had a population of 77,616 in 1860, Cleveland accounting for 43,417 of this number. If one estimates that one out of every five persons was available for service, the maximum supply of men in the county would have been about 15,600. Cuyahoga actually furnished roughly 10,000 men or approximately 64 percent of her potential military manpower. Of these, some 1,700 died on the battlefield or in prison, and another 2,000 were crippled or disabled.

Cleveland had volunteers in 77 infantry, 12 artillery, 3 cavalry, and 2 naval units. She furnished 432 officers of infantry, 104 of artillery, 57 of cavalry, 7 of navy, and 21 staff officers—a grand total of 621 commissioned officers.

While the great majority of soldiers were enlisted men, the draft accounted for 8,750 men in Ohio. When the number of volunteers proved insufficient, a drive for recruits began, early in July 1862, to fill the reduced ranks of various regiments. Cuyahoga County commissioners borrowed $50,000 to be paid as bounties of $50 each to recruits. In a further effort to avoid a draft, Cleveland was divided into wards, each with a quota for enlistment. Additional funds were raised, but even a bounty inducement failed to supply enough enlistees at this time.

The first Cleveland draft, in October 1862, lasted six days, with a few wards exempt because they had filled their quotas. Some persons attempted to avoid service. "Men who have been passing for 38 or 39 years of age, have suddenly owned up to 45," it was reported, "while young bucks who have passed with the girls for 20 have shrunk to the other side of 18." As much as $700 was paid by a draftee for a substitute to enter the service. On one occasion, a Cleveland mob destroyed a box containing the names to be drawn for service, but no general resistance to the draft was encountered. A second draft occurred in the city in January 1864. The wards again tried to fill their quotas with volunteers, but only the fourth ward was successful. In the remaining ten wards of the city, 500 men were drafted.

Some fourteen Ohio regiments included 4,630 men from the city. Five other regiments included another 1,012 Clevelanders, while the remaining Cleveland volunteers were widely scattered in many other units. A study of only the regimental histories of the group of nineteen indicates that some Clevelanders participated in virtually every major engagement of the Civil War. They fought at Bull Run, Chancellorsville, and Gettysburg; Shiloh, Chickamauga, and Missionary Ridge; Atlanta, Nashville, and Petersburg. War-weary Cleveland men were in the ranks when Lee surrendered to Grant. Three hundred Clevelanders were killed in action in the Union navy while serving in blockading squadrons on the Atlantic coast or in the ironclad fleet of the Mississippi. . . .

Cleveland was also the scene of two major political meetings early in the Civil War. On May 3, 1861, a conference of governors from states west of New England convened at Angier House at the invitation of Governor Dennison of Ohio. Morgan of New York and Yates of Illinois were too busy to attend and sent agents, who met with Dennison, Morton of Indiana, Curtin of Pennsylvania, Randall of Wisconsin, and Blair of Michigan. The governors were critical of the national administration's inefficiency in raising, organizing, and equipping troops, and its general lack of coordination. At Cleveland, they agreed to address President Lincoln on the need for more men, more efficiency, more enthusiasm, and a concrete plan of campaign. The state executives, closer to the people than the national government, felt that popular enthusiasm should be immediately utilized; they designated Alexander Randall as their spokesman. In the evening, Cleveland citizens gathered outside the Angier House for an impromptu serenade. Mayor Flint introduced Governor Dennison, who in turn presented Curtin, Randall, and Blair to speak. General McClellan wisely declined to address the crowd after so much political oratory.

Lincoln recognized the challenge to his authority as commander in chief posed by the governors' meeting in Cleveland. On May 4, he issued a proclamation through the War Department, dated May 3, 1861, calling for forty regiments of volunteers, increasing the regular army by eight regiments, and asking for eighteen thousand new sailors. The move had two results: (1) state militia were no longer called for ninety days, but for three years, or for the duration of the war, and would be under the president's authority; and (2) governors might commission officers, but the president would direct the army. As the months passed, the governors realized that by this act Lincoln had taken command. The Cleveland Conference of Governors had compelled him to assert his presidential powers.

How much the situation had changed is revealed by the circumstances of a second Cleveland meeting of governors in July 1862. McClellan had been defeated before Richmond in June. To avoid panic, Lincoln asked for more troops in the East, so western armies and Washington, D.C., defenders need not be moved. It was arranged that Secretary of State Seward should meet with the governors and explain Lincoln's plan. The governors should ask Lincoln for 150,000 troops, and the president would issue a call immediately. Meanwhile, Secretary of War Stanton agreed to advance $25 to recruits from the bounty of $100 which they were to receive at the end of their service. Seward persuaded Governor E. D. Morgan of New York and Governor Andrew of Massachusetts to support the plan. This insured success in the East. Seward then returned to Washington on urgent business, but sent Brigadier General C. P. Buckingham, confidential Assistant Adjutant General to Secretary of War Stanton, to meet with western governors in Cleveland on July 4, 1862. He telegraphed Stanton: "Have met Governors Tod (Ohio), Morton (Indiana), Blair (Michigan), and Salomon (Wisconsin), and Temple of Kentucky. All feel right and will do their duty." Lincoln then called for 300,000 troops in order to be sure of enough men.

The people of Cleveland were often subject to rumors of a possible Confederate invasion of the city by way of Canada. War did come close to Cleveland in November 1863, when Canadian refugees and Confederates plotted to free war prisoners on Johnson's Island in Sandusky Bay, take over federal gunboats, and bombard lake cities. The One Hundred and Twenty-Eighth Ohio Volunteers, including three hundred Cleveland men, suppressed the plot by timely action. Secretary of War Stanton, acting on advice from the British minister, Lord Lyons, notified by telegraph Mayor J. N. Masters of Cleveland and ten other lake city executives of this plot. Masters replied quickly: "Have taken the matter before the military committee here and we shall take prompt measures to prevent any invasion of this city." About thirty Confederates armed with revolvers and bowie knives made an abortive move in the vicinity of Johnson's Island on September 19, 1864, by capturing the steamers *Island Queen* and *Parsons*. One of the principal conspirators was caught and jailed immediately. Cleveland authorities were promptly alerted but nothing further transpired. Cleveland proper was never in real danger of raids or full-scale attack during the Civil War....

Although the earliest settlers of Cleveland thought little about slavery, men of Cleveland and the Western Reserve soon became quite outspoken on the subject. Both abolitionists and colonizationists (who believed in sending emancipated slaves to Liberia) resided in the Reserve. Joshua Giddings, a free-soiler, represented Cleveland in Congress from 1843 to 1853, and helped John Quincy Adams in the latter's fight to repeal the gag rule and allow discussion of antislavery proposals. In the fifties, he helped to form the Republican party and to write its first platform. Giddings was an intimate friend and former law student of Elisha Whittlesey, Ohio Whig congressman from Canfield, one of the forgotten first citizens of the Western Reserve. With the exception of Clay, Whittlesey was the most important man from the West in the American Colonization Society, and for a number of years was the chairman of its executive committee. Another important figure was Albert Gallatin Riddle, of Geauga County, who called the first free-soil convention in Ohio. After removing to Cleveland in 1850, he became prosecuting attorney, and later defended the Oberlin slave rescuers (1859) in the famous Oberlin-Wellington case. He was Cleveland's congressman for one term (1861–63). Riddle felt that the free states were equally responsible with the slave states for the existence of slavery in the District of Columbia. In an impassioned speech he urged that the institution be outlawed in the nation's capital.

No mob violence occurred in Cleveland during the Civil War era, although it was threatened once when a runaway slave girl, Sarah Lucy Bagby, was seized by the United States Marshal on January 19, 1861, in the home of L. A. Benton on Prospect Street, where she was employed as a servant. Sympathetic Clevelanders tried unsuccessfully to purchase her freedom. After a hearing, the United States commissioner returned her to her owner to take back to Virginia. A mob gathered at the jail, but to no avail. Sarah Lucy Bagby was the last slave returned from the North under the Fugitive Slave Law.

Strongly abolitionist, the community welcomed the Emancipation Proclamation, and the *Leader* considered it not only a war measure but a death blow to the Confederacy and "a magnificent stride toward the day of Universal Love and Brotherhood." During the Northern Ohio Sanitary Fair of 1864, 2,675 persons signed a petition for general emancipation and an amendment to the federal constitution, and the *Leader* urged the formation of a Women's Loyal League in Cleveland.

EDWARD T. DOWNER

Civil War Prisons: Johnson's Island

In October 1861, Lieutenant Colonel William Hoffman of the Eighth U.S. Infantry was appointed Commissary General of Prisoners in the Department of the Quartermaster General. His first assignment was to establish a new depot for prisoners of war in order to relieve the unsatisfactory and crowded prisons at Fort Warren, Fort Lafayette, Governor's Island, and elsewhere. Quartermaster General M. C. Meigs had suggested the Put-in-Bay Islands in Lake Erie north of Sandusky, Ohio. Hoffman visited the islands but found them unsatisfactory. They lay too close to the Canadian border, they were too remote from the mainland, and the owners of the cleared land were unwilling to give up their vineyards. Instead, Hoffman recommended "an island in Sandusky Bay opposite the city."

The site he proposed was Johnson's Island, three miles north of the city of Sandusky and a half mile south of the Marblehead Peninsula, which, extending in a westerly direction for a distance of fifteen miles, created the fine Sandusky Bay. The island lay not far out in Lake Erie, but in the protected waters of the bay. It consisted of 300 acres of clay and loam soil, from two to eight feet deep, underneath which was solid limestone. Hoffman recommended it because forty acres of land already cleared would afford an excellent site, the fallen timber would serve as fuel, and the camp could be easily supplied from the mainland by boat in the summer and over the ice in the winter. Moreover, he explained, "the proximity of the city [Sandusky] would prevent any possibility of a rising upon the guard." And, finally, one half of the island "can be leased for $500 a year with the entire control of the remainder."

To Southern boys who had never seen snow and who found walking on ice a precarious experience, Johnson's Island presented a frigid and forbidding prospect during the winter months. As one remarked, it "was just the place to convert visitors to the theological belief of the Norwegians that Hell has torments of cold instead of heat." But to the inhabitants of the cities along the shores of Lake Erie—Toledo, Cleveland, and Sandusky—the weather conditions on the island were little different from those to which they were accustomed, and these temperatures could scarcely be called arctic. Meteorological statistics for nearby

Kelley's Island, eight miles north of Johnson's Island, gave the mean temperatures, 1860–64 inclusive, as 32.04 F. for December, 28.08 F. for January, and 29.47 F. for February. The shores and islands in and about Sandusky Bay would be popular summer resort areas for many years. A Confederate prisoner wrote in June 1862, "the lake breezes rob the summer sun of its heat, the view of the city, lake and neighboring islands is fine . . . and altogether it is a salubrious pleasant place." Another added: "Where persons are well protected, in substantial homes, suited to the climate, well fed and clothed, it is a healthy locality."

Plans for the prison were approved and the contract let in November 1861. The work was to be completed by February 1862, at a cost of no more than $30,000. The prison was located on a cleared area of approximately fifteen acres on the southeast shore of the island. The area was surrounded by a plank stockade fourteen feet in height, with four-inch spaces between the upright planks on the bay side. When finally completed, the prisoners' quarters comprised thirteen two-story, barrack-type, frame buildings, each known as a "block," facing each other across a 150-foot street. Each block was 120 feet by 28 feet, designed to accommodate 250 men. Buildings for the garrison were located outside the prison yard.

The buildings were constructed of a single layer of knotty drop lumber nailed to upright beams. Without ceiling or plastering, the warped weatherboards, with cracks in between, offered a thin wall of protection against the bitter winds sweeping across Sandusky Bay. By the winter of 1864–65, however, most of the blocks had been ceiled.

Water was obtained at first from two surface wells, but pipes from the bay were later installed. When the wells became exhausted or when the pipes were frozen, the prisoners carried their water from the bay. Latrines (or "sinks") could be dug only to a depth of five or six feet, for deeper vaults required difficult and expensive blasting through the limestone rock. With no provision for drainage, the shallow vaults quickly filled, and new ones were constantly needed. An inspector reported that most of the space behind the blocks was filled with abandoned sinks, carelessly covered with dirt.

The first prisoners arrived in April 1862. For the first two months the depot received prisoners of all types: officers, enlisted men, and civilian political prisoners. In June, however, by direction of the secretary of war, the commanders of prisoner-of-war posts were instructed to send all officer-prisoners to Sandusky. From that time on, Johnson's Island became virtually an officers' prison, although some forty-fifty civilians and enlisted men could always be found in the stockade. In December 1863, it was reported that there were at the depot 287 general, field, and staff officers and 2,274 company officers.

Prominent among the inmates was Major General Isaac Trimble, who had lost a leg in Pickett's charge at Gettysburg. Among other Gettysburg captives were Brigadier General James J. Archer of A. P. Hill's corps, taken on the first day of the battle, and Colonel Henry Kyd Douglas, at times a staff officer under Stonewall Jackson and Jubal Early. Among other well-known prisoners were Colonel

Charles H. Olmstead, the defender of Fort Pulaski, and Brigadier General J. W. Frazier, who had been forced to surrender at Cumberland Gap on September 9, 1863. Also confined for brief periods were Brigadier General John Marmaduke from Missouri, M. Jefferson (Jeff) Thompson, and some of John Hunt Morgan's officers, seized in the Ohio Raid of 1863. Among the latter was Basil Duke, Morgan's brother-in-law and second in command of the raiders.

Estimates of the total number of officers confined in the forty months during which the prison was in operation vary from ten thousand to fifteen thousand men. In the first twenty months (May 1862, to December 1863, inclusive) 7,371 prisoners were confined at Johnson's Island. The precise number for the subsequent twenty months is not recorded. Yet as this was the most active period in the history of the depot, it can be assumed that the number added during this time was near to that of the previous twenty months. Conservatively, at least twelve thousand Confederate officers were unwilling guests at Johnson's Island.

The population varied widely from month to month. In the first months the number of prisoners increased until the cartel agreement on prisoner exchange was adopted, after which it declined to as low as seventy-three in May 1863. With the collapse of the cartel and the consequent stoppage of exchanges, the number of inmates again began to rise. During the twenty-four months from July 1863 to June 1865, the minimum occupancy was 1,710 and the maximum 3,256, with a general monthly average of 2,549.

Four of the buildings, or "blocks," which housed the prisoners were divided into small, comfortable, ceiled rooms. The remaining nine buildings were partitioned into two large rooms below and three above, with a small room attached to each for cooking purposes. Arranged along the walls were three tiers of bunks, each bunk accommodating two men. At the end of the room were a number of plank mess tables, each designed for ten men. The single room served as a living room, mess hall, storeroom for clothes and rations, and a sleeping apartment. In September 1864, two mess halls and a wash house were built on the recommendation of an inspector who described the unsanitary conditions resulting from cooking, eating, storing rations, and washing in the living quarters.

Each room was provided with a wood-burning stove, which one prisoner stated, "kept the room fairly comfortable within a certain range, except in very cold weather." The prisoners all complained of suffering from the cold in the winter, particularly during a bitter January 1864, when on at least two days the thermometer fell to twenty-five degrees below zero. The wood which was supplied was green and not sufficient to keep fires burning. At this time General Trimble protested in writing to the commander of the post that "in my own room we have been many hours without fire."

The only ventilation was by means of windows insufficient in number for the fifty-eighty men packed in each room. In the summer months, the prisoners sought air by cutting small holes in the walls near their heads, to which the commissary general of prisoners objected—although he conceded the need "to make openings for ventilation."

Bunks were supplied with straw ticks, and each prisoner was given a blanket if he did not have enough of his own. In 1863, at least, additional blankets were issued upon complaint "so that each bunk for two men has an average of three blankets." In 1864 it was reported that "all have blankets," but early in 1865 the superintendent of the prison complained of a "deficiency of blankets." Moreover, in the winter of 1864–65, he reported "half of the prisoners without straw" because the "quartermaster's stores had not come forward sufficiently before navigation was closed by ice." Evidently, it was the policy of the commissary general of prisoners to keep the prisoners warm, but there were frequent gaps between policy and performance.

Prisoners were permitted to receive clothes from friends and relatives, provided the cloth was gray and the design was not in the nature of a uniform. Moreover, they could purchase clothes from the sutler as long as his store was in operation. Those who had no means of obtaining clothes themselves, or through relatives, were issued extra clothing by the quartermaster—but only "if recommended by the medical officers." In the cold of January 1864, an inspector noted that "few complain seriously of having insufficient clothes, although all need and should be supplied with overcoats." But prisoners later told of insufficient blankets and clothing for men unaccustomed to cold weather, especially those without funds or generous friends and therefore subject to the whims of their captors.

From 1862 to early 1864, the quantity and quality of the food was satisfactory both to prisoners and to federal inspectors. In fact, at one time the rations were ordered reduced because they were found to be too ample for men leading sedentary lives. The savings from these withheld issues were applied to the purchase of stoves and to the prison fund, which was used primarily to furnish the men with tobacco, stamps, and stationery. Late in 1863, General William Orme, a prison inspector, wrote that "the supply of food is abundant and of good quality, the bread being good wheat bread." To supplement the monotonous army ration, prisoners were permitted to receive boxes of food from friends and relatives, and to purchase supplies from not only the prison sutler but outside sources as well. One Confederate wrote: "Our men having plenty of money live as well in the way of eating as we ever did." Another man, confined from October 1863 to February 1864, gave a similarly good report of fare at Johnson's Island. "The food we received . . . was not, except at times, such as a prisoner had a right to complain of."

In the spring of 1864, however, a radical change took place. Rations were reduced sharply and heavy restrictions were placed on purchases. The sutler's store was removed, along with the liberty of purchasing supplies from mainland firms. Regulations went into effect even limiting the written requests sent to relatives for food. "I remember," one prisoner stated, that the new daily ration "consisted of a loaf of bread and a small piece of fresh meat. Coffee was unknown." He added that as a result of months of hunger, his weight dropped from 140 to 100 pounds. The September 1864 diary of another prisoner contained the following note: "Rats are found to be very good for food, and every night many are cap-tured and slain."

In November, three Southern physicians who were serving as prisoner-surgeons at the depot petitioned the commander of the post for an increase in the ration. A statistical check, they pointed out, showed that the ration issued to a prisoner was six ounces less than that required under the orders of the com-missary general of prisoners, and that "instances are not infrequent of repulsive articles being greedily devoured—rats, spoiled meat, bones, bread from the slops, etc." The post commander asked for permission to allow prisoners to purchase vegetables, but Washington denied the request, except in cases "when they are necessary as antiscorbutics."

This more rigorous treatment of the Johnson Island prisoners cannot be ex-plained on the grounds of any shortage in the available food supply, inadequate transportation facilities, or lack of funds. The changes coincide in time, how-ever, with the widely circulated atrocity stories about the ill treatment of Union soldiers in Southern prison camps. Therefore, one finds it easy to believe that these harsh measures were in response to the public clamor for retaliation, or at least as insurance against the coddling of Rebel prisoners. Writing in July, the commissary general of prisoners asserted: "It is not expected that anything more will be done to provide for the welfare of Rebel prisoners that is absolutely nec-essary."

The policing of the prison was a constant problem. Acting Medical Director Charles T. Alexander wrote: "Seeing the camp, you would not know whether to be most astounded at the inefficiency of the officer in charge of the prisoners' camp or disgusted that men calling themselves gentlemen should be willing to live in such filth." Filth appears to have been the condition everywhere. As the barracks rooms served for the storing and cooking of food, as well as for the washing of clothes, everything was greasy and "dirty soap-suds met you on every turn." A nauseating stench permeated the air, rising from overflowing sinks, un-collected garbage around the kitchens, and open drains clogged with slop. The flat country offered little natural drainage, and dirty conditions are referred to in every inspection report.

Prisoners offered the scarcity of water as an excuse for these conditions; prison officials explained them on the grounds that "the prisoners being nearly all offi-cers makes it difficult to obtain the necessary amount of 'dirty work' from them." Trimble protested to the post commander that such degrading duties as digging sinks and loading garbage by officers were "contrary to the usages of war among civilized nations," and pointed out that such menial tasks were not inflicted on federal officer-prisoners in Richmond. One prisoner recalled that even sawing fuel wood was a fatiguing duty, "not that there was much to saw, but that most of us were not used to it."

While these proud Southern officers were reluctant to perform such fatigue duty, they showed remarkable ingenuity in manufacturing articles of all kinds. As an escape from prison ennui, they fashioned rings from gutta-percha and charms from shells picked up along the beach. One prisoner made a violin from material gathered from the woodpile. Each man seems to have built a chair for himself on which he carved his name, the number of his regiment, and the state from which he came. Many of these chairs were not just of the rustic type, but were quite artistic, some having split bottoms made from leather from old boots, cut into strings and neatly interwoven. Their only tool was a jackknife. The smaller articles furnished a cash return to the manufacturer when sold on the outside (with the camp guards serving as middlemen).

For exercise and recreation, the prisoners had the free use of the yard between the barracks buildings. "The prisoners nearly every evening are engaged in a game they call 'base ball' which notwithstanding the heat they prosecute with persevering energy," one man noted. "I don't understand the game but those who play it get very much excited over it." Snowball fights occupied the winter months. In one notable battle, Isaac Trimble commanded one of the sides and Jeff Thompson the other. Unfortunately, the outcome of the engagement is not recorded, although it is known that Thompson was taken prisoner but subsequently exchanged.

Those less athletically inclined passed the monotonous hours by playing cards and chess, reading, and singing. In the summer of 1864, a number worked small gardens. They were permitted to receive any books except geographies, military histories, or military treatises. By pooling their individual collections, they were able to operate a circulating library of from "500 to 800" books, magazines, and novels.

In describing a typical day in his prison life, one prisoner wrote: "Then the newspapers came in, the *Sandusky Register,* a dirty, falsifying sheet, as black with Abolitionism as Erebus; *New York Herald,* and *Cincinnati Enquirer.*" From friends they received copies of Southern papers. This privilege caused some concern to the prison authorities, as the prisoners expressed overwhelming preference for this "disloyal" material. There was no limit to the number of letters they could write or receive, but in the interest of censorship the length of the letters was restricted to one page.

Those musically inclined organized a minstrel band which they named the "Rebellonians"; and those with histrionic talent were able to join the "Thespians." The latter group staged a performance entitled "The Battle of Gettysburg," which enjoyed a successful run of three weeks.

Despite the unsanitary conditions of the camp, the health record among the prisoners was reasonably good. The medical services were under the direction of Dr. T. Woodbridge, described as a "man of no mean professional ability" with a "kind and gentle temper," but not well fitted "to force obedience to his orders in the proper conduct of the hospital or in the sanitary management of the camp." Nevertheless, the few comparative figures available indicate that the general health of the Johnson's Island prisoners was considerably better than was that of those in most of the other Union prisoner-of-war posts.

In November 1863, Johnson's Island lost 16 men by death out of 2,381; in this same month, Camp Morton at Indianapolis lost 40 men out of 2,831. From the date of opening in April 1862, through December 1863, Johnson's Island had a death rate of only 2 percent (127 of 6,410 prisoners). When contrasted with a comparable 8.4 percent for the infamous Fort Delaware, or the 4.5 percent at Point Lookout, this percentage is extremely low. The record for 1864–65 appears to have been even better, with only ninety-four deaths in twenty months.

The total number of deaths during the whole life of the Johnson's Island prison was 221 from among approximately 12,000 men. The commander of the post estimated that 90 percent of the deaths were caused by pneumonia, typhoid fever, camp fever, and dysentery. During 1862–63, twenty-six cases of smallpox resulted in four deaths. In one of his reports, Chief Surgeon Woodbridge called attention to the obvious fact that many of the prisoners arrived at the camp "with their health impaired by previous disease, exposure, and bad diet."

The hospital contained beds for sixty-eight patients; only in the fall of 1863 was it crowded. During the months from September to December of that year, the health conditions were at their worst. The hospital was filled to overflowing and the deaths numbered fifty-nine, which was more than one-fourth of the total for the entire forty months of operation. Except for this period, the sick reports show never more than sixty-two hospital patients in any one month. In January 1865, at which time the number of prisoners reached the maximum, the number on the sick list was only fifty-seven men.

Even before the prison was completed, William S. Pierson, a Yale graduate and the mayor of Sandusky, was placed in charge. Though not a military man, he was commissioned first a major and then a lieutenant colonel. As soon as it was decided to establish the depot, the governor of Ohio was requested by the secretary of war to "raise for the service of the United States a select company of volunteers for duty as a guard." Four companies were recruited and organized; and these 400 men, called the "Hoffman Battalion," served as the guard from the spring of 1862 until January 1864, when six more companies were added. Having reached full regimental strength, the ten companies became the 128th Ohio Volunteer Infantry. The unit remained at Johnson's Island as the principal guard until July 10, 1865, when the prison was virtually closed. During the first two years the "Hoffman Battalion" was led by Lieutenant Colonel Pierson. Upon reaching full regimental size, the unit was placed under the command of Colonel Charles W. Hill, who had seen field service in western Virginia and had been adjutant general of Ohio.

Although one prisoner wrote that "the officers and guards with rare exception, were civil and considerate," General Trimble complained to the post commander that "our officers have been frequently 'fired on' by day and night." Trimble's complaint appears to have been well founded, for the prison reports mention the wounding by the sentries of a number of prisoners and the killing of at least two. Much of the shooting seems to have been caused by two rules: no visiting between wards after 9:00 p.m., and all lights out after 10:00 p.m. A prisoner told of the shooting and killing of one lieutenant. "Hearing retreat sounded, he started to his room. The sentinel fired and killed him." Another wrote that "on one or two occasions drunken sentinels on post fired into wards through weather boards at candles that had been lighted." One rule which caused the prisoners a good deal of discomfort was a prohibition against more than two men visiting the privies at a time. Another source of irritation was the row of stakes, thirty feet from the stockade, that marked the "deadline" beyond which they were forbidden to take a single step even to avoid the mud.

Johnson's Island was separated from the nearest mainland by a half-mile of water in the summer, solid ice in the winter, and soft ice floes in the spring and fall. Confronted by such a seemingly impassable obstruction, only the boldest dared attempt escape. In his final report, the commissary general of prisoners gave twelve as the entire number of escapees from Johnson's Island, which, compared with other Union prisons, was an excellent security record. Fort Delaware, another island prison, reported fifty-two escapes.

Attempted escapes were more frequent during the winter months when the ice was firm, and cold guards huddled in their sentry boxes. However, a successful winter escape required luck in scaling, unnoticed, the fourteen-foot stockade, the stamina to negotiate a half-mile-long trek across the rough ice in the pitch darkness, and finally, the ability to elude the unfriendly civilians who populated the area. Few places existed in that bleak enemy country where grayclad Rebels could find shelter or guidance. A number of prisoners, dressed in blue uniforms, simply walked out of the big gate with fatigue details or garrison soldiers. Helpful comrades always delayed detection by answering roll call for the absentees.

It was not the fear of escape by individual prisoners, but rather organized revolts among the prisoners (with help from Confederate sympathizers in nearby Canadian ports) that kept the prison authorities in a constant state of alarm. For example, the post had been in operation but a few weeks when, on June 18, 1862, Adjutant General Lorenzo Thomas sent a warning to the post commander: "A scheme is reported to be on foot in Canada by Southern sympathizers to release the prisoners on the island. Be on your guard." Major Pierson, the post commandant, replied with information that the prisoners had a military organization, were planning to revolt, and "will have abundance of transportation from Canada." In a rationalizing postscript he added: "There was no dissatisfaction with their treatment which creates this disposition, but it is the result of the restless spirit of a set of very bad rebels." A company of federal soldiers rushed to the island from Camp Chase to meet this emergency, which proved false.

In November 1863, Lord Lyons, British ambassador to the United States, notified Washington that a plot was on foot to surprise Johnson's Island, release the prisoners, and proceed with them in an attack on Buffalo. Great excitement swept all along the lower Great Lakes region. General Jacob D. Cox, commanding the Ohio Military District, hastened to Sandusky from his Cincinnati headquarters. He ordered up two batteries of artillery and placed them on Cedar Point, a peninsula from which the guns could command the entrance to Sandusky Bay. Governor David Tod rushed six companies to the Twelfth Ohio Cavalry (dismounted) to Sandusky, and the Navy Department moved the U.S.

Steamer *Michigan* (fourteen guns) to Johnson's Island. Presumably, the plotters were frustrated by this display of military strength; in any event, the rumored attack did not materialize.

The fear of a hostile move from Canada continued for some time afterward. In the following January, five regiments of the Third Division, Sixth Army Corps, were assigned to duty at Sandusky. With this addition the garrison numbered 2,238 men, which was greater than the number of prisoners confined at the time. The troops not only built fortifications and maintained defenses against outside attacks by both land and water, but also performed picket duty and guarded prisoners.

The long-anticipated attack from Canada erupted at last in September 1864. On September 19, the assistant provost marshal at Detroit informed Captain John C. Carter, commanding the U.S. Steamer *Michigan*, that "parties will embark today at Malden [on the Canadian side of the Detroit River] on board the *Philo Parsons*." He added an assurance that officers and men of the *Michigan* had been bribed by a man named Cole.

The provost marshal's information was to a degree correct. On the morning of September 19, a detail of thirty paroled or escaped Confederate soldiers and sailors, armed with revolvers and bowie knives, took passage on the steamer *Philo Parsons*, which plied the Lake Erie islands. At Kelley's Island they seized the vessel and with it set forth for Middle Bass. Soon they met and took over the *Island Queen*, another passenger boat, which they sank after discharging the passengers (thirty-five of whom were unarmed Ohio militiamen). That night they stood on the deck of the *Philo Parsons* at Middle Bass Island and looked across the water for a rocket signal from the gunboat *Michigan*, which lay a few miles away. At the signal they were to board and capture the *Michigan*.

The rocket was to be set off on orders from one Charles H. Cole, a Confederate agent charged with the job of laying the groundwork at Sandusky and Johnson's Island. For weeks he had been living in Sandusky, posing as a Philadelphia banker, although he was actually a paroled officer from Bedford Forrest's cavalry. With lavish entertainments he had won his way into the good graces of the officers at Sandusky and those on the steamer *Michigan*, and so had been a frequent and a welcome visitor both at the prison and on the *Michigan*. The action at Sandusky was to open with a gala dinner to the officers of the *Michigan* aboard the ship. The event was scheduled for the same evening that the attacking party on the *Philo Parsons* would be arriving at nearby Middle Bass. The host was to be Charles Cole; a number of landlubber guests would be his accomplices. With the ship's officers paralyzed from drugged champagne, the signal to the *Parsons* would bring the boarding party and the *Michigan* would be a prize of the Confederate States of America.

On that same evening, members of Ohio copperhead organizations were to arrive by train at Sandusky. They were to seize the arsenal, then arm themselves and the prisoners on Johnson's Island. Attacked by land and water, with a prisoners' revolt from within, the prison guard would be overwhelmed and the prisoners released. A Confederate army made up of Northern copperheads and Rebel officers, assisted by the only armed vessel on the lower Great Lakes, would soon be marching to capture and sack the cities along the shores of Lake Erie.

This fantastic scheme proved to be a miserable fiasco. The conspirators were betrayed into the hands of the U.S. provost marshal in Detroit, who sent warnings to the authorities at Sandusky. Cole was arrested at his hotel in the afternoon. There was no dinner on the *Michigan,* and consequently no rocket. Seeing no signal, the men on the *Philo Parsons* suspected that the plot had been discovered. They lost their nerve and compelled John Yates Beall, their leader, to sail back to Canada. Trains arriving at Sandusky were thoroughly searched, but the expected companies of fighting men were nowhere to be found.

Although Cole, on his visits to Johnson's Island, must have tipped off the leaders among the prisoners, no disturbance occurred within the prison walls that evening. The superintendent of the prison did not even mention the incident in his weekly report, being much more concerned about a severe windstorm which a few days later unroofed some of the blocks and injured a number of the prisoners.

Reasons existed for these frequent alarms about incursions from Canada. Confederate Commissioners Jacob Thompson and Clement C. Clay were active in organizing Southern sympathizers north of the border. Amply supplied with funds, they were in close alliance with the leaders of secret Ohio disloyal organizations, said to number over one hundred thousand men. These activities, however, turned out to be only sound and fury, and resulted in nothing. No effective force was ever mobilized in Canada, and the Ohio disloyalists confined their efforts only to sub rosa meetings, drilling, and oath taking. At no time was the security of Johnson's Island prisoners ever in serious jeopardy.

Much of the wretchedness at Johnson's Island can be traced to shortsighted planning at the outset. In the winter of 1861–62, when the prison was being designed and constructed, a mammoth army assembled at Washington to advance on Richmond and crush the Southern rebellion. Hence, like so much of Civil War planning, the Johnson's Island project was in the nature of an expedient, intended to be temporary and inexpensive. The jerry-built quality of the buildings (void of foundations) clearly indicates that the camp was not intended for any lengthy service. The nearby fallen trees, it was thought, would furnish ample fuel during the brief life of the prison, and the owner of the island would be glad to collect the kitchen scraps to feed his hogs.

Contrary to all expectations, the frail, cheap, and hastily built structures were forced to stand against the fierce northern Ohio gales of three long winters. A camp planned to accommodate 1,000 prisoners was later to house several times that number. Prisoners who were to be held only for a few weeks pending exchange were compelled to remain for from twelve to sixteen months, and in some cases longer. The small garrison of 400 men grew into a force of 2,200—

two regiments in size. With the departure of the last inhabitants in July 1865, the anticipated short-lived Johnson's Island depot for prisoners of war had had a long and lively existence of forty months.

Prisoners were the helpless victims of laxity in the operation of Johnson's Island. Seldom if ever were all of the camp facilities in full working order. The quarters and grounds were never properly policed, supplies were constantly short, the beef was often rancid, and the fuel wood was green. The water pipes were frequently frozen or out of order, and the sanitation problems were never solved.

William S. Pierson, who commanded the post until supplanted in January 1864, was a loyal, conscientious officer, yet a man with no military training. With a small staff and a meager working force, he was responsible for the guarding and disciplining of the prisoners, the maintenance of the buildings and grounds, and for all commissary and quartermaster services. Such a demand called for a versatility rare among even experienced field officers.

Brigadier General H. D. Terry of the Sixth Army Corps, who succeeded Pierson, showed little enthusiasm for his prison assignment. As Lieutenant Colonel John Marsh commented in an inspection report: "General Terry is an intelligent, clever gentleman, but quite as fond of a social glass of whiskey as of attending to the duties of his command." He then added that "little judgment is exercised in the management and discipline of the prison." Colonel Charles W. Hill, who commanded during the busy period of 1864 and early 1865, complained to Washington of his "enormous amount of work." He called attention to his many duties in disciplining and instructing troops and prisoners, and "policing, building, road-making, draining, and repairs."

In an apparent effort to achieve a more efficient operation, the commissary general of prisoners, in the spring of 1864, ordered the appointment of a superintendent of the prison, who was required to submit weekly reports on the condition of the prison and prisoners. If inspections and reports could accomplish perfection, Johnson's Island would have been an ideal institution. It was visited, inspected, and reported on almost continually. Army medical officers wrote detailed accounts of their findings, listed deficiencies, and recommended improvements—despite the fact that few of their recommendations resulted in any positive action.

Washington would allow the local authorities very little discretion. This policy of remote control engendered inevitable delays, frustrations, and misunderstandings. Authority to move a section of the stockade a few paces, allowing prisoners to purchase potatoes and onions from the sutler, permitting crippled and sick prisoners to eat in their quarters—all such minor matters required Washington's approval. The request of a Sandusky priest to visit the camp to minister to the spiritual needs of Catholic prisoners could be granted only upon a permit from the commissary general's headquarters in Washington. The occupants of some of the blocks offered to provide the labor and materials for lining the thin walls of their wards with ceiling. While they received the hearty approval of the commander of the post, the commissary general vetoed the proposal on the ground that "to put the requisite tools and lumber in the hands of the prisoners would much facilitate their efforts to escape." He suggested that the cracks between the boards "be closed up with a plaster of clay."

Constantly in the minds of the authorities was the necessity for economy, for they were always fearful of public criticism if any large expenditures were made for the comfort of Confederate prisoners. Even in the initial planning, one of the important considerations for locating the prison on Johnson's Island was the fact that the land could be rented for the mere sum of $500 a year, while the cost of building the project was only a few thousand dollars. Orders issued at a later date by the commissary general specified that the structures "must be of a temporary and cheap character." In over three years, the only additions and improvements introduced consisted of a slight enlargement of the prison area and lining the walls of some of the blocks, two new mess halls, a wash house, and an extra water pump. Ironically, surrounded by Lake Erie, the water supply was inadequate, a constant source of complaint by the prisoners, and the subject of comment by many inspectors. A reservoir supplying clear water pumped from the bay could have been installed for a meager $7,000. Such a water system would have solved the difficulties of sanitation and would have provided an ample supply of water with which the buildings and their occupants could have been kept clean. But no one seemed to have the courage or the initiative to endorse such a large outlay of funds, even though the project could have been financed from the prison fund.

There was misery aplenty on Johnson's Island, but the prison certainly was far from being the worst of Civil War compounds. The health record was good and, up to the last few months of 1864, the food ration was sufficient and could be supplemented by private purchases. The prisoners, especially those from the Deep South, found their quarters cold. Yet they were as comfortable as members of the garrison, some of whom were housed in tents. The men were given as much freedom as security would permit. They engaged in many recreational activities, were able to obtain reading material, and to receive letters and newspapers from home. Except in a few cases, they were not ill treated by their captors. On the other hand, being ordered about by Yankee privates must have been humiliating to those proud officers. "Our rolls," wrote one prisoner, "are called by a sergeant of eighteen years of age, who, with an impudent air, orders, 'Fall in, boys, I'm in a hurry,' and this to his seniors in age, rank, position, and everything that constitutes a man, soldier, and gentleman."

Most of the time the physical discomforts of the prisoners were caused primarily by bad management, not design, on the part of the authorities. But their greatest distress was not so much physical as it was mental. The mere fact of being restricted to an isolated island far from civilian life must have been depressing in itself. Moreover, the southerners were in a harsh, strange climate, far different from that of their beloved and sunny homeland. Their minds were filled with thoughts of home and friends, the dull routine of prison life offering little else to think about. Even good food and a comfortable bed would not have cured the agonies of homesickness—and, underneath, was a deep-seated restlessness nourished by a feeling of frustration in being so useless to the cause in which they believed.

Today Johnson's Island is a lonely but lovely spot with no permanent inhabitants, although efforts are being made to develop it into a summer resort. Time has obliterated all traces of the prison buildings, the stockade, and block houses. The only memory of sad Civil War days is the little cemetery near the northeast point of the island. The cemetery covers an acre of ground, shaded on one side by a beautiful grove of trees. This grassy plot, surrounded by an iron fence, holds the graves of 206 Confederate soldiers and a few enlisted men who died on the island while prisoners of war. Each grave is marked by a headstone of Georgian marble on which is carved the name of the soldier and that of his regiment, except for a few who are unknown. At the entrance, on a marble base, stands the bronze figure of a Confederate private soldier, peering out over the waters of the bay. This statue, unveiled in 1910 and named "The Outlook," is the creation of Sir Moses Ezekial, world-famous Richmond sculptor who also designed the well-known figure of Stonewall Jackson on the campus of the Virginia Military Institute in Lexington, Virginia.

After the war the cemetery was greatly neglected, except when it was cleaned up for Memorial Day exercises, which for years were conducted by the Sandusky McMeans Post of the G.A.R. In 1889 a party of editors and public officials from Georgia visited the island. They found the wooden grave markers rotting away with the names rapidly being effaced. By private subscription they obtained the funds out of which they had the present marble headstones carved and placed on the graves. The cemetery is now the property of the United States government and is maintained by the Department of the Interior.

Building the Railroads

Before the canal system in Ohio was well under way, men were already talking about railroads. They continued to talk about them for a generation. The canals were serviceable but slow—eighty hours from Cleveland to Portsmouth. Reckless drivers of stagecoaches had been known to reach a speed of eight miles per hour. Imaginative men like the citizens of Sandusky and of Cleveland looked into the future and predicted that the time would come when trains would hurtle across the surface of Ohio at a speed of fifteen miles an hour. One Ohio city refused to allow a debate on this issue in 1828 with the simple statement, "If God had designed that his intelligent creatures should travel at a frightful rate of fifteen miles an hour, by steam he would have told it through His holy pamphlet. It is a device of Satan to lead immortal souls down to Hell." Twenty years later trains out of Sandusky actually ran sixteen miles per hour.

Sandusky had taken the lead in railroad-mindedness among Reserve towns. It had lost its strong bid for the lake terminus of one of the canals. These had gone to Cleveland and to Toledo. Toledo likewise had the first railroad in the west—a thirty-three-mile-long stub of oak track to Adrian, Michigan, opened in 1836. Not wishing to be completely bypassed in this internal development of Ohio, Sandusky men sponsored the idea of a railroad running south between the two canals to the Ohio River via Bellevue, Tiffin, Carey, Kenton, and Springfield. There it would join the Little Miami Railroad and achieve through-service to Cincinnati. They got a charter from the legislature on New Year's Day 1832 for the enterprise, which they named the Mad River and Lake Erie Railroad. The proposal created excitement and enticed subscribers to buy its bonds. One of them was Ralph Waldo Emerson, who invested some of his lecture money in the venture.

Amid great festivities the first earth was ceremoniously turned in September 1832. However, the beginning was premature. The 1830s were difficult years, culminating in the great panic of 1837 when many of our citizens were on a dole of a shovelful of potatoes for a week's allowance. Nonetheless the Sandusky people kept at work, and by 1839 they had a few miles of usable track. By 1841 they had succeeded in pushing their rails back across the low ground south of Sandusky, following an old fur trader's trail through the forest walls and up over the old beach ridges to Bellevue, a distance of sixteen miles. In that year there were only thirty-six miles of railroad in Ohio. The rails were sawed white oak with a thin strap of iron spiked to the surface. The construction was crude; the ends of these iron straps would work loose, and sometimes actually jab through the floor of the cars and injure a passenger.

By 1842 the road was opened to Tiffin. Charles Dickens, that year, after his most unhappy stagecoach trip from Columbus to Upper Sandusky, during which he thought he would be killed or at least have most of his bones broken, was pleased to board the cars at Tiffin for the rest of the journey to the lake. In his *American Notes* he wrote, "At two o'clock we took the railroad; the traveling on which was very slow, its construction being indifferent, and the ground wet and marshy; and arrived at Sandusky in time to dine that evening." Recalling Read's journey south from Sandusky by stagecoach, we note the improvement in travel. The citizens of Cleveland waited another seven years to see the first train enter their city.

In the 1846 edition of Henry Howe's *History of Ohio*, enlivened by nearly two hundred of his own quaint sketches of people, towns, and roads, there are but two pictures of trains—one in Xenia and the other at Kenton. The Mad River Line, still inching its way south, had just reached Kenton. Howe shows a tiny, wood-burning engine drawing four small, four-wheeled cars through the village. The engine had been shipped by canal and lake from the East to the port at Sandusky. All the early locomotives had names like ships. This one was called the *Sandusky*. It was the first to run in the Reserve. The directors were so proud of it that they fired its boiler and blew its whistle for hours, even though no track was ready for it to run on when it arrived in July 1838. Those in use on the Cincinnati end of the line—the Little Miami Railroad—had come up the river by way of New Orleans. These two roads made connection late in 1846; they provided a more rapid 211-mile route from Lake Erie to the Ohio River.

Not content with this progress, the enterprising Sandusky men planned and began construction on another route cutting through the richer wheatlands of the Reserve by way of Monroeville to Mansfield, a distance of fifty-six miles. The road reached Mansfield in 1846 with one accommodation and one express train each day. On January 8, 1851, it entered Newark. Sandusky, for this achievement, received the high distinction of editorial acclaim from her rival Cleveland. The *Daily True Democrat* wrote, "Sandusky deserves every praise. No city of her size has shown more enterprise or done more." It was largely through the efforts of Sandusky that the miles of track in Ohio had lengthened from 36 in 1841 to 299 in 1850.

Cleveland seemed to many people to have gone to sleep. The newspapers of the era are constantly enlivened with indignant or ironical outbursts from their readers. They say it is time for Cleveland to stop talking and build roads. When the Mad River and the Little Miami railroads met, one citizen wrote wryly that Clevelanders could now go from the lake to Cincinnati by rail—by sailing over to Sandusky City to catch the train! The temper of the Clevelanders may be gauged by this flavored item from the *Daily True Democrat* on April 4, 1848:

> Not far from this city may be seen, and could have been during all the past winter, a solitary man, with pickaxe and spade, digging into the bowels of the earth. Every now and then he would raise his eyes to the task before him and groan in agony. And, reader, what do you think is his object? Why, he is building a railroad from Cleveland to Columbus! Poor fellow! To keep the charter alive, he is obliged to labor on without "cessation." Surely the prospect brightens; and the citizens of Cleveland may soon expect to ride to the Capital on a railroad.

These criticisms were, as they usually are, quite unjust. They ignored the gigantic risks, as well as the difficulties of finance, right of way, charters, management, and materials faced by the sponsors. They did not know how earnestly and farsightedly the Cleveland leaders were working on these problems. But they did know, of course, about the stupendous failures already made in a day when there were no precedents or experience to serve as a guide, when each venture had to learn about railroad building the bitter way.

While Sandusky was putting down track to link itself with Cincinnati, Cleveland had built what it optimistically and generously called the Cleveland and Newburgh Railroad. It was opened for traffic in 1838. It ran from a stone quarry near the present Adelbert College, down Euclid Avenue to the Public Square. The road was nothing more than a tramway down a rutted, dusty, or mud-soggy street. The grandiose charter authorized this great railroad to carry passengers and freight "by the power and force of steam, animals, or other mechanical force, or by a combination of them." Two horses, as a matter of fact, furnished the propulsive force. And two trips a day exhausted all the demand for transport. A single passenger-coach accommodated all the passengers. The freight was stone and lumber which was dumped into the Public Square. The road was soon abandoned, but the ties and rails lay in the street and rotted in the mud. It was an inauspicious beginning for the rail center of the Reserve.

The Reserve had also witnessed the catastrophe of a second undertaking in which its citizens lost heavily. This was the mad scheme to build the Ohio Railroad on stilts. The story reads like a concoction in some juvenile romance, but it is a matter of record and may be read in detail in C. P. Leland's Western Reserve tract, *The Ohio Railroad: That Famous Structure Built on Stilts*. A group of sixteen prominent citizens, including John W. Allen, P. M. Weddell, Rice Harper, Eliphalet Austin, Charles C. Paine, and Herman Ely, organized the company at Painesville in April 1836. They thought they could avoid the heavy expense of grading and graveling a railroad bed by placing the tracks on two rows of piles driven into the ground and sawed off to grade. The new road would run from the eastern edge of the Reserve to the mouth of the Maumee River. Two great trade centers would be built, one on the Grand River near present Fairport, and the other on the Maumee.

The legislature granted them a charter and extraordinary privileges. They could issue money like a bank—and they did, with a loss of several hundred thousand dollars to the holders of their paper. They were also granted the backing of state credit—with a loss to Ohio of $249,000. The ease with which the company got pledges of support of almost two million dollars indicates the spirit of speculation of the age. The people were so eager for transportation that they willingly believed that any scheme, however fanciful, to move people or goods through the mud and forests would certainly succeed.

The engineering on the road was also in keeping with the vigorous but blundering imagination of the 1830s. A pile driver with a half-ton iron hammer pounded the two rows of poles into the ground. A circular saw cut the tops off at the proper height. A sawmill followed along behind the pile drivers preparing stringers eight by eight inches and fifteen feet long for the rails. These were laid on crossties held in place by cedar pins. Iron straps were laid on the stringers. Workmen labored away on this contraption west of Fremont and in the Reserve between Cleveland and Huron, while the management worried through the panic of 1837 and the mounting troubles that brought on the complete collapse in 1843. For its pains and its money the Reserve got fifteen miles of stilts which rotted so slowly that they continued to stick up out of the ground like grim tombstones through the next half century.

These experiences, however, did not stifle the energies of the Reserve. The ambitious villages in the interior—Ravenna, Hudson, Jefferson, Medina, Elyria—continued to cry for outlet. Few people were thinking of a continental network of railroads. They were still in the stage of trying to connect their own towns and counties with a Lake Erie port, the Ohio River, or the canal. In Ohio their thoughts ran north and south rather than from east to west. Cleveland, as the center of the Reserve, was the logical terminal and natural leader. Why, they demanded again, doesn't Cleveland do something?

Cleveland was doing something. The papers kept announcing still another meeting to be held in the courthouse to discuss ways and means. Good men were formulating the plans. There was John W. Allen, that prominent and tireless public servant of the city, whom we have already met as banker. Despite his connection with the two railroads just mentioned, he was one of the leaders in the proposal for a railway to Columbus and Cincinnati, and became president of the C.C. & C. There was Henry B. Payne, one of Cleveland's leading citizens. He had come out from Hamilton, New York, in 1832 as a young lawyer. Interested in all sorts of enterprises, he was a director or stockholder in eighteen companies. He worked with Allen for city improvement and public waterworks. Payne married a Cleveland girl, the daughter of Nathan Perry, the son of one of the first Reserve families and owner of large areas of Cleveland and Lake County real estate. He served as a director of the proposed C.C. & C. Railroad. There was Leonard Case, who became president of this railroad. As a boy he had migrated to a farm in the Reserve near Warren. He had been crippled by illness, but went on to become a surveyor, land agent, and a lawyer. He came up to

Cleveland in 1816. He became president of the Commercial Bank. Case foresaw the growth of Cleveland and invested wisely in real estate downtown and in the suburbs. He was president of the village of Cleveland from 1821 to 1825. The vast fortune which he accumulated passed to his son Leonard, Jr., who in turn founded and richly endowed the Case School of Applied Sciences, now Case Institute of Technology, and gave to Cleveland many cultural benefactions.

There was Richard Hilliard who had come out from New York to the Reserve in the 1820s to go into the dry goods and grocery business. He prospered mightily and became president of Cleveland in 1830. He saw the usefulness of the Flats and bought up a large share of this land to be developed for manufacturing. Hilliard worked with Allen, Payne, and others to improve the city, and now he joined them in the effort to get the C.C. & C. started. There were also Alfred Kelley's capable brother Thomas, and Cyrus Prentiss, who became president of the Cleveland and Pittsburgh road, and many other such men vigorously promoting the railroads.

These men were not easily discouraged or defeated; they conceived large ventures, and they were trusted by their fellow citizens. They got their railroads for Cleveland and the Reserve. The charter granted by the legislature in 1836 had been forfeited—one reason for the vexation of the citizens expressed in the newspapers. It was revived in 1845, and for the next three years the directors tried to get together enough capital to begin the work. Subscriptions were slow in coming. Various people suggested that if Alfred Kelley would take the presidency, they would subscribe. In August 1847 Richard Hilliard and Thomas M. Kelley went to Columbus to see Mr. Kelley. The physical trip itself was all the argument anybody needed to establish the urgent need of rail connections between Cleveland and the state capital. It could be made only by stagecoach or by canal, and it required two days over rough roads. Winter closed the canals and discouraged all but the most pressing travel by road.

They found Kelley in his handsome and comfortable Greek-revival stone mansion which he had built on East Broad Street in 1836. He was looking forward to some years of leisure and peace, and a chance to reorganize his private affairs which had suffered for the public welfare. His brother and Hilliard talked with him late into the evening urging him to accept the presidency of the C.C. & C. Kelley said no. Mrs. Kelley also said no. She thought she and her children were now entitled to see something of Mr. Kelley. As Hilliard was leaving, he said to Kelley, "I appreciate your reasons for declining our request, and I admit we have no claims on you. This project, however, is very important to Cleveland and the State, and should it fail because you decline to take hold of it, will it not be a source of regret the residue of your life?"

Kelley became president a few days after this meeting, and just three years and six months later he rode the first through train into Cleveland from Columbus.

Those years were almost as strenuous for Kelley as his canal-building days. He held a meeting in Cleveland to explain the program for building the road. Subscriptions poured in. They soon reached $3,000,000 worth of stock. Cleveland itself put up $200,000. Kelley, grown so familiar with the lay of the Ohio land, helped the engineers to locate the 145-mile route and the right-of-way. On September 20, 1848, he and a dozen others went down to the terminal site in Cleveland and turned a few spadefuls of earth to symbolize the beginning of the project. While he organized all the intricate details of the contracts, finances, and materials, that lone man, ridiculed by the paper, was continuing to keep the charter valid. Kelley himself went to Wales to get some of the iron for the rails. Some of it was shipped in by way of the St. Lawrence River and the Lakes. He bought 7,000 tons in the East, and the *New York Tribune* announced that the price had gone up from $3 a ton to $5. Kelley had this road built not of oak with strap-iron surface, but with the new solid iron T-rails of the general type now standard.

Once the construction got started, the parallel rails marched down across the Reserve at a good rate. Two trains each day were running down to Wellington in midsummer 1850. By the end of the year the road had reached Crestline. By the end of January the Cleveland papers were dramatically reporting from day to day the approaching completion of the C.C. & C. On January 31, 1851, they announced, "only thirteen more miles to go"; on February 18, "last mile of the C.C. & C. completed." Kelley and Mayor William Case of Cleveland had laid the last two joining rails and hammered in the last spike, while a crowd looked on and cheered, a cannon fired salutes, and the whistle of the little engine tooted. The first train then moved across the rails and into Cleveland at seven o'clock that evening.

Such an epoch-making achievement, of course, called for a full-dress celebration. Since it wasn't the Fourth of July, the next best date was selected. That was Washington's Birthday. The city firemen (after rehearsal), the Cleveland bands, and the local militia in full uniform turned out to greet the special train from Columbus. It bore 428 officials, dignitaries, and private citizens, headed by the governor, Cleveland's own Reuben Wood, affectionately known as "the tall chief of the Cuyahoga." They were greeted with cheers, cannon salutes, and bank music, and then conducted to the Public Square for the speeches. The *Herald* summed up the general spirit in the flowing periods of that day.

> On Saturday, as we saw the Buckeyes from the banks of the Ohio and the rich valleys of the Miami and the Scioto mingling their congratulations with those of the Yankee Reserve, upon contemplation of an improvement, which served to bring them into business and social connection, and to break down the barriers which distance, prejudice, and ignorance of each other had built up, we felt that the completion of the Cleveland, Columbus & Cincinnati Railroad would be instrumental in accomplishing a good work for Ohio, the value of which no figures could compute.

During the three months before June 1, the intercultural and commercial link carried 31,679 passengers. The cars were drawn by engines manufactured in Cleveland by the Cuyahoga Steam Furnace Company. On September 22, this rising concern delivered the eleventh locomotive for the C.C. & C.

The construction of the railroad, in addition to bringing Alfred Kelley back to his old home town, was the occasion for the arrival of a man who was to become one of the city's great figures. He was Amasa Stone, general benefactor and special patron of Western Reserve University. This Massachusetts farm boy, while still a young man, had become famous as a builder of railroads and of the Howe Truss Bridge, which he helped to design. He had joined with Frederick Harbach and Stillman Stitt to build railroads in New England. Kelley persuaded him and his company to undertake the entire contract for the Cleveland to Columbus trackage. He accepted the job of superintendent of the road and moved to Cleveland in 1850. From then until his death in 1883, he was a director in several leading banks, president of many railroads, and restlessly engaged in ironworks, woolen mills, and a dozen other manufacturing activities. He designed and built the old Union Passenger Depot. He was a friend and counselor of Abraham Lincoln. He became a multimillionaire. His only son, Adelbert, was drowned in the Connecticut River while he was a student at Yale. In his memory, Amasa Stone gave to Western Reserve College, then located at Hudson, a half-million dollars on condition that it move to Cleveland and name its college of liberal arts Adelbert College.

Judging by the emphasis of the Cleveland newspapers, the Reserve was even more interested in the proposed rail line between Cleveland and Pittsburgh. A charter had been granted for it in 1836, but it had shared the same trouble which the other companies had encountered, and, like them, did not get organized until 1845. Construction began down at Wellsville (on the Ohio River) in July 1847, and at the Cleveland end in February 1849. Exactly two years later the road had reached Hudson. In celebration, the delegation that had come to Cleveland for the opening of the C.C. & C. were taken for an excursion ride over this portion of the C. & P. to visit the village of Hudson. The track, not yet ballasted, was rough and the travel slow. The train on the return trip jumped the rails and was delayed until late that night. Hudson had not been able to feed all its guests, and they arrived in Cleveland weary, famished, and less sure of the benefits of steam locomotion. Ravenna, thirty-eight miles from Cleveland, greeted the opening of the road into its precincts in March 1851. During the first week of April, 1,363 passengers were carried on the new coaches. The following year the two sections were joined and a through road opened to the southeast. The trip required thirty-six hours.

These roads were all geared to the south. To connect the Reserve from east to west and with Erie, Buffalo, and New York, the Cleveland, Painesville, and Ashtabula Railroad Company was organized. Alfred Kelley was one of the directors and later president of the road. Amasa Stone was the builder, as well as a director and later the superintendent. The rails reached Painesville on November 20, 1851. A big delegation of Cleveland people in "two fine cars" rode over for the grand opening. The mayor made a speech. As the line neared completion to the Pennsylvania border, the *Daily True Democrat* again voiced the spirit of the day. On comes the iron bank linking us closer, it said. "The Reserve, as glorious a land, and as free as the sun shines upon, will wake up to new life under these railroad openings." At the same time the line to the west was edging its way to Berea and Elyria, through Lorain County and the Firelands, and across the swamps toward Toledo.

This rapid account of progress minimizes some of the troubles Kelley was having to realize his dream of free-flowing rail traffic from Michigan and Cincinnati through Cleveland to New York. One of his difficulties must be recorded as a part of essential railroad history as well as an illuminating insight into the character of this driving personality. It came about in this way.

When George Stephenson designed and built the first locomotive in England, he chose for no apparent reason at all to set the axle length at four feet, eight and a half inches. That caprice determined the distance between the rails on the first tracks. The Pennsylvania Main Line, the B. & O., and the New York Central to Buffalo adopted the English gauge. A southern road across New York terminating at Dunkirk had laid its tracks six feet apart. Other early roads chose gauges of four feet three, four feet seven, four feet nine, and five feet. The engine *Sandusky* was built to a four-feet ten-inch gauge. It set the standard in Ohio, for the legislature made it unlawful to build any other gauge in the state. Kelley's roads, therefore, were laid with rails four feet ten inches apart. All this variety caused inconvenience to travelers and expense to shippers, for they had to unload themselves or their goods at the end of one line and load again on another. It cost as much to make these transfers as it did to run a train an additional fifty miles. But many workers had jobs at transfer points.

The Cleveland, Painesville, and Ashtabula Railroad was supposed to extend into Pennsylvania to Erie, there to connect with the two roads for New York. The New York Central had used the English standard gauge to Buffalo, but wished to extend its line to Erie to meet the Ohio road on the four-feet-ten gauge. The city of Erie was determined to preserve a difference in gauges in order to get the business of unloading and reloading all the passengers and freight that passed through. It passed a "gauge law" requiring that all roads running from Erie to the New York state line be either four feet eight and a half inches or six feet wide, and all between Erie and Ohio four feet ten. Because Kelley took the New York Central's side in the controversy, he was refused authority to continue the C.P. & A. into Pennsylvania.

Kelley was not one to accept defeat from such a narrow and provincial attitude. The larger ends of the Ohio railroads were dependent on eastern connections. Kelley explored all the possibilities. He discovered that the Franklin Canal Company of Pennsylvania had a charter which gave it the right to construct a railroad instead of a canal if it chose to do so. Kelley then bought a controlling interest in this company, transferred it to the C.P. & A., and went on building his railroad. Erie got an injunction against him. When the court examined the charter, it found that it was in order—except for the first five miles from the Ohio line. Kelley was stopped again. He went through the five miles, made friends with the landowners, and succeeded in buying a right-of-way through most of the area. In some cases he personally bought whole farms. He got from the local officers of the townships the right to cross highways with his tracks. And in November 1852 he ran the line into Erie.

The citizens there threatened to mob him if he came to town. He promptly drove into Erie and walked about the streets. One brick was thrown, but Kelley was not molested. The heated opposition of Erie continued for a time, and they actually tore up track to prevent the roads from joining. But time was on Kelley's side, the union was effected, and by 1854 the law was adjusted to protect these steps on the road to progress. Kelley thereupon retired from active railroad business, again to seek a period of rest after seven of his most strenuous years. He had the satisfaction of seeing the main routes through Ohio served by a fair network of canals and railroads with Cleveland as the center. The entire lake front from Bank Street (West Sixth) to the Cuyahoga was taken over by the railroads, and long docks reaching into the harbor joined the rails with the steamers and schooners of Lake Erie.

One other important road was completed before the Civil War despite vicissitudes as great as those just described. This was the Cleveland and Mahoning Valley Railroad, chartered in 1848, and completed to Youngstown in 1857, just as this section began to take on primary importance as an iron center in the midst of a region of coal. It ran through Newburg, Solon, Aurora, Mantua, and Warren. By this time, too, the small roads were being gathered into larger units, which, during the reconstruction period, became the great New York Central, the Pennsylvania, the Baltimore and Ohio, and the Erie systems. " 'Consolidation' is the order of the day," the Canal Board wrote in 1855. "The immense railroad system of Ohio is rapidly becoming a unit." It was reaching into every county of the Reserve to stimulate manufacture and trade. Before the Civil War stopped construction, Ohio had 2,788 miles of railroads. No other state had so much.

When we get to thinking about these great systems with their present luxurious cars, we forget just what the first trains were like. A glance at the early prints brings us back to the reality. The engines look like old-fashioned sawmill boilers on wheels. The tall ornate smokestacks pour out smoke from the acres of forest cut down to feed them. The engineer, standing on an open platform, unprotected except for his stovepipe hat, drives the train along the uneven track at fifteen to twenty miles an hour, dragging a few swaying carriages behind him. The slaughter of wildlife and livestock along the way is so heavy that it causes protests and cries for protection in the newspapers, and it soon brings about the "cowcatcher" on the front of the engine and cattle guards at country lanes. The passengers sit on hard seats on elongated stagecoaches, some of which have observation platforms. The engine puffs smoke and cinders back into their faces. People get killed up there when they fail to heed the warning of the conductor and get knocked off by a low bridge. And inside, some of the passengers are so annoyed by the undisciplined children whose parents take them out "for an airing of a few hundred miles" that they write a letter of protest to the papers. They don't think little boys and girls should be permitted to climb uninvited into ladies' laps, soil their dresses, eat molasses candy and wipe their fingers on gentlemen's trousers, or climb noisily over the backs of the seats in the cars. Can't such behavior be stopped?

It couldn't be stopped, but nonetheless more and more passengers rode the ever-lengthening coaches behind ever-bigger and more powerful engines over heavier, safer, and smoother tracks. And increasing wealth for Cleveland and the Reserve rolled in on the new iron wheels.

FREDERICK D. WILLIAMS

Garfield's Front Porch Campaign: The Mentor Scene

The news from Chicago electrified the little Ohio village. People cheered, displayed banners and bunting, waved flags, and talked excitedly. At the railroad depot they erected an arch inscribed on one side, "OUR TOWNS-MAN, JAMES A. GARFIELD," and on the other, "JAMES A. GARFIELD, OHIO'S FAVORITE." Flush with pride, they planned a fitting welcome for their neighbor, the newly nominated candidate for president. How Garfield's nomination was to affect life at his home and in the village of Mentor, few could have imagined early in June 1880.

Mentor, with a population of about two hundred, was situated on a railroad that ran along the southern shore of Lake Erie to Cleveland, some twenty miles to the west. During the campaign thousands of people, including many dignitaries, rode the Lake Shore Railroad to the Mentor depot, a neat little structure "of the Swiss cottage style." Nearby were a large wooden church, a general store, a small hotel, and a livery where visitors often rented horses and carriages to reach Garfield's home, which was about a mile and a half west, on the north side of a tree-lined dirt road.

The home was a newly restructured, three-story, freshly painted, white frame house, across the front of which stretched a long wide porch. Between the house and the picket fence flanking the road was a tree-shaded lawn with a croquet course. Across the road lay a meadowland. The farm, soon to be known to the nation as Lawnfield (the name originated with newspaper reporters), consisted of nearly one hundred sixty acres. The house, yard, garden, orchard, barns and other buildings took up about twelve acres, another seventy were cultivated, and the rest were woods and pasture. In the back of the house a lane cut across level ground to a point beyond the orchard, then descended gradually to the railroad. During the campaign, trains sometimes stopped and let off groups of people to walk the lane to Garfield's house.

The owner of Lawnfield was known to everyone as General. His Civil War military career had helped him win a seat in Congress as representative of Ohio's nineteenth district, a position he held for seventeen years. In early 1880, when he was elected to the United States Senate, he was and had been for several years the leader of the Republican congressional minority. In June he was one of Ohio's delegates-at-large to the Republican national convention.

Long before the delegates met in Chicago, Garfield was being mentioned as a dark-horse candidate, but he went to the convention to help prevent the nomination of Ulysses S. Grant for a third term and to deliver the nominating speech for fellow Ohioan John Sherman. After thirty-five ballots failed to break the deadlock between stalwart Republicans backing Grant, and anti-Grant Republicans, most of whom supported either Sherman or James G. Blaine of Maine, the convention nominated Garfield—a move that left him pale and stunned. Stunned too were 306 die-hard Grant men. In silent disbelief, they and their leader, Senator Roscoe Conkling of New York, watched the crowded hall become a bedlam. Inevitably, the verdict left the Republicans seriously divided. Of no help in repairing the damage was the selection of Chester A. Arthur, a New York stalwart, as vice presidential candidate. Arthur's inclusion on the ticket offended liberal Republicans without appeasing the Grant-Conkling faction.

Garfield's trip home from the convention was by way of Hiram, where his wife Lucretia ("Crete") met him. Hiram was her birthplace. There, while attending the school that is now Hiram College, they fell in love, and there, in 1858, they were married. For the next fourteen years their home was in Hiram. They were now the devoted parents of four sons and a daughter, all of whom were together at Lawnfield during part of the campaign. At that home, purchased in 1876 and loved by every member of the family, Garfield and his wife arrived late in the evening of June 11, while the village slept.

Tradition forced presidential candidates to stay home and make no political pronouncements. Garfield, an extraordinary speaker and effective campaigner, chafed at such "established usage," as he once put it. "If I could but take the stump and bear a fighting share in the campaign," he told his diary, "I should feel happier." Newspapers urged him to "take the stump," but so religiously did he observe protocol that he told members of a Republican Clubs committee, gathered in the library of his home, that he could not discuss political subjects with them. Yet he made many speeches to delegations that called at his home and to nonpolitical gatherings elsewhere, including crowds along his route to and from New York City, where he met in early August with a large body of Republican leaders.

Another tradition was an acceptance letter by each candidate. Garfield's, issued on July 10, contained no surprises for those who knew him. Carefully prepared with a view to reuniting his party, the letter touched upon leading issues, including two very sensitive ones—Chinese immigration, which, to the delight of the West Coast, he favored restricting, and the civil service, on which he equivocated, displeasing party liberals who favored reform, and failing to impress stalwarts who liked the spoils system.

The Democratic candidate, nominated two weeks after Garfield reached home, was General Winfield S. Hancock, a well-liked Civil War hero with no political experience. The nomination of William H. English as his running mate added no strength to the ticket, not even in English's home state of Indiana. Garfield learned of Hancock's nomination while strolling over his farm with Charles E. Henry, a close friend and longtime political advisor. Henry recalled that Garfield did not want Hancock "assailed by personal abuse," and that Hancock advised Democrats "to follow the same course." Despite their concern for decency, each candidate was abused. The personal campaign against Garfield was particularly vicious. Hostile papers denigrated him as a deceitful, vacillating man whose blind loyalty to party, inability to lead, and record of corruption made him unfit for the presidency.

On a typical day at Lawnfield, the candidate rose at about six, worked on his massive correspondence, welcomed visitors (many were encouraged at the village livery not to call until after noon), and scheduled and oversaw work on the farm. More often than not guests joined the family for meals, which were enlivened by a game in which Garfield spelled words from the book *Three Thousand English Words Usually Mispronounced* for each person in turn to pronounce. Some responses brought hearty laughter and good-natured teasing, all of which Garfield found pleasant diversion and help toward "a purer speech." Other diversions included croquet, lawn tennis, cards, reading, group discussions and singing, and this or that farm chore. During the busy but pleasant months of the campaign the candidate seldom retired much before midnight.

At his farmhouse Garfield helped map campaign strategy, raise money, and allocate party funds. He also summoned people to Mentor to discuss problems or to receive special assignments, managed a number of crises, appeased uneasy or disgruntled individuals and factions, and called for progress reports from various parts of the country. Each day brought stacks of letters which were screened by three assistants—Thomas Nichol, George U. Rose, and Joseph Brown—who responded to such things as congratulatory messages and requests for photographs and autographs. Garfield dictated most of his letters and signed nearly all outgoing mail, the handling of which took him several hours each day.

The bulk of this work was done in the office, a one-room, one-story structure situated a little to the rear and east of the house. In the center of the office stood a wood stove. Most of the remaining space was taken up by three tables, piled high with correspondence, bundles of documents, books, and newspapers. On the table sat a telegraph machine with wires running out to the road where they tapped the lines of the Western Union and the Atlantic and Pacific Telegraph Company. A full-time operator, helped occasionally by an assistant, sent and received dispatches.

Although a steady flow of callers interrupted work, play, and meals, Garfield remained cordial, courteous, and relaxed. One reporter found him in the office "attired loosely in his working clothes—a sack coat, rather brief in the taffrail, a neat pair of bluish trousers, slippers, and such et cetera as might characterize a cleanly man who is never too busy to forget his toilet, and not so fond of dress as to let it interfere with his comfort while at work." Through the first weeks of the campaign he was besieged by biographers and reporters seeking written material and interviews, and by artists wanting sittings. For several days in August he sat for John H. Witt, an irksome chore which Crete made bearable by reading to him. The painting turned out well: Garfield thought it was the best ever done of him; the artist called it his finest portrait.

Making the pilgrimage to Mentor were legions of people, some of whom Garfield had not seen for years. From Iowa came Lorenzo S. Coffin, who had taught at Geauga Seminary when Garfield and Crete were students there, and who now labored "like a missionary" to get Garfield to stop smoking. From Illinois came a former classmate at Geauga who in 1850 had asked Garfield's opinion about the providence of God in sickness and death. From Indiana came President Otis A. Burgess of Butler University, a fellow Disciple and preacher now faithfully at work converting Hoosier Disciples to Republicanism. Others came: Williams College classmates, soldiers and former soldiers of all ranks, bankers, businessmen, politicians, and farmers. In this procession were hundreds of people who had to be lodged overnight. Since neither the local hostelry nor the hotels in nearby Willoughby and Painesville could accommodate everyone, the villagers did "a thriving business entertaining strangers." And at Lawnfield, putting up overnight guests sometimes forced Garfield's boys to "hit the hay" in the barn.

Occasionally, callers provided unexpected entertainment. The erratic behavior of one individual, a self-styled "professor" named Zedaker, surprised and amused the entire household. Fortunately he sent to the *Cleveland Leader* an account of the trip which included his call on Garfield. First he went to Garrettsville (which he spelled "garitville"), then made an overnight stop at Little Mountain, a resort for well-to-do people of the Cleveland area. There, as he put it, "I had the pleasure of danceing upon the evening of my arrival," and composed a poem of fifteen verses "on the beauties of the place." The next morning, he rode a hack to Lawnfield and presented his "poem book" to Garfield. Zedaker explained that he and his host had never met, but that "each knowing other by fame before this," Garfield invited him to dinner. After eating, the "professor" recalled, "I was then envited to declaim and sing, from witch I delivered the Wild mountains an original oration, and sung two original songs—Lucy's Lamb and the Shenango river. I fund the gen in good health and quite cheerful." For his part, Garfield left this account of the episode: "The *soi disant* 'Prof.' Zedaker of Youngstown, Warren and Cleveland came and dined, and then gave us the most amazing exhibition of egotism I have ever seen."

Another eccentric visitor came from Painesville, where he had gotten a ride from a reporter. Following a discussion with Garfield, the newsman remembered his passenger in the carriage. Garfield went to him and asked what he wanted. According to the reporter, the man said: "Well, you see, general, I was in the war, an' awhile ago I made an application for a pension on account of my chronic diaree, . . . but the claim agent he slid 'er along t' Washntn, an' that's the last I've heard about it, an' by brother he said . . . you'd fix it fer me." Garfield, whom the reporter believed wanted to laugh, "gently and with utmost kindness" explained that the process took time, advised the man to get in touch with his congressman, and said that he would try to do so himself. Undeterred, the man said that he "kept agoin' to a 'pothecary shop an' gittin the same kin' o' drugs all the time." With that, the reporter shook the reins and said goodbye. As the carriage began to roll, the passenger turned, watched Garfield cross the lawn, and said: "Might a know'd it—might a know'd it. Soon's a man gits up in the world he gits proud." On the ride to Painesville, the man's "chronicality cammandeered his speech organs," the nub of his gripe with Garfield being, "I can't see why he won't do it, for funds is damn low with me."

The highlight of the drama at Lawnfield unfolded in late September when Grant, Senators Conkling and John Logan, and Congressman Levi P. Morton, treasurer of the Republican National Committee, arrived from Warren. With them were prominent Ohio Republicans and a battery of reporters. Conkling was the most powerful Republican in the state of New York, whose electoral votes were essential to Garfield. Following Grant's defeat at Chicago, Conkling had sulked, contributed nothing to the presidential campaign, and did not show up at New York City to meet with Garfield, who had gone there ostensibly for a strategy session with Republican leaders, but primarily to soothe the senator's feelings. At length, under pressure and out of self-interest, Conkling agreed to help. An important part of his effort was a speaking tour in the Midwest. It began at Warren, where he addressed about forty thousand people without mentioning Garfield "in any generous way." After completing the speech, he and his party of stalwarts boarded a train for Mentor. Upon their arrival a mounted company of guards, bearing torchlights, formed an escort and lighted the way over the muddy road to Lawnfield.

Before the watchful eyes of reporters and about two hundred curious and excited people—residents of Mentor and nearby places—Garfield greeted his guests with handshakes and warm words of welcome. Then he led them into the house, where they met Crete and Garfield's mother, had a stand-up lunch, and engaged in polite conversation. Since Grant was the man most people were interested in, Garfield arranged for everyone inside to meet him. He then led the former president, Conkling, and Logan onto the porch and introduced them in that order to the crowd outside. Each acknowledged applause appropriately but made no speech. A violent thunderstorm drove the dignitaries back into the house, but they left within an hour of their arrival in Mentor.

In the days that followed, Democratic newspapers gave a lot of space to what they called the "Treaty of Mentor," but neither they nor anyone else ever produced evidence of bargains made or agreements reached during the visit. It is important to note, however, that Conkling's Warren speech gave Garfield's campaign a much needed boost, and the brief call at Lawnfield a helpful nudge.

Delegations large and small, made up of people from all walks of life, piled onto trains and headed for Mentor. Most groups called late in the campaign. One day, about five thousand appeared at the farm. Usually, upon arriving, a spokesman for the group made a brief presentation. Then Garfield responded with a short statement neatly tailored for the occasion. Now and then he got off a comment praising the Republican record or mentioning some specific accomplishment he was particularly proud of. But he made no political speeches.

Early in September, ninety-five ladies and gentlemen representing various commercial enterprises arrived from Indianapolis. They came, their spokesman declared, to honor a self-made man who overcame adversity and with God's help shaped his own destiny and pursued the right. Garfield was particularly concerned about Indiana, which, like Ohio, held state elections in October. Indiana had gone Democratic in 1876 and was now in the doubtful column. Early in the campaign Garfield began stressing the need to carry the state. A victory there, he insisted, would ensure New York in November. But Conkling and his followers, believing that the Republicans could not take Indiana, preferred concentrating on New York. Garfield disagreed, held his ground, and Conkling gave in. The Republicans then went all-out, captured Indiana, and won even more impressively in Ohio. These triumphs, three weeks before the national elections, offset Republican losses suffered earlier in Maine's state elections.

A week after those victories, five hundred Lincoln Club members of Indianapolis, led by a band, arrived at Lawnfield. Wearing linen dusters and three-cornered straw hats as a burlesque of the expensive costumes worn by members of the Democratic Jefferson Club of their city, they heard their spokesman affirm their commitment to Republican principles and promise Garfield an Indiana majority of 10,000 votes. Garfield thanked his visitors, praised Indiana's contributions to national development, and declared that the victories in the Indiana and Ohio state elections signified a revival of the spirit of the Revolution, Abraham Lincoln, universal liberty, and just and equal law all over the land. At the end of the speech, the Hoosiers gave three cheers, fired a cannon, shook hands with their host, and departed.

Garfield's campaign crossed paths twice with the campaign of Fisk University's Jubilee singers, a group of Negroes who toured the United States and abroad to raise money for their financially distressed school. At Chautauqua, New York, where Garfield stopped on his return from New York City, the singers moved him deeply with their doleful spirituals, sung so beautifully that he wondered if the tropical sun had not distilled its sweetness and slavery its sadness into such touchingly melodic voices. Seven weeks later, on September 30, the singers called at Lawnfield, had coffee and fruit, and sang to a living room audience of family and neighbors. Led by Frederick J. Loudin, who had been a student in Crete's class twenty-five years earlier, they sang "their finest pieces," a "vibrant but mournful" repertoire that penetrated the very souls of the listeners. Some wept openly. Then, overcome by emotion, Garfield spoke, beginning in low, conversational tones, explaining "his understanding of the needs and aspirations of a race out of place." His concluding remark came "in ringing tones": "And I tell you now, in the closing days of this campaign, that I would rather be with you and defeated than against you and victorious."

When four hundred First Voters called from Cleveland to pay their respects, Garfield joked that he had always considered himself a young man, and still did, even though they were about to vote in their first presidential election, and he had voted before they were born. Turning serious, he delivered a stirring tribute to the nation and democracy. "Right here in this yard," he declared, "is a splendid specimen of American sovereignty, the roof and crown of this world of sovereignty. Enlarge it into the millions of men who vote and you have the grand, august sovereign of this last and best-born of time, the American Republic." His parting shot was an expression of confidence that his young audience would guard the sanctity of the ballot-box and keep the Republic pure and free.

But Garfield was no champion of feminism, and he believed that preserving the sanctity of the ballot-box required the exclusion of ballots cast by females. Accordingly, he delivered to nine hundred ladies from the Cleveland area, who arrived in the rain under a canopy of black umbrellas, a special "at home" message. A visit like this, he told them, could only occur in our democratic country where those who govern remain at home, sending servants out to perform the work of government. In the Civil War, he explained, there were three forces: the army that fought; those who paid and supplied the army; and those at home, mostly women, who labored and loved and inspired the nation in its hour of peril. In all great public work, he said, "the will of the Nation resides in the hearts and homes and by the firesides of the fifty millions of people, and there by the hearthstone nearest to the heart of our sovereign, the people, it is the woman's great and beneficent power to impress itself upon the national will. I greet you for having brought the spirit of home to my home," for showing by this visit "the growing power of home upon American public life, and for it and all that it means, I thank you with all my heart." Presumably, the ladies returned to their homes with a new sense of power, a new awareness of how much they were doing at their hearthstones to shape the nation's destiny. At any rate, Garfield commented in his diary, with apparent satisfaction, that he delivered to the ladies "a brief address setting forth the relation of women to American public life."

What he said to eight hundred Clevelanders, who came by special train, had a different focus. The group was made up of business and professional men and included city officials and Congressman Amos Townsend. Businessmen, Garfield reminded them, could get no insurance policy guaranteeing them prosperity during the next four years, but a great political organization could protect them against the evils of "bad legislation" and "bad finance." He praised the accomplishments of American labor and capital, and assured his guests, including "the blacks" in the group, that the country regarded each of them as the equal of any man, anywhere.

Many in the delegation had chuckled when they noticed that the seventh car in their train was numbered "329." That number, seen everywhere during the campaign, represented the sum of money Garfield was said to have received as dividends on stock in Crédit Mobilier, a company whose corrupt practices, made public in 1872, had scandalized the nation. Democrats scribbled "329" in just about every place imaginable, and in a few places that were unimaginable, during the 1880 campaign. To them, the number symbolized Garfield's tainted public career.

But to one hundred fifty Youngstown iron workers who braved a steady drizzle and arrived at Lawnfield "with a band, and wearing badges with '329' on their hats," the numerals stood for Garfield's three years in the Union Army, two years in the Ohio Senate, and nine terms in Congress. Garfield told the workers that tools were probably as good an index as any of the progress and intelligence of a civilization, and that they were largely engaged in tool-making—in making products for the defense, independence, and well-being of their country—"a great, material and patriotic work which the Government should protect and defend for the good of all."

No sooner had the Youngstown delegation left on that wet and busy day, than another arrived with a band and glee club. Then came one hundred Britton Iron and Steel workers of Cleveland. By late afternoon, when Lake County infantry and cavalry units appeared, the drizzle had become a steady downpour. As darkness closed in, so did fifteen hundred guards, mounted and on foot. Using the meadowland across the road as a parade ground, they formed two great columns. At that point, Garfield came outdoors, climbed into his carriage, and reviewed the troops, while scores of people, their vehicles clogging the road, looked on. After Garfield retreated to the dry warmth of his house, the military units marched and drilled in the flickering glow of lanterns and torches, fascinating the crowd who stayed and watched.

Welcoming some callers gave Garfield and Crete a few emotional moments. To twelve hundred Western Reserve veterans, he spoke eloquently of their noble struggle for freedom and national unity, and told them that their spirit and character and impressions would live at his home forever. On another occasion, two hundred men and women from Portage County were invited into the house. "There were so many old neighbors and friends," Garfield noted, "that Crete had her first cry in public while receiving them."

On a chilly afternoon in a wind-driven snowfall, Garfield stepped onto his porch in a heavy overcoat and a black felt hat to greet five hundred German Republicans from Cuyahoga county. He praised the record of the Germanic people and said that the best elements of their race and other races were coming to America and making her a stronger nation. Following a reference to the recent completion of the Cathedral of Cologne, which had been under construction for 630 years, he told the Germans that they had come to the United States, not to erect a Gothic building from the quarries of the Rhine, but to build free institutions, the shaping and improving of which was an ongoing process.

Two weeks before the election a New York City newspaper, *Truth*, jolted the nation by publishing a letter from J. A. Garfield to H. L. Morey, the subject of which was "the Chinese problem." The letter acknowledged the right of employers to buy the cheapest labor available and supported continuing immigration of Chinese laborers. Those views conflicted with the ones expressed in Garfield's letter of acceptance and had the potential to damage his campaign, especially on the Pacific coast where anti-Chinese feeling was intense. There were anxious moments at Lawnfield, for Garfield could not be sure that one of his assistants in Washington, who was helping with his correspondence in January 1880, had not written and mailed the letter on his own. But a careful check of the files in Washington turned up nothing. Meanwhile, Garfield obtained a lithographic facsimile of the letter, found it to be a "manifestly bungling attempt" to copy his hand and signature, and publicly denounced it as a forgery. Whether the letter hurt Garfield more than it helped him is debatable. What can be said with certainty is that he handled the matter admirably and exonerated himself before the election.

Election day was clear, bright, and unusually quiet at Mentor. Garfield spent much of the forenoon dictating and writing letters. John P. Robinson, next-door neighbor and longtime friend, arrived on the noon train from Cleveland, talked with Garfield and Crete about the work they wanted done on the farm, and at two o'clock the men drove to the town hall and voted. On the way back, Garfield settled some dairy accounts at the cheese house. At home he found telegrams indicating a "peaceful election and heavy vote." Returns began coming in about six o'clock. A little later, friends, neighbors, and reporters began arriving. Through the evening, men crowded into the little campaign office, smoked, spat on the floor, and cheered when the latest returns in Northern states came over the wires. By 11:00 p.m. it was clear that New York had gone Republican. At midnight, twenty-four people sat down to a splendid meal of "canvassbacks—oysters-and-ham in champagne." Three hours later, confident that he had been elected, Garfield closed the office and went to bed.

Two days after the election Garfield wrote to John Sherman thanking him for his help: "The success of the election is very gratifying. The distrust of the solid south, and of adverse financial legislation, have been the chief factors in the contest. I think also that the country wanted to rebuke the attempt of the Democrats to narrow the issue to the low level of personal abuse."

Garfield could have mentioned another kind of abuse—physical abuse to his property. A neighbor, aware of what was happening at Lawnfield, opined that it was "the curse of a candidate for high office to have the visitors he does not want, while those he would like to have often remain away out of pity." Garfield, of course, had visits both from good friends and total strangers. Whatever the case, so uniformly gracious was his hospitality that all visitors felt right at home. And some behaved badly. Members of more than one delegation scattered over the farm, helping themselves to vegetables and apples. Many of the German Republicans carried away seeds, and a few of the over-enthusiastic ones "pulled turnips, carrots, small squashes, and other mementoes to carry home."

The *Chicago Times* reported that the residents of Lawnfield were well, but their carpets and furniture, new a few months earlier, were "worn and muddied," while the "stripped garden and orchard...plainly confess the sad tale of too many callers." The paper added, however, that since Garfield would soon live in the White House, use public furniture and dishware, and have his annual salary increased from $5,000 to $50,000, there was good reason why his family "should not worry excessively about the irreparable damage to their carpets." The Democratic *Cleveland Plain Dealer* said simply that it would "cost Garfield half his first year's salary to put his premises in order."

While newspapers assessed the damage done by campaign visitors, an army of reporters, anxious to avail themselves of the good copy at Lawnfield, and legions of office-seekers, aware of the patronage Garfield commanded, packed their bags for a trip to Mentor.

The Funeral of the Century:
James A. Garfield

The train, for a change, was running ahead of schedule, but its most distinguished passenger neither cared nor noticed. It was a funeral train and it was carrying the body of James Abram Garfield, late president of the United States, from Washington, D.C., to his final ceremonies and ultimate resting place at Cleveland, Ohio.

Only seven months earlier another train had taken Garfield, then full of life and hope, from Ohio to the capital, where he would take up his new duties as president. What happened then was well known—perhaps the best-known, most closely followed story of the century. Garfield's assassination by an unhinged religious fanatic and the wounded president's three-month struggle with death coincided with a revolution in communications technology. The telegraph, wire services, high-speed printing presses, and other devices of mass journalism combined to turn Garfield's ordeal into the first "media event" of modern times.

Never before in peace time had Americans all over the country so avidly followed the same unfolding story step by step, finding in their common preoccupation an unprecedented unity of purpose and interest. They read the same medical bulletins, shuddered simultaneously at the gruesome details of the illness, and shared a common revulsion at the insane antics of the assassin, Charles Julius Guiteau. Even Garfield, on his sick bed, marvelled at the publicity he had engendered and expected the public soon to tire of the story. Instead, all throughout the summer of 1881 the nation marked time as it watched the events in the sick room at the White House.

When the end came, the shared emotions that had been roused by this saga had to find some outlet. Extravagent displays of mourning and solemn memorial ceremonies marked the end of this three-month national obsession. The culmination was to be this final internment at Cleveland.

Cleveland was chosen by the president's widow because of its close association with the events of her late husband's life. He had been born fifty years earlier in a humble log cabin on the outskirts of that city when it had been little more than a frontier village. Many of his friends and associates still lived there, and Garfield himself had recently bought a house at Mentor, Ohio, only a few miles to the east. Although Cleveland had never been within the borders of Garfield's congressional district, it was the chief city of Ohio's Western Reserve, an area he had represented at Washington for over seventeen years. Burial at Cleveland was akin to coming home.

The president had died on September 19, 1881, at a summer resort on the New Jersey shore. From there his body was returned to Washington by a special train. The route of that train was marked by lines of mourners who silently hailed its passage with bowed heads. Buildings and bridges along the right-of-way were draped in black, and church bells tolled the mournful cargo as it rolled by. At Princeton the college students scattered flowers along the roadbed and gathered the crushed petals as relics after the train had passed.

Such extravagant displays of grief would become commonplace in the following week. Even blasé Washington, D.C., succumbed to the fever. Chief Justice Morrison R. Waite, the entire cabinet, and two presidents (Chester Alan Arthur and Ulysses S. Grant) met the train at the depot and stood at attention as the coffin was transferred to a hearse for its journey up Pennsylvania Avenue to the Capitol. It was the same route Garfield had taken only a few months earlier for his inauguration, and the crowds which lined the street were as densely packed as on that happier day. On that occasion a hearse had somehow gotten caught up in the parade, causing the superstitious to shudder. Now a hearse was the center of attention, and it slowly rolled down the avenue to the beat of muffled drums. The coffin was placed in the very middle of the Capitol rotunda, which had been hastily draped in black and piled high with flowers. An oversize wreath of white rosebuds from Queen Victoria commanded particular attention.

State funerals were no novelty for Washingtonians but this one was special. Over seventy thousand citizens waited in line up to three and a half hours for an opportunity to shuffle past the open coffin for a final glimpse of the fallen leader. That glimpse was not an edifying one. The embalmer's efforts proved inadequate to the Washington heat. Patches of the president's face had turned blue and his mouth was twisted into a sardonic smile. Women fainted and grown men sickened at the sight.

At eleven o'clock on the morning of September 23 the crowd was cleared and the bereaved widow spent a lonely hour with the body of her late husband. After her vigil she ordered the casket closed and so it remained. At three o'clock the memorial services began. Garfield's last hours in Washington were spent in much the same manner as his life there—surrounded by oratory.

The coffin was then borne out of the Capitol and returned to the train for its final journey westward. That train departed from the same Baltimore and Potomac station in which Garfield had been shot. In order to spare the widow the unhappy associations of that site, the engineer considerately stopped the train a few miles down the tracks and allowed her to board separately.

The little train of only seven cars evoked a competitive spirit among the various cities along its route as each hoped to outdo the others in ostentatious displays of civic mourning. Since most of the train's journey was traversed at night, much of this effort was wasted. Unlike Lincoln's funeral train, which had stopped for ceremonies at each principal city along its route, Garfield's was halted only for the necessities of the locomotive. Even so, crowds gathered at each depot along the way. At one, a long line of Civil War veterans fell to their knees as the train sped by. Pennsylvania coal miners, still grimy from their day's work, waited in the dark for a sight of the funeral car. Bonfires illuminated grade crossings and bells and cannon broke the stillness of the night.

Following the funeral train by a respectful twenty minutes was a train loaded with congressmen and other dignitaries. A third special train, crammed with journalists, brought up the rear of the procession. As it was crossing a bridge at Beaver Run, Pennsylvania, it plowed into a work party, killing six. They sped quickly past the scene of the accident without even bothering to clean the blood off the locomotive. The reporters were too anxious to attend the president's funeral to stop for humbler tragedies.

The lead train reached Pittsburgh at dawn. If it continued at its present pace it would arrive in Cleveland around nine in the morning. This would be embarrassingly early. Cleveland officials in charge of the arrangements had not expected a funeral train to act like an express. Even though a gang of almost one hundred men had been working around the clock (illuminated at night by the newly invented electric light), the funeral pavilion on Public Square was not yet ready. (Nor would it, in fact, be finally completed until some days after the funeral was over.)

Consequently, those in charge of the funeral train had to mark time. They meandered around northern Ohio for the rest of the morning, following a twisted, roundabout route. At Wellsville the train met a special car carrying Ohio's governor, Charles Foster, and a group of prominent Ohio politicos. Foster wanted his car hitched to the funeral train but Attorney General Wayne Mc-Veagh, who was in charge of the arrangements, peremptorily refused. A nasty scene ensued, with Foster claiming jurisdiction over all trains within his state and McVeagh standing firm for federal supremacy. The cause of states rights met another defeat, and Foster and his party were compelled to find seats in the crowded cars of the funeral train.

As Cleveland neared, the crowds along the trackside grew thicker, and the last mile or two was solidly lined with spectators. Not all of them were native Clevelanders. The three-day ceremony would attract an estimated quarter-million people, a hundred thousand more than lived in the city. It was claimed that "no city in America, of equal size, ever attempted to feed and lodge anything like the number of people which will demand such service of Cleveland during the next three days." Visitors descended on the city in such abundance that all hotel rooms were snapped up at once. A United States senator who tried to pull rank to obtain a room was turned away by an unimpressed desk clerk. "The woods are full of them," he disdainfully said of senators. So were the rooming houses, tourist homes, and even private residences which had been pressed into service to house the overflow crowd.

Cleveland was clearly enjoying its moment in the sun. "Among all the cities of the earth," an enthusiastic newspaper asserted, "Cleveland today occupies the first place in the attention and interest of the civilized world." Rising to the challenge, Clevelanders turned their city into a temporary necropolis. Nineteen out of twenty wore some badge of mourning, and the streets and buildings were so lavishly laden with black that to the *New York Herald*, the "Forest City" had changed to "the Sable City."

Not to be outdone, the funeral train that finally arrived at 1:21p.m. was so lavishly draped in black crepe that only the windows were visible. Every bit of brightwork was covered. Over the boiler head rode an outsize portrait of the late president. It too was framed in black crepe.

The president's widow emerged supported by Secretary of State James G. Blaine and her oldest son, Harry. An honor guard of eight sergeants from the Second U.S. Artillery carried the silver-trimmed coffin to its hearse. The hearse was escorted by soldiers from the railroad station to Cleveland's Monumental Park, as Public Square was then called. This was a large, open quadrangle in the center of the city which when Garfield was a boy had been used by grazing cattle but was now reserved for more solemn civic occasions. It was dominated by a hastily constructed pavilion, on the same site and of similar design to the one which, fifteen years earlier, had briefly sheltered the coffin of Abraham Lincoln on his last journey to Springfield, Illinois.

A dozen pallbearers, all of them Clevelanders, transferred the coffin from the hearse to this pavilion. Each of these men had been associated with Garfield in one phase or another of his remarkably varied career. James H. Rhodes had taught alongside Garfield at the Western Reserve Eclectic Institute (now Hiram College); Charles Henry had been Garfield's student, then a soldier in Garfield's Civil War regiment and, finally, his old colonel's lieutenant in the political wars of the nineteenth Ohio congressional district. Edwin Cowles had promoted Garfield's political career in the pages of his newspaper, *The Cleveland Leader*; Daniel P. Eels had contributed money to further that career; and former Congressman Richard C. Parsons had almost destroyed that career by dragging Garfield into an unsavory paving-contract scandal. Others were old friends and members of the church in which Garfield not only prayed but preached: the Disciples of Christ.

Together, they carried their friend's remains into the pavilion and placed it upon a raised platform. This pavilion, or catafalque, measured forty-five feet on each side. Its shape was square, with a thirty-foot-high archway on each side to facilitate access. From each of the pillars which supported that arch was stretched a canopy which tapered to seventy-two feet above ground level. On top of that rested a globe (looking like a black maraschino cherry on a giant sundae) and on top of *that* brooded a twenty-four-foot-tall gilt angel whose wing tips hovered ninety-six feet above the ground.

Every inch of the catafalque was covered with some reminder of mortality. This was not an age which believed in stark simplicity. Flags, banners, and shields were placed at strategic locations. The names of the states ran up the columns and cannon, their muzzles draped in black, crouched at every corner. Flowers were everywhere—an estimated three thousand dollars worth. Cleveland's supply was exhausted and had to be supplemented by two boxcars from Cincinnati. Tuberoses, begonias, ferns, and immortelles were piled in profusion inside the pavilion and spilled over into the adjacent park. The floral tributes required two full newspaper columns to give what the author apologetically called a "meagre" description. They were arranged to form crosses, masonic symbols, messages ("Gone But Not Forgotten" in white immortelles) and altar pieces representing "The Last Sheaf," "Gates Ajar," "The Union Forever," and other such sentiments.

Amidst such lush surroundings, the coffin itself seemed almost indecently bare. It was graced only by a pair of palm branches arranged in a V (for victory) and by Queen Victoria's wreath. At the head of the casket someone had propped a placard bearing a motto of unknown origin:

> Life's race well run,
> Life's work well done,
> Life's crown well won;
>   Now comes rest.

A military honor guard stood at frozen attention around the coffin. With their high busbies, broad epaulettes, and white belts crossed at the chest, they looked for all the world like the tin soldiers from Babes in Toyland, adding a fantasy touch to the solemn scene.

On Sunday the catafalque was thrown open to the public. The line of viewers at times stretched across the Superior viaduct and up Pearl Street on the city's west side. While the Marine Corps band played mournful dirges, the procession filed through the pavilion six abreast at a brisk 140 persons a minute. They came all day, through the night, and into the morning of September 26.

At dawn that morning the streets of Cleveland were already crowded. By 8:00 a.m. even foot traffic was paralyzed on Euclid Avenue. That street, which was to be the route of the afternoon's procession, was decorated as much for a festival as for a funeral, presenting "a curious compound of Sabbath and popular holiday." Street vendors peddling souvenirs and refreshments lightened the tedium of waiting but added an incongruous note of commerce to the proceedings.

Precisely at 9:00 a.m. soldiers halted the procession of viewers, much to the indignation of those who had waited hours for an opportunity (now lost) to see the casket. The services began at ten. The mourners had already taken their seats around the catafalque. The dignitaries included eighteen United States senators, forty congressmen, former President Rutherford B. Hayes, future President Benjamin Harrison, and a contingent of governors, mayors, generals, and admirals. The Garfield family came when all was ready. Most visibly affected was the late president's aged mother who threw herself, weeping and praying, upon the coffin.

The day was already hot and sultry. There was no shade nor ice water for the mourners. None was more visibly uncomfortable than General Winfield Scott Hancock, the man Garfield had defeated for the presidency almost exactly a year earlier. At the Battle of Gettysburg, Hancock had displayed such cool non-chalance that he had won the nickname "The Superb," but now, his dress uni-form soaked with perspiration, he loudly moaned that the heat was unbearable.

The services began with the Episcopal burial service read by Bishop G. T. Be-dell. In life, Garfield had scorned Episcopalian formality for the simpler piety of the Disciple brotherhood, but it was decided that he should be sent to his Maker in a more decorous fashion. After various prayers and hymns, the funeral oration was delivered by a Disciple minister, Isaac Errett. This was an appropriate choice. Errett and Garfield had been young preachers in the same church a quarter-century earlier, and even though Garfield had left the pulpit for a worldly career their friendship had remained undimmed.

Errett took as his text: "And the archers shot King Josiah, and the King said to his servants, have me away, for I am sore wounded." He expounded on this theme for over forty minutes in the steaming heat. Even the newspapers were compelled to admit that the services "were rather long and somewhat tedious." The vast crowd outside the park displayed surprising patience and good order, even though they could see little and hear nothing. At his peroration Errett wept openly, as did many of the spectators, Hancock most conspicuously.

The eulogy was followed by a rendition of "Ho! Reapers of Life's Harvest," one of the many hymns claimed to have been the late president's favorite. After a benediction the coffin was carried by ten soldiers to a funeral car, and the mourners took their places in carriages for the procession to Lake View Ceme-tery, five miles to the east. The funeral car was a top-heavy conveyance, capped by a mock funerary urn perched twenty feet above street level. It was, of course, heavily draped with black broadcloth, showing no touch of color except for the white-tipped plumes bobbing from the twelve black horses who slowly pulled it up Euclid Avenue. They were led by six grooms, all black.

Euclid Avenue was then primarily residential. The lower portion was lined with the posh homes of Cleveland millionaires whose constant boast was that their address was on what was commonly called "The Most Beautiful Street in the World." On this day its sidewalks were packed ten to twenty people deep. Every window was occupied, as were the doorsteps, porches and, despite the heat, even the rooftops. The solemnity of the past few days had spent itself and the crowd displayed a festive spirit. Their attention was absorbed by the many celebrities in the procession, whose names they excitedly called out as each passed. "There is evidently a greater desire to see the distinguished living than to pay homage to the illustrious dead," one cynic concluded. Secretary of War Robert Todd Lincoln, son of an earlier martyred president, was a particular ob-ject of curiosity.

The funeral procession was so long that its head reached the cemetery gates just as its tail was leaving Monumental Park. When it was halfway through its course a violent rain storm burst upon the city. The spectators quickly scattered and the now waterlogged cortege made its way to the cemetery in semi-privacy. The soggy draperies on the funeral car dragged in the mud and caught in its wheels.

The services at the cemetery were brief. An oration was delivered by J. H. Jones, chaplain of Garfield's Civil War regiment, and the closing benediction was given by Burke A. Hinsdale, a one-time student of the late president's and a lifelong friend. The coffin was placed in a flower-laden vault guarded by soldiers in the presence of the small group of dedicated mourners who had braved the storm. After the multitudes of the past few days it seemed somehow strange that Garfield, as one orator elegantly put it, should take "his seat in the parliament of the skies" in silence, "darkness, gloom and desolation."

So came to an end what the *Boston Globe* hailed as "The Most Impressive Funeral Ever Witnessed in America." The cost of the extravaganza was estimated at $247,650, but that figure was clearly a grossly inflated estimate; the verifiable expenses seem to have been less than one-sixth of that amount. Years earlier, when Garfield had been a young man, he had recorded his indignation at an ostentatious tomb: "I could not but feel . . . that it was an unnecessary expense which might have relieved the sufferings of hundreds." Fortunately for his peace of mind he was spared the necessity of witnessing his own magnificent and expensive funeral celebration.

Additional Reading

Akin, Edward N. *Flagler: Rockefeller Partner and Florida Baron*. Kent, Ohio, 1988.

Cardinal, Eric J. "Antislavery Activity in the Western Reserve," *The Western Reserve Magazine* 6 (September-October, 1979): 37-44.

Condon, George E. *Cleveland: The Best Kept Secret*. Garden City, 1967.

Leech, Margaret and Brown, Harry J. *The Garfield Orbit*. New York, 1978.

Oates, Stephen B. *To Purge This Land With Blood*. New York, 1970.

Peskin, Allan. *Garfield*. Kent, Ohio, 1978.

Rose, William G. *Cleveland: The Making of a City*. Cleveland, 1950.

Shriver, Phillip R. *Ohio's Military Prisons in the Civil War*. Columbus, 1964.

Siebert, Wilbur H. *The Mysteries of Ohio's Underground Railroad*. Columbus, 1951.

Stewart, James. *Joshua Giddings and the Tactics of Radical Politics*. Cleveland, 1970.

Trefousse, H. L. *Benjamin Franklin Wade*. New York, 1963.

Wheeler, Robert A. *Pleasantly Situated on the West Side*. Cleveland, 1980.

Wyatt-Brown, Bertram. *Lewis Tappan and the Evangelical War Against Slavery*. Cleveland, 1969.

PART IV

A Changing Legacy: Industrialism, Ethnicity, and the Age of Reform

On the evening of October 16, 1879, John Hay, journalist and former secretary to Abraham Lincoln, held a reception at his elegant Euclid Avenue mansion. His guests were the political, economic, and cultural notables of the day—President of the United States, Ohioan Rutherford B. Hayes, Mentor's General James A. Garfield, Cleveland lawyer, U.S. Congressman R. C. Parsons, and Euclid Avenue moguls of business and industry Amasa Stone, Samuel L. Mather, W. J. Boardman, and Henry B. Payne. They were invited to honor Hay's journalism teacher William Dean Howells, novelist, critic, and editor of the *Atlantic Monthly*, who started his career in the Western Reserve town of Jefferson working in his father's newspaper office.

This glittering assembly represented the high-ranking leadership with Western Reserve connections in the closing decades of the nineteenth century—star-studded, halcyon days for Cleveland and the Reserve. One hundred years earlier at the end of the eighteenth century, Moses Cleaveland had reached the mouth of the Cuyahoga and predicted that the "town on the bank of Lake Erie" would prosper. In an 1886 issue of *Harper's New Monthly Magazine*, Edmund Kirke wrote: "If we stand on the precise spot where General Cleaveland landed on that summer day in 1796, and look about us for a moment, we shall be able to form some idea of the great wealth and immense activity of this teeming hive of industry." He looked to the high bluffs on the outer edges of the valley and remarked about the city built there, but "here, along the bed of the river," he said, "is the industrial heart of Cleveland."

The "irregular valley" under a mile wide that followed "the windings of the river and doubling itself several times" afforded a long line of dock front. Following the valley, one scanned hundreds of acres covered by ship and lumber yards, planing and flour mills, iron foundries and factories, oil and chemical works. "Here ten thousand machines move night and day in ceaseless hum, sending away, upon the numerous rail tracks which everywhere interlace the district, iron in its various forms." Kirke counted six great rail lines that entered the valley bringing tons of raw materials and bearing from it thousands of cars of manufactured products.

The air was punctuated and saturated with the sounds of industry: "the frequent scream of the steam-whistle, the ceaseless whir of the heavy machinery, the constant coming and going of the loaded trains with harsh grating of their iron wheels." To the right of the main branch was another valley skirting a narrow stream which for one and a half miles was crowded with woolen factories and slaughter and packing houses. Farther up the Cuyahoga was another stream called Kingsbury Run and at its mouth, and covering several acres, were the works of The Standard Oil Company. "A marvel of commercial enterprise," exulted Kirke, "a mammoth corporation that, it was said, had bought out rival establishments, made its own terms with railroads while enriching them by its traffic, to control the crude oil market of Pennsylvania and the refined oil market of the world."

In "Personalities of An Era...Intersections," Gladys Haddad casts John D. Rockefeller and relationships to Flora Stone Mather, Cleveland philanthropist and Euclid Avenue contemporary, and Ida Minerva Tarbell, "muckraker" journalist and author of *The History of The Standard Oil Company*, in a narrative that illuminates the controversial issue of the acquisition and accumulation of personal wealth and its distribution and application for the general good. Peter Jedick, in"When Euclid Avenue Was Somebody," offers a directory of habitats on Cleveland's Millionaires' Row and a candid chronicle of the pursuits of its rich and famous.

Fortunes were being made in iron ore, coal, steel, and oil by Chisholm, Otis, Stone, Mather, Rockefeller, and Hanna. The shipyards of Cleveland built vessels that plied the lakes and seas with products of local industry and farms to markets throughout the world. Fifty-five percent of the ore shipped from Lake Superior was received at the Western Reserve ports of Cleveland, Ashtabula, Conneaut, Fairport, and Lorain. In turn, each one of these ports was a hub for transshipments from the rich agricultural areas of the Reserve's heartland.

Men of vision and wealth launched new business enterprises and enlarged mills and factories. Jobs were plentiful. In the rising tide of immigration came the workers—Bohemians, natives of Czechoslovakia; Finns to Fairport Harbor; and Hungarians who displaced the Germans and Irish in the factory district. In the consolidation of shops and factories, larger numbers of workers came together and united for their mutual benefit by agitating for higher wages, better working conditions, and shorter hours. Workers in the mills and on the farms saved their earnings. Banks flourished in the Western Reserve.

These were prosperous times! Leisure activities stretched across the seasons. Cleveland's "first" families held sleigh races on Euclid Avenue. With the first snowfall, well-to-do drivers, bundled in buffalo robes, began racing their fastest horses. The bicycle became popular with the advent of the "safety" and its two wheels of equal size following the hazardous high-wheeler. Sports activities were popular—ice-skating, roller skating, tennis, football, and baseball.

On October 8, 1890, Samuel Livingston Mather died, a pivotal figure who exemplified the Western Reserve's New England legacy. Born in 1817 at Middletown, Connecticut, he had come to Cleveland in 1843 in the interest of Western Reserve lands belonging to his father, Samuel Mather, Jr., the only stockholder in the pioneering Connecticut Land Company whose descendants were to be of tremendous influence in the city's future. A lawyer, Samuel Livingston Mather was fascinated by the discovery of iron ore in the Lake Superior region. He raised local capital to organize the Cleveland Iron Mining Company in the early fifties, directing its mining and shipping activities, and then became president in 1869. The company was the parent of subsequent industrial concerns that had vast operations in the great Marquette ranges of the Iron Mountain district—Marquette Iron, Cleveland Boiler Plate, and the American Iron Mining Company. Mather was a director of the New York, Pennsylvania and Ohio Railroad Company, and one of the original directors of the Merchant's National Bank. His courage to venture into unexplored opportunities characterized the life of this pioneer industrialist who created wealth and power for Cleveland. The legacy of Samuel Livingston Mather was manifested in his sons Samuel and William Gwinn, who inherited his business acumen, civic responsibility, and humanitarian spirit.

The eyes of the world focused on Cleveland in 1884 when the first electric streetcar went into operation. Citizens, however, had to be satisfied to ride horsecar lines for another decade. The city was trying to support a confusion of competing street railway lines. Clashes over plans and policies precipitated the famous feud between Tom Johnson and Mark Hanna that continued for more than two decades. Eugene Murdock's "A Couple of Giants" studies Johnson and Hanna from their origins through their careers and contributions to the life of the Western Reserve. Their legendary feud cannot obscure the roles that these dramatically contrasting men played in the development of the regional reputation of northeastern Ohio. Tom L. Johnson came to Cleveland in 1879 and acquired wealth through the invention of street railway devices and his association with traction companies. Identified with the slogan "home rule, three cent carfare and single tax," he was elected Cleveland's mayor four terms and later served two terms in Congress. He inspired interest in municipal government, and during his administration (1901–1909) the idea for grouping public buildings surrounding a central mall, called The Group Plan, became a reality. Marcus Alonza Hanna entered business and street railway ownership by marriage to the daughter of an industrialist. In a multi-faceted career he became a coal and iron executive, banker, builder of a steamship line, owner of the city's opera house, and newspaper publisher. A dominant force in the Republican party, Hanna took charge of putting William McKinley in the White House in 1897, and in the same year was himself elected to the United States Senate.

On March 4, 1897, William McKinley became the twenty-fourth president of the United States. He was born in 1843 in the Western Reserve town of Niles, where his father was in the iron foundry business. At the outbreak of the Civil War, young McKinley left school teaching and enlisted in the Twenty-third Ohio Volunteer Infantry commanded by Rutherford B. Hayes. After the Battle of

Antietam, he was commissioned and mustered out in 1865 as a major. He studied law, established residence in Canton, and opened his practice. He entered politics and in 1876 helped elect his old commander, Rutherford B. Hayes, president. That same year he was elected to Congress and later reelected twice. Soon after coming to Washington, McKinley aligned himself as a representative of the nation's dominant industrial group desiring high protective tariff rates. This won him the friendship of Marcus A. Hanna, controlling power of the Republican machine in Ohio who supported him for the governorship for two terms starting in 1891.

In the intense presidential campaign of 1896, William McKinley, backed and counseled by Mark Hanna, opposed Democrat William Jennings Bryan, the principal issues being protective tariffs and free coinage of silver. Touring Union generals, torchlight parades, journeys to Canton, and oratorical exhibitions on Public Square marked the Cleveland campaign. From his home in Canton, McKinley conducted his political operation in the style of fellow Ohioan James A. Garfield by giving "front porch" addresses to visiting delegations. McKinley's slogan "a full dinner pail" and "cash on the barrelhead" produced a bracing electoral victory and smashing popular majority.

The gravest issue during McKinley's presidency concerned relations with Spain. Americans demanded intervention in Cuba with an eye toward seizing the island and other Spanish territory. On February 15, 1898, the destruction of the USS *Maine* in the Havana Harbor led to a declaration of war. An easy victory over Spain gave rise to the reputation of Commodore George Dewey, who destroyed the Spanish fleet at Manilla, and Lieutenant Colonel Theodore Roosevelt, whose Rough Riders mounted the heights at San Juan. By December, Spain had withdrawn from Cuba, ceded it along with Puerto Rico, Guam, and the Philippines to the United States, and "the splendid little war," as Secretary of State John Hay called it, was over. The quick and decisive victory marked the end of Spain's New World empire and gained respect at home and abroad for the rise of the United States as a major power.

In early November 1900, twenty thousand men marched in the McKinley-Roosevelt parade on Euclid Avenue. Cleveland chronicler William Ganson Rose reported, "Rough rider hats and white duck suits were prominent. Full dinner pails were carried on floats and on marchers' shoulders. An elephant ambled along in a procession that included thirty-eight bands. Two old-time horsecars were reclaimed to operate where men carried canes with red, white and blue streamers." In the election, voters overwhelmingly supported William McKinley for president and Theodore Roosevelt for vice president.

William McKinley paid his last visit to Cleveland on September 5, 1901, while on his way from Canton to Buffalo to attend the Pan-American Exposition. He reached the Union Depot shortly after noon, addressed the group assembled to greet him, and visited with Senator Mark Hanna. The next day at a reception at the Exposition in Buffalo he was shot by anarchist Leon Czolgosz. He died just over a week later on September 14. Northeastern Ohio's Western Reserve had the unfortunate distinction of being home to two of the three assassinated presidents. In a twist of fate McKinley died of his wounds just five days before the twentieth anniversary of the death of James A. Garfield.

Elaborate preparations had been made to receive President McKinley in Cleveland as the most distinguished visitor to the Thirty-fifth Encampment of the Grand Army of the Republic. Instead, the white columns in the Public Square were entwined with streamers of black as a symbol of the city's grief. The GAR parade, in which over fifteen thousand Civil War veterans marched, was one of the most impressive occasions Cleveland had known. More than two hundred thousand people watched as Senator Mark Hanna took the president's place in the reviewing stand, and when "the Ohio boys in blue" marched by, he fell into line with them.

Cleveland was on the verge of the Automobile Age—an age that threatened bicycles, buggies, and surries and ended the romantic era of horses and carriages. Alexander Winton was twenty-five when he came to Cleveland in 1885 from Scotland. Here he organized the Winton Bicycle Company and turned out bicycles at the rate of fifty per month. His bicycle brought a high price because riding was the fashion and the demand was great. By 1898 Alexander Winton had changed the name of his shop to the Winton Motor Carriage Company and was one of the first to make an internal-combustion motor car. The Winton was a one-lunger, reportedly "very elegant in appearance, fashioned after the pattern of an engine runabout and lacking little but the shafts and whipsocket." It carried two passengers at a speed of ten miles an hour.

Contained within the boundaries of the Western Reserve, in contrast to the accelerating inroads of industrialism and modernization, were communities in which the steady trot of the horse metered life's daily events. Thomas L. Newcomb's "Northeastern Ohio's Mennonite and Amish Folk" traces the history of these religious groups and their introduction to the Western Reserve counties of Ashtabula, Geauga, Trumbull, and Portage where they remain to suggest the diversity of the region's population.

Cleveland celebrated its centennial in 1896 and gave witness to the strides that the wilderness village had taken in its first century. Candlelight had been replaced by electricity. Stage coaches and canalboats had been exchanged for express trains and automobiles. Log cabins had been superseded by mansions and sky scrapers. At the same time, William Ganson Rose observed, "Nationality influences had almost obliterated the mark of the New England pioneers." Immigrants were swarming into the industrial districts where Cleveland had won its reputation as a prosperous city. Swelling the ranks of those from Great Britain and Germany, the new century brought Swedes, Russians, Austrians, Italians, and Slavs. Workers lived in the old dwellings and tenements of the industrial districts where soot and smoke blanketed the congested areas. Housing was inadequate, and in this unhealthy environment disease, crime, and manifold welfare problems developed. Cleveland's charitable organizations were overwhelmed by the demands, assisted as they were, by the agencies established by immigrant groups for relief of their own. In his explication, "Social Reform and Philanthropic Order in Cleveland, 1896–1920," John J. Grabowski shows how by utilizing the ethical structure of Protestant Christianity and the principles of efficient management, "Cleveland was able to meet and ameliorate many of its urban needs and problems in a manner which avoided both systemic disruption and social chaos."

The turn of the century witnessed many changes in the physical appearance as well as in the general character of the city. The grandeur that was Euclid Avenue began to fade, as did its west side counterpart, Franklin Avenue, where leaders of industry occupied magnificent residences shaded by great elms, oaks, maples, and hickories that characterized Cleveland as the Forest City. Cleveland's bid for size and importance left its marks as commerce and industry pushed out from the central city. The fine old homes were abandoned by families seeking the beauties of the peaceful countryside; the attractiveness of the city suffered as the charm of the outlying communities grew. Decentralization was quickening. The interurban electric railways that operated out of Cleveland carried passengers over a two-hundred-mile network to the Western Reserve communities of Berea, Elyria, Oberlin, Norwalk, Medina, and Painesville.

In 1912 Woodrow Wilson was elected the twenty-seventh president of the United States. Within two years the European war started that soon became a World War with the entrance of the United States on April 16, 1917. Under Cleveland's Newton D. Baker, secretary of war, began the greatest troop movement in modern history, as American soldiers were transported across the Atlantic in what proved to be the most important influence upon final victory. Patriotic fervor ran high throughout the Western Reserve. Parades, rallies, and meetings on city and town squares supported Liberty war bond drives and war chest campaigns to aid the boys "over there." Measures were introduced to conserve light, power, gasoline, and products essential to war production. Rationing programs were launched for meat, wheat, and sugar; war gardens were planted. From the beginning of war preparations, Cleveland industry led in output. This brought to Cleveland a problem identified and described by state legislator Harry E. Davis:

> War industries induced a mass movement of colored workers into Cleveland which almost completely submerged the older elements of the colored population. Industry sent agents into the South to recruit labor, and they were brought to Cleveland in carloads. Many of them came with only the clothing they were wearing, with no preparation for housing, and with little idea of the problems they must inevitably encounter.

Kenneth L. Kusmer, in *A Ghetto Takes Shape*, maintains that the residential segregation of urban blacks at this time formulated the focus for "crystalization of the pattern of discrimination" that resulted in the "flowering of racism." In "Racism at High Tide," Kusmer states that "Cleveland, a city more liberal than most, managed to avoid the racist excesses that plagued other communities." In the critical period of the city's second decade, he delineates the response of whites that began with the Great Migration.

Word that the Armistice had been signed came to Cleveland early in the morning of November 11, 1918. Factories let out workers, stores closed, and church bells and factories brought rejoicing people into the streets to parade in celebration. Immediately, thoughts turned to reconstruction and the change-over to peacetime economy. Jobs were predicted for veterans and all workers, many of them women, who were needed to fill the orders for the resumption of production and the demand for housing and for public improvement programs. The impression was that the wartime boom could be depended upon to con-tinue in peacetime. Manufacturers bought new machinery, and enlarged plants; wages rose and prices escalated. The transition from war to peace seemed com-paratively easy in the first months after the conflict, but new difficulties were to be faced as time went on.

Early in the twentieth-century administration of Cleveland's Tom L. Johnson, Daniel H. Burnham, architect and planner of White City at the World's Colum-bian Exposition, was a consultant for The Group Plan of buildings that Johnson wanted to put in the heart of the city to erase a blighted area and situate his vi-sion of civic and artistic achievement. Burnham's statement expressing the aims of the architects and engineers embodied the spirit and promise of the future that carried on the legacy that had created Ohio's Western Reserve. "Make no little plans; they have no magic to stir men's blood and probably themselves will not be realized. Make big plans; aim high in hope and work, remembering that a noble, logical plan once recorded will never die, but long after we are gone will be a living thing asserting itself with growing insistence."

Personalities of an Era...Intersections:
Rockefeller, Mather, Tarbell

Ida Tarbell recalled as a young girl "the marvel" of a family trip to Cleveland from their Rouseville, Pennsylvania home—an "advantage" afforded by early rewards of the burgeoning oil industry. In 1868 renowned among Cleveland's sights was its residential "millionaires' row" Euclid Avenue. At the corner of East Thirteenth Street stood the palatial mansion of Amasa Stone. Westward on "the Avenue" at East Fortieth Street was the home to which John D. Rockefeller had just moved his young family.

Two notable women born within five years of each other at the midpoint of the nineteenth century were Flora Stone Mather (1852–1909), philanthropist and daughter of Cleveland industrialist Amasa Stone, and Ida Minerva Tarbell (1857–1944), journalist and daughter of farmer-carpenter Franklin Tarbell. Their intersections with John D. Rockefeller (1839–1937) lend focus to their contrasting roles and the position of women in nineteenth-century America.

In the twenty-five years before her death in 1909 at fifty-seven, Flora Stone Mather achieved a remarkable record for philanthropy. She was a major benefactress of the College for Women of Western Reserve University and supported the establishment of schools, colleges, and church missions in this country and abroad. She founded one of Cleveland's first social settlements, Goodrich House, and was instrumental in the development of the Temperance League, Consumer's League, Day Nursery and Kindergarten Association, Children's Aid Society, and Home for Aged Women. In an ultimate accolade for 1909, a *Cleveland Leader* editorial eulogized, "Mrs. Mather achieved a career of which any man might well be proud."

After a fifty-year career as a highly productive journalist, Ida Minerva Tarbell was remembered for her *History of the Standard Oil Company* published in 1904. Her reputation was established at the turn of the century through mass-circulation publications, especially *McClure's Magazine*, where the Standard Oil history first appeared. Ida Tarbell grew up in the oil regions of western Pennsylvania, where her father was an independent oil operator shortly after the discovery of oil there in 1859. *The History of the Standard Oil Company* concerned the threat to traditional institutions represented by corporate capitalism, an issue she had personally experienced. The book, for which Ida Tarbell was hailed "muckraker," has been recalled by some as the signal that put a stop to unregulated monopoly in the oil industry.

Flora, the youngest child of Amasa and Julia Gleason Stone, was born in 1852, two years after the family that included Adelbert and Clara came from Massachusetts to settle in Cleveland. Amasa Stone had achieved a notable record as a contractor and bridge builder in the East, which recommended him for opportunities in the West. He took advantage of the opportunities offered in the rising flood of national expansion and in a business career of forty years amassed a considerable fortune. In 1849, he contracted to build the Cleveland, Columbus &Cincinnati Railroad and following its completion became successively superintendent, then president, and established Cleveland as his home. He built an empire around railroads and, with his business acumen, broadened his interests to score successfully with banking, telegraph lines, and heavy industry. The Civil War brought his enterprises into a focus that made him a millionaire.

With the discovery of oil in Pennsylvania in 1859, the business of drilling wells and refining oil expanded rapidly during the war. In 1865, thirty Cleveland oil refiners were joined by young John D. Rockefeller, who, with Samuel Andrews, formed a company. Undaunted by local competition, Rockefeller studied the Pennsylvania refiners who held a substantial lead and reasoned this was due to relatively low transportation costs and the proximity of production and refining. Freight rates were fundamental elements in gaining advantage over both local and sectional competitors. In 1868, John D. Rockefeller enlisted Henry M. Flagler to negotiate a rebate with Amasa Stone's Lake Shore Railroad for Pennsylvania oil region shipments to Cleveland. In 1870 when The Standard Oil Co. was created Amasa Stone held 500 shares, symbolizing the liaison of railroads and oil.

In 1871, a severe depression in the oil industry compelled Rockefeller to propose a cooperative federation of all oil refining units to eliminate excess refining capacity and ruthless competition. It was a scheme to expand The Standard Oil Co. so that it could command the refining industry as a whole. Large bank credits were required, and Rockefeller had good ratings with Cleveland's institutions. Amasa Stone was prominent among bankers who lent support for Standard Oil to absorb thirty Cleveland refineries.

Flora Stone was educated with Clara, her older sister, at the Cleveland Academy, built by her father and led by the city's most notable educator, Linda Guilford. In 1881 Flora Stone and Samuel Mather, longtime friends and neighbors, were married, uniting two of Cleveland's wealthiest Euclid Avenue families. Flora and Samuel Mather had four children—Samuel Livingston, Amasa Stone, Constance, and Phillip Richard.

Amasa Stone exemplified the nineteenth-century business baron whose life was underscored by struggle, achievement, and command. In an era when colleges sought millionaires, Amasa Stone became the major benefactor for Western Reserve. In 1880 he agreed to give Western Reserve College $500,000 to move from Hudson to Cleveland. His gift carried conditions: control of the board of trustees, supervision of building construction, and selection of the college name—Adelbert—in memory of his son. Three years later, in 1883, tormented by blame for a railroad tragedy, physically impaired by a carriage accident, and emotionally exhausted by the toll of his life's labors and the death of his son, Amasa Stone took command for the last time and ended his own life.

Amasa Stone's will designated the distribution of an estimated eight million dollar estate, in the form of securities, to his immediate family and relatives. Institutional beneficiaries that received cash amounts were Adelbert College, the Home for Aged Women, and the Children's Aid Society. Flora, who had continued to make her home with her parents after marriage, became the dispensing hand of a large inheritance.

In a family tradition of financial support for Western Reserve, Flora Stone Mather made her first large gift to Adelbert College in 1888; she endowed its first chair of history in the name of Hiram C. Haydn, her pastor and the university president. At his inauguration, Haydn announced the end of coeducation and the plan for its replacement. Adelbert College was to be for men only; a women's college in close proximity and in every respect equal to it would be created. Her brother's name, Adelbert, would forever be linked with the men's college. Flora Stone Mather worked generously on behalf of the women's college; one day her name would be given to it.

Flora Stone Mather chose the role of philanthropist and in the nature and quality of her efforts became a social activist. She used "good works" to invest her personal energies in the establishment and administration of policies that reminded many of a ministry. She explained: "I feel so strongly that I am one of God's stewards. Large means without effort of mine have been put into my hands; and I must use them as I know my Heavenly Father would have me, and as my dear earthly father would have me, were he here."

Responsive to the problems arising from industrialization and acting on her feminist convictions of advocacy for women and children, Flora Stone Mather shortly before her father's death initiated correspondence with John D. Rockefeller for support of the Cleveland Day Nursery and Kindergarten Association of the Young Ladies Branch of the Women's Christian Association. In 1883, she wrote: "We have three nurseries under our care and we feel that with our increased experience they ought to increase not only in numbers but in usefulness." Three years later, Mrs. Mather informed him:

This has been our most successful year, at least so far as the Perkins Nursery is concerned. That is the largest and best appointed in every way, and through the summer we had as many as thirty-eight children some days. Even in this winter weather when the women have less opportunity for obtaining work by the day we have had as many as twenty-seven and eight children a day, all we can manage with our present arrangements.

In 1888, sending his annual gift of fifty dollars, Mr. Rockefeller's note addressed Mrs. Mather:

Dear Madame:
With best wishes for the success of the good work and gratitude that there are true and
faithful ones who conscientiously stand by it.

That same year Mrs. Mather asked Rockefeller to solicit from the Sunday school
of his Euclid Avenue Baptist Church on behalf of the Day Nursery and Kindergarten Association. In 1893 she acknowledged his annual gift: "We are endeav-
oring to make our kindergartens more effective this year. We feel sure that no
influence is stronger in its neighborhood than the ideal kindergarten and we
want to approach that ideal as nearly as possible."

From 1884 to 1904 John D. Rockefeller gave a total of $18,930 to the Cleve-
land Day Nursery and Kindergarten Association. After 1893 his annual gift increased with the creation of a facility in the Mayfield Road Italian neighborhood and named for Alta, his daughter, who took personal interest in its
growth and development.

In 1910, upon receipt of the memorial volume prepared by Samuel Mather for
his wife, John D. Rockefeller wrote of Flora Stone Mather: "Her beautiful life
and works were always an inspiration to us, as well as to so many others. Her
memory will ever be dear to the multitudes she blessed. There is no one to take
her place in the city she loved."

Ida Minerva Tarbell, the first child of Esther and Franklin Tarbell, was born in
1857 on the farm of her maternal grandparents in Erie County, Pennsylvania.
The discovery of oil in Titusville in 1859, which transformed the character of
northwestern Pennsylvania from agricultural to industrial, gave Franklin Tarbell,
with his carpentry skills, a financial opportunity. Producers desperately needed
oil storage facilities, and he designed and built a wooden tank with a capacity of
500 barrels of crude oil. He soon had his own shop and the beginning of financial security for his family. To Rouseville in 1860 he brought his wife and children, where prosperity enabled a move from the oil-laden air of the valley to the
green hills above.

Schooling in Rouseville was irregular, and Ida's education came from her own
reading and observation of life, much of which was crude and colorful in contrast to the Protestant sanctity of the devout Tarbells. Born Presbyterians, they
joined the congregation of the First Methodist, the only church in town. In
1870, when she was thirteen, Ida Tarbell's family moved to the prosperous Oil
Creek Valley town of Titusville, where she entered public school and excelled in
science.

While Ida was in high school, The Standard Oil Co. and a group of allied refiners from outside the Oil Regions contrived with the railroads to take control
of the oil industry from its developers by rigging freight rates in their favor,
thereby ruining their competitors because of prohibitive transportation rates.
When the scheme of the so-called South Improvement Co. was uncovered in
1872, the entire region erupted in violent protest, and the syndicate was abandoned. Transportation rebates, however, remained a basis for the oil monopoly
that was rapidly achieved by The Standard Oil Co. Managerial efficiency and

imaginative innovations in business methods originated by the corporation's numerous partners had its genius in John D. Rockefeller.

Ida's father was by then one of the independent oil producers who remained adamant against Standard Oil despite the financial reverses that brought his demise in the industry. Resentment amounting to hatred of the Standard Oil methods became a state of mind in the region, and Ida Tarbell, then fifteen, shared the outrage over the invasion by outsiders of the industry they considered rightfully theirs. Discriminatory freight rates granted to a few constituted a violation of the rights of many and threatened the egalitarian tradition of American democracy. This was the position Ida Tarbell, thirty years hence, would articulate on behalf of the people of her region in *The History of the Standard Oil Company*.

As a girl, Ida was strongly influenced by the woman's rights movement, some of whose leaders, including Frances Willard and Mary Livermore, were guests in the Tarbell home. Listening to talk of marriage, Ida envisioned entrapment and vowed never to marry. Education became for her the symbol of freedom. In 1876 she entered Allegheny College, one of five women students and the only female in the freshman class. Unfazed by the ratio, she determined to show what a woman could accomplish academically in competition with males.

Following her Allegheny graduation in 1880, Ida Tarbell taught for two years at the Poland (Ohio) Union Seminary, then returned to Meadville, where she joined the staff of *The Chautauquan*, an influential monthly publication with a wide circulation in the Middle West. For many years the Tarbell family vacationed on the shores of Lake Chautauqua, New York, where from Methodist origins had grown a formidable cultural institution that now offered, by correspondence, a very popular curriculum equivalent to a four-year college course. *The Chautauquan* provided contact between students and course leaders. Ida moved through its ranks to become managing editor and in the process learned the skills of magazine production that were basic to her subsequent journalistic endeavors with *McClure's* and *The American* magazines.

In 1891, after eight years, she left the confines of work and locale to study in Paris, in keeping with her feminist outlook, the role of women in the French Revolution. A "femme travailleuse," she found an intellectually stimulating circle of friends and, to meet expenses she contributed articles to American periodicals such as *Scribner's* and *McClure's*. She joined the staff of the latter in 1893 upon her return to New York and there established her reputation as a journalist with a series on Napoleon and Abraham Lincoln.

In 1900, Ida Tarbell, daughter of the Pennsylvania Oil region, was assigned a series for *McClure's* on the development of the Standard Oil Trust. Despite her careful research and attempted objectivity, the rage of times past surfaced as she chronicled the manipulations which had marked Standard's early history. Privately, an indignant Rockefeller denied Ida's version. He refused to reply publicly to the articles in *McClure's*. "Not a word," he insisted, "not a word about that misguided woman!" Her powerful indictment published in book form as *The*

History of the Standard Oil Company in 1904 created a sensation and achieved for her the basis of her reputation. She was one of a number of writers exposing corruption in all phases of American life and hence the name "muckraker."

Despite her personal hostility toward Standard Oil, Ida Tarbell found much to praise in John D. Rockefeller and in her history wrote:

> There was no more faithful Baptist in Cleveland than he. Every enterprise of that church he had supported liberally from his youth. He gave to its poor. He visited its sick. He wept with its suffering. Moreover, he gave unostentatiously to many outside charities of whose worthiness he was satisfied. He was simple and frugal in his habits. He never went to the theatre, never drank wine. He gave much time to the training of his children, seeking to develop in them his own habits of economy and charity. Yet he was willing to strain every nerve to obtain for himself special and unjust privileges from the railroads which were bound to ruin every man in the oil business not sharing with them.

According to Allan Nevins in his biography of Rockefeller, Ida Tarbell's history of Standard Oil was "the most spectacular success of the muckraking school of journalism, and its most enduring achievement."

In 1906 Ida Tarbell left *McClure's* and with others purchased *The American Magazine*. After its sale in 1915 she became a popular lecturer on the Chautauqua circuit, and based on her fame with the Standard Oil history, drew large crowds who heard her address righteousness in business and other issues such as unemployment, the Versailles Treaty, League of Nations, and disarmament. For twenty-five years she travelled, lectured, and wrote, and in 1937 she was writing her autobiography when John D. Rockefeller died at ninety-seven. The woman who had been his nemesis lived seven more years, enjoying the tranquility of her Connecticut farm.

When Euclid Avenue Was Somebody

Dwelle Butts, Cleveland's busdriving ego-booster, swings his green Cleveland Tours coach onto Euclid Avenue for the final leg of his two-and-a-half-hour trip. He beeps wildly to draw my attention and pulls out of the flow of traffic coming off Liberty Boulevard to pick me up. I'd been waiting to hitch a ride down what was once known as the most beautiful street in the world, Euclid Avenue, to see what traces of that age still remain.

I take the seat directly behind our host. Behind me are two elderly black ladies, both native Clevelanders rediscovering their city. Across the aisle is a middle-aged couple from New York and their teenage daughter.

The intrusion over, Butts quickly slips back into his rat-a-tat documentary. His first comment on the once grand boulevard is about Winston Willis, the black entrepreneur who had developed the East 105th-Euclid area into a thriving entertainment center, and his second is about Bob Hope, who sold newspapers on the same corner the first time the area was a thriving entertainment center fifty years ago. Butts casually mentions that the area was once known as Doan's Corners. It was named after Job Doan, who owned most of the surrounding land long before either Winston Willis or Bob Hope arrived on the scene. Doan built a tavern on Euclid Avenue when it was still an Indian path that followed Lake Erie's old shoreline all the way to Buffalo.

Then, in 1815, Buffalo Road was renamed Euclid Avenue within the city limits. Why? Because it was the main thoroughfare to the outlying township of Euclid.

Ten years after the name change, new settlers were still clearing the land, but they left enough trees for the village that would become known as the "Forest City." A new arrival sailing into the mouth of the Cuyahoga would have trouble believing anyone lived nearby. A few church spires were his only clues. But in the 1820s something happened that would change forever the destiny of the small settlement of farmers and tradesmen along the banks of a crooked little river. Cleveland was chosen as the northern terminus of the Ohio Canal and quickly became a center of trade and industry. Within years the once marshy flats of the Cuyahoga Valley became a dense mass of iron mills and lumberyards.

The Civil War gave industry its great impetus, and for the first time in the country's history there was an opportunity for many to amass great wealth. And Cleveland, at the crossroads of the industrial revolution, was the place to make it. Along with great wealth came a tremendous purchasing power and Cleveland's instant millionaires turned their newfound riches in one direction, Euclid Avenue.

Butts knows his route and teases his riders with an offhand remark. "We're now approaching what was once Millionaires' Row. Every now and then you'll see the remains of an old mansion." Then, almost as the word mansion slips past his lips, the University Club, T. S. Beckwith's old mansion, appears out of nowhere. It's set far enough back from the road that if you weren't looking for it you wouldn't notice it.

Millionaires' Row, just like the rest of the city, grew in bits and pieces. Sam Williamson started it all. He arrived in Cleveland in 1810 and built the city's first tannery near his home by the Cuyahoga River. A few years later, looking for more room for his growing family, he built a new home at Euclid Avenue and Public Square. Little did he realize the trend he was setting. Sam Williamson lived to see Cleveland grow from a hamlet of fifty-seven persons to a city of two hundred thousand.

Other residents followed his lead as the population swelled in a southeasterly direction. But the first step in converting the simple country road into a classic boulevard was taken by Truman P. Handy, better known as "the first banker of Cleveland." Handy was the cashier of the Commercial Bank of Lake Erie, Cleveland's first bank, organized in 1816.

By 1842, after his bank had failed once and then reopened, he had become successful and was ready to build a new home. He chose a lot on Euclid at about East Nineteenth Street, but his old neighbors tried to talk him out of moving so far away from his place of business. Despite their objections, he built what was then considered the finest residence in Cleveland. And, as a prominent civic leader, he encouraged other notables to build "out in the country" even though Euclid was still a cinder road, and the Erie (East Ninth) Street intersection was so muddy and rutted from stagecoach wheels it was called "the frog pond."

Handy's friends followed his advice. Family after family of the city's emerging aristocracy chose Euclid Avenue for their homes. It became the "in" place to live. A stranger wanting to know who the most powerful men in Cleveland were in the last half of the nineteenth century had merely to stroll down Euclid and ask who lived where.

The three decades after the Civil War were both Cleveland's and Euclid Avenue's golden era. The hardships of the pioneer days had been left behind, while the evils of the machine age still lurked over the horizon. It was a time, according to Ella Grant Wilson's Famous Old Euclid Avenue, "when horse cars rattled over cobblestone streets, when women's skirts trailed in the dust and when downtown was west of Public Square." And "almost every man wore whiskers and a rubber collar. Bustles, balloon sleeves, and funny hats were in vogue for women. The tallest building in town was six stories, saloons and grog shops almost rubbed elbows, and horses, hitched tandem, pranced down Euclid Avenue in the shade of stately elms."

It was the stately elms, and the residences beneath them, that made Euclid Avenue world-famous. In 1860 John Fiske, a popular writer, described the avenue in a lecture before the Royal Society of Great Britain: "Bordered on each side with a double row of arching trees, and with handsome stone houses of sufficient variety and freedom of architectural design, standing at intervals of one to two hundred feet along the entire length of the street...the vistas reminding one of the nave and aisles of a huge cathedral."

The majestic elms were from the Forest City's original forest, and it was a liberal sprinkling of these trees plus an ornate landscaping of the huge grounds between the homes which made Euclid Avenue unique. It seemed more like a park than a street.

While America's nouveau riche were building brownstone fronts along New York's Fifth Avenue and other such streets, Cleveland's newly rich were pioneering the suburban concept. The eastern cities were borrowing their building ideas from London (city folks), while Cleveland was being true to its heritage (country folks). And, as country folks might do, it wasn't uncommon to find the family cow grazing along the avenue's spacious front lawns.

Warren Wick remembers one such cow interfering with his boyhood plans to build a tennis court at the corner of Sterling (East Thirtieth) and Euclid. Wick, an eighty-eight-year-old retired investment banker, whose flashing blue eyes reveal youthful exuberance, grew up in a yellow and white house where the United Way Services building now stands at 3100 Euclid. The cow was owned by his next-door neighbor, William A. Leonard, Episcopal bishop of Ohio. He grazed the cow in the empty lot where Warren and his friend, Elton Hoyt, envisioned a lawn tennis court. In the spirit of the times Bishop Leonard shortened the cow's towline so the boys could mark off their court in the far corner of the property.

Wick's older brother, Dudley, was a budding scientist and used their home as a testing ground for his experiments. While electricity was still a virtually unknown phenomenon, he installed a burglar alarm system, electric starters for the gas lights, and his own dynamo. While attending Central High School, he assisted Dr. Dayton Miller of old Case School of Applied Science in developing the first X-ray machine in the U.S. Dudley took the country's first X-ray, a shot of his own left hand, on February 14, 1896. He died tragically nine years later from overexposure to the rays.

Both Warren Wick and Reveley G. Beattie, another native of that era, remember Euclid's being portrayed as "the most beautiful street in the world" in their schoolbooks. This tribute, eagerly repeated by the city's natives, was given avenue by Bayard Taylor, an American traveler and author who visited Cleveland frequently. He stated that only the Prospekt Nevsky in St. Petersburg (today Leningrad) matched its beauty. Others compared it with the Champs Elysees in Paris and the Unter den Linden in Berlin. It was claimed that "no other avenue in the world presented such a continuous succession of charming residences and such uniformly beautiful grounds for so great a distance."

If a Clevelander was visiting another city, the first reaction he invariably received was, "Ah, Euclid Avenue." Its fame was such that a butler, Samuel Milliken, once received a letter from Europe addressed simply, "Samuel Milliken, Euclid Avenue." There was no need to add anything further.

Such bouquets hardly could be unnoticed. Euclid Avenue became more than a civic asset; it was a spiritual reservoir, the American dream stretched out along a cobblestone boulevard for all the world to sit back and pay homage. Its grandeur testified to the nineteenth-century business philosophy of Social Darwinism, the application of Darwin's famous "survival of the fittest" evolution formula to social organization. The new ruling class, the industrialist and the investment banker who made their fortunes in the industrial revolution, believed they got where they were because they deserved it and those who didn't, didn't. "God gave me my money," explained John D. Rockefeller. And Rockefeller was only one of Cleveland's wealthy who owned a home on Euclid Avenue.

That these homes were built to last forever was never questioned. They were to be used as centers of great social and political gatherings since, by the era of Reconstruction, Euclid Avenue's residents were exerting tremendous power not only on the local scene, but at the national level.

Daniel P. Eells made his fortune developing railroads. In 1881 the library of his Euclid Avenue estate was the scene of a conference between him, Marcus Hanna (another Euclid Avenue resident and later U.S. senator), and William McKinley, who went on to become governor of Ohio, and, in 1897, president of the United States.

On the corner of Euclid and North Perry (East Twenty-first) stood Senator Henry Payne's massive stone house. In his gabled residence with its stone-railed portico, railroads were planned, Civil War Reconstruction organized, and political strategy developed.

Up Euclid, on the corner of Case (East Fortieth), Colonel Sylvester T. Everett in 1883 built the most costly home yet. The railroad magnate-financier used his brownstone mansion to entertain Presidents Grant, Hayes, McKinley, and Taft, as well as such captains of industry as Andrew Carnegie and J. Pierpont Morgan.

Across Case from Everett's, General Grant could be remembered picking Malaga grapes from Jeptha H. Wade's famous garden. The benefactor of Wade Park, who began his career as a portrait painter, built his fortune consolidating telegraph companies into Western Union. The seven monumental pillars used as cornerstones for his iron fence cost $1,000 apiece, a fabulous sum.

Even the backyards were unique. Charles Brush, developer of the arc light, lived where the Arena now stands. His basement laboratory was powered by an enormous backyard windmill. Tom L. Johnson, successful millionaire turned radical mayor in 1901, kept an ice skating rink in his Euclid backyard to entertain distinguished guests and neighborhood youth, in that order. Statesmen, scientists, financiers, and industrialists lined both sides of the boulevard in a wide array of architectural achievements.

But the one mansion which symbolized both Euclid Avenue's glory and tragedy was Samuel Andrews' castle. Andrews, whose process for refining crude oil provided the key to Rockefeller's Standard Oil Co. empire, took three years to build a thirty-three-room mansion with castle-like towers and turrets. Such was his belief in the street's reputation that he had all his furnishings imported from England in anticipation of a visit from Queen Victoria. Not only did Queen Victoria fail to show, the Andrews' themselves moved out within a few years. Their thirty-three-room white elephant, complete with 100 servants, was too much for even a Standard Oil magnate to support. The empty castle was known as "Andrews' Folly" until it was replaced by a miniature golf course in 1923.

Yet Andrews' fantasies of a visit from Queen Victoria were not so farfetched for a Euclid Avenue habitué. Distinguished visitors routinely appeared here. Cleveland, on the basis of its economic strength, had moved into the forefront of national affairs. Its Euclid Avenue upstarts were influencing the seats of power formerly held by southern planters and northern merchants, the old aristocracy of inherited wealth.

Obviously the old aristocracy didn't take a particularly sympathetic view to the newcomers. John Hay's novel, *The Breadwinners*, illustrates this view. Hay, secretary to President Lincoln and later secretary of state under McKinley, spent five years in Cleveland after marrying the wealthy Amasa Stone's daughter, Clara. Stone wanted his daughter near him while he was ill and also wanted Hay to do something more manly than write for a newspaper. (Hay was on the staff of the *New York Tribune*.) So Stone built a fashionable residence for the couple next to his own mansion on Euclid and Brownell (East Fourteenth). At the time, Stone declared he was "building a barn for my Hay" which was exactly the kind of comment that nauseated the blue-blooded diplomat. Hay wrote *The Breadwinners* during his Cleveland stay and published it anonymously as a social study. His in-depth view of the personal lives of the Euclid Avenue residents was intended as a criticism of their crassness. Instead, it revealed the resentment of the old order at being dethroned.

Of course their life-style was extravagant. What was one to do with those great piles of greenbacks? The income tax and welfare state were generations away. Philanthropy was a full-time profession.

But Ella Grant Wilson gives us an indication of the dollar's more mundane uses. As one of Cleveland's leading florists, she was welcome on Millionaires' Row. She tells of one seven-course meal for seven millionaires and their wives where the table's linen, service, and floral arrangements were changed with each course. "In those days, wines were served with each course, and I think the guests must have been pretty mellow by the time they had finished the famous brands set forth."

Julia Raymond, in her "Recollections of Euclid Avenue," details the feminine life-style in the age of Saturday baths:

> I asked mother what young ladies did in the years after school before they settled down to married life. No one "came out" in those days. Were there any committees? No. Or sewing circles?...As a matter of fact none of the girls could sew well except Jessie Taintor...The young ladies made their beds and dusted their room and on Saturdays cleaned the ornaments in the what-nots that stood in every parlor. Finally Mother said, they were elevated to arranging the flowers. But, besides these, no tasks seem to have been expected of them.

She recalls her mother once receiving a diamond ring for baking a loaf of bread.

Despite the great material gulf separating the Euclid residents from the rest of Cleveland, there was one ritual that all Clevelanders shared in, and it added immensely to the street's reputation: the Euclid Avenue sleigh races, a six-week, nonstop informal winter festival.

The sleigh driver might have been a Rockefeller, a Hanna, a Bolton, or an Otis, but the spirited races were open to everyone who owned a horse. There were no official starters, no timers, and no judges. Applause from the crowds that lined the sidewalk was the only reward for winning. The races were purely spontaneous. A driver would move slowly eastward from Erie Street and then turn at Perry or maybe Case and line up an opponent. Heading westward the two sleighs would charge neck and neck back to Erie with the possible intention of having an exciting brush with a friend or foe who had been singled out beforehand. And while the local aristocracy dominated the scene in elegant two-horse sleighs, complete with driver, footman, and charcoal foot warmer, others came from as far away as Doan's Corners.

Warren Wick remembers trying to hook his sled on the back of John D. Rockefeller's sleigh as it sped down to the Euclid Avenue Baptist Church each Sunday morning at exactly 10:10. He and his friends would try to hitch up to the sleigh only to receive a taste of the footman's whip. "It used to sting, but us kids kept trying," Wick recalls.

Today, the sleigh races, like the gaslights that kept them going through the night, long since have fallen victim to the machine age. Today's stately elm is a stark telephone pole, its branches covered with harsh electric lights, tangles of wires, and voltage regulators. Gazing across the University Club's front lawn, where T. S. Beckwith's family could once watch the sleigh races, one can instead watch the Belmont Motor Hotel's blinking red neon sign. The spacious lawn is half cement parking lot and although a few trees remain, they seem out of place. The mansion itself, reserved for University Club members, reveals its age with peeling white paint. The old stables are a locker room and the back lawn is a tennis court. The one remaining tie with the avenue's golden era is the black iron fence that borders the front sidewalk.

As Butts' tour sneaks under the East Fifty-fifth Street railroad overpass, we remember what was once "the most beautiful street in the world." As we enter the land of barred storefront windows Butts becomes uneasily silent. There is little he can say. I want to break the silence by telling how Sam Huntington, one of Cleveland's original land owners,was supposedly attacked by a wolf pack back when the East Fifty-fifth Street intersection was a swampy forest.

Instead, we approach Cleveland State and the last reminder of Millionaires' Row. Above the deep cut beneath the avenue where Innerbelt traffic flows, Samuel Mather's forty-five-room mansion sits like a ghost house on an artificial hill. The one-time Mather estate was taken over by the Cleveland Automobile Club in 1940, and was expropriated by Cleveland State University for administrative offices in 1968.

Perhaps CSU can succeed where Samuel Mather failed. In 1907 the descendant of Puritan ministers Cotton and Increase Mather commissioned the prominent Cleveland architect Charles F. Schweinfurth (who also designed Trinity Cathedral at East Twenty-second) to create the most expensive home ever built in Cleveland. Mather, who made his fortune mining iron ore, hoped that such a great investment at such a late date would forestall the avenue's desertion by Cleveland's first families. But as both Dan Harbaugh, a seventy-three-year-old retired banker who grew up near Euclid and Bolton (East Eighty-ninth), and Warren Wick recall, "the Heights" had already replaced Euclid Avenue as the place to live. New forms of architecture already were supplanting Schweinfurth's massive Romanesque style. The retreat to the suburbs had begun. The old gang was definitely breaking up, and one by one the old residences were overcome by that greatest of all evils, creeping commercialism.

Back in 1870 when Millionaires' Row was just beginning to take form, a couple of Bostonians planned to open a dry goods store on the corner of Euclid Avenue and Public Square. Local commercial prophets scoffed. Everyone knew the high-class retail section of Cleveland was Superior Street. But William Taylor and Thomas Kilpatrick pinned their hopes on a brand new merchandising concept, "the one-price system."

They publicized their new idea in the *Cleveland Herald* on the day of their grand opening. "Our goods are bought in the present low market and will be sold exclusively at the one-price system at popular prices." This meant the same price would be given each customer on the same piece of goods. Prior to the Taylor-Kilpatrick policy an item's final price was the product of a bartering exchange between customer and merchant. Their method caught on, their store was a success, and Euclid Avenue's destiny was changed forever.

Slowly but surely other commercial enterprises inched up the boulevard. In 1871 Burrows' book store opened several blocks east of Public Square. In 1873 the Standard Block, home office of Standard Oil, was erected on the north side of Euclid. By 1895 Henry Chisholm's mansion between Bond (East Sixth) and Erie was razed to make room for a new fourteen-story sandstone office building. It marked the beginning of the end of the glory that was Euclid's.

Why wasn't anything done once these evil omens began to appear? One attempt was made to preserve the avenue. On April 19, 1897, city council passed a resolution making Euclid Avenue a boulevard and placing its care under the Board of Park Commissioners. The resolution recognized the street's worldwide reputation and stated the hope that Euclid Avenue could be maintained as a magnificent parkway connecting the center city with a new park system that one day would encircle the city.

But too much money already had been invested in Euclid Avenue's success as a commercial enterprise. Within weeks, over thirty lawsuits were filed in common pleas court contesting the constitutionality of the resolution and demanding property damages up to $100,000 if the resolution was upheld.

Three years later the park commission gave up its ill-fated task and asked the city to rescind the resolution and dismiss the court cases. The same philosophy that created the wealth to build Euclid Avenue had ensured its destruction. By the 1930s John D. Rockefeller's symbol of wealth and accomplishment was razed to make room for a gas station and parking lot. A new generation of investors demanded their share of God's blessings, and in the process a proud avenue was destroyed. Most of the mansions were razed in the years after World War II to make way for cheap office buildings and even one warehouse.

That Euclid Avenue could have been preserved is not mere speculation. The few remaining mansions that have been converted to meet new needs offer convincing proof. Their success illustrates that the avenue's destruction was never necessary, only profitable.

EUGENE C. MURDOCK

A Couple of Giants: Mark Hanna and Tom Johnson

It is unfortunate, in a way, that Mark Hanna's statue is not located on Cleveland's Public Square rather than at University Circle on the East Side. For if it were, then two of the giants of Cleveland history would face each other across the green, just as they faced one another for more than twenty-five years in business and politics. As it is, Tom L. Johnson, millionaire, street railway magnate-turned reform mayor, sits alone. That is, unless you wish to count the ancient Moses Cleaveland, the city's founder, who stands in front of the Terminal Tower.

On the other hand, it is probably more fitting that the present arrangements continue. For powerful as he was, both in state and national politics, Hanna never quite got a firm grasp of the local political temper. He had his followers, and he wielded his influence, but his control of the Republican organization in Cleveland never compared to Tom Johnson's strength in Democratic and independent circles. Moreover, Johnson was mayor of Cleveland for nearly ten years (1901–10), during which time he restructured the city in the mold of Progressivism, despite Hanna's efforts to preserve the existing order.

Johnson was born into a Kentucky family of moderate means in 1854, but in the course of the Civil War everything was lost. The family had financial problems after the war, too, and when Tom was fifteen he decided to go out on his own. He had no opportunity for a formal education, but a keen mind and a mechanical bent brought him quick success. He learned the fundamentals of the street railway business in Louisville. While there he invented a coin farebox, which he was able to market and which brought him several thousand dollars. While trying to sell his farebox in 1876, he was induced to buy the Citizens Street Railway Company in Indianapolis. Although this was a dilapidated run-down facility when he bought it, he sold it about ten years later for $800,000.

Meanwhile, he purchased street railway lines in Cleveland and would later operate transit systems in Brooklyn and Detroit. Johnson also invented a "girder groove rail" for urban railways and built a small steel plant in Johnstown, Pennsylvania, for the manufacture of the rail and other track devices. By the time he was twenty-five years old his fortune was estimated at more than a million dollars.

It was in Cleveland in the early 1880s that Johnson first encountered Mark Hanna. Hanna was not a self-made man as was Johnson, but his business skills were just as sharp. He was born in New Lisbon, Ohio, in 1837, and moved to Cleveland in 1852, where his father and uncle established a produce commission house. Mark rose to a position of importance in the concern, but it went bankrupt after the Civil War. In 1867 he joined his father-in-law's organization which was engaged in the coal and oil business. The company successfully expanded its interests in coal, oil, iron, and lake shipping as Hanna gradually assumed control. In 1879, through his wife's family, he inherited the West Side Street Railway Company in Cleveland, which was the very year that Tom L. Johnson came to town.

During the Gilded Age of industrial and urban growth, men of vision and rough methods were building up vast fortunes as they developed the country. While Hanna and Johnson did not operate on quite the same scale as Andrew Carnegie and John D. Rockefeller, they were much like their more celebrated fellows. They were men of imagination, they possessed an astute business sense, they were organizers, and they were leaders of men. They knew exactly what they wanted to achieve and fought hard to achieve it.

This was illustrated by an incident which occurred in 1885. Johnson secured a twenty-five-year franchise renewal on one of his street railway lines from the Cleveland City Council, which apparently caught Hanna by surprise. As the renewal had an adverse effect on Hanna's lines, Mark invited Tom to lunch at the Union Club, where he proposed that they form a partnership. Hanna explained that he was not primarily a street railway man—that he had not wanted his line, but had inherited it. He argued that his influence among the bankers and familiarity with politics, added to Johnson's street railway know-how, would make them an unbeatable combination. Flushed with victory, Johnson declined the offer. "We would make good opponents," he said, "but poor partners."

Electrification of street railways—either by overhead wire or underground cable—commenced in 1889 and 1890. This advance greatly enhanced the value of all street railway lines and led to a demand for their consolidation. At one time there were eight lines in Cleveland (Johnson owning two of them), but by May 1893, after various consolidations, only two lines remained. The Cleveland Electric Railway, in which Johnson shared ownership, controlled 60 percent of the street railway trackage in the city. The Cleveland City Railway, in which Hanna shared ownership, controlled the other 40 percent.

After these consolidations, Hanna approached Johnson with the idea of resolving several long-standing disagreements among the former companies. "Now that we've all consolidated, Tom, you and I might as well take up some old matters of dispute between us and get them settled."

"Certainly," Johnson replied. "By our consolidation agreement all disputes are to be referred to the president (of the Cleveland Electric Railway), so all you have to do is to see your friend, Horace Andrews."

Hanna got the point. Andrews was a bitter enemy of his. With an oath he slammed out of the room. Johnson and Hanna were never friends, but they did respect the other's business methods. It was not quite the same in the field of politics.

In 1895 Hanna retired from most of his business operations—he retained the street railway—and devoted all of his energies for the next year and a half to making William McKinley president. In this task he was eminently successful. His careful pre-convention planning which insured McKinley a first ballot nomination at the 1896 Republican convention has long served as a textbook model.

Hanna's political talents had developed steadily during the previous ten years, but he had concentrated largely on the elevation of other people to high office. Having succeeded in putting his friend McKinley in the White House, he now sought high office himself—the United States Senate. After McKinley named the aging Senator John Sherman to be secretary of state, the governor of Ohio, Asa Bushnell, appointed Hanna to fill out the two remaining years of Sherman's term in the Senate. Hanna was reelected for a full term beginning in 1899.

For some years Johnson had been dissatisfied with business and was searching for some new outlet. He found it in Henry George and his teachings. He had first heard of George in 1883 and was won over at once by the man's deep humanity. He was also speedily converted to George's economic views as embodied in the "single tax." This was a tax on land values, which George felt was the only equitable tax. If people only had to pay taxes on the unearned increment of their land, sufficient revenues would be available to run the government, and no one would be unjustly deprived of income he had earned by his own efforts. Since no other taxes would be necessary, this tax on land values came to be known as the single tax.

Johnson admitted to George that the wealth he had acquired in the street railway and steel business was ill-gotten in single tax terms, and that maybe he should quit the game. His mentor advised against it, saying that as long as the system permitted him to make vast sums of money he should do so, but that he should then contribute some of his wealth to "the cause." So Johnson stayed in business. In fact, it was not until after George's death in October 1897, that Johnson decided to divest himself of all business connections. It was his feeling that since the single tax movement had now lost its leader, it was his duty to assume command.

Johnson had served two terms in the United States House of Representatives from his Cleveland district from 1891 to 1895 and had at that time tried to advance "the cause." He found, however, that the little band of single taxers was badly outnumbered and that their collective impact was negligible. On leaving Washington he asserted that Congress was no proper battleground for the great struggle to right the socio-economic wrongs of the day. That fight must be carried on at the local level. At this time Johnson sold all his street railway holdings in Cleveland and for the next five years devoted much of his time to his street railway properties in Brooklyn and Detroit.

It so happened that in 1900 a battle was raging in Cleveland over a twenty-five-year franchise renewal grant to Mark Hanna's Cleveland City Railway Company well in advance of the expiration of the franchise. It was the kind of manipulation Johnson had benefited from many times as a street railway owner, but now he was on the other side. Hanna did not get his franchise renewal because of the popular outcry against it, but the incident galvanized Tom Johnson into action. He announced that he was available for public office. The Democratic party nominated him for mayor of Cleveland in February 1901, and the people of Cleveland elected him to that office the following April.

Having abandoned business to fight "privilege," Johnson was now ready to begin the battle. He suffered much abuse from his former business contemporaries, as well as from politicians and private citizens for this change of view. But to some observers of that day and to some historians of this day, Johnson's conversion was an honest and sincere transformation. The impact of Henry George's personality and teachings was sufficient to explain the turnabout. In the final analysis, what the man actually did, rather than what he had been, and the price he paid to do what he did, should be the measure. At the end of his "Nine Years War With Privilege" Tom Johnson was a broken man, both in his financial and physical states. No longer was he the millionaire street railway magnate. There were times during that war when he might have gone back into business and recouped some of his losses, but he chose to continue his fight to make Cleveland a better place in which to live, whatever the cost might be.

Johnson's new career in politics as a reform mayor brought him head to head against his old nemesis of street railway days, Mark Hanna. Hanna still controlled the Cleveland City Railway Company, but was more famous as United States senator and the most influential figure in President McKinley's coterie of advisers. Although the murder of McKinley in September 1901 led to the erosion of Hanna's power at the national level, he was still a man to be contended with at the time of his death in February 1904.

The final chapters in the Tom Johnson-Mark Hanna fray centered on two issues: the Federal Plan ouster suit and Nash Code in 1901 and 1902, and Johnson's bid for the governorship in 1903. A short history lesson is necessary to understand the first of these disputes. Under the 1851 Ohio Constitution, charters for the government of every city in the state had to be drafted by the state legislature. And all such charters had to be "general," that is the legislation must not authorize one type of charter for Cleveland, another for Youngstown, a third for Dayton, and so forth. This would constitute "special" legislation. In practice, however, the legislature began to classify cities by population and to draft "general" charters for each classification. Some of these were ludicrous. For example, one such classification embraced all cities with populations between 27,690 and 27,720. Youngstown was the only city which qualified. By 1901 there were twelve classifications and ten of these had only one city.

One of the categories applied to Cleveland. In 1891 a measure drawn up by Cleveland lawyers and students of municipal government providing for the Federal Plan was adopted by the state legislature. While obviously a species of "special" legislation, it came to be regarded as a model for municipal government. It provided for a strong mayor with the power to appoint all his cabinet officers. Authority and responsibility were fixed. It contrasted favorably with the Board Plan of government in force in Cincinnati, where power and responsibility were diffused. Mark Hanna, apparently, never thought much about special legislation or the Federal Plan before. But now with Tom L. Johnson mayor, a man who advocated a lot of wild, radical ideas, like the three-cent fare, home rule, and the single tax, Hanna decided something should be done about it.

Johnson had become interested in the three-cent fare idea for street railways when it was tried by Mayor Hazen Pingree of Detroit in 1895. He was not won over to it then, being the manager of a street railway company himself, but the idea took root. As mayor he was ready to try it. In his 1901 campaign he repeatedly stressed his intention to oppose the Cleveland Electric Railway Company and the Cleveland City Railway Company in their quests for twenty-five-year and thirty-year franchise extensions at the five-cent rate. He promised to bring them to terms with a three-cent fare.

During the first six months of his term, from spring until fall 1901, Johnson was preoccupied with his fight for tax reform. He had no expectation of instituting the single tax, but he did intend to make tax rates more equitable. He enjoyed only marginal success in this first bout with "Privilege." By autumn he was ready to begin his campaign for a three-cent fare. The battle commenced the night of December 9, 1901, when Councilman Fred Howe introduced a three-cent fare ordinance into the Cleveland City Council. Two days later, December 11, a suit was filed in the Ohio Supreme Court to void the Federal Plan charter of Cleveland on the grounds that it was "special" legislation. The case took six months to work its way through the court, during which time the city proceeded with its plans for a three-cent fare.

It required no great imagination to determine what forces were behind the Federal Plan ouster suit. It was actually initiated by an obscure attorney, but the real influences were the public service corporations of Cleveland and Mark Hanna. The lawyer conceded that he had consulted with Hanna as well as other Republicans and anti-Johnson Democrats before filing the suit, and added that his purpose was to wreck the frame of government which gave such power to people like Johnson.

But most knowledgeable people seemed to feel that the Supreme Court would uphold the Federal Plan. They were mistaken, for on June 26, 1902, the court declared the Federal Plan charter unconstitutional because it was "special" legislation prohibited by the state constitution. Tom Johnson, although bitter at the partisan motives behind the suit, agreed that it was probably best that special legislation be abolished. The need now was to draw up a new municipal code based on something akin to the Federal Plan. What the Federal Plan ouster meant was that the charter of every city in the state of Ohio was invalid because all of the charters were special legislation. Thus a new municipal code for the state would have to be enacted at once. The Supreme Court deferred execution of its order until October 2, 1902, to permit the legislature to draft a new code. In the intervening period any ordinances adopted or actions taken in any city were subject to review by the court.

When the state legislature convened in special session on August 25, Republican Governor George K. Nash presented his proposal for a new municipal code. The plan had been worked out at a series of meetings at Put-in-Bay among the leading Republicans of the state, Mark Hanna among them. Although a number of lawyers and experts on municipal government went to Put-in-Bay to argue for the Federal Plan as a basis for the new code, they got an unsympathetic hearing. The draft submitted by Nash to the legislature embodied the principal elements of the Board Plan of government. Deliberations on the Nash Code, as it was called, lasted about two months, and though there was opposition to it, the measure passed and was signed by the governor in late October.

The new code provided for enlarging city councils (which would probably make them more difficult to control), the creation of an elected Board of Public Service, and an appointed (with the approval of council) Board of Public Safety. The president of council, auditor, treasurer, and solicitor were all to be elected by the people. Elections were to be held in April 1903, and the new officers would assume their duties on the first Monday in May. Meanwhile the Supreme Court stayed execution of its order abolishing the old governments until the new ones took over.

Mark Hanna had won his first big battle with Johnson in the political sphere. He had been instrumental in (a) the overthrow of the Federal Plan which had enhanced the mayor's powers, and (b) establishment of the loose Board Plan, which was likely to diminish the mayor's powers. No longer, or so it appeared, did Hanna have to worry about three-cent fares undercutting his own street railway properties, or the eventual municipal ownership of all street railways.

But was Hanna's triumph really so complete? If he thought it was, he reckoned little with the great hold Johnson had already secured on the minds and hearts of many Clevelanders. The mayor's fight for tax reform, the three-cent fare, and lesser improvements, plus the attempts to destroy his influence through the Federal Plan ouster suit had won the support of many who had been skeptical of his purposes when he first took office. But the true referendum on Johnson's performance would take place when he ran for reelection in April 1903.

At the Democratic party's city convention in March, Johnson was renominated along with his hand-picked slate of officers. Thus if the party could carry the election, the mayor would have his own cabinet in spite of the Nash Code. When the results of the election were in, Johnson had won a decisive endorsement. Although he received forty-eight fewer votes than in 1901, he defeated his Republican opponent, Harvey Goulder, by a 5,985 plurality. So unhappy were the people with the Republicans and their ouster suit, and so pleased were they with what the mayor had done and might have done except for the ouster suit, that they gave Johnson his own cabinet and an absolute Democratic majority in the council. Though the city would be operating under the Nash Code within a month, Johnson had as tight a grip on the administration as before, and Mark Hanna had not won this first fight after all.

Moreover, Johnson's success in Cleveland and the weakness of the Democratic party statewide at once raised talk of his running for governor. Soon after his re-election, *The Public* noted that "On all hands it is conceded that Johnson is the logical Democratic candidate." The mayor, however, had no desire to enter the race. The party was divided, the opposition would misrepresent his political and economic views, and there seemed little chance of carrying the state. Why make the run? In late June he stated that there was little likelihood the Democrats could win the governorship, but they might gain a seat on the Supreme Court and a working majority in the legislature. The latter was important because Mark Hanna would be up for reelection to the Senate, and in those pre-Seventeenth Amendment days, senators were elected by state legislatures.

The pressure from within the liberal wing of the state Democratic party mounted, however, and in early August Johnson reluctantly announced his candidacy. He was nominated for governor at the state convention August 26, and his platform, which favored home rule and just taxation while opposing the Nash Code and the Republican party's links with great corporations, was adopted handily. But there were numerous conservative Democrats who did not like all of this, and they promised to either sit out the election or support the Republicans.

The breach within the Democratic ranks was a severe one, and even efforts by the national leader, William Jennings Bryan, who spent several days in the state in early September, failed to mend it. The Republicans, meanwhile, lost no time in exploiting Democratic difficulties. In a number of counties Republicans offered their support for local Democratic candidates in exchange for Democratic support for the Republican state ticket. Consequently, when Johnson arrived in a number of places, he received cool, almost insulting, receptions from local Democrats.

The Republicans nominated Myron T. Herrick, president of the Society for Savings Bank in Cleveland, for governor. But their most prominent campaigner was Mark Hanna. He no doubt felt certain that Herrick would win the governorship with little trouble, but that his own reelection would be more difficult to secure. Therefore he spent many days and nights on the campaign trail. In fact, the campaign seemed to be more of a contest between Johnson and Hanna than Johnson and Herrick. In general, the Democrats emphasized Johnson's program and attacked Hanna. The Republicans, on the other hand, emphasized national prosperity, for which, they argued, Hanna was largely responsible. Despite this priority given to national concerns, Hanna hit hard at Johnson on several occasions.

At Chillicothe on September 19 he characterized the mayor as "a carpetbagger followed by a train of all the political vagrants of Ohio, with a crazy quilt ticket and pretending to stand upon a pessimistic, socialistic, anarchistic platform."

At Sandusky on September 29 he charged "that Tom L. Johnson is the national leader of the Socialist Party. Under the guise of the cloak of Democracy he is striving to accomplish results simply to satisfy a personal ambition and to meet his own selfish ends. I beg of you to rise and kill the attempt to float the flag of socialism over Ohio."

And in Lima on October 2 he summarized his thoughts on what a Johnson victory would mean, declaiming that when you "vote for the Tom L. Johnson socialistic ticket. . .you vote for the absolute destruction and ruin of your American institutions and for utter chaos in this country."

It is unlikely that any respect Johnson may have had for Hanna when they were business competitors survived these attacks. The mayor was bitter at being misrepresented. "They make these charges," he complained, "but they never pick out plank after plank and say what's wrong. Not since they have started their campaign have they picked out a single plank and criticized it. They have never made a specific charge."

Hanna himself could hardly have believed that American civilization was really on the line in the 1903 Ohio gubernatorial campaign, but his flaming rhetoric achieved his goal. In rural areas—and in some urban centers as well—his remarks carried conviction, and after the speeches in Chillicothe, Sandusky, and Lima, Johnson was no longer a serious threat to win.

When the votes were tabulated following the November 3 election, Tom L. Johnson turned out to be the most badly beaten candidate for governor since the Civil War. Herrick had amassed a plurality in excess of one hundred thousand votes. The Republicans even carried Johnson's home Cuyahoga County, which sent a solid Republican delegation to the state legislature. In retrospect, it was conceded that Ohio was not quite ready for Tom L. Johnson. A few years later it might have been, but in 1903 his ideas seemed too new and radical, while Hanna's influence across the state was too great to be successfully challenged.

And so it was that Mark Hanna won the second and biggest battle between himself and Tom Johnson. But as with his first victory, it was a short-lived one. True enough, Johnson's hopes of becoming a state and perhaps a national leader were blunted, but he continued on as mayor of Cleveland for six more years, during which time he saw a number of his goals attained. Home rule, the three-cent fare, and more equitable taxation all came in time—after they had lost some of their "anarchistic-socialistic" flavor. Mark Hanna did not live to see these changes, for he passed away in 1904. Had he lived it would have been worth a fat thirty-year street railway franchise to see which of the two giants would have won the day.

THOMAS L. NEWCOMB

Northeastern Ohio's Mennonite and Amish Folk

If you are a resident of northeastern Ohio, or have traveled there extensively, you are, no doubt, acquainted with the Old Order Amish. These quaint religious separatists have held the interest and curiosity of the American public for the two hundred years since they arrived on our continent. And, if you have been in "Amish country" in the area of Geauga and Trumbull Counties, you might have seen some incongruous sights. As you take in the picturesque scenery you might see a black buggy drawn by a sprightly horse. In the carriage itself, you see a bearded man dressed in dark blue or black, wearing a wide-brimmed black hat. Next to him sits a serene-looking woman, dressed in black bonnet and shawl. If you identify these people as "Amish," you are correct.

In the same glance, however, you may see a family dressed in similar attire driving by in a plain auto. In a parking lot in Middlefield or Chardon, your discerning eye may see many "plain people," as they are often called. You will notice that some are dressed in similar, yet different, clothing. Some drive buggies, others autos. Why the difference in colors and styles of these people?

Some may have told you that the buggy drivers are "Amish" and the car drivers are the "progressive Amish." Others might bring up the name "Mennonites." Who are these people, and what do they believe? Where did they come from, and how are they alike and/or different? Let us take a careful and accurate look.

Our journey into the world of the plain people will be multifold, and it will be based on fact. Although there is widespread publicity and literature concerning these people, much of it is inaccurate or misinterpreted. Let us first go back to the beginning of the this heritage, to its source in Europe.

The Amish and Mennonites trace their cultural heritage to the Reformation period in Europe in the 1500s. This was a time of great religious turmoil, both in the Protestant and Catholic churches. In Switzerland in the early 1500s, following the example of such religious reformers as Martin Luther and Ulrich Zwingly, a group of peasants started fellowshipping together under the leadership of a few educated students of the Bible. This Bible-based worship in the language of the common people was well received by the public. Critical of the teachings of the formal churches of the time, this group met in homes, streets, and any other shelter that proved convenient. Early leaders were Felix Manz, George Blaurock, and Conrad Grebel. This group, calling themselves "Brethren," held to simple Bible teachings which included a Christ-centered life, nonresistance, separation of church and state, simple living by Bible doctrine, and adult believers' baptism. This radical stand caused great friction between the Brethren and both the Catholic and Protestant churches. Because of the fact that converts to the new movement were rebaptized for scriptural reasons, the new group was nicknamed "Anabaptists" by outsiders. Severe persecution followed. Most leaders and many followers were captured, jailed, or tortured to death. The church survived, however, under new peasant leaders. In the area we now call Holland, a similar movement began under two brothers, Obie and Dietrich Philip. Obie later recanted after capture, but Dietrich continued as an early leader and writer. Later, a converted Catholic priest, Menno Simons, joined the Holland group. Simons became a famous preacher and inspired writer for his group. His efforts and later his attempts at unification of the numerous Holland movements gained the church the name "Mennists" and eventually "Mennonites." The Swiss group was slower to unite with the Holland group, and retained the name "Brethren" for some time.

The Swiss Brethren were finally driven from Switzerland to France and Germany by persecution, leaving a small faction behind. Once in the Pallatinate region, the Swiss Brethren united under the Dortrecht Confession of Faith with the Holland Mennonites. The Swiss Brethren in Switzerland did not, however, unify at this time. It was a situation that caused the genesis of a new church group. In 1692-93, problems arose between the Pallatinate Mennonites and the Swiss Brethren over certain articles of doctrine. The German and French church bishops (believed to include about twenty individuals) delegated a young Bishop, Jacob Amman, to go to Switzerland to meet with Hans Reist, elder bishop of the Swiss Brethren, to work out these problems.

Amman was a dedicated, passionate Christian. He made three trips to meet with Reist, yet they could not agree on the three or so points of doctrinal contention. Finally, in 1693, Amman and a select group of conservatives broke off from the main group and started meeting together on their own. The Amish today derive their name from Jacob Amman, the young bishop who founded a new Anabaptist church. Later, it is strange to note, Reist's group unified with the "Mennonite" group. Amman's group did not, and maintained a very conservative stand in their doctrines. Thus we see that the Amish and Mennonites came from all over Europe, and that they are a Christian movement. It is also worthwhile to note that contrary to popular belief, the Amish came out of the Mennonites, not the Mennonites out of the Amish.

Persecution of the sects continued, and following the invitation of Quaker William Penn, the Amish and Mennonites started migrating to North America in the early 1700s. This movement lasted well into the 1800s. The first North American areas to receive the groups were Pennsylvania and Ontario, Canada. The area near Lancaster, Pennsylvania, and outer regions is the oldest American

Amish and Mennonite settlement. Since coming to America, the Amish and Mennonites have spread out over some thirty states and have divided into several divisions or groups, each with its own beliefs and interpretations of doctrine. The Old Order Amish (horse-and-buggy Amish) are the most conservative and are found in North and Central America. There are approximately seventy to eighty-five thousand Old Order Amish. They use horse and buggy for travel, wear somber plain clothes, generally use no electricity or telephones in their homes, reject most modern movements or influences, and meet in each other's homes for worship.

There are also about six thousand "Beachy" or "New Order" Amish in North, Central, and South America. This group is named for a Pennsylvania bishop who originally allowed some modern conveniences into his church, such as electricity, telephones, autos, and some variation in clothing styles. The Beachy Amish are still easily recognizable, however, as conservatives.

The Mennonite Church is much more diverse, with an approximate world membership of eight hundred thousand. Mennonites are found in other countries, but most are located in America. The many groups range from quite contemporary to very conservative. In general, however, the Mennonite church is becoming more contemporary and is, in most cases, much more progressive than the Amish groups. Most Amish and Mennonite groups, it seems, do recognize each other as religious "cousins." It is actually different interpretations of the same Bible and traditional doctrines that differentiates the churches.

A wide range of the Amish and Mennonite churches is observable in the northeastern Ohio settlement. The area of highest concentration centers around the following counties: Geauga, Trumbull, Ashtabula, and northern Portage. The main area of land is a strip approximately twelve by twenty-six miles, not including outside edges, which are expanding with the growing population. The Amish population of the area is about sixty-five hundred, the Mennonite population about four hundred. Both of these figures include children and are based on current estimates.

The first Amish and Mennonite settlements were in the Holmes County area in our state. This area is now the largest Amish/Mennonite settlement in America. Migration started in the early 1800s from Pennsylvania to the Holmes County area. The Amish and Mennonite population of the area is now estimated to be in the area of thirty thousand, including children. (Figures are from current estimates and reports.) As land became scarce in southern and central Ohio, the Amish migrated north. The first settlers arrived in the Geauga area in 1886.

Since past articles have concentrated mainly on the Amish, let us now take a closer look at the Mennonites in this geographic area. In the Geauga-Trumbull-centered settlement are five Mennonite churches. This does not include churches in areas such as Cleveland, Youngstown, Hartville, and Aurora. The Geauga-Trumbull area churches all evolved out of the Old Order Amish church for doctrinal or contemporary reasons. This is a general sociological tendency for all conservative Amish and Mennonite groups—there is a certain percentage of upward spiral from more conservative to less conservative churches. Membership in the Geauga-Trumbull Mennonite churches now also includes those from pure Mennonite or other cultural heritages. Please note also that both the Amish and Mennonite churches believe in adult baptism into church membership upon confession of faith. Thus, children are not included in church population figures unless noted as such.

There is one Beachy Amish or Amish-Mennonite church in the Geauga area. These "progressive Amish," as they are often called, meet in a church house located on Georgia Road, just outside of Middlefield. These Amish-Mennonites use some modern conveniences such as telephones and limited applications of electricity, as well as unadorned (usually black) cars. The group meets in a church house, unlike the Old Order, who continue to use each other's homes for services. The Zion Fellowship has a membership of fifty and is composed primarily of ex-Old Order families and others from different backgrounds. The Beachy Amish church is more organized than the Old Order. They hold regular, large, interchurch fellowship meetings and also have a well-organized mission and a disaster relief effort. Adult men generally wear the beard, although it is trimmed, which is forbidden in the Old Orders. Men also usually wear suspenders and straight cut dress coats without the lay-down contemporary collar. Dress for women includes a long, conservatively designed cape dress and the head covering or "prayer cap." Unlike the Old Order Amish, who prefer hook-and-eyes and pins for clothing, the Beachy Amish allow use of buttons and zippers. Colors of clothing are generally unpatterned earth colors, avoiding reds, pinks, and louder shades. This is much like the Old Order choice of colors for clothes.

Maple View Mennonite Church, founded as a mission effort in 1947 by Mennonites from Hartville, is the oldest of four churches in the Geauga-Trumbull settlement. It is located northwest of Middlefield on the Burton-Windsor Road.

Since coming into the Western Reserve, the Amish and Mennonites have blended in well and are generally respected as God-fearing, good citizens. The Old Order Amish are generally a farming people, although some are carpenters, hand craftsmen, or local factory workers. Women, usually become housewives after marriage, but some open small home businesses such as book or craft shops. The Amish do not vote or take public office, yet they pay their taxes and are law-abiding in their way of life. They are good farmers and respected craftsmen. Mennonites are found in many different occupations in the Western Reserve: farmers, teachers, truck drivers, factory workers, carpenters, professionals and others. Generally reluctant to take public office or to vote (depending on how liberal the church), Mennonites are also good, law-abiding citizens. Amish and Mennonites are quite charitable, giving much for relief work in and outside our country; they are well known for their own relief and emergency services rendered without prejudice to those in need in our area and across the country.

Perhaps the biggest stumbling block for the Amish and Mennonites is the contention that sometimes exists between them. Because a certain percentage of Old Order and Conservative members move to a more contemporary order, the churches are sometimes critical of one another. It is really a small scale of the endless liberal/conservative question in American life.

Since the Amish and Mennonites are still a growing population in America and Ohio, it is unlikely that they will eventually blend into contemporary society. A people with a 300-year-old heritage that has survived in the Old Orders and Conservatives with little change is not likely to be assimilated into American society. Likewise, it is no doubt important for the more contemporary Mennonites to help bridge the space between the conservative churches and modern society.

A number of contemporary issues face the northeastern Mennonites and their Amish "cousins." One is their ability to maintain their own interpretation of the following general articles of faith (this annotated list is not exhaustive and not peculiar to all groups): Christ-centered life; nonconformity and nonresistance; closed communion service; foot-washing services (an Amish practice); services in members' homes; submission and pacifism; mission outreach activity in Mennonites; purity and holiness of lifestyle; no alcoholic drinking or smoking; no business or working on Sunday; Amish and Conservative practice of no musical instruments during worship; women's wearing of the prayer cap or devotional covering; women never cutting their hair in Amish and Conservative Mennonite groups; plain clothes and modest dress; headship belief of God-Christ-Man-Woman. Although not all groups hold to these practices, it is worthwhile to note that those who do, defend the doctrines with Bible passages.

Another important issue is that of education. Mennonites, in general, accept higher education but prefer Christian schools and teachers. There are many Mennonite parochial schools in Ohio; one is located in Middlefield and operated by the Beachy Amish church. More conservative Mennonites believe in an eight-year education, like the Old Order Amish. In the early 1900s Amish and Mennonite schools came under great pressure from the state concerning minimum standards. In the 1970s, however, a Supreme Court case lifted most state sanctions on the Amish and Mennonite parochial schools. The Amish and many Mennonite parents view teachings in higher public school education as a threat to the religious beliefs of their society.

It would also be appropriate to mention Amish and Mennonite languages here. The original language of the Amish and Mennonites was a German dialect. This is often called "Pennsylvania Dutch" today, although it is a distinct German dialect. Slowly, as it has become more contemporary, the Mennonite church has been losing the use of this dialect. Only the Old Order Amish and a few Conservative Mennonite groups still use the Pennsylvania German dialect. Though it is written, Pennsylvania German is basically a spoken language. The Old Order Amish and Old Order Mennonites alone still use it as the native tongue of their home and society. This is true to the point that many Amish children speak no English until they begin school. Conservative Mennonites may speak Pennsylvania German, but do not use it as their main language. Old

Order Amish church services are held in Pennsylvania German with Bible reading from the High (or formal) German Bible.

Mennonites, particularly the conservative groups, are taking steps to provide social activities for their youth that will encourage them to refrain from too much interaction and exposure to outside society. This concern for maintaining the stability of the young people in their groups is also shared by the Old Order Amish. Leaders of both sects are trying to maintain a balance between inter-church experience and outside exposure for their adults and children.

Lastly, the growing size of Amish and Mennonite culture is a very important issue. In northern Ohio alone, land for Amish and Mennonite farmers and young households is becoming expensive and scarce. While contemporary Mennonites can find work and land in outlying areas within the normal limits of modern society, Conservatives and the Amish are less likely to wish to move to the outskirts of a settlement when the cohesiveness of their society is so vital. Necessity often causes new settlements or church districts to spring up, but it is feared that as the church spreads out and is more exposed to the outside world, it may come to resemble its modern surroundings, thus threatening the unity of the church. The extent of this concern is rather proportionate to the conservative emphasis of the church group.

These are real people who have lived in northern Ohio for nearly one hundred years. They are generous people, contributing to local fire funds, donating to local charity, and giving much aid on their own. They add to the local economy with their patronage and their own butcher, craft, and furniture shops, carpentry work, and produce stands. They ask less from modern society than do most people. They pay taxes, obey the laws, and are fundamental Christians. They have added backbone to the Western Reserve with their quiet but forceful reminder of a simpler, more fundamental, God-fearing life. You will find them to be open and friendly to the sincere who wish to know them better.

When you drive through the rolling farmland near Middlefield or Burton, admiring the wheat shocks in the fields, passing an occasional buggy, and smiling at the barefooted, plainly dressed children playing in their yards, remember that these people are as human as all of us. Very few Amish or Mennonites take foolish pride in their different way of living, but most outsiders who come to know them are glad to have an opportunity to understand and appreciate the "plain people" of northeastern Ohio in their many forms.

JOHN J. GRABOWSKI

Social Reform and Philanthropic Order in Cleveland, 1896–1920

The most important and effective manifestation of the social gospel movement in the United States and in Cleveland was the social settlement house. The settlement served as the primary instrument for the advocacy of social reform measures during the Progressive Era. Settlements have been aptly characterized as "spearheads for reform," although settlement work did not involve benevolence or charity, per se. Rather than attempting to ameliorate social problems by the provision of material aid, the settlements sought to cure these problems by eliminating their causes. The basic premise of the settlement movement was the actual residence of well-educated settlement workers within depressed areas of the city. By sharing the living conditions of the urban poor, the workers would learn the roots of urban problems. Using their own knowledge and skills, these individuals hoped to eradicate the problems at their sources and to educate the neighborhood residents so that they might overcome their condition. The desire to create an urban village lay at the heart of many settlement efforts. Those involved in the settlement movement believed that urban neighborhoods could overcome their problems if they established the network of mutual aid and sharing considered to typify small-town life.

The movement which began in England quickly spread to the United States. By 1900 there were nearly one hundred settlement houses in the nation, five of which were located in Cleveland. Four of these early enterprises, Hiram House, Goodrich House, Alta House, and the Council Educational Alliance, have left behind them substantial information concerning their origins, supporters, personnel, and policies. This information makes possible a survey of their divergent, yet similar characteristics.

Hiram House, established in July 1896, is generally considered to have been the first true social settlement in Cleveland. The idea for the settlement originated in a YMCA study class at Hiram College in Hiram, Ohio. Affiliated with the Disciples of Christ Church, the college attracted students with both religious and academic interests. The class chose to study the social settlement movement and, encouraged by lectures from luminaries such as Graham Taylor, founder of the Chicago Commons Settlement, decided to examine the possibility of starting a settlement house in Cleveland, some fifty miles to the north. A visit to the city convinced the students, most of whom were from small towns, that such work would be needed: "We went to Whiskey Isle; there we found saloons, prostitution, open sewers, and all in all everything was not very good. We went back to Hiram College with the report that Cleveland needed a settlement very bad."

Seven members of that class began actual settlement work following graduation in June 1896. They took up residence in a rented house in the Irish quarter near Whiskey Island on the City's West Side. They began kindergarten classes and started planning for educational classes directed toward all age levels in the neighborhood. Pamphlets issued by the students while at this location emphasized the Christian, social gospel basis of the work and clearly outlined their idealistic goals. The hope of Hiram House, they said, "is to become part of the life of its own ward becoming so by personal helpfulness. In helping the masses, its wish is to help remove the cause of distress, further than this we do not commit ourselves to any social program regarding the vexed industrial and economic problems of the day." Other early publications solicited support from the general public for the work in the name of Christ.

Protestant Christianity could not long prosper in an Irish Catholic neighborhood. By the autumn of 1896 pressure from local priests forced the settlement to relocate. It moved to the Haymarket district on the East Side. This was the center of the city's Jewish community, and despite some early protests by the residents of the area the settlement managed to take root. Its initial locations in this area, a series of rented houses along Orange Avenue, provided Hiram House with enough space to continue and expand its programs. The workers again began a kindergarten to which they added a day nursery, high school classes for older youths, debating clubs, excursions to parks, and a summer camp. Most of these programs were directed toward educating the people of the neighborhood and providing them with the intellectual means to rise above their environment. Other programs, such as camping and excursions, were attempts to physically remove people, especially children, from the crowded conditions and debilitating atmosphere of the inner city.

The staff carried on its work without substantive support from any single institution. Hiram College provided its good wishes and a continuous flow of student volunteers, but no financial support. Funds came primarily from collections taken up in rural churches by one of the original student volunteers, George Bellamy. Initially financial solicitor for the settlement, Bellamy assumed control of all work in 1897and retained it until his retirement in 1946.

Bellamy came from a religious family of moderate means. He was born in Cascade, Michigan, in 1872, descended on his mother's side from colonists who had arrived in 1620. Several relatives were active in the Disciples of Christ Church, and his older brother, William, a Hiram graduate, served as a minister for that denomination. Bellamy followed his brother into the ministerial course at Hiram, earning all of his college expenses through summer jobs and part-time employment during the school year. His interest in social settlement work was sparked in 1895 by a chance meeting with Graham Taylor while at a Chautau-qua lecture. Years later he would credit his conversion to the social gospel to a vision he had had in church while still a youth.

Bellamy's convictions were tested to the limit during his first several years at the settlement. He worked without pay, having given his savings to the settle-ment. He was often rebuffed when he attempted to solicit funds from the major churches in Cleveland because the enterprise he represented was viewed as so-cialistic. One church official told Bellamy, "You ought to be ostracized from [for] living among such people. God never intended to save such people. You should shove them off in a corner and let them be there and rot." Fund-raising was suc-cessful only among small Disciples congregations in the rural towns surrounding the city. They contributed money as well as flowers for distribution in the bleak city neighborhood.

Despite the youthful dedication and idealism committed to the settlement, Hiram House prospered only after Bellamy found a substantial secular source of funds. A meeting in 1898 with a prominent jurist and member of the Disciples of Christ Church, Henry White, paved the way for this change. White contrib-uted money, but more importantly, he formed an executive committee to oversee the affairs of Hiram House. By 1900 the committee had evolved into a board of trustees that consisted primarily of prominent businessmen, most of whom were important enough to be listed in the city's *Blue Book*. The board of trustees served to legitimize Hiram House as an institution worthy of support. Within two years it solicited sufficient funds, including substantial donations from John D. Rockefeller and Samuel Mather, to build and equip a four-story structure for the settlement at East Twenty-seventh Street and Orange Avenue. The guaran-tee of support allowed Hiram House's budget to grow from $2,210.31 in 1898 to $6,860.00 in 1900, to $12,745.60 in 1905, and to $20,614.10 in 1910. More im-portantly, Samuel Mather, perhaps the city's richest citizen, became a member of the board during this period and took an unflagging interest in the work of the settlement.

Having such wherewithal, Bellamy was able to expand programs and activities which he believed would eliminate the problems plaguing his neighborhood. A new publication, *Hiram House Life*, initially offered a forum for studies of local problems. A playground constructed at the rear of the settlement building pro-vided much-needed open space for the neighborhood. The ample structure had rooms which were used by clubs and classes as well as by other organizations, such as the Visiting Nurse Association and a branch of the Cleveland Public Li-brary. New staff, including a playground director, a director of boys' work, and a neighborhood visitor, similarly extended the settlement's work and its utility. By World War I, Hiram House provided play areas for children, meeting rooms for clubs (mainly for children), weekly entertainments, a gymnasium, and voca-tional education and homemaking classes within its facilities, as well as head-quarters for nurses and workers who visited the sick and needy in its surrounding neighborhood.

The ethnic background of Hiram House's clientele was changing, too, during this time. As the Jewish immigrant population prospered and moved out of the Haymarket district, Italian immigrants began moving in, beginning about 1905. They, in turn, were eventually replaced by southern blacks, who began moving to Cleveland in large numbers during the First World War.

Relieved by the successful efforts of his board of trustees from the constant task of soliciting funds, Bellamy became involved in various nonsettlement activities directed toward social reform. For example, he made some effort to rid the neighborhood of Harry Bernstein, its corrupt ward boss. He also became an active member of the Cleveland Council of Sociology, an organization comprised of clerics, charity workers, and others, which was devoted to the discussion of the social issues of the day. He served on two committees of the chamber of commerce, both of which were dedicated to the elimination of particular social ills: the chamber's Bath House Committee of 1901 studied the lack of bathing facilities in the inner city and successfully implemented a program for the construction of bathhouses; and its Committee on the Housing Problem of 1903-4 surveyed housing conditions in the city and made recommendations for a revision of the city's housing code.

As late as 1905, Bellamy also remained active in the Disciples of Christ Church. He used a speech at a church convention that year to set forth his strong social gospel idealism and to decry the criticism of reform-minded clerics by the church establishment: "The representatives of the most advanced religious thought, no matter how God-fearing or how conscientious, have by no means passed the period of church discipline or rebuke. This lack of freedom in religious thought and study has hindered a wholesome, righteous growth of religious understanding."

The growth of Hiram House had consequences for both Bellamy's social thought and the institution itself. As it grew, Hiram House drifted away from the concept of "personal helpfulness." Certainly neighborhood residents could meet and work with staff members, but these workers were much less neighbors in themselves. They were professional employees who answered to the demands of an institutional bureaucracy. As early as 1902, Hiram House had eleven different departments directed largely by paid staff rather than by student volunteers. These employees reported to George Bellamy. By 1910 Bellamy was an administrator of an institution removed, for the most part, from close contact with its clientele. As an administrator responsible to a board of trustees, he had to ensure that his operation ran smoothly and that its backers were pleased with both its progress and programs. To these ends he devised settlement programs which were popular, and he personally abstained from causes or issues which might irritate his supporters. Popular programs drew large numbers of people to the settlement and thus seemed to prove its worth to its patrons. Therefore, by World War I, Hiram House had come to concentrate on recreational programs which would appeal to the children in the neighborhood. It tended to avoid programs which were educational or which were directed at adult immigrants, as the former would be unpopular and the latter dealt with a clientele which was difficult to attract in large numbers.

While Hiram House would come to be characterized as one of the city's most conservative settlement houses, Goodrich House, the second settlement in the city, was perhaps its most liberal. This social settlement evolved from a series of boys' clubs and classes held in Cleveland's First Presbyterian (Old Stone) Church in the mid-1890s. Located on Public Square, the church had one of the city's oldest and most prestigious congregations. The classes and clubs, which attracted children from the congested, run-down neighborhood to the north of the church, were directed by Elizabeth and Edward W. Haines, Elizabeth being the daughter of the church's pastor, Dr. Hiram C. Haydn.

As the work seemed to fill a major need in the neighborhood, the church began planning its expansion. Central to this planning was Flora Stone Mather, a member of the church, the wife of Samuel Mather, and the daughter of Amasa Stone, railroad builder and industrialist and one of the city's most influential men in the immediate post-Civil War period. Wealthy in her own right, Flora Stone's marriage to Samuel Mather allowed her to become the benefactor of a variety of charitable and educational agencies. Goodrich, however, was her most important charitable interest. Upon her death in 1909, her husband noted, "There was nothing she ever did in which she was more interested than Goodrich House."

Originally, Flora Mather proposed that she would construct a parish house in which the church could undertake neighborhood work. However, the lack of land immediately adjacent to the church and a feeling that the scope of such work might soon overwhelm the church led to a reconsideration. Since 1893, Mather had carried on a correspondence with Professor Henry E. Bourne of Western Reserve University in which they discussed social settlement work. Bourne apparently used this correspondence to assist her in understanding settlement work. She had probably first learned of settlement work through a friend, Lucy B. Buell, a former resident of the College Settlement in New York. The physical problems of constructing a parish house and her correspondence with Bourne led Mather to propose the construction of a fully equipped settlement in the general neighborhood of the church. When Goodrich House finally began work in May 1897, it operated out of a new building constructed expressly for it at St. Clair and East Sixth Street. Flora Mather had paid for the structure and for a number of years thereafter underwrote the cost of the settlement's operations.

The programs in the new building were supervised by Starr Cadwallader. Cadwallader, a graduate of Union Theological Seminary in Utica, New York, had worked briefly at Union Settlement before coming to Cleveland. During his five-year tenure at Goodrich House, he directed the agency in many of the standard areas of settlement work. The structure housed a bowling alley, baths, laundry, library, and meeting rooms which were made available to neighborhood residents and to a variety of clubs and social groups. Cadwallader and his staff also attempted to improve neighborhood conditions by lobbying for cleaner streets and encouraging area residents to plant home gardens.

However, quite unlike Hiram House, Goodrich House became known as a public forum for the discussion of social reform issues; records indicate, for example, that a young socialist club met at the facilities. Some of the meetings held at Goodrich House led to the creation of such reform-oriented groups as the Consumers' League of Ohio, and the Legal Aid Society, as well as the creation of a separate, rural boys' farm for housing juvenile offenders. Among the settlement residents who took part in such discussions were Frederick C. Howe and Newton D. Baker, both of whom left the settlement for positions in Tom L. Johnson's mayoral administration.

Goodrich had a board of directors as soon as it had a building. Composed largely of people affiliated with the First Presbyterian Church and their friends, this body did little, if anything, to challenge the somewhat radical events at the settlement. Dr. Haydn presided over the first board, which included Flora and Samuel Mather, Elizabeth and Edward Haines, Professor Bourne, and Lucy Buell. By 1905 Cadwallader, Howe, and Baker, all of whom had left the employ of the settlement, had joined the board. James R. Garfield, son of President Garfield and law partner of Howe, also served on the board during the early years of the settlement.

The tightly knit nature of this board and its ties to the church rather than to business, were probably two factors which allowed Goodrich to pursue a more radical course than Hiram House. That the settlement existed because of Flora Mather's largess is, however, a more important factor. Whereas Bellamy had a number of donors to please, Cadwallader had only Mrs. Mather and his rather small board to consider when directing the settlement. Then, too, Hiram House was Bellamy's creation; its failure would be his failure. Cadwallader could, and did, walk away from Goodrich whenever he pleased. In his case, the social goals he wished to achieve took precedence over loyalty to any particular institution.

Goodrich was an institution from the first day it opened its doors. Its funding, operations, and physical structure grew simultaneously. As such it proved to be both sound and remarkably flexible. When the population of its neighborhood began to decline around 1908, it was easily able to move its operations to a new location at East Thirty-first Street and St. Clair, some twenty-four blocks to the east. Mather had expressly provided for such a contingency when she deeded the settlement to its board:

> I desire the house to be used for a Christian Social Settlement so long as, in the judgment of the trustees, that is a useful and needful work in the neighborhood; but if ever in their judgment there was a time when to continue such work, there would be a waste of energy the trustees may dispose of the property. If it should be deemed wise by the trustees to discontinue the work there I wish them to use the funds, including the proceeds of any sale of the house, to carry on the work in some other downtown locality.

Though the liberal nature of Goodrich could not be written into its articles of incorporation, it nevertheless seemed to be an integral part of the settlement. Cadwallader's work seems to have set the liberal tone for the settlement. There-

after it would tend to attract new headworkers of a similar mien. Five headworkers followed in rather quick succession when Cadwallader left Goodrich in 1904.
The rapid turnover ended in 1917 when Alice Gannett, formerly of Henry
Street Settlement in New York, took the position and held it until 1947. Gannett continued to strengthen Goodrich's liberal reputation. During her career
she served as president of the Ohio Consumers' League and the National Federation of Settlements, and was active in the League for Human Rights.

Alta House, which began settlement work in Cleveland's Little Italy district
in 1900, provided yet another example of the diversity of the settlement and reform impulse in Cleveland. Sequestered in a compact ethnic neighborhood, it
exhibited none of the neighborhood activism which characterized the very early
years of Hiram House nor the liberal leanings characteristic of Goodrich and its
staff. Nor was Alta the creation of youthful idealism or a church.

Alta House reflected the expressed needs of the neighborhood as acted upon
by social gospel idealism. Mothers in the Little Italy district attempted to establish a day nursery in the mid-1890s. Many of them worked in the vineyards in
the east of the city and needed day care for their children. They appealed to the
Cleveland Day Nursery Association for help. Louise (Mrs. Marius E.) Rawson of
the association directed its efforts to assist the Italian mothers. Rawson, a New
England-born school teacher, began the nursery in a small cottage, which the
work soon outgrew. Relocated in a larger structure, the nursery expanded to include boys' clubs, mothers' clubs, and cooking classes, and again strained the capacity of its quarters. At this point, Rawson began to search for funding to
provide a permanent, larger building for the work. She approached John D.
Rockefeller for that aid.

Rockefeller was a natural choice. He was wealthy and a devoutly religious
man. As such, he made his money available to a number of worthy causes in and
outside of Cleveland—whether his philanthropy signified a social gospel-like desire to help his fellow men or followed the tradition of benevolence by the
wealthy cannot be stated with any certainty. Most important in Rawson's plans
was the fact that Rockefeller, when in Cleveland, daily traveled through the Italian district on his way to and from his estate in Forest Hills.

Rockefeller proved amenable to assisting the undertaking. In 1898 he agreed
to build a structure for the work being carried on by Rawson. During the discussion and construction phases, the work projected for the new building grew well
beyond the confines of a nursery and evolved into a settlement.

Rockefeller's hopes for the settlement were in the best tradition of the social
gospel movement. He expressed them in a letter he sent to the dedication ceremony for the building in 1900: "May the spirit of the Christ Child dwell within
this house, built primarily for the children, and may that same spirit of love go
out with each one who passes through its doors and be broadly disseminated in
the surrounding homes." While Rockefeller's letter spelled out the Christian
foundations of the endeavor, a second letter from his daughter, Alta Rockefeller
Prentice (after whom the settlement was named), explicitly stated its purpose:

"The work for which it stands, namely that of helping to educate your children mentally, morally, and physically, and through them aiding in every effort to elevate and purify home life and the life of the neighborhood is very dear to me."

Katherine E. Smith, formerly of the Rivington Street Settlement in New York, came to Cleveland to head the work at Alta House. Work in the new structure focused primarily on child-oriented activities. It included a day nursery, a kindergarten, boys' clubs, girls' classes in sewing, millinery, and cooking, a school for eighteen crippled children, and a gymnasium. In addition, a medical dispensary, a resident visiting nurse, public baths, a public laundry, and a playground were provided.

Smith answered to a board of trustees which included J. G. W. Cowles, a real estate dealer who lived in the Heights area just above the settlement; Paul L. Feiss, one of the officers of the Joseph and Feiss clothing company; John D. Rockefeller, Jr.; Alta Rockefeller Prentice; Professor Matoon M. Curtis of neighboring Western Reserve University; Belle Sherwin, daughter of a prominent family and a leading figure in various reform movements; Maude O. (Mrs. William) Truesdale, the wife of an assistant professor at Western Reserve University; and Louise Rawson.The board certainly did not represent the religious element, nor, excepting the Rockefeller contingent, did it lean particularly on the wealthiest families of the city. The presence of Rawson and Truesdale, neither of whom represented money or social status, was unusual, but was an acknowledgment of the Day Nursery Association's role in the creation of Alta House, as well as of Truesdale's strong educational programming.

Alta House had no need to combat social evils such as poor housing, overcrowding, or open sewers. The housing stock of the neighborhood was largely new, having been erected by the Italian immigrants during the last decades of the nineteenth century. It was almost a rural area, five miles from the center of the city. Its only industries were a streetcar carbarn and the monument works of Joseph Carabelli. The settlement's task, therefore, naturally centered on the social, academic, civic, and sanitation education of the immigrants. Smith may have chafed at these apparently pedestrian duties. Her first annual report, for example, indicated an interest in starting a social reform club for young boys. The record does not indicate if she accomplished this. However, classes in English, sewing, cooking, and hygiene, as well as physical education programs, were still strong, if indirect, means of social reform, for they seemed to guarantee the training of useful, healthy future citizens who would be assets to the community.

The Rockefeller family continued to support Alta House until 1921, at which time John D. Rockefeller, Jr., asked to be relieved of its annual costs. Because of the long-term interest of the Rockefellers and the insular nature of the Little Italy neighborhood, Alta House was quite dissimilar from either Hiram House or Goodrich House. Yet it still shared the Christian seed of these organizations as well as their dedication to social reform in one guise or another.

KENNETH L. KUSMER

Racism at High Tide:
Cleveland, 1915–1920

The increasing residential segregation of urban blacks after 1915 was accompanied by an intensification of white hostility and a crystallization of the pattern of discrimination that had begun to take shape before the war. Both were in large part the result of what one historian has called the "flowering of racism" that occurred during the 1920s. To be sure, a few scholars were beginning to build a scientific critique of the racist theories that had been formulated at the turn of the century. But the average white person continued to believe in black inferiority; and as black sociologist Charles S. Johnson lamented in 1923, "False notions, if believed, . . . may control conduct as effectively as true ones." During and immediately after World War I, whites vented their fears and frustrations in a series of vicious race riots; the two worst riots alone, in East St. Louis and Chicago, were responsible for eighty-five deaths and over a thousand injuries. Although this type of extreme violence fell off sharply after 1919, lesser forms of white hostility did not. The white quest for racial purity found its embodiment in a rejuvenated Ku Klux Klan, an organization which directed its propaganda at Catholics and Jews as well as blacks. Founded in 1915, the new Klan was as much a northern as a southern phenomenon, and at least one-third of all Klansmen could be found in urban areas. By 1924 at least one million whites had joined the organization, and in several localities the Ku Klux Klan became a force to be reckoned with.

Cleveland, a city more liberal than most, managed to avoid the racist excesses that plagued other communities. During the tense summers of 1917 and 1919, interracial violence did break out on several occasions, but these encounters did not, luckily, escalate into racial warfare. Nor was the Ku Klux Klan an important factor in Cleveland's racial scene. During the 1920s, a small local chapter was organized, but Klan membership in the city never exceeded two thousand (Chicago may have had fifty thousand Klansmen at one time), and local authorities remained hostile to the secret organization. But there was still a noticeable increase in race prejudice in the city after 1915. Before the war the black population of Cleveland was small and easily overlooked. By 1920 it could no longer be ignored. As black migrants entered the mills and foundries of the city, whites sometimes felt that their jobs were threatened. At the same time, the expansion of the ghetto made white home owners fearful for the value of their property and the stability of their neighborhoods. The result was a sharp rise in racial tension and an increase in institutional discrimination.

The initial response of many whites to the Great Migration was one of fear. White journalists, who previously had for the most part avoided any discussion of the city's black community, now took a more hostile view of the race. In the spring of 1917 one white newspaper printed a scare article which warned Clevelanders of the "danger of the spread of small pox, hookworm, and other diseases prevalent in the South, as a result of the Negro influx." Throughout the year, two Cleveland newspapers, the *News* and the *Leader*, continued to stir dangerous emotions by allowing the terms "nigger" and "darkey" to appear in print. In 1919, a year of anti-black violence throughout the nation, these two papers fanned the flames of racial discord by publishing blatantly prejudiced articles. Both papers made derogatory remarks about the all-black 372d Regiment when it returned to Cleveland after the signing of the peace treaty. During the "red summer" of 1919, the *News*, a leading daily, printed a front-page sensationalistic article on lynchings and blamed the racial disturbances that were spreading across the country on " the active and systematic proselyting [sic] done among the colored workers of the South by Bolshevists." Such copy was hardly designed to promote racial harmony.

Mass circulation newspapers were not the only media that reflected (and influenced) the deepening antagonism toward blacks that surfaced during the war. The popularity of the racist films *The Nigger* and *The Birth of a Nation*, both of which came to the city in 1917, were signs of a growing anti-Negro sentiment among the white population. *The Nigger*, as described by the *Advocate*, contained "huge mob scenes and race riots" and was filled "with the crack of the white man's whip and the scream of the blacks." A cheap but gaudy production, it was the less popular of the two motion pictures. *The Birth of a Nation* was more invidious because of its high technical—if not moral—qualities. Produced by D. W. Griffith, *The Birth of a Nation* was quickly recognized as an outstanding example of the art of film-making. The subject matter of the film, however, was volatile; based on a caustically racist novel by Thomas Dixon, it portrayed blacks as ignorant brutes and glorified the original Ku Klux Klan as the righteous upholders of white civilization in the South. *The Birth of a Nation* was eventually banned from Cleveland, but not before it had become a box-office hit in several theaters.

White politicians, sensitive to the changing temperament of the electorate, equivocated on the issue of civil rights or dangerously played upon the racist emotions of voters for their own political advantage. In 1917 William Finley, the state chairman of the Democratic party in Ohio, attempted to gain support for the Democratic ticket by associating Republicans with the migration of southern blacks that was then under way. Blacks were traditionally Republican, and Finley claimed that the Ohio GOP was assisting in the "colonization" of thousands of poor black migrants for the purpose of increasing the Republican vote. A similar claim, made against the Republicans of East St. Louis in 1916, was one of the underlying causes of the bloody race riot that occurred there the following year. Such racist propaganda was not limited to the party of Woodrow Wilson. In Cleveland the Republican successor to Mayor Newton D. Baker, Harry L. Davis, implied in a speech in 1917 that the Central Avenue area had developed into a vice district because blacks were naturally degenerate. Davis steadfastly refused to appoint black clerks to City Hall during his administration or to choose a black as an assistant police prosecutor or member of the mayor's Advisory War Board—despite the fact that one of the board's functions was to deal with the immediate problems resulting from the influx of black migrants during the war. In 1920, race once again became an election issue when several candidates for local office distributed racist literature claiming that blacks would not be satisfied until they could "dominate" Cleveland.

Fears of black "domination" were more than simply false; they actually amounted to an inverted view of race relations in the city. Politically, blacks had gained little as a result of their consistent support of the Republican party. From 1915 to 1930 a string of Republican administrations in Cleveland refused, with few exceptions, to appoint Afro-Americans to anything but minor positions. In the area of municipal services, black neighborhoods were consistently short-changed. In the Central and lower Woodland Avenue districts, recreational facilities were scarce, garbage and rubbish removal were often irregular, and the streetcars were notorious for their poor service and shoddy conditions—despite the fact that the Central line was one of the most profitable in the city. During the twenties, Cleveland adopted the city manager form of government (it was the largest metropolis to do so), yet the vaunted "efficiency" of this system of administration did not seem to work to the benefit of the black community.

As far as police protection was concerned, black people could without contradiction say that they received both too little and too much. Throughout the postwar period no effort was made by City Hall to clean up the gambling and prostitution rackets on Central Avenue. The number of police assigned to black sections of the city was inadequate, and when the police received reports of crimes they were often slow to arrive on the scene. "It is only on rare occasions," complained Harry C. Smith, that "policemen are seen in 'the roaring third' [as whites called the Central area] and then as a rule, after some crime has already been committed." On the other hand, when police did enter the ghetto to make an arrest or to patrol the area, they often seemed unnecessarily brutal. In 1917 Smith noted that "flagrant and barbarous beating-up of Negroes" was an all too common occurrence with white officers. "Since the influx from the South," Smith reported a few years later, "there has been a growing tendency upon the part of the police, both public and private, to kill members of the race sought for committing crimes and misdemeanors." Police were "too quick to shoot" if the suspect was a black and they were not overly concerned about harming bystanders if they had the misfortune of being black. Undoubtedly, part of the problem was the small number of black patrolmen; in 1919 only seven of the city's thirteen hundred police officers were blacks, and eleven years later there were still only twelve blacks on the force.

In 1919 a small incident symbolized the state of race relations in Cleveland in the wake of the Great Migration. With the city's tradition of fairness to blacks in mind, the NAACP in that year chose Cleveland as the site of its annual convention. "We were not in the cotton fields of Louisiana," Mary White Ovington wrote in retrospect, "but in the City of Cleveland of the State of Ohio, that had bred abolitionists, and started Oberlin." At the same time that Miss Ovington was exulting over the heritage of northern freedom, however, James Weldon Johnson, field secretary for the NAACP, was being refused service in a Cleveland restaurant because he was black. The irony of the situation was symptomatic of the continuing deterioration of the city's liberal racial climate during the postwar era: the abolitionist heritage of Cleveland's past was rapidly being supplanted by the reality of its discriminatory present.

Nowhere was this increasing discrimination more evident than in the unequal treatment blacks received in the city's restaurants, theaters, and other places of public accommodation. As the black population expanded out of its original area of settlement, white restaurant owners, like some white property owners, often tried to "hold the line" against the advancing black tide. They used a variety of tactics. Some simply refused blacks altogether, and a few of these had the effrontery to place "white only" signs in their windows. Others discouraged black patrons by giving them poor service. Still others served blacks but charged them higher prices; one Greek restaurant owner blandly informed a black customer that he would be glad to serve him but would have to charge him four times the regular price of a meal. Previously liberal downtown restaurants and hotels also began to exclude Afro-Americans more frequently, although they faced no threat of "invasion." Even prominent black visitors were not always able to find adequate hotel accommodations. When Robert R. Moton, Booker T. Washington's successor as head of the Tuskegee Institute, came to Cleveland in 1923 to address the Chamber of Commerce, officials at the Statler Hotel told him that they would be able to accommodate him only if he agreed to take his meals in his room. In a number of exclusive establishments, however, skin color remained an important factor in determining who would be admitted. Light-skinned blacks could still eat at many of the city's better restaurants during the twenties, but Charles W. Chesnutt (who himself had a very fair complexion) noted in 1930 that he did not "know more than one place downtown where [he] could take for luncheon a dark-colored man." Not all of the increase in restaurant discrimination, it should be noted, was the result of a conscious policy of management. In many cases waiters and waitresses acted on their own initiative in refusing to serve Afro-Americans. The white Waiters' Union was one of Cleveland's most intensely racist labor organizations.

Discriminatory practices were not limited to hotels and restaurants. Theaters often refused to admit blacks, segregated them within the theater, seated them in the balcony, or charged them higher prices. Blacks could, of course, ride the city streetcars. But a local taxi company attempted to restrict its service to whites only, and by the end of the twenties the Greyhound Bus Company was making blacks sit in the back of buses traveling to the South.

Racial lines also hardened in recreational facilities. Cleveland's two main amusement parks, Luna Park and Euclid Beach Park, continued their established policy of restricting the use of their facilities by blacks to a small number of days each summer. Social agencies involved in recreation frequently introduced a policy of segregation where none had existed before the war. "Some of the settlement houses," Jane Edna Hunter remarked, "alternate their camp periods, sending the Negro children out to the camp for one period and the white children for another." The YMCA restricted black participation in its activities to one branch on Cedar Avenue in the 1920s, and the YWCA continued its policy of excluding blacks altogether. Blacks also encountered a considerable amount of discrimination in public facilities. At the city beach nearest to the ghetto, Gordon Park, blacks were segregated, while they were excluded altogether from some other beaches. At the instigation of Thomas Fleming, the black councilman, the city did construct a bathhouse on Central in 1919 at a cost of $45,000. It was apparent, however, that the black community was being shortchanged when the city announced construction of a similar facility in the ethnic St. Clair Avenue area with a price tag of $125,000. Surveying the Central Avenue bathhouse shortly after it opened, the editor of the *Gazette* pronounced it "cheaply constructed." "*Anything*," he concluded, "seems good enough for *colored* people, as far as Fleming and the Davis Administration goes."

As before the war, black Clevelanders achieved only partial success in forcing white establishments to end discriminatory practices. Blacks actually brought more civil rights suits in the 1920s than ever before, and they did force a number of white restaurants and downtown theaters to open their doors to black people. Those of the race who sought redress in the courts, however, were hindered in a number of ways. They continued to be stymied by narrow interpretations of the Ohio Civil Rights Law. In 1918, for example, a black man brought suit against a Euclid Avenue restaurant owner who refused him service. The jury, however, ruled in favor of the proprietor, apparently on the ground that the black man "was not a bona fide patron but was merely there for the purpose of stirring up trouble." Such circuitous reasoning made "test cases" against discriminatory establishments difficult and in some instances rendered the Civil Rights Law null. Blacks encountered less hostility and prejudice from white judges and lawyers than from juries. "Juries are prejudiced," one black lawyer reported, "and if a personal injury case is worth $5,000 the jury would give a colored man, in my opinion, $2,000 or possible $2,500." One of the hindrances to equal justice in Cleveland was the fact that fewer blacks served on juries than their percentage of the population would seem to warrant. Blacks complained that—whether by design or accident—too few of their race were called to jury duty and that many who were called were "excused." "Only ceaseless insistence on the enforcement of law," the black *Call and Post* editorialized in 1928, "will prevent the Ohio Civil Rights Statute from becoming a dead letter." Such continual vigilance, however, was bothersome, difficult, and often expensive; few blacks had sufficient time, funds, and tenacity to indulge in such tactics. As Charles Chesnutt laconically put it, "One does not care to have to bring a lawsuit or swear out a warrant every time one wants a sandwich or a cup of coffee."

Cleveland's hospitals and schools also mirrored the rising tide of discrimination after 1915. Before the war, little noticeable discrimination was seen in hospital policies. During the Great Migration several hospitals adopted the procedure of segregating black and white patients in separate wards; during the next decade many other hospitals in the area followed suit. In addition, some medical institutions reserved only a designated number of beds for black patients. The number of spaces reserved was sometimes woefully inadequate. "These hospitals," a group of blacks complained in 1927, "ask doctors on requesting admission of patients whether the patient is white or colored, and frequently the answer is: 'there are no colored beds vacant.' " At the peak of the wartime migration, one institution, Charity Hospital, belied its name by refusing to accept black patients who could not pay for their treatment in advance. Although there is no evidence that this policy became standard procedure in later years, while in force it was most disconcerting to black Clevelanders.

The color bar against black doctors and nurses remained as firm in Cleveland hospitals as it had been before the war. Most Cleveland hospitals refused to allow black physicians on their staffs or to provide training programs for black interns. This eventually led to an unsuccessful attempt by a group of black doctors, politicians, and businessmen to establish an all-black hospital. But at the end of the twenties, there was still no hospital in the city which would accept black interns or nurse trainees. Only two hospitals had black doctors attached to their staffs.

The changes that occurred in the policies of Cleveland's educational institutions as a result of the migration were more subtle. The city's public schools had been integrated for many decades, and to a large extent they remained this way during and after the war. With the exception of the city's trade schools, which discouraged black attendance because of the exclusionary policies of many union apprenticeship programs, the schools and colleges of Cleveland remained open to both races on a nondiscriminatory basis. During the peak month of the wartime migration, however, several school principals sought to establish segregated classes *within* their schools, and one head of an all-white school refused to accept a black teacher who had been assigned to his district. Yet there is no indication that either of these policies became accepted practice or amounted to anything more than a temporary aberration. During the twenties black teachers not only increased steadily in numbers but remained fairly well integrated in the system. In 1929 eighty-four black instructors taught in forty-one different schools, most of them in predominantly white neighborhoods.

Nevertheless, a subtle process of discrimination did begin to affect the public schools. Two of the city's technical high schools—Jane Addams Vocational

School and the Cleveland Trade School—had no black students at all. The third, East Technical High School, although located in the heart of the ghetto, was only 4 percent black in 1929. As the ghetto consolidated and expanded during the twenties, some schools became predominantly black. On the eve of the Great Depression, 89 percent of Cleveland's black junior high school students were enrolled in only four (out of a total of twenty-three) schools; and fully 61 percent of all black senior high school students attended a single institution, Central High. In 1931 whites made up only about 3 percent of the student body at Central. The gradual development of segregation in the schools after World War I was, initially, a by-product of the shifting demographic patterns of the city; as blacks moved into neighborhoods in larger numbers, nearby schools naturally gained in black enrollment. By the early 1930s (it is difficult to determine exactly when the policy began), however, the Board of Education was beginning to reinforce and accelerate this trend through artificial means. In 1933 blacks complained that most black children on the East Side were being forced to attend Central High, even though many lived much nearer to other schools. A few years later, it was charged that white students who lived in the Central High district were permitted to transfer to other schools. This policy of selective transfers, which would continue for several decades, often placed a considerable hardship on students, since it sometimes forced them to attend a school that was several streetcar lines away from their home. Ironically, in the 1960s and 1970s, whites would vigorously oppose the busing of children for the purpose of creating racial balance in the schools, whereas over thirty years earlier, the Board of Education had already established a program of busing (or its equivalent), not for the purpose of ending segregation but as a means of furthering it.

As schools became predominantly black, their curricula often changed from an emphasis on liberal arts to a stressing of skills of a more mundane nature. The changes that occurred at Kennard Junior High School during the twenties are a good example of this process. In 1924 the school's student body was 31 percent black in composition; in 1930, as a result of the white exodus from neighborhoods near the school, blacks constituted 60 percent of the students. As the racial balance of the school shifted, administrators gradually altered the curriculum. They dropped foreign languages altogether; intensified course offerings in certain types of industrial work; cut back on the number of available electives; and placed more emphasis on "sewing, cooking, manual training, foundry work, and sheet metal [work]." In Central High School the same transformation was occurring. In 1933 the Cleveland branch of the NAACP discovered that over half the tenth-grade students at Central were receiving no training in mathematics at all. Most of the home economics courses at the school emphasized laundry work, and such electives as Spanish, German, bookkeeping, and stenography (standard fare in other high schools) had been dropped from the curriculum. These changes in course offerings undoubtedly lowered the expectations of black students and oriented them, at an early age, toward lower-paying, less prestigious occupations. Once a powerful force for equality and integration, the public schools had by 1935 become yet another factor leading to two separate but unequal worlds of race.

With the growth of prejudice evident in so many aspects of life in Cleveland after 1915, it was almost inevitable that violent encounters between blacks and whites occur. Before the war, the city had been relatively free of interracial violence; but now whites were more willing to use intimidation, mob action, and even terrorism in the face of an assumed threat to their homes and jobs.

It was during the tense summers of 1917 and 1919 that anti-black violence in Cleveland reached a peak. Several times lynchings or a race riot seemed imminent but miraculously failed to materialize. In June 1917, two incidents occurred within the span of a single week. The first took place in the predominantly white neighborhood near East Seventy-first Street, far from the main area of black settlement. The trouble began when a white woman began to complain loudly that a black had insulted her. A crowd of whites soon gathered and started to harass and then to chase the black man, who sought refuge in a nearby house. By the time a patrol wagon arrived on the scene, a menacing crowd of two hundred whites had gathered and were preparing to storm the house, capture its black occupant, and lynch him. Only the somewhat belated appearance of the police prevented bloodshed. Less than a week later, a near riot occurred in the lower Central Avenue district. No one seemed to know how the trouble began, but by the time the police were summoned "scores of Negroes and foreigners were fighting with fists, clubs, and stones." After these two outbursts of racial hostility, Harry C. Smith feared that a major clash between blacks and whites was inevitable. Not one to mince words, he urged his readers to "purchase a regular army riot gun and plenty of ammunition" for self-defense.

In the summer of 1919, anti-black violence again flared up in Cleveland. This time the attackers directed their fury at children rather than adults. On three separate occasions mobs of white men and boys stoned groups of black youngsters. The first incident occurred when a group of black children were riding a streetcar through a white neighborhood; the second and third while parties of black youths were swimming in one of the local park lakes, a recreation spot some distance from the ghetto and usually not frequented by blacks. Luckily, in none of the incidents were there any serious injuries. For many weeks afterward, however, the racial atmosphere of the city was taut with fear. Commenting on the two occurrences at the park lakes, the editor of the *Gazette* cautioned his readers that "this is just what started the Chicago riot" and again urged black Clevelanders to prepare to defend themselves. Fortunately, Smith's premonition proved to be without foundation, and the "red summer" of 1919 ended without a major racial confrontation in Cleveland.

Given the intensification of racial prejudice and the propensity of some whites to resort to violence against blacks, why did no race riot take place in Cleveland during the migration years? A comparison with Chicago—which did experience a violent race riot in 1919—shows that a number of factors must be taken into account. First, Cleveland's industries were far more diversified than

Chicago's. In Chicago the stockyards served as a focal point of racial hostility be-tween black and white workers; in the Lake Erie metropolis no such focal point existed. In addition, Cleveland was fortunate in that its black steelworkers were almost completely unionized during the crucial year 1919. By refusing to act as strikebreakers, blacks in Cleveland temporarily undercut a major source of racial strife. The residential pattern of black settlement in the city also was important in preventing a riot. In Chicago, black workers found it necessary to pass through hostile ethnic neighborhoods on their way to work; this made them easy prey for white mobs. In Cleveland, however, as the black ghetto consoli-dated after 1915 it abutted the main industrial district, and most blacks could go to and from work without straying very far from the predominantly black (or at least integrated) sections of the city. Despite the hostility of white ethnic groups, blacks in Cleveland had considerably more opportunity for expansion than the hemmed-in South Side black belt of Chicago. The streets directly to the east of the original area of black settlement were occupied primarily by Russian Jews, British immigrants, and native white Americans. Though far from unprejudiced, most of these whites were not anti-black in the violent, defensive manner of suburbanites and those ethnic groups living to the south and southeast of the ghetto; and when black expansion became a necessity after 1915, they were will-ing to allow the peaceful movement of blacks into their neighborhoods. The ex-istence of this "escape valve" reduced the possibility of contested neighborhoods and lessened tensions in the city during a critical period of race relations.

Finally, in assessing the differences between the two cities one cannot under-estimate the effects of the slower development of the ghetto in Cleveland. In Chicago, the black belt had taken shape by 1910 (perhaps earlier), and on the eve of the wartime migration a gulf had opened between the two races that has not yet, to this day, been bridged. Sociologists have noted that personal experi-ence with blacks is an important factor in shaping white racial attitudes, and that those who have the least contact with members of the opposite race often harbor the most intense prejudice. Conditions in Chicago before the riot nur-tured such intolerance. There, says historian William Tuttle, Jr., "because of ex-treme residential segregation, there was a paucity of social interchange between the races. Consequently, there was a decided lack of interracial understanding." In spite of increasing evidences of racism in Cleveland during the prewar years, the city's black community was not nearly as isolated as was Chicago's in 1915; the existence of integrated schools and neighborhoods kept open crucial lines of communication between the races and helped check the racial paranoia that re-sulted in a bloodbath in Chicago.

By the end of the 1920s, however, most of these lines of communication had been effectively closed. With the new racism in public facilities and the increas-ing ghetto-ization of the black population more evident with each passing year, Cleveland was coming to resemble other metropolises in its prejudicial treat-ment of black citizens. This fact was a painful one for older black residents of the city to accept. "Time was," said black politician and civic leader George

Myers despairingly in 1928, "that Cleveland was the freest from race prejudice and the fairest city in the United States not excepting Freedom's birthplace Boston. Today we have only two unrestricted privileges left, the Ballot and the Public Schools." The same year, the black *Call and Post* editorialized: "Daily it becomes more apparent that the virus of southern race prejudice is bearing its malignant fruit in this cosmopolitan city of Cleveland. With amazing rapidity it is spreading through the very arteries of this city—once famous for its liberality to minority groups."

The comparison of Cleveland with the South was apt, and it pinpointed an important national trend. Among whites, something of a consensus in favor of racial separation emerged in the postwar era. "There seems to be a concerted effort," Robert W. Bagnall, the NAACP's director of branches, wrote in 1925, "to force segregation on Negroes all over [the United States]." The "Southern Way," remarks C. Vann Woodward in his discussion of racial discrimination in the twenties, "was spreading as the American Way in race relations." Nevertheless, while the distance between North and South on the race question had narrowed, essential differences still remained. Blacks, as George Myers pointed out, retained the right to vote in the northern states, and in Cleveland they would soon use their increased numbers as a political tool to gain concessions from city government. Furthermore, the separation of the races never became as complete in Cleveland as it did in many of the southern states. No system of "racial etiquette" took root in the North in the twenties—there were no Jim Crow streetcars, Jim Crow drinking fountains, or Jim Crow bibles for witnesses in court, and northern blacks were not required by custom to constantly show deference to whites in day-to-day contacts between the races.

Why did Cleveland not become like Atlanta, Charleston, and Mobile, where the principle of segregation was applied rigidly, dogmatically, to almost every facet of life? The question is not one that can be answered with absolute certainty, but two important factors, at least, must be taken into account. First, a portion of the white community continued to adhere to the tradition of tolerance and egalitarianism that at one time had been dominant. Influential white liberals included Russell Jelliffe, codirector of the interracial settlement house that would later become known as Karamu House, and Charles F. Thwing, president of Western Reserve University. Both were active in the NAACP, and Jelliffe served on a number of interracial committees during the 1920s. Although it is clear that Thwing and Jelliffe were not representative of most whites, they did speak for a constituency that was able to exercise some restraint on the growth of segregation and intolerance in the city.

Perhaps a more important factor that has been neglected was the nature of urban life in the North. The intricate subtleties of the race system common throughout most of the South simply could not be adapted to life in huge, industrialized, impersonal northern cities such as Cleveland. Beyond a certain point in urban development, the separation of the races in public and private facilities becomes inefficient, expensive, and dysfunctional to the operation of a modern industrial metropolis; by 1920, Cleveland, Chicago, and other large northern cities had long since passed that point. Paradoxically, however, the same dynamic urban growth that made segregated streetcars and certain aspects of racial etiquette almost impossible also rendered them largely unnecessary. In contrast to the South, where in many cities the growth of ghettos was retarded, in the North blacks were rapidly becoming residentially isolated from the rest of the population. Thus in northern cities informal contacts between the races in daily life were becoming less and less frequent. Because most blacks now lived in a circumscribed section of the city, there was less need for the formal establishment of separate streetcars, schools, and so on: de facto segregation, resulting from the growth of the black ghetto, was accomplishing in many instances the same end.

Additional Reading

Campen, Richard N. *Architecture of the Western Reserve 1800-1900*. Cleveland, 1971.

Davis, Russell H. *Memorable Negroes in Cleveland's Past*. Cleveland, 1969.

Goulder-Izant, Grace. *Rockefeller, the Cleveland Years*. Cleveland, 1975.

Howe, Frederick C. *The Confessions of a Reformer*. New York, 1925.

Ingham, Mary. *Women of Cleveland and Their Work*. Cleveland, 1893.

Johnson, Tom L. *My Story*. Seattle, 1970.

Nevins, Allan. *John D. Rockefeller*. New York, 1959.

Orth, Samuel P. *A History of Cleveland, Ohio*. 3 vols. Chicago, 1910.

Wittke, Carl. *We Who Built America*. Cleveland, 1939.

Epilogue
New England and the Western Reserve in the Nineteenth Century: Some Suggestions

An array of scholars have shared their thoughts, and from the discipline of each of them we have gained perspectives on factors that have helped to make this region distinctive. It is fair, then, to tell you of my own perspective. As a local historian and director of a local history institution, I would underscore the validity and necessity not only of the study of regional historical and cultural developments, but local and community ones as well. I would like to proceed to a brief precis of the initial and following early Euramerican settlement patterns in Connecticut's Western Reserve, and some suggestions about the impact that that pattern had upon nineteenth-century cultural development in the section.

I think that one of the most interesting aspects of the Western Reserve is that, as a definable region, it was the result of a political and arbitrary imposition rather than of natural or geographical causes. That New England's influence was instrumental in forming and defining the cultural foundations of the Western Reserve has been a long-accepted and obvious tenet. Writing in 1840, when the region was only just beyond the frontier stage, Ravenna editor Lyman W. Hall remarked that the Reserve was "in its education, in its leading habits, sympathies [and] feelings, New England in miniature." In 1873, standing before a meeting of Geauga County Historical Society, Congressman James A. Garfield observed that "there are townships on this Western Reserve which are more thoroughly New England in character and spirit than most towns of New England today." In a turn of the century *Atlantic Monthly* article, Rollin Lynde Harte noted that in the Reserve "is the Puritan regimen of Massachusetts and Connecticut condensed and exaggerated. In what other part of the country, save in antique New England, could you have brewed such a strenuous leaven." In *Years of My Youth* William Dean Howells recalled "that remarkable group of counties in northern Ohio called the Western Reserve," a region of which "the population was almost purely New England in origin, either by direct settlement from Connecticut, or indirectly after the sojourn of a generation in New York State."

Speeches, articles, memoirs, and other writings from the latter half of the last century and the first years of the present one are studded with observations similar to these. The Western Reserve as NEW ENGLAND IN MINIATURE or, indeed, as MORE NEW ENGLAND THAN NEW ENGLAND ITSELF has become commonplace wisdom. I would like to say that I have not catalogued these thoughts in order to dismiss or destroy them. Especially in terms of the nineteenth century—"the world the settlers made"—I see no reason to revise that wisdom. Instead, I would like to suggest ways in which our understanding of the cultural foundations of the Western Reserve, and New England's undoubted influence upon them, may be refined.

The initial imposition of "New England culture" upon the Western Reserve was the result of a number of factors. Most important of these were a singular pattern of land acquisition and settlement, and of intent. For mostly arbitrary reasons, I will discuss the latter of these first.

When the states which held claims to western lands by virtue of colonial charter or purchase from Indian tribes ceded them to the federal government in the 1780s, several retained small areas for their use. Connecticut reserved a portion of land running 120 miles west from the Pennsylvania line and from the forty-first north latitude to the southern shore of Lake Erie—a hefty chunk of land totalling more than three million acres (3,333,699). Thus from the outset, the Western Reserve would be a creature of the Commonwealth of Connecticut. When Moses Cleaveland's surveying party crossed the Pennsylvania line into the reserved territory, apparently providentially on the Fourth of July, 1796, the general ordered appropriate celebrations of the event. The men fired a fifteen-round salute, one for each state of the Union, and then a sixteenth, for "New Connecticut." Cleaveland then broke open a cask of "grog" and offered several Independence Day toasts. The first was for the president of the United States; the second was the "*state* of New Connecticut" (my emphasis). We need not read too great a significance into the revelry of a surveying team to realize that such expressions were a clear indication that the implantation of a New England stamp—more precisely, a Connecticut stamp—upon the Western Reserve was neither accidental nor haphazard. It was, indeed, a modified repetition of the initial impulse to carry an "errand into the wilderness" that brought Puritan settlers to Massachusetts Bay in the first place. When settlers from New England came to the Reserve, they brought their cultural baggage with them not unconsciously but quite deliberately. Again to quote James A. Garfield, "In many instances, a township organization was completed and their minister chosen before they left home. Thus they planted the institutions and opinions of old Connecticut in their wilderness homes [and] nourished them with an energy and devotion scarcely equalled in any other quarter of the world."

An often cited but still pertinent example was that of Hudson. David Hudson of Goshen, Connecticut, experienced a religious visitation that, in description, was not unlike the religious experiences of the Visible Saints of seventeenth-century New England. Hudson's visions instructed him to be "guided by four basic controlling ideals of religion, morality, law observance, and education." In 1799 Hudson and five co-proprietors purchased a township in the Reserve. In

June of that year, after an arduous journey, Hudson discovered and occupied his land for the first time. That first night, lying in the open in a downpour of rain, Hudson was filled with a spirit of "grateful pleasure," peace and joy. Several months later, he returned to Connecticut to fetch his family and to recruit set-tlers for his oasis in the wilderness. By January 1800, he was ready to return to the Reserve permanently. On the eve of departure, Hudson was sleepless and filled with forebodings of the dangers of the "extreme frontier." "But after pre-senting my case before Israel's God and committing all to his care," he con-cluded, "I cheerfully launched out the next morning upon the great deep." Upon arrival, he found the party he had left in Ohio had survived, and he im-mediately called the new and old settlers together for a thanksgiving service. In 1802, the township was officially named Hudson. That same year, a Congrega-tional Church was founded and a school opened. The next year saw the con-struction of a sawmill, and within five years David Hudson and his family were living in a neat frame house in what had literally been a trackless wilderness. Within a score more years Hudson led the way in founding Western Reserve College in Hudson, which was self-consciously designed to be the "Yale of the West." Robert Shackleton, who wrote of the Western Reserve for *New England Magazine* in 1896, saw in Hudson "that most charming of New England towns, Concord." It is perhaps to place too fine a point on the observation to add that even today Hudson remains emblematic of the Reserve's Connecticut heritage, and with a strict architectural code intends to preserve such associations.

Can we generalize from the case of Hudson? Certainly David Hudson was an exceptional man, and the development of his township was not precisely repli-cated elsewhere. But, save for Hudson's driving organizational genius and inspi-rational leadership, the pattern of planned settlement was repeated time and again. Burton, also settled in the first decade of the nineteenth century, was ini-tially populated almost exclusively by emigrants from Cheshire, Connecticut. Indeed, in 1806 when young Peter Hitchcock determined to make his way in the unsettled west he decided to go to Burton precisely because it was peopled by neighbors and acquaintances from home. In 1798, Alexander Harper, of Dela-ware County, New York, led several families to what became Harpersfield in Ashtabula County. During the next decade a steady trickle of immigrants came to Harpersfield from the same district. Charles Curtiss, for whom Charlestown in Portage County was named, came to Ohio in 1811, joining the families of Chauncey Curtiss, Linus Curtiss, and Levi Sutliff who had settled there the year before. In 1815, four other families, numbering fifty-six persons, joined the Cur-tiss clan. Thus by 1820, in addition to other accessions, the community con-tained a nucleus of better than one hundred residents from fewer than ten families, all hailing from the same section of New England. In Windsor, Ashta-bula County, among the earliest settlers were thirteen families from Tolland, Connecticut. And so it went throughout the Western Reserve.

Once in the new country the settlers continued, again very deliberately, the process of introducing and nurturing New England institutions upon the new land. In 1801, the Reverend Joseph Badger penned a petition to the territorial legislature for the creation of an institution of higher learning in the Western Reserve. "It is wished by the people in general in this part of the Territory," he wrote, "that something might be done to bring forward a literary establishment." At the time there could not have been more than one thousand residents in the entire Western Reserve. This petition failed, but two years later the first General Assembly of the new state of Ohio acted favorably on a similar request from "a number of proprietors of land" in the Reserve seeking to organize to "support of a seminary of learning" there. The legislature authorized the incorporation of the Erie Literary Society which acted as institutional agent to encourage the founding of a college. The efforts culminated in 1826 with the establishment of Western Reserve College, but the point to underscore here is that organized, institutionalized efforts to do so dated from the initial settlement of the first communities.

In practice, too, the New England stamp upon education in the Reserve was unmistakable. "In the pioneer days we come upon no trace of a character who is familiar in many Southern States and in parts of Ohio," remarked Burke A. Hinsdale in the 1890s. "I refer to the Scotch-Irish schoolmaster. The New Connecticut Yankees had no use for him." Instead, "Presbyterian and Congregational ministers did good educational service in those days."

Indeed, the Missionary Society of Connecticut was diligent in serving all the needs of New Connecticut. "From the first settlement of New Connecticut," noted an 1807 report of the Society, "the Trustees have thought it their duty . . . to pay particular attention to that country." A similar report in 1812 remarked that "the Connecticut Western Reserve has received the greatest attention of the Society." Indeed, during the first sixty years of the Society's existence, 30 percent of all missionaries appointed were sent to the Western Reserve (84 of 277).

Thus the early, overwhelming transferral of New England cultural norms was due greatly to these deliberate processes. The organized settlement of new towns by families already related by kinship, previous associations and, often, common purpose meant that they almost immediately developed a sense of community so often present in frontier settlements. It also meant that the degree of cultural transferral would be great; portions of existing New England communities were grafted as complete or semi-complete social organizations upon lands previously unbounded and undivided. The very early organization of institutions in the Reserve to nurture New England culture meant that the efforts would succeed.

This institutional transplantation of New England culture accounted for its strength in the Western Reserve. But instrumental in the *continuing* pervasiveness of that legacy was the distinctively random pattern of land acquisition and dispersal that shaped Western Reserve settlement. The stereotypical pattern of the "western movement" in America was a relatively steady push of population westward (or northward or southward or, in the case of Maine, even eastward) into unsettled frontier regions just beyond more established communities. The process was irregular, depending upon geographic features, Native American resistance, and fluctuations in national economic and political factors. Typically, though, pioneers ventured from settled areas into geographically contiguous regions just beyond the cutting edge of the frontier. Even in instances of long migrations beyond the established frontier through hostile and uncharted lands to a distant destination (such as transcontinental forays to California and Oregon in the 1840s and 1850s), once in the new land, pioneers' settlement patterns were determined by the desirability of specific locales, natural resources, hostile Indians, and other immediately relevant conditions.

Such patterns were not at work in the settlement of the Western Reserve. Several factors combined to make the settlement pattern of New Connecticut atypical.

First, there was no Native American population within the area capable of mounting resistance to white settlement. Aboriginal groups who had occupied the northern Ohio country had all been dispersed by the time Europeans first penetrated the region. By the eighteenth century, the Indians of Ohio were all refugee populations—groups already displaced by European intrusion or related inter-tribal warfare. For a variety of reasons, none of these groups heavily reoccupied northeastern Ohio, an area that one colonial mapmaker (1755) described as "the seat of war, the mart of trade & chief hunting grounds of the Six Nations" (that is, the Iroquois Confederation). Northern Ohio, then, was an area of Native American activity and contention, but none of the tribal or sub-tribal groups became strongly entrenched in the section that was to become the Western Reserve. By the end of the American Revolution, the power of the Six Nations had been vastly reduced, and the Ohio tribes had also been "battered by the forces of war." During the last years of the eighteenth century, however, these Indians joined in a loose but effective confederation which, for a time, was able to block Euramerican penetration of the Ohio country. This confederation was defeated by the army of General Anthony Wayne at Fallen Timbers in 1794, and the resulting Treaty of Green Ville (1795) opened eastern Ohio for white settlement. Confederation chiefs, whose tribes' strength lay to the west and south, acquiesced in the creation of a treaty line through Ohio that in the Reserve ran from Lake Erie south along the Cuyahoga River. This meant that the western portion of the Reserve was still claimed by the tribes, but that the entire eastern portion was at once thrown open to settlement. The few scattered Indians who did remain in northeastern Ohio had been long since militarily nullified, and presented more a curiosity than a threat to the pioneers. In 1806, renewed negotiations with the tribes resulted in further concessions by the Indians. In the Treaty of Fort Industry, the remaining portion of the Connecticut Western Reserve, among other lands, were ceded by the Indians. These developments meant that the settlers of the Reserve encountered no hostile bands of Indians to stymie their penetration of first the eastern portion, or, a decade later, the entirety of the Reserve.

Meanwhile, in Connecticut, the Reserve was transferred by the state into the hands of private investors. The western half-million acres were set aside for the benefit of Revolutionary War sufferers in the state whose property had been put to the torch by the British—the "Fire Lands." The remaining portion of nearly three million acres was sold to a group of investors: the Connecticut Land Company. Investments by individuals ranged from a few hundred dollars (Sylvanus Griswald, $1,683) to well over one hundred thousand dollars (Oliver Phelps, $168,185). In all, fifty-seven investors purchased shares in the company's property, all while the land itself remained unsurveyed.

After Moses Cleaveland's expedition of 1796 and a subsequent one led by Seth Pease in 1797, the land east of the treaty line was measured and bounded for the first time, and ready for division among the shareholders. The territory was to be divided according to the monetary investment of each man, but great care was taken that none would receive undesirable property. An extremely complex formula was devised by which above average, average, and substandard lands were "equalized" by combination with each other. The investors then divided their land by blind lottery. Investors received blocks of land—sometimes more than one, depending upon the amount of their investment and the equalization process—purely by chance, and for the most part, sight unseen. After the division, each proprietor became responsible for his own holding. The actual settlements which followed, therefore, were widely scattered. Settlement did not commence at the Pennsylvania line and inch westward, or at the lakeshore and push southward, or proceed along some natural avenue like a river or even a ridge. Rather, each settling party made its way to a site determined arbitrarily by chance, or by purchase from among the fifty-odd proprietors. And in some instances, the desire to colonize New Connecticut made any knowledge of the land itself decidedly secondary. When David Hudson and his co-proprietors, enflamed with the idea of establishing a godly commonwealth in the wilderness, enthusiastically made their way west, it mattered little to them where their property exactly was. Indeed, so trackless were the wilds into which they came that it took them six days to discover the boundaries of the township once they arrived. En route, Hudson's party encountered Benjamin Tappan and Elias Harmon and his family, also on their way to the Reserve. The party shared the journey from Buffalo to Ohio. Under other circumstances, these pioneers might have fallen in together, pooling their strengths and resources for the benefit of them all. Instead, once in New Connecticut, they separated, each going to his own respective plot: Hudson to Hudson; Tappan to Ravenna; the Harmons to Mantua. In such fashion the initial settlements in the Reserve were established many miles from each other, although the founding of many of the earliest communities were contemporaneous. Other townships remained unsettled for years. Proprietors who owned portions of more than one township due to the equalization formula could naturally put their energies and resources in the development of the one they believed the most promising—but at the expense of the others. Also, individual proprietors established specific conditions for their lands not present elsewhere. During the first decade of the nineteenth century, land was offered and sold in Geneva Township, Ashtabula County, for $1.50 per acre. At the same time, Christopher Leffingwell and Daniel Coit were offering property in their southern Ashtabula County town (later Orwell) for $5.00 per acre. Perhaps unsurprisingly, Orwell had no permanent settlement until after the War of 1812. In Hartsgrove Township of the same county, the proprietors made no attempt to market the land for years, and settlement was so spotty that the town "was for many years the hunting ground of the settlers of the neighboring townships... While adjoining localities were denuded of their timber and gave evidence of the advance of civilization, this township, for more than twenty years after the arrival of the first settlers, remained an unbroken wilderness."

When the western portion of the Connecticut Land Company's holdings became available for settlement by Indian cessation, the process of division was similar. Likewise, the Firelands were parceled by lottery among the Sufferers and the heirs. There were, therefore, three major divisions within the Western Reserve: the eastern portion of the Connecticut Land Company's holdings opened to settlement by the Green Ville Treaty Line; the western portion of the company's holdings, opened by the Treaty of Fort Industry; and the Firelands. But the method of land acquisition and division was such that in *each* of these subsections the actual pattern of settlement was crazy quilt. While major portions of the Reserve were opened for colonization at a time, the actual settlements—the colonies—remained quite isolated. Settlement, wrote the Reverend Carroll Cutler in 1876, was relatively steady after 1800. The pioneers, however, "did not... locate near each other and thus form strong communities...but scattered over the while [wild] region so as to greatly increase their privation, dangers and hardships." Such separation created more than hardship, it created too an atmosphere in which cultural continuity, stability, even insularity, would be fostered. The deliberate implantation of New England cultural norms into communities that, by the very processes of the settlement, would remain isolated from even their most immediate neighbors, helped to perpetuate both autonomy and that aura of "antique New England," to repeat the phrase of Rollin Linde Harte.

This process seemed to make the region as a whole impervious to change. Indeed, some observers attributed the evident cultural continuity that they sensed to a lingering isolation, and an absence of change. When James Garfield spoke of the New England traits that were characteristic of the people of the Reserve, he offered a reason: "Cut off as they were from the metropolitan life that has gradually been molding and changing the spirit of New England, they preserved here in the wilderness the characteristics of New England as it was at the beginning of the century. This has given to the people of the Western Reserve those strongly marked characteristics which have always distinguished them." A generation later, an alumnus of Western Reserve Academy recalled Hudson as a "transplanted academic village amid the rolling richness of Middle-Western woodland and farming country [which] was what New England had been half a century before and would have remained but for the importation of Southern European mill hands." Such an observation, of course, failed to recognize, among other things, the presence of "Southern European mill hands" and other non-Yankees who were and had been present throughout the Reserve.

A 1916 Cleveland Public School System report characterized Cleveland as "one of the most foreign cities in the United States. Of the 50 cities having a population of over 100,000 at the time of the last census, only seven... contained a larger proportion of foreign inhabitants. Cleveland's foreign population would constitute by itself a city larger than any other in the state of Ohio except Cincinnati." Such change was confined neither to Cleveland nor to the twentieth century. The Ohio Canal, constructed in the 1820s, was not known as the "Irish Ditch" accidentally. The men who came to dig the canal remained to bring wives, families, and parish priests to New Connecticut. Akron, a town virtually created by the canal, as well as Ravenna and Cleveland, all had Irish neighborhoods by the 1830s. Also by the 1830s, German-born immigrants made up sizeable minorities in the southern Portage County towns of Deerfield, Rootstown, and Randolph. In 1829, there were enough German Catholics to support the organization of a German-language Catholic Church in Randolph. In the 1870s, the German-speaking population of the county was substantial enough to warrant the printing of data in a county atlas in both English and German. During the 1870s and 1880s, the smaller lakeshore cities of Lorain, Fairport, Ashtabula, and Conneaut all experienced an influx of European immigrants to work on the docks, in the mills and on the railroads. In 1872, the *Ashtabula Sentinel* noticed that "among our railroad operatives is to be found a considerable number of Finlanders—a class of people that have but recently made their appearance among us." Attracted first to the ports of Ashtabula Harbor and Fairport Harbor, by the 1880s Finns were working in Youngstown steel mills, on rail lines, and on lake steamers. By 1900, 97 percent of the Finnish-born population in Ohio lived in the Western Reserve.

Nor was change in the Reserve confined to European immigration. Both Youngstown and Akron experienced phenomenal industrial growth in the last quarter of the nineteenth century. Akron, created by its strategic position at the watershed of the Ohio Canal, was never the stereotypical New England settlement. A transfer point on an important north-south avenue, Akron, from its earliest days, received not only goods but people from the interior of Ohio and in fact the entire Ohio River Valley. Youngstown, connected by river to Pittsburgh, also always had important ties outside the Reserve.

These examples constitute something more substantial than exceptions that prove the rule. The Western Reserve was not, as Garfield supposed, "cut off from metropolitan life," but rather, from the mid-nineteenth century on, very much a part of it. Yet Garfield was not wrong when he characterized the prevailing cultural flavor of the region as that of New England. The combination of deliberate processes by earliest pioneers coupled with the separated, isolated fashion in which the communities developed permitted the Reserve to experience the processes of industrialization, immigration, and urbanization without transforming the cultural continuity of the region as a whole. This is not to say that the newcomers left no mark. In politics, for example, the importance of foreign-born and first-generation voters was substantial, particularly in local elections. In

1860, the foreign-born voters in Cleveland presented a solid phalanx against Abraham Lincoln, due primarily to nativism and prohibitionism on the part of the local Republican party. In the 1880s, Walter Dickinson, of Randolph, gave a similarly ethnic explanation for political developments in his community:

> The politics of this township are now, as they were away back in the forties, Democratic. The change from Republicanism to Democracy has been slow but sure, owing to the prolific nature of our Catholic German population. The way new voters, who have just come of age, present their ballots at every election is surprising. The Yankees "can't hold a candle" to them in this natural increase. Well, we all know how this class of people vote.

The effect of such political developments were generally of only local importance in the nineteenth century. The Western Reserve as a region retained, as Garfield and so many others observed, a pervasive atmosphere of New England, throughout the nineteenth century and into the twentieth. No one would argue that the Western Reserve remains a bastion of Yankee Puritanism in the last quarter of the twentieth century. Yet even today, the built environment, the town- and country-scapes, the regular five-mile-wide gridwork pattern of townships established by the Connecticut Land Company's surveyors are still present, tangible reminders of New England influence.

The challenge to us, as students of our region's history and culture, is not to miss the rich cultural diversity and ethnic variety that has long characterized so many Western Reserve communities by concentrating too heavily on that Yankee heritage. For too long, written regional and local histories of the Reserve have emphasized the latter to the near exclusion of the former. We can sympathize with the Sandusky physician and historian Ernst Von Schulenburg, who observed in 1889 that "although the German population of Sandusky seems almost the same as that of the native-born and has become a powerful factor in the religious, political and social life of the city, yet it is surely striking that in all the local histories which I have seen, the German element was either completely ignored or at best treated as a step child." Von Schulenburg went on to remedy that situation, by penning *Sandusky Then and Now*, which he subtitled *With Special Regard to Local, German Situations*. We, too, must look beyond the obviousness of the region's New England influence, even in the nineteenth century, to important, other threads of regional culture. Using the methods of the new social history, as well as nearby and community history; collecting, exhibiting, and interpreting objects of material culture; preserving buildings and other structures are the means, and the opportunity, to discover, record, and appreciate the true richness of Western Reserve history and culture.

Contributors and Editors

ELROY M. AVERY (1844–1935) was Superintendent of East Cleveland Schools in the 1870s. He wrote several textbooks and in 1918 *A History of Cleveland and Its Environs*.

JEFFREY P. BROWN is Assistant Professor of History and Director of the Public History Program at New Mexico State University at Las Cruces. He publishes on the old Northwest and early Ohio in *Ohio History, Journal of the Early Republic, Northwest Ohio Quarterly*, and *Old Northwest*.

ERIC J. CARDINAL is Director of the Lake County Historical Society. He has written on Ohio's pre-history and Civil War periods for *The Ohio Archaeologist, Western Reserve Studies, Northwest Quarterly, Ohio History, Lake County History Quarterly*, and *The Western Reserve Magazine*.

JARÉ R. CARDINAL is Director of Education for the Lake County Historical Society. She has written on Amerindian and local history for *The Ohio Archaeologist* and *The Western Reserve Magazine*.

CLARENCE H. CRAMER (1905–1982) was Professor Emeritus of History at Case Western Reserve University, where he also served as Dean. He wrote several biographies, including one of Newton D. Baker, and institutional histories of Case Western Reserve University, its several schools and the Cleveland Public Library.

KENNETH E. DAVISON is Professor of History and American Studies at Heidelberg College and author of *Cleveland During the Civil War, Forgotten Ohioan: Elisha Whittlesey 1783–1863, The Presidency of Rutherford B. Hayes*, and *Ohio's Heritage* with James L. Burke.

EDWARD T. DOWNER (1893–1968) was Registrar Emeritus at Case Western Reserve University. An authority on Ohio's role in the Civil War, he contributed to *Civil War Prisons, Civil War History*, and wrote *Stonewall Jackson's Shenandoah Valley Campaign 1862*.

WILLIAM D. ELLIS is Editor of *Inland Seas* and author of *The Cuyahoga* and *Land of the Inland Seas*. He was a contributor to *Early Settlers of Cleveland*.

JOHN J. GRABOWSKI is Curator of Manuscripts at the Western Reserve Historical Society. He is the Editor of the *Ohio Archivist*. He is co-editor with David D. Van Tassel and contributor to *Cleveland: A Tradition of Reform* and Managing Editor of the *Encylcopedia of Cleveland History*.

GLADYS HADDAD is Professor of American Studies at Lake Erie College and Director of the Lake Erie College Press which publishes *Western Reserve Studies: A Journal of Regional History and Culture*. She has published in *The Gamut* and *The Western Reserve Magazine*.

HARLAN HATCHER is President Emeritus of the University of Michigan and formerly professor and administrator at Ohio State University. A regional specialist, he wrote *Lake Erie, The Great Lakes, The Buckeye County: A Pageant of Ohio*, and *The Western Reserve: The Story of New Connecticut in Ohio*.

GRACE GOULDER IZANT (1893–1984) was a journalist and wrote for *The Plain Dealer*. A long-time Hudson resident, she authored *Hudson's Heritage* and pursued regional subjects in *This Is Ohio, Ohio Scenes and Citizens* and *John D. Rockefeller: The Cleveland Years*.

PETER JEDICK is a Cleveland fireman and free-lance writer. He has published in *Cleveland Magazine, The Sunday Magazine* of *The Plain Dealer, Sun Newspapers*, and *Cleveland Press*.

GEORGE W. KNEPPER is Professor of History and University Historian at The University of Akron. His published works include *Akron: City At The Summit, An Ohio Portrait*, and articles in *The Western Reserve Magazine, Old Portage Trail Review, Northwest Ohio Quarterly*, and *Western Reserve Studies*.

KENNETH KUSMER is Associate Professor of History at Temple University and Editor of *The Temple University Historian*. He publishes on American social history since 1850, and is the author of *A Ghetto Takes Shape* and articles for the *Journal of American History* and the *Journal of Interdisciplinary History*.

HARRY F. LUPOLD is Professor of History at Lakeland Community College. He is the author of *The Latch String Is Out: A Pioneer History of Lake County, Ohio, The Forgotten People: The Woodland Erie*, and articles in the *Negro History Bulletin, Inland Seas, Ohioana Quarterly, The Western Reserve Magazine*, and *The Civil War in the North*.

EUGENE C. MURDOCK is Professor of History Emeritus and College Historian at Marietta College. He has published *One Million Men: The Civil War Draft in the North, Ohio's Civil War Bounty, Patriotism Limited 1862-1865*, and written for *The Western Reserve Magazine*.

THOMAS L. NEWCOMB is an elementary school teacher in the Bloomfield Mesopotamia Local district in the heart of the Amish Mennonite country. He has published on Amish education in Ohio for *Internal and External Perspectives on Amish Mennonite Life II*, for the University of Essen, Germany, and written articles for *The Western Reserve Magazine* and *Bend of the River Magazine*.

ALLAN PESKIN is Professor of History at Cleveland State University. He is the author of *North Into Freedom: The Autobiography of John Malvin, Free Negro, 1795–1880* and *Garfield*, which received both the Ohioana and Ohio

Academy of History Publication awards. He has written for *The Historian, Journal of American History*, and *Encyclopedia of Southern History*.

PHILLIP R. SHRIVER is President Emeritus and Professor of History Emeritus at Miami University in Ohio. He authored *George A. Bowman: The Biography of An Educator, The Years of Youth: Kent State University 1910–1960*, and has written for *Timeline, Encyclopedia of Southern History, Dictionary of American Biography*, and *Notable American Women*.

THOMAS A. SMITH is Chief of Research at the Rutherford B. Hayes Presidential Library and author of *Oulanie Thepy: The Golden Age of Harbour Town, Vermillion, 1837 to 1879*. He has published in *The Western Reserve Magazine*.

ROBERT WHEELER is Professor of History at Cleveland State University and author of a series of articles on Western Reserve agriculture, industry, towns, and culture from 1800 to 1860 published in *The Western Reserve Magazine*. He wrote *Pleasantly Situated On the West Side: An Economic and Social History of the Ohio City Area 1800–1878* for The Western Reserve Historical Society.

FREDERICK WILLIAMS is Professor of American History at Michigan State University. He co-edited with Harry Brown *The Diary of James A. Garfield*, wrote *The Wild Life of the Army: Civil War Letters of James A. Garfield*, and wrote on Garfield for the *Lake County Historical Quarterly*.

Index